SEEK THE PEACE OF THE CITY

THEOPOLITICAL VISIONS

SERIES EDITORS:

Thomas Heilke
D. Stephen Long
and C. C. Pecknold

Theopolitical Visions seeks to open up new vistas on public life, hosting fresh conversations between theology and political theory. This series assembles writers who wish to revive theopolitical imagination for the sake of our common good.

Theopolitical Visions hopes to re-source modern imaginations with those ancient traditions in which political theorists were often also theologians. Whether it was Jeremiah's prophetic vision of exiles "seeking the peace of the city," Plato's illuminations on piety and the civic virtues in the Republic, St. Paul's call to "a common life worthy of the Gospel," St. Augustine's beatific vision of the City of God, or the gothic heights of medieval political theology, much of Western thought has found it necessary to think theologically about politics, and to think politically about theology. This series is founded in the hope that the renewal of such mutual illumination might make a genuine contribution to the peace of our cities.

OTHER VOLUMES IN THE SERIES:

Stanley Hauerwas and Romand Coles
Christianity, Democracy, and the Radical Ordinary: Conversations between a Radical Democrat and a Christian

Gabriel A. Santos
Redeeming the Broken Body: Church and State after Disasters

Bryan C. Hollon
Everything Is Sacred: Spiritual Exegesis in the Political Theology of Henri de Lubac

Nathan R. Kerr
Christ, History and Apocalyptic: The Politics of Christian Mission

Seek the Peace of the
CITY

Christian Political Criticism as Public,

Realist, and Transformative

RICHARD BOURNE

 CASCADE *Books* · Eugene, Oregon

SEEK THE PEACE OF THE CITY
Christian Political Criticism as Public, Realist, and Transformative

Theopolitical Visions 5

Copyright © 2009 Richard Bourne. All rights reserved. Except for brief quotations in critical publications or reviews, no part of this book may be reproduced in any manner without prior written permission from the publisher. Write: Permissions, Wipf and Stock Publishers, 199 W. 8th Ave., Suite 3, Eugene, OR 97401.

Portions of this book were published as "Governmentality, Witness and the State: Christian Social Criticism with and beyond Yoder and Foucault," in Jeremy Bergen and Anthony Siegrist, eds., *Power and Practices* (Scottdale, PA: Herald, 2009); and "Witness, Democracy and Civil Society: Reflections on John Howard Yoder's Exilic Ecclesiology," *Ecclesiology* 3.2 (2007) 195–213.

Cascade Books
A Division of Wipf and Stock Publishers
199 W. 8th Ave., Suite 3
Eugene, OR 97401

www.wipfandstock.com

ISBN 13: 978-1-55635-642-1

Cataloging-in-Publication data:

Bourne, Richard.

    Seek the peace of the city : Christian political criticism as public, realist, and transformative / Richard Bourne.

    xvi + 330 p. ; 23 cm. Includes bibliographical references and index.

    Theopolitical Visions 5

    ISBN 13: 978-1-55635-642-1

    1. Political theology. 2. Christianity and politics. 3. Yoder, John Howard. I. Title. II. Series.

BR115.P7 B670 2009

Manufactured in the U.S.A.

For Kristen

Contents

Preface ix

Acknowledgments xi

Abbreviations xiii

CHAPTER 1 There Is Another King: Mission and Public Theology in a Plural World 1

CHAPTER 2 Political Criticism and the Vulnerability of the Particular 40

CHAPTER 3 The Cruciformity of the Cosmos: The Christological and Eschatological Basis for Realism 81

CHAPTER 4 The Ecclesiology of Nonviolent Witness 122

CHAPTER 5 Doxology and Social Change: The Subversive Citizenship of the Messianic Community 157

CHAPTER 6 Eschatology, Exile, and Election: A Theology of Governmental Power With and Beyond Yoder 207

CHAPTER 7 Towards a Peaceable Civility 262

Bibliography 297

Index of Names and Subjects 325

Preface

This book began as a doctoral dissertation undertaken at the University of Exeter, completed in 2005. It became apparent early on in the research process that my desire to explore the public and political complexion of Christian critique would lead me to John Howard Yoder. In so doing it led me also to numerous conversations, wide-eyed realizations, periods of insomnia, and some gradual (and occasionally grudging) changes of mind. Encountering Yoder is not always a comfortable process, and it is all the better for that.

It became equally apparent that I could not bring myself to just write *about* Yoder. I firmly believe that works "on" Yoder are best, not when he is described and discussed, but when he is used for ends beyond, but in sympathy with his own projects. To that end, both this book and the thesis on which it is based seek to place Yoder into forced but fruitful dialogue with a range of concerns in both theology and political theory. I take from Yoder the notion that the desire to "keep Christian politics Christian" (to adapt a phrase from Stanley Hauerwas) and the desire to keep it "public" are not mutually exclusive options. Rather, both desires can only be satisfied through an extended reflection on the relation of social and political criticism to the reality of a nonviolent, patient, forgiving, and reconciling God.

This book is an attempt to see what happens when *that* reality is allowed to touch contemporary accounts of public discourse, social transformation, statehood, and civil society. At no point does it pretend to be a complete account of the disquieting and transformative impact I have come to expect in those encounters. It is my hope that the reader may find a suggestive quality to these explorations; the first breaths of one answer to the question that guided the thought of Yoder and many who are influenced by him—what if we take seriously the claim that what the Church has always said about Jesus is the key to how we might live, and in so doing continue to "seek the peace of the city" (Jer 29:7).

Acknowledgments

Throughout any long-term research project one inevitably accrues an enormous range of debts of gratitude. This book would never have reached completion without the financial assistance of the AHRB Doctoral Award, and various contributions from the Saint Luke's College Foundation. My thanks also go to the staff of the London Mennonite Centre for their hospitality and for making their library available to me. Without the collection of Yoder's unpublished writings available there my research would be significantly poorer. Equally, the library of the Faculty of Divinity of the University of Cambridge was generous enough to grant borrowing rights to an interloper from Exeter.

Through their guidance and patience my doctoral supervisors, Tim Gorringe and Paul Avis, are responsible for my avoiding both stylistic and substantive errors. Needless to say, those faults that remain are attributable only to me. Thanks also go to those participants in various conferences and postgraduate study days at which the themes set out here received their first public airing. Mark Wynn and Sam Wells examined the doctoral thesis, and provided encouragement and feedback. Phillip Blond, Stanley Hauerwas, Craig Hovey, Karl Möller, and many others offered enthusiasm and encouragement during the process of converting a doctoral dissertation into a book.

Thanks also to Charlie Collier, Diane Farley, and the editorial team at Cascade for their patience in awaiting an overdue manuscript. My sincere thanks go to all my colleagues and students at both the University of Cumbria and at Leeds, Trinity and All Saints. They have endured, with apparent or polite keenness, far more talk of witness, nonviolence, power and governmentality, than I could ever have hoped for. Such themes infuse and underlie my forays into preaching too, so my thanks extend also to those at St. Thomas's Church, Lancaster, who have offered their own appreciation for the fragments and hints they encounter.

It would take far too long to list all those whose friendship has sustained me through recent times. I shall always be grateful to friends and family alike who, while often bemused by the details of my work, consistently offered encouragement and welcome distraction. In the time it has taken to produce this book I have lived in the Southwest (Exeter), East Anglia (Cambridge), Southeast (Surrey and London), and Northwest (Lancaster) regions of England. In each of those settings I have found faithful friends, times of delight, and a ready supply of good coffee or single malt. Again, there are far too many to name, but the kindness, patience, and support offered by Charlie and Imogen Adkins at a particularly challenging episode in that history cannot go unmentioned.

Special mention should go to my father, for always knowing why theology matters; to my brother, for being less convinced that it does; and to my mother, who didn't mind as long as I was happy. To all of these go my thanks. This book is, however, dedicated to the woman who entered my life after the first incarnation of the work was complete; but whose generosity, gentleness, and most of all joy have been a constant feature of its transfiguration into its current state. Her patience with an absent, frustrated, distracted, and tired husband warrants far more than a simple dedication can express. Such as it is, this is for Kristen.

Abbreviations

Works by John Howard Yoder

AE   "Armaments and Eschatology." *Studies in Christian Ethics* 1:1 (1988) 43–61.
ARS   *Anabaptism and Reformation in Switzerland: An Historical and Theological Analysis of the Dialogues Between Anabaptists and Reformers*. Kitchener, Ontario: Pandora, 2004.
AT   *Authentic Transformation: A New Vision of Christ and Culture*. With Glen Stassen and Dianne M. Yeager. Nashville: Abingdon, 1996.
BH   *Balthasar Hubmaier: Theologian of Anabaptism*. Scottdale, PA: Herald, 1989.
BP   *Body Politics: Five Practices Before the Watching World*. Scottdale, PA: Herald, 1992.
CAW   *Christian Attitudes to War, Peace and Revolution: A Companion to Bainton*. Elkhart, IN: Co-Op Bookstore, 1983.
CCP   *The Christian and Capital Punishment*. Newton, KS: Faith and Life, 1961.
CHRN   "Chapters in the History of Religiously Rooted NonViolence: A Series of Working Papers of the Joan B Kroc Institute for International Peace Studies." Unpublished papers, 1996.
CWS   *The Christian Witness to the State*. Newton, KS: Faith and Life Press, 1964.
DPR   *Discipleship as Political Responsibility*. Translated by Timothy J. Geddert. Scottdale, PA: Herald, 2003.
FC   *The Fullness of Christ: Paul's Vision of Universal Ministry*. Elgin, IL: Bretheren, 1987.
FTN   *For the Nations: Essays Public and Evangelical*. Grand Rapids: Eerdmans, 1997.
HCPP   *He Came Preaching Peace*. Scottdale, PA: Herald, 1985.

JCSR	*The Jewish-Christian Schism Revisited.* Edited by Michael G Cartwright and Peter Ochs. London: SCM, 2003.
KBPW	*Karl Barth and the Problem of War.* Nashville: Abingdon, 1970.
LMS	*The Legacy of Michael Sattler.* Scottdale, PA: Herald, 1973.
MAB	"Meaning After Babble: With Jeffrey Stout Beyond Relativism." *Journal of Religious Ethics* 24 (Spring 1996) 125–138.
NS	*Nevertheless: Varieties of Religious Pacifism.* Revised Edition. Scottdale, PA: Herald, 1992.
OR	*The Original Revolution: Essays on Christian Pacifism.* Scottdale, PA: Herald, 1998.
PJ	*The Politics of Jesus: Vicit Agnus Noster.* Second edition. Grand Rapids: Eerdmans, 1994.
PK	*The Priestly Kingdom: Social Ethics as Gospel.* Notre Dame: University of Notre Dame Press, 1984.
PMMR	"'Patience' as Method in Moral Reasoning: Is an Ethic of Discipleship 'Absolute'?" In *The Wisdom of the Cross: Essays in Honour of John Howard Yoder,* edited by Stanley Hauerwas et al., 24–42. Grand Rapids: Eerdmans, 1999.
PT	*Preface to Theology: Christology and Theological Method.* Grand Rapids: Brazos, 2002.
RP	*The Royal Priesthood: Essays Ecclesiological and Ecumenical.* Edited by Michael G. Cartwright. Grand Rapids: Eerdmans, 1994.
THW	*To Hear the Word.* Eugene, OR: Wipf & Stock, 2001.
WWYD	*What Would You Do? A Serious Answer to a Standard Question.* Expanded Edition. Scottdale, PA: Herald, 1992.
WWU	*When War is Unjust: Being Honest in Just-War Thinking.* Revised edition. Reprint, Eugene, OR: Wipf & Stock, 2001.
YHIC	"You Have It Coming: The Legitimate Social Function of Punitive Behaviour." Elkhart, IN: Shalom Desktop, 1995.

Works by Karl Barth

CD	*Church Dogmatics.* 13 vols. Translated by G. W Bromiley and T. F. Torrance. Edinburgh: T. & T. Clark, 1956–1975.

Works by Stanley Hauerwas

AC	*After Christendom: How the Church Is to Behave If Freedom, Justice, and a Christian Nation Are Bad Ideas.* Nashville: Abingdon, 1991.
ATN	*Against the Nations: War and Survival in a Liberal Society.* Minneapolis: Winston, 1985.
BH	*A Better Hope: Resources for a Church Confronting Capitalism, Democracy, and Postmodernity.* Grand Rapids: Brazos, 2000.

CET	*Christian Existence Today: Essays on Church, World and Living in Between.* Durham: Labyrinth, 1988.
DF	*Dispatches from the Front: Theological Engagements with the Secular.* Durham, NC: Duke University Press, 1994.
PF	*Performing the Faith: Bonhoeffer and the Practice of Nonviolence.* Grand Rapids: Brazos, 2004.
RA	*Resident Aliens: Life in the Christian Colony.* With William Willimon. Nashville: Abingdon, 1989.
STT	*Sanctify Them in Truth: Holiness Exemplified.* Edinburgh: T. & T. Clark, 1998.
TPK	*The Peaceable Kingdom: A Primer in Christian Ethics.* Notre Dame: University of Notre Dame Press, 1983.
TWC	*The Wisdom of the Cross: Essays in Honour of John Howard Yoder.* Edited by Stanley Hauerwas, Chris K. Huebner, Harry J. Huebner, and Mark Thiessen Nation. Grand Rapids: Eerdmans, 1999.
US	*Unleashing the Scriptures: Freeing the Bible from Captivity to America.* Nashville: Abingdon, 1993.
VV	*Vision and Virtue: Essays in Christian Ethical Reflection.* Notre Dame: Notre Dame University Press, 1981.
WGU	*With the Grain of the Universe: The Church's Witness and Natural Theology—Being the Gifford Lectures Delivered at the University of St Andrews in 2001.* London: SCM, 2002.
WW	*Wilderness Wanderings: Probing Twentieth-Century Theology and Philosophy.* Boulder, CO: Westview, 1997.

Works by John Milbank

BR	*Being Reconciled: Ontology and Pardon.* London: Routledge, 2003.
TST	*Theology and Social Theory: Beyond Secular Reason.* Oxford: Blackwell, 1990.
WMS	*The Word Made Strange: Theology, Language and Culture.* Oxford: Blackwell, 1997.

Works by Oliver O'Donovan

BI	*Bonds of Imperfection: Christian Politics, Past and Present.* With Joan Lockwood O'Donovan. Grand Rapids: Eerdmans, 2004.
DN	*The Desire of the Nations: Rediscovering the Roots of Political Theology.* Cambridge: Cambridge University Press, 1996.
RMO	*Resurrection and Moral Order: An Outline for Evangelical Ethics.* Leicester: InterVarsity, 1986.
WJ	*The Ways of Judgment.* Grand Rapids: Eerdmans, 2005.

CHAPTER 1

There Is Another King:
Mission and Public Theology in a Plural World

"It was the Jewishness of Jesus, the rootage of his message in the particular heritage of Abraham, Moses, and Jeremiah, which . . . made it good news for the whole world. . . . Only the Jew Jesus, by announcing and accomplishing the fulfilment of God's promises to the Jews, could send out into the world a people of peace open to the Gentiles. Only the Jewish claim that the one true God, known to Abraham's children through their history, was also the Creator and sustainer of the other peoples as well, could enable mission without provincialism, cosmopolitan vision without empire."[1]

—John Howard Yoder

Turning the World Upside Down in the City of Idols

Consider two accounts of missionary encounter, the first is scriptural and the second contemporary. An angry mob sets the city of Thessalonica in uproar, dragging a man named Jason before the city authorities and shouting . . .

> These people who have been turning the world upside down have come here also, and Jason has entertained them as guests. They

---

1. Yoder, "Jesus the Jewish Pacifist," in *JCSR*, 69–89, 75.

> are acting contrary to the decrees of the emperor, saying that there is another king named Jesus. (Acts 17:6b–7)

Having been driven out of the synagogue at Thessalonica, and thence from Berea, the apostle Paul waits in Athens for the arrival of Silas and Timothy. While there he becomes distressed to see a city full of idols. With characteristic vigor he sets about the persuasion and disputation through which he aims to propagate the gospel.

> So he argues in the synagogue with the Jews and the devout persons, and also in the marketplace every day with those who happened to be there. Also some Epicurean and Stoic philosophers debated with him. Some said, "What does this babbler want to say?" Others said, "He seems to be a proclaimer of foreign divinities." (This was because he was telling the good news about Jesus and the resurrection.) So they took him and brought him to the Areopagus and asked him, "May we know what this new teaching is that you are presenting? It sounds rather strange to us, so we would like to know what it means." Now all the Athenians and the foreigners living there would spend their time in nothing but telling or hearing something new . . . (Acts 17:17–21)

Why begin with Athens? Certainly there is a *prima facie* resemblance to the modern conception of the "marketplace of ideas." Yet the constraints of such a metaphor—its conformity to a propositional and commercial notion of discourse, and the understanding of democratic formation that goes along with it, point to equally important dissimilarities. In both settings, however, the conditions and nature of truthfulness are placed in question by the disquieting annunciation of "another king."[2] It is that commonality—the unsettling quality of gospel "truth," and the mission of the Church through which it has effect—which unites Athens and contemporary contexts. This will become clearer as we examine our second story, and then undertake the extended methodological excursus that forms the heart of this chapter. These stories of mission frame the ensuing claims for the political-critical nature of the Christian community founded on this very public truth, the gospel of Jesus Christ.

In 1974, when Lesslie Newbigin retired to England after thirty-eight years of ministry in India, like Paul in Athens he became distressed. Newbigin was shocked to find a culture that lacked hope; or rather, as

---

2. Bernard Williams provides a clear reflection on the limitations of the notion of a "marketplace of ideas" in his account of truthfulness and critique in liberalism. Williams, *Truth and Truthfulness*, 213–19.

he came to see it, a culture that had created a void by driving God from the public sphere. But no void can exist for long. "If God is driven out, the gods come trooping in."[3] His previously positive reading of the missionary opportunities afforded by secularization had altered. Britain, he says, had become a pagan land. In losing the theocratic assumptions of Christendom, British culture has ceded dominance to a vision of pluralism in which "dogma" has been "entangled with coercion, with political power, and with the denial of freedom—freedom of thought and of conscience".[4]

For Newbigin, the distinction of public from private, of fact from value, had become, borrowing a phrase from Peter Berger, the dominant "plausibility structure." It follows from the quest for Descartes's "false ideal of an indubitable knowledge," which in turn has relegated religion to a private realm from which it could no longer offer any significant social critique.[5] But Christian witness cannot defend the gospel by the domestication of its claims to the regnant plausibility structure. Which is to say that, following Christianity's earliest cultured despisers, the public truth of the gospel inevitably turns the world upside down. Dogma, then, is not to be associated with the denial of the freedom of thought that Enlightenment thinkers sought to wrest from theocratic control. Rather, the response to plurality (as a phenomenon distinct from the normative construal of it given in "pluralism") should, says Newbigin, see the gospel as public truth—not a truth to be possessed, enforced, guarded, or imposed, but a truth to be told.

> The truth is that it is the dogma rightly understood, namely the free gift of God's grace in Jesus Christ, which alone can establish and sustain freedom of thought and of conscience. We must affirm the gospel as truth, universal truth, truth for all peoples and for all times, the truth which creates the possibility of freedom.[6]

To appeal for a recovery of the public truth of the gospel may all too easily appear as nostalgia for a by-gone age, the age of Christendom. My assertion, in this book, of the public truth of the gospel is not akin to the lamentation of Job that, under the now lost favor of God, the people "listened to me, and waited, and kept silence for my counsel" (Job 29:21).

3. Newbigin, *Unfinished Agenda*, 249. See also Kettle, "Lesslie Newbigin."
4. Newbigin, *Gospel*, 10.
5. Newbigin, *Truth to Tell*, 50.
6. Newbigin, *Gospel*, 10.

Even if Job's lamentation of his role ever befitted the church, it certainly cannot be said to do so now. Equally, our use of the rhetoric of the book of Acts may come too easily unless theologians can meet the task of further explicating what it means to say that the gospel "turns the world upside down." In such a task there is neither virtue nor necessity in easy caricature of the world as it appears in what may loosely be termed a "pluralistic" (or, more properly, "plural") framework. Nor, therefore, is there cause for triumphal or crusading claims for the present impact of the truth of the gospel. Indeed, as this book develops, I shall argue that such crusading conceptions of gospel truth are inadequate to its nature as a truth of *witness*. In particular, the witnessing character of public theological truth, especially the eschatological claim that "there is another king," is most appropriately found in the traits often associated with the Anabaptists and other "peace" churches (though present throughout the range of Christian traditions)—nonviolence, hospitality, and patience.

We shall return to the importance of a particular kind of eschatology for a fruitful understanding of Christian social and political criticism in later chapters. Before we do so two tasks lie ahead. First, we shall examine how the social critique that inevitably ensues from the claim of the "truth" of the gospel may fit within, and itself reshape, the theoretical frameworks and descriptions of the supposedly "post-secular," "post-modern," "post-liberal" and "post-Christendom" situation, which constitute our context. Second, we shall consider the extent to which the plausibility structure of many attempts at a public theology fail to take account of the way that eschatology and Christology "turn the world upside down," and, in that failure, inevitably, as Newbigin puts it, "domesticate" the gospel.

The claims that occupy us in these first two chapters of the book are simply:

1. that Christian truth possesses an inherent drive to social and political criticism;
2. that all such criticism is situated within the everyday life of the Christian community;
3. that such criticism is therefore "public" in the sense that the gospel itself is "public"; and finally,
4. that theological analysis concerning the public nature of ecclesial political criticism must begin with the notion of witness.

From the Areopagus to Secular Space

Contemporary debate locates itself around a series of dualisms and polarities. On a synchronic axis space is divided into discrete realms—the secular public space and the (sometimes) religious private space. The diachronic axis follows either a two-fold or three-fold progression—from medieval to modern, and on to postmodern; from religious to secular, and on to post-secular. The announcement of a new King unsettles all other spatial constructions and aeonic divisions. The terms "modern" and "secular" possess both descriptive and prescriptive aspects, which cannot be easily disentangled. The decline of religious practices as the linchpin of social identity is often taken for granted, and the (Cartesian) subject possessed of (a Kantian) autonomy appears, to many, so basic a description of humanity as to be self-evident. The modern world, so the narrative goes, emerged from the maelstrom of bloodshed and disunity seen in the "wars of religion" of sixteenth- and seventeenth-century Europe. In place of this disorder, the Peace of Westphalia (1648) marked a transition to forms of unity established by the contracting of individuals to a loyalty to the nation-state.[7] Religion continued to lose ground as a locus of coercive power and is largely confined to the emerging realm of "private" concern. The coupling of the emancipatory intent of the Enlightenment project with the privatizing of religious concern impacted both the popular imagination and the apparently scientific norms of sociology. Indeed, it has done so to such a degree that the earliest apologists for the phenomena of "secularization" successfully passed anti-religious sentiment off as the irrefutable description of modernity.

More sober descriptions of the nature and extent of religious decline tend to highlight the diversity and limitation of the applicability of the epithet "secularization." It is not, then, the decline of the religious *beliefs* of individuals that comes under immediate suspicion, but the pivotal and even determinative influence of religious *institutions*. The two moments of secularization are, then, the emergence of a non-religious basis for individual rationality and autonomy, and the resultant reaction against Caesaropapist patterns of Christendom as determinative of the social order. Importantly, this tying of a broader pattern of modernization to the process of secularization requires advocates to restrict its application largely to Western, even European, contexts. The process of modernization

---

7. See Toulmin, *Cosmopolis*.

is said to entail a decline of religious concern to a largely epiphenomenal status. One of secularization's most emphatic apologists, Bryan Wilson, thereby claims that a transition occurs from a "communal" to a "societal" form of social organization, which has occasioned, for religious bodies, a loss of social significance.[8] "Whereas religion once entered into the very texture of community life, in modern society it operates only in interstitial places in the system."[9] Yet such descriptions of the impact of modernization tend towards a functional (Durkheimian) view of the role of religion that often fails to take account of the diverse ways in which religious groups may affect the moral order. However, I shall contend throughout that the lack of privileged access to the ruler's ear, through the substantial differentiation of society, does not entail the loss of all influence, and may well portend a more faithful practice of critique. Such a practice is unlikely to be well received by those accounts still committed to models of secularization construed as a transfer of authority, influence, or significance from religious to non-religious bodies.

Two factors give occasion for the more explicitly theological and radical account of public political criticism to be developed here. First, the dubious empirical and historical basis and the clear ideological and normative functions of the putative "great separation" are increasingly subject to significant analysis.[10] Second, we must note the rise of accounts of the critical enterprise that, contrary to liberalism, stress their situated and particularistic nature. When this latter is subjected to some significant theological transformation we will find the starting point for our development of an account of Christian political criticism as public, realist, and transformative. The remainder of this introductory chapter will explore these two factors in turn.

Public Religion and Secular Space

The persistence of religion as a public force is shown in José Casanova's important *Public Religions in the Modern World*. Casanova helpfully distinguishes between three often-conflated moments of the term secularization. Thus "secularization" has come to mean:

8. Wilson, *Religion in Sociological Perspective*, 148–79.

9. Ibid., 155.

10. The term "great separation" is taken from the popular polemic of Mark Lilla's *The Stillborn God*.

1. The process of "differentiation" whereby social structures shift towards an increasing level of organizational complexity and modal distinction. The "secular" spheres of the (capitalist industrialized) economy and the state gain a significant, though varying, degree of autonomy from religious institutions and norms.

2. The decline of religion per se. The description of the loss of religious affiliation and practice that extrapolates the history of certain, largely "Caesaropapist," aspects of Western European religiosity to an often global paradigm. The wider application of the "Enlightenment critique of religion."

3. The privatization of religion. The "depoliticizing" process supposedly attendant upon modern differentiation, whereby the drive to specialization locates religion as germane solely to the subjective quest for meaning.

While "differentiation" is largely taken to be an accurate description of the development of a modern industrialized capitalist system, both the "decline" and the "privatization" of religion easily shift from descriptive to prescriptive mode. They then slip into a normative stance that seeks to curtail any "illegitimate" incursions of the religious into the public sphere.[11] This is achieved, in part, through a series of unjustified preferences: for a liberal polity founded on a separation of public and private realms; for the nation-state as the sole appropriate mode and bearer of political sovereignty; and for "Protestant" subjectivist accounts of religion. I maintain that all three of these preferences are contingent and problematic. The account of public, realist, and transformative Christian political critique developed in this book will demonstrate an alternative to all three. The separation of public and private spheres will be shown to operate on a false and attenuated notion of publicity. The statist bent of such political theory will be shown to be selective, limiting, and often damaging. The subjectivist picture of religion we will come to see not so much as "Protestant" per se, but as the pietistic variant of Protestantism from which our more public and political variant must distinguish itself.[12]

---

11. Casanova, *Public Religions*, 11–39.

12. I follow Yoder in marking a distinction between "pietism" naming a tendency to eschew social and political concerns, and historic Pietists, for whom such concerns were often extremely important. See Yoder, *CWS*, 84–88. I am grateful to Charlie Collier for discussion on this point.

Even when one traces the roots of decline in religious affiliation through this long process of modernization it seems likely that the current state of religious life, and importantly for our purposes, its public role, has been significantly altered in the latter half of the twentieth century. Callum Brown highlights how the thesis of gradual decline does not sufficiently account for the dramatic impact of rapid social change in the 1960s. He claims that the public influence of Christianity in Britain was undermined by a decaying structure of cultural reproduction. The role of the Christian narrative in the formation of the identity of British women, having already become somewhat attenuated, is resolutely broken in the cultural shifts of the 1960s. Thus the mechanism for the transmission of the Christian narrative necessary for a dominant "discursive" public role disappeared.[13]

Of course, the nature of this religiosity, whose decline Brown identifies, is not to be directly equated with the object of theologians' normative ecclesiological reflections. As well as attempting to explain the decline in churchgoing, Brown is highlighting how British culture, *in se*, ceased to regard itself as "Christian." As we shall see, that is hardly the same thing as saying that Christianity, understood as the guiding religious claims of those communities who aim to embody the truth of the gospel in a life of discipleship, is itself lacking in public influence.[14] Nevertheless the link between Christian belief and Christian belonging inevitably impacts the scale, nature, and effect of the church's public mission. It is here that churchgoing may reflect wider social and cultural shifts that have impacted upon the levels of participation in a variety of modes of public life, both political and religious.[15]

Some of the most persuasive reflections on secularization identify aspects of the social imaginary that, by enabling these social and cultural shifts, serve to direct, restrict, and shape public religious presence. Secularization is better conceived of not as a transfer of authority from

---

13. Brown, *Death of Christian Britain*.

14. Brown acknowledges something similar, although he expresses it in largely pejorative terms. He concludes the book thus: "This is not the death of churches, for despite their dramatic decline, they will continue to exist in some skeletal form with increasing commitment from decreasing numbers of adherents. Nor is it the death of belief in God, for though that too has declined, it may well remain as a root belief of people. But the culture of Christianity has gone in the Britain of the new millennium. Britain is showing the world how religion as we have known it can die" (ibid., 197–98).

15. See Davie, *Religion in Britain Since 1945*; Beckford, *Religion and Advanced Industrial Society*.

religious to non-religious bodies, but as the creation of a space in which religious modalities are normatively construed and constrained.[16] Secular space is not the value-neutral arena, adjunct to which we find the waiting room in which modern private religion is held. It is the factory in which private religion is produced. In articulating a spatial view of secularization, Charles Taylor has argued that we move to a modern social imaginary structured around notions of popular sovereignty;[17] an imaginary that is free from mediating institutions and hierarchically structured coteries of public influence. Talal Asad is right, in my view, to argue that this form of secularism does not so much usher in a society of direct access to governance as replace some practices of religiously based political-public mediation with another diverse set of secular mediations.[18] It is not, then, so much the absence of religion from the public square as the reshaping of that presence. This reshaping is historically and politically contingent. "The social" as we have it is the invented "all-inclusive secular space" that permits and even requires the constant redefinition, re-tasking, maintenance, and policing of "religion."

The dominance of the modern nation-state itself emerges out of attempts to create an undifferentiated sociality and easily identifiable political unity. To support its own nascent authority the nation-state robes itself in the garb of a regal savior.[19] In order to do so it had to privatize religion, domesticate transcendence, and thus render believer and church docile to the power and purposes of the state. The much-vaunted liberal tolerance of Western political secularism is founded on a vision of social solidarity achieved in the nation. But this national loyalty is constructed not just through the twin processes of the simplification of the competing laws of gild, Church, and feudal principality on the one hand and, on the other, the encouraged rise of capitalism through the sponsoring of new economic practices—the creation of currency, trade law, and a system of subsidies and protections for businessmen without affiliation to Church and guild.[20] At the same time it is enabled through the thoroughly intolerant and illiberal exploitation of the fear of religious minorities by those

---

16. See, for example, Taylor, "Modes of Secularization," and also in remarkable detail in *Secular Age*.
17. Taylor, *Modern Social Imaginaries*.
18. Asad, *Formations of the Secular*, 5.
19. See Cavanaugh, "Fire Strong Enough to Consume the House."
20. Nisbet, *Quest for Community*.

seeking to entrench power and bolster authority.[21] But this is far from a matter of concern only to those with an eye to historiography. It sets the tone for contemporary discussions of plurality and multiculturalism. As Charles Mathewes rightly identifies,

> [t]he belief that "the liberal state" is the response to the challenge of pluralism gets things the wrong way round; pluralism is a problem only when you have a monotheism of the state, when the state claims to be the only game in town as regards power and authority. Without such an essentially aggrandizing political structure, diversity in belief, and heterogeneity on the ground, is much less difficult. Pluralism is a central problem for modern states not because of pluralism, but because of modern states.[22]

The Kantian approach to religion and the dominant modern variants of secularization that flow from it all identify sectarian Christianity as the key danger[23]—for this is painted as the enemy of cosmopolitanism and social cohesion. We shall see, however, that charges of sectarianism ill fit the defense of public Christian critique delineated here. Ironically, however, that epithet may well befit liberal secular modalities of private religion. In Kantian, Lockean, and Rousseauean forms of argument, religion was dangerous in its supposedly inherent drive to division. Toleration was thus only granted to those who accepted a "protestantized," i.e., privatized and individualized, view of religion.[24] This vision remains central to discourses of democratization and nation-building today.[25]

The celebrated postmodern turn has not led us away from such constrictions. Incredulity toward metanarratives is rightly identified by Jean-François Lyotard as the major "condition of knowledge" in highly developed, largely plural, societies. The loss of the credibility of grand narratives leads to the celebration of long suppressed differences, a restoration of the little narrative, the *petit récit*, as the "quintessential form of imaginative invention."[26] No doubt these developments have given us con-

21. Marx, *Faith in Nation*.
22. Mathewes, *Theology of Public Life*, 155.
23. Connolly, *Why I am Not a Secularist*, 32.
24. Walzer, *On Toleration*, 67.
25. For example, Saba Mahmood argues persuasively that the account of secularization dominant in contemporary American politics, as given expression in the 1998 International Religious Freedom Act, seeks to achieve a drastic redefinition and constraint of religious subjectivities. See Mahmood, "Secularism, Hermeneutics and Empire."
26. Lyotard, *Postmodern Condition*, 60.

cepts and analyses that allow us to identify the productive and disciplinary aspects of secular culture (to use terms clearly indebted to Foucault). But the account of Christian political criticism to be developed in this work cannot simply embrace "postmodernism"—not least because there is no determinate object to embrace. By its very nature the "postmodern" is difficult to pin down. It is elusive, amorphous, and diversely understood. Whether or not the postmodern refers to a distinct era subsequent to that of modernity, runs parallel to it, or represents a phase within the bounds of modernity itself, is an area of contestation I do not intend to discuss here. Even if, as I am not, one is sufficiently persuaded that its beginning(s) mark the end of modernity, postmodernity should not be taken as just another stage, for, as Terry Eagleton puts it, postmodernism

> . . . cannot really come to a conclusion, any more than there could be an end to post-Marie Antoinette. It is not, in its own eyes, an "historical stage," but the ruin of all such stagist thought.[27]

But as a celebration of otherness, subjectivity, disorder, and a humanity seen in all its heterogeneous glory, postmodernism can come close to the utter nihilistic collapse presented in the Nietzschean antecedents of the philosophy of deconstruction. It claims to lay bare the pathological failures that lie behind modernity's boasts of inclusion and universality, but, in doing so, comes dangerously close to undermining all emancipatory effort through its celebration of plurality as of absolute value. Eagleton is incisive in his judgment that such invocations of difference all too easily reflect a privileged social location where there is little to lose through "proclaiming the virtues of undecidability."[28]

Frederic Jameson and David Harvey have both pursued a similar line of critique. For Jameson, postmodernity represents "the cultural logic of late capitalism,"[29] where culture is subsumed under categories of commodity production with their incessant demand for the novel, the "latest thing." This is a zeitgeist peculiarly suited to the propagation of a consumerist hegemony (an issue to which I shall return at the end of the book). Harvey describes this shift in mass-consumer culture as the basis for the "rootedness" of postmodernism in daily life. He traces the development of postmodernity to a shift from Fordist economics to a

27. Eagleton, *Illusions of Postmodernism*, 29.
28. Ibid., 5, cf. 127.
29. Jameson, *Postmodernism*.

regime of "flexible accumulation." Fordist economics, with its focus on homogenization, rationalization, and mass production serving a culture of mass consumption aided the expansion of U.S. geo-political dominance. Nevertheless its inherent link with Keynesian methods of fiscal control meant it was unable to cope with the inherent "overaccumulation" tendencies of capitalism. This heralded a system based more on fictitious capital (credit) that required a shift towards a regime of "flexible accumulation." The advent of new technologies, the development of "flexible" and "mobile" working patterns, and a "service-based" economy are all trends of this shift in emphasis towards the continual manufacture of a desire for disposable consumer items. The point is, as Harvey puts it, capitalism did not invent "the other" but it certainly made use of and promoted it in highly structured ways."[30] "Precisely because capitalism is expansionary and imperialistic, cultural life in more and more areas gets brought within the grasp of the cash nexus and the logic of capital circulation."[31]

What hope then for a fully public and religious form of political criticism in such circumstances? Certainly there may be some hope of vanquishing the damaging impact of an uncritical acceptance of the secularization thesis in its strongest form. Zygmunt Bauman talks of postmodernity as a "re-enchantment of the world," restoring the mythic elements that modernity sought to exclude.[32] David Martin notes the new scope allowed for public religious belief once the two bases of secularization are brought into question. He argues that the establishment of religion, in the sense of Caesaropapist notions of Christendom, is largely waning, and the rationalist underpinnings of the Enlightenment project have been thrown into disarray.[33] However, much postmodern discourse is equally as dismissive and virulently anti-religious as the apologists for secularization. The differentiation, which forms the crux of the link between modernization and secularization, has continued apace under the postmodern condition.[34] The spontaneity, fragmentation, and superficiality of the cultural milieu have encouraged a commodification of

---

30. D. Harvey, *Condition of Postmodernity*, 104.
31. Ibid., 344.
32. Bauman, *Intimations of Postmodernity*, x.
33. Martin, "Secularization Issue," 473. Cited in Bruce, *God Is Dead*, 233–34.
34. See, for example, Heelas, "Introduction."

religious belief—a reduction to the market niche of "spirituality" with its preference for eclecticism, individualization, and relativity.[35]

Stanley Hauerwas points to the inadequacy of either "modernity" or "postmodernity" as a cultural moment in which a fully Christian social vision can be at home.

> Modernity, drawing on the metaphysics of a transcendent god, was an attempt to be historical without Christ. Postmodernity, facing the agony of living in a history with no end, is a denial of history. In the wake of such a denial, the only remaining comfort is the shopping mall, which gives us the illusion of creating histories through choice, thus hiding from us the reality that none of us can avoid having our lives determined by money.[36]

The importance for Christian political criticism of "being historical" *with Christ* is the central problematic of this book.

A Theology of Immanent Critique

The cautionary note sounded here regarding postmodernity must not mute the importance placed on the second factor we have identified in contemporary postsecular accounts of public religious critical practice—namely the stress on the situated and particular nature of that practice. I suggest that, contrary to the extremes of postmodern historicism, an account of immanent or situated critique is essential to the continuation of moral discourse in any realist sense. I argue that the basis of such discussions in accounts of the plurality of contemporary western moral and political discourse calls for a theological transformation and resolution. Thus the particular and communal site of *moral* realism poses a further challenge for Christian political criticism, which can only be met by a parallel commitment to *theological* realism.

In order to begin to establish this conclusion I shall briefly engage with a number of contemporary writers all of whom have sought to describe both religious and moral language as in some way "community-dependent." I will argue in the remaining pages of this chapter that the political- and social-critical nature of the truth of the gospel is dependent upon its communal setting. I reserve for the next chapter the contrast

---

35. See, for example, Carrette and King, *Selling Spirituality*.
36. Hauerwas, "Christian Difference," in *BH*, 39.

between this approach and the less particularist, more universalizing, approaches of the procedural accounts of what, following Christopher Eberle, I shall call "justificatory liberalism."[37]

Although I have described those thinkers with whom we are presently concerned as united in an understanding of moral language as community-dependent, the nature, degree, and consequences of that dependence vary from writer to writer. The writers with whom I am concerned are Alasdair MacIntyre, John Milbank, Michael Walzer, and John Howard Yoder. Rather than dealing with them sequentially, it will be more fruitful to engage with them thematically. First I will engage with the philosophical understandings of moral language and pluralism, as given by Walzer and MacIntyre. I will then engage with the theological implications of these arguments through considerations of Milbank and Yoder. This, of course, is not to imply that theology bears a secondary or methodologically subsequent place to such philosophical accounts—quite the opposite. It is through an understanding of the theological implications of such theorizations that one can move beyond the problematic aspects of such theoretical enterprises. It will become evident through this discussion that it is with Yoder's approach that I most closely identify. The remainder of the book will therefore constitute an in-depth comparative exploration of Yoder's theology. It will not, however, be a simple work of exposition. Rather, by means of excavation, dialogue, comparison, and contestation, I will seek to deploy Yoder's theology in the service of an account of Christian political critique that exceeds and compliments his own published concerns.

To begin an enquiry into realism and Christian political criticism, as we have, with the theology of mission presages a trend towards broadly "historicist" forms of thought. That is to say, it is committed to the historical contingency of its discourse—the all-important factor of "context."[38] It is not, however, "historicist" in the stronger, more dogmatic, sense of a commitment to a particular historically derived and realized teleology, as found most famously in Hegel's insistence on history as the arena for the progressive realization of *Geist*. Equally it is not fully historicist in the alternative sense that views all teleology as suspect or redundant and thereby drifts into relativism.

---

37. Eberle, *Religious Conviction in Liberal Politics*.
38. Stout, *Flight From Authority*, 256–72.

The claim that so persuasively underwrites John Howard Yoder's distinctly non-theoretical theology is nicely expressed by one of his best, and most recent interpreters. Craig Carter describes Yoder as a thoroughgoing historicist "except at the point of the incarnation."[39] I concur and suggest that Yoder's theology is characterized by a dynamic understanding of the historical character of revelation, and of its embeddedness in the work of the Holy Spirit in the Church. This leads Yoder to make an important distinction between "relative relativism" and "absolute relativism." The former simply denotes the (providential) inevitable "relativity" attendant upon the encounter between diverse peoples and viewpoints within a plural setting.[40] The latter, by contrast, denies the possibility of any assessment, validation, or accountability.

Such absolute relativism appears to be the precipice down which some postmodern thinkers gleefully fling themselves. Its "modern" converse would be the search for a transcendent or universal foundation upon which to build an edifice of certainty. Understood in such stark terms, historicism would naturally eschew all foundational claims. Of course the contrast is overplayed, but the charting of a path between these dangers is not so simple. Ironically, as Yoder adeptly points out,

> [t]he absolute relativism of the politically correct, when based in a particular (subcultural) denial of the availability of any common norms, is a foundationalism turned in on itself.... Unbelief about communicability is self-fulfilling.[41]

For Yoder, anti-foundationalism is a form of "methodologism"—it seeks a basic starting point from which to assert control.[42] Even the denial of all foundations is itself a foundation. Indeed, as Eagleton has argued with respect to postmodernism in general, it may be a foundation for a peculiarly bourgeois form of "liberal" toleration. If anti-foundationalism, in its stringency, collapses back into a covert foundationalism, then an ad hoc openness to dialogic encounters (of the sort anti-foundationalism precludes a priori) may be better termed "non-foundational."

> Ultimate validation is a matter not of a reasoning process which one could by dint of more doubt or finer hair-splitting push down

---

39. Carter, *Politics of the Cross*, 72–74.
40. Brad Kallenberg provides a stimulating account of relativism in Kallenberg, "Gospel Truth of Relativism."
41. Yoder, "Absolute Philosophical Relativism is an Oxymoron."
42. Yoder, "Walk and Word."

one story closer to the bedrock, but of the concrete social genuineness of the community's reasoning together in the Spirit.[43]

Both foundationalism and anti-foundationalism become forms of ideological closure which themselves prohibit or constrict the performance of political critique. As Slavoj Žižek observes, historicism grasps "the endless play of substitutions" as they are placed within the single field of action—the contingent.[44] "Historicity proper," by contrast does not impose a single structural principle of the possibility or impossibility of an action. Non-foundational accounts of historicity may, I suggest, permit the apparently ad hoc to be genuinely ad hoc and not merely the most recent in a series of encounters with either bald contingency or a singular immanent historical movement. Nonetheless, if political critique is to be both genuinely ad hoc and yet realist, the historicity of such performances must be asserted in relation to the founding event that makes them possible. Here we may heed Žižek's suggestion, contra historicism, that "[t]he truly radical assertion of historical contingency has to include the dialectical tension between the domain of historical change itself and its traumatic 'ahistorical' kernel qua its condition of (im)possibility."[45] To do so, I argue, it must be a practice of political critique articulated as a response to and participation in the nonviolent, patient, reconciling action of God. It must thus be formed around the dogmatic triad of Christology, eschatology, and ecclesiology. Here, major contemporary accounts of the situated critic are found wanting.

Particular Moral Discourse in a Plural Setting

Let us consider the theological basis for understanding the ad hoc encounters that characterize critical engagements in a plural setting. Alasdair MacIntyre famously characterizes the failure of the Enlightenment project as attendant upon the utter fragmentation of contemporary moral discourse. In attempting to discern a universal rational foundation for moral thought, the architects of the Enlightenment discarded all particular accounts of the telos of human life.[46] Without such an account, knowl-

---

43. Ibid., 83.
44. Žižek, "Class Struggle or Postmodernism?" 112.
45. Ibid., 111–12.
46. MacIntyre gives the extended example of the ninth edition of the *Encyclopaedia Britannica* as an attempt at such a unitary system of rationality. MacIntyre, *Three Rival Versions of Moral Enquiry*, 16–17.

edge of basic human goods became problematic. A catastrophic breach occurred between socially embodied practices on the one hand, and conceptions of moral conduct on the other. What we are left with is a series of surviving linguistic fragments from older traditions—fragments that no longer "make sense."[47] The prevalence of apparently irresolvable moral and political disagreement attests to this dire situation. MacIntyre puts it evocatively—"Deprive children of stories and you leave them unscripted, anxious stutterers in their actions as in their words."[48] His landmark *After Virtue* begins the necessary program of recovery through the reclamation of the Aristotelian notion of the virtues in relation to teleology. MacIntyre criticizes the suppression of moral differences through manipulation and rhetoric that he detects as a defining moment in liberal polities. Instead, he argues, a vital and healthy plural society requires vibrant communal existence. The recovery of such a communal setting is necessary in order to nurture the historical memory and extended "practices" in which the virtues can once again flourish. Nevertheless, *After Virtue* is famously pessimistic about the possibility of recovering such vibrant communal life on a large scale.

Like MacIntyre, Michael Walzer's thought makes a central place for the communal setting of moral discourse. His *Spheres of Justice* argues that the shared understandings operative within political communities display an "internal moral logic" within diverse "spheres." These societal spheres, such as education, welfare, money, or politics, display a high degree of autonomy in relation to the notion of justice. That is to say, in a liberal Western society, the notion of justice with regard to education and with regard to welfare cannot, pace John Rawls, be united under a singular simple banner such as "justice as fairness."[49] Rather the autonomy of each sphere requires a divergent understanding of justice—for education that would include principles of equal opportunities and the reward of merit; for welfare, the distribution of benefits according to "socially recognized needs." By contrast with "simple equality," as a basic distributive principle, Walzer advocates "complex equality." A notion of "complex equality" will therefore attempt to maximize the possibility of

47. MacIntyre, *After Virtue*, 6–11; *Whose Justice? Which Rationality?* 1–6; *Three Rival Versions of Moral Enquiry*, 5–7.

48. MacIntyre, *After Virtue*, 216.

49. Walzer, *Spheres of Justice*. Walzer responds here to Rawls's *Theory of Justice*. Rawls's theory has undergone substantial development and some significant change in later works, see *Political Liberalism*.

justice within these spheres, but may need to tolerate significant injustice and disparity within one or two of its spheres in order to do so.[50]

Further, these diverse needs are dependent on the social and cultural setting. For example, in contemporary America the ownership of bicycles or access to a gymnasium are largely factors to be judged according to the goods and values of leisure pursuits in an affluent modern capitalist setting. However, in the Netherlands, where little urban car use is possible, the public provision of bicycles appears a more appropriate, i.e., "just," use of public money. Equally, the provision of free and open gymnasia in ancient Greece was a prerequisite for the formation of citizens and smooth running of the public sphere in a city-state.[51] Nevertheless it is not always clear in Walzer's account how the differentiation, in an extension of our earlier sense, of Western liberal societies into such autonomous spheres may afford a workable form of "complex equality." Indeed, it is certainly the case that in advocating these specific divisions between education, money, politics, leisure, education, and family, Walzer reflects a more sanguine approach to the "thick" construction of communal life of contemporary liberal society than many, including myself, think justifiable.

The use of the term "thick" here represents another important aspect in the affirmation of communal particularity in relation to contemporary moral and political discourse. Walzer follows Clifford Geertz and Gilbert Ryle in characterizing particularity as "thickness," with the "thin" thereby representing substantially denuded forms of discourse. This provides a point of contrast with the Enlightenment project's assertion of the normativity of universalized moral claims, which for Kant was based in a rationalist ontology of human personhood, and, for forms of justificatory liberalism, becomes rooted in the procedural conditions for, or the very nature of, communication itself.[52] Indeed it is natural to assume that one cannot expect those formed within other traditions and narratives to fully understand the particular justifications one gives for particular laws, policies, or norms. Nonetheless, this does not require the denigration of public particularity. The particular may be partially translatable. The movement from particularity to public discourse is, says

---

50. Walzer, *Spheres of Justice*, 3–30.

51. Examples here are taken from Trappenburg, "In Defence of Pure Pluralism," 348.

52. For a clear and concise account of such a shift, see Gascoigne, *Public Forum and Christian Ethics*, 15.

Walzer, a mediation between "thick" and "thin."[53] It is fundamentally a hermeneutical process.

Immanent Criticism

By contrast, the commitment to some form of cultural transcendence means that those seeking to accommodate this insight into a revivified Enlightenment schema can do so only by continuing to assume, occasionally in rather dogmatic form, a pejorative picture of the critical potential of cultural particularity. Seyla Benhabib has demonstrated a willingness to accept the traditioned nature of the substantive presuppositions that motivate assent to the guiding principles of universal moral respect and egalitarian reciprocity.[54] Benhabib also argues that an ability to distance oneself from those traditions is indispensable, in order to allow for the self-critical practices essential for public ethical debate. Without such distance, Benhabib claims, communitarians will be unable to discern where the emphasis on formative tradition diverges from "an endorsement of social conformism, authoritarianism, and . . . patriarchalism."[55]

It is important not to move too hastily to rebuttal here. The pejorative picture of concerns for tradition (in a non-MacIntyrean sense) that evoke connotations of parochialism, narrowness of thought, and a conservative resistance to change, do represent an ever-present danger. Indeed, much so-called "communitarian" thought remains vulnerable to accusations of philosophical inaccuracy in its account of how critical practices relate to the interrelationship of self and community. It is for such reasons that MacIntyre has emphatically distanced himself from the designation "communitarian." For MacIntyre, communitarianism remains fundamentally, and fatally, optimistic about the promise of the nation-state. Any misplaced optimism in the liberal nation-state fails because of an internal contradiction in that institution's claim to moral neutrality. On the one hand, the state disavows any particular account of moral teleology, claiming for itself merely the role of efficacious bureaucracy, while on the other hand, enforcing ultimate claims on loyal citizens in the name of the common good, which it cannot itself sustain. To lay down one's life on behalf of the common good of the nation is, therefore,

---

53. Walzer, *Thick and Thin*.
54. Benhabib, *Situating the Self*.
55. Ibid., 74.

akin to "being asked to die for the telephone company."[56] However, the celebration of the revival of small-scale communities is not, in and of itself, a sufficient alternative. MacIntyre therefore seeks an account of how a variety of goods are to be integrated into the life of the whole. In order to achieve the integration of such goods, the communitarian's desire for the nation-state to adopt a more substantive (communitarian) account of the common good courts facism. For MacIntyre, it is through the process of dialogue in a peaceful and open environment that such an authentic civil ordering can come about.[57]

That said, let us now consider a rejoinder to the presumption of the putative objectivity gained through detachment. "The view from nowhere," in Thomas Nagel's phrase, is characterized by the attempt to attain an impersonal perspective detached from particularity and thus often fails to accommodate the traditioned nature of the self.[58] As we shall see in our fuller discussion in the next chapter, Jürgen Habermas begs the question when he insists that the minimal conditions required for discursive consensus are in some sense prior to, or more basic than, any particular stance taken within that discourse. Not only is it questionable that minimal rules precede maximal engagements, but the social structure and political arrangements that are required for the maintenance of these rules of engagement themselves represent a culturally thick discourse—which, as Walzer notes, leaves very little chance for substantive change beyond "local adjustments." "The thin morality is already very thick—with an entirely decent liberal or social democratic thickness."[59]

Of course, these conditions are essential to the self-description of the liberal order. Importantly, as Miroslav Volf has said, the project of inclusion represents a modern, Western conception that is itself violently exclusionary.

> Those who are conveniently left out of the modern narrative of inclusion because they disturb the integrity of its "happy ending" plot demand a long and gruesome counter-narrative of exclusion.

56. MacIntyre, "Partial Response to My Critics," 303.

57. For a useful discussion of this and associated problems, see a brief but clear discussion in Fergusson, *Community, Liberalism, and Christian Ethics*, 125–30.

58. Nagel, *View from Nowhere*.

59. Walzer, *Thick and Thin*, 11–15. Notably John Rawls came to be more willing to concede the "thickness" of such liberal conditions, through his inclusion of liberal politics in the concept of a "reasonable comprehensive doctrine." See Rawls, *Political Liberalism*, and *Law of Peoples*, especially the essay "Idea of Public Reason Revisited," 129–80.

> ... The undeniable progress of inclusion fed on the persistent practice of exclusion.[60]

How then, in the face of the failure of the liberal claims to inclusivity and universal emancipation, is the situated critic to escape the dangers of social conformism? Jonathan Allen rightly rejects the implication of an inappropriate cultural loyalty within the endorsement of the situated critic:

> Immanent criticism is only conservative or limited at the outset and in the sense that its radicalisation occurs over time. But it is always capable of being radicalised. Elites cannot control the terms and symbols which they put into social circulation or inject into the world of moral discourse.[61]

Such symbols are the vehicles of political discourse. The exclusionary politics of the dominant can be subverted through what James Scott calls the voicings of the "hidden transcripts" of the subjugated and excluded.[62] It is, I suggest, in such actions, at least as much as in the open invitation to a pre-existent departicularized public sphere, that the emancipatory goal of liberalism may be sufficiently embodied. To anticipate the concerns of the next chapter, let us take as our example Jürgen Habermas's "ideal speech situation"—where all affected parties participate within justificatory discussion of norms. The recognition of the radical liberative potential of situated, tradition-constituted criticism requires a substantial theological radicalization of Habermas, which locates the emancipatory intent of his project on a rather different foundation. I shall return to the elaboration of this shift in the next chapter; for now it is enough to note that Scott's own discussion of the "ideal speech situation" seems to corroborate aspects of this reading.

> If we were to proceed in terms of Habermas's analysis of the "ideal speech situation," the hidden transcript would represent the whole reciprocal conversational reply of the subordinate, which, for reasons of domination, cannot be spoken of openly. Habermas excludes, by definition, all "strategic" action and dominated discourse from the ideal speech situation and hence, from the search for rational consensus. What domination achieves, in

---

60. Volf, *Exclusion and Embrace*, 59–60.
61. Allen, "Situated Critic or the Loyal Critic?" 38.
62. Scott, *Domination and the Arts of Resistance*.

this context, is the fragmentation of discourse, so that much of what would be cohesive, integrated discourse is sequestered into the hidden transcript of the dominant.[63]

We shall see as we progress that the immanent nature of social and political criticism is closely tied to the possibility of emancipatory politics. That link is itself a significant characteristic of the way that the theology of mission, with which we began, must chart its course guided by a peculiarly theological form of realism. The arena in which both the subversion of symbols and the emergence of Christian publicity take place is no abstract theater set aside for entertaining rhetorical dueling. Rather the inclusion of the disenfranchised, subjugated, excluded, and dominated is itself an incomplete signification of the coming of the Kingdom of God. In relation to Jesus's life and ministry, this is what Ched Myers calls the "war of myths"—in which the way of the cross "subverts the dominant symbol systems of both imperial Rome and Palestinian Judaism."[64] Then, as now, this unsettling announcement of another king is, in the best sense of the word, "ideological," or, perhaps less pejoratively, "political." Before we can test these theological claims we need to see more clearly how the construals of immanent criticism themselves require a greater degree of theological precision.

Theological Transformations 1: Walzer on Prophecy

Walzer advances a concept of the "subversiveness of immanence" whereby the critic should be "a little to the side, but not outside: critical distance is measured in inches."[65] Moral argument, for Walzer, is best seen as interpretation, rather than either discovery or invention.[66] Detached criticism, as derived from discovered or invented moral standards, is seen as inherently coercive. "It presses practitioners toward manipulation and compulsion . . . insofar as the critic wants to be effective, wants to drive his criticism home (though the home is, in a sense, no longer his own), he finds himself driven to one or another version of an unattractive politics."[67] In contrast Walzer affirms that a noncoercive public sphere is

63. Ibid., 38 n. 36.
64. Myers, *Binding the Strong Man*, 14–21.
65. Walzer, *Interpretation and Social Criticism*, 61f.
66. Ibid., 21–22.
67. Ibid., 64.

essential for the flourishing of social criticism. Toleration, he says, "is not a formula for harmony: it legitimates previously repressed or invisible groups and so enables them to compete for available resources."[68]

This sort of inclusion is, he claims, a "prophetic" act. The biblical prophets provide Walzer with an exemplary embodiment of his conception of the subversiveness of immanence. Walzer advances a view of prophecy (which he takes to be little more than critique) as a social practice not limited to the men or texts themselves, but to the whole prophetic message and its wider reception. The normal procedure of social criticism, as it has been historically realized, is not that of detached critics—for as Walzer notes, we expect and readily dismiss criticism from outsiders. It is only from inside that the critic can tear aside the veil of the lies we tell about ourselves.[69] This necessarily implies an imperative to (critical) openness to the reception of what Paul Tillich called "reverse prophetism" in the ecclesial community.[70] Walzer says:

> Social criticism in maximalist terms can call into question, can even overturn, the moral maximum itself, by exposing its internal tensions and contradictions. . . . Social critics commonly start from where they stand, win or lose, on their own ground. . . . [disputes] that arise within a particular society and culture have to be settled—there is no choice—from within. Not without suggestions from outside, not without reference to other maximal moralities, but by and large through . . . interpretive arguments.[71]

The authority of the prophet was rooted not in his or her own critical abilities, nor was their critique based in a universalist natural law; it was integrally related to the history of the community's relationship to God. This is why Max Weber's account of prophecy is inadequate; for it deracinates individual charismatic authority from this wider history.[72] Walzer rightly notes that prophecy must function in relation to a shared history if it is to evoke memory, incite indignation, and move hearers to repentance.

Ironically, a "thicker" account of Judaeo-Christian practices of prophecy seems necessary if the role of this shared history is to function

68. Walzer, *On Toleration*, 107.
69. Walzer, *Thick and Thin*, 42.
70. Tillich, *Systematic Theology*, 3:209f.
71. Walzer, *Thick and Thin*, 47, 49.
72. See, for example, Plant, *Politics, Theology, and History*, 26–28.

correctly. There is inevitably a paucity of the *theological* thickness I argue is necessary here—most specifically there is both an impoverished eschatology, and the absence of the category of ecclesiology. Where Weber's account of prophecy does not place the prophet in an ongoing tradition and shared history, Walzer's account of prophecy does not lack a communal site but nonetheless fails to give sufficient attention to the specific missiological dimension of the *elected* community of Israel and the Church. The categories of prophet and community become general figures for the situatedness of the critic in any thick setting. But, prophecy, like all charisms, is orientated firstly for the building up of the church (1 Cor 14:1–4).[73] Prophecy, as Oliver O'Donovan claims, is the archetypal charism—it is through the individual prophetic figure addressing the Church that the prophetic message extends to the world. "The individual prophet, like all who exercise a charism, does not address the world immediately, but the church, and, by contributing to the church's prophetic identity, addresses the world through the church."[74] The charismatic nature of prophetic criticism is linked to a wider context of missionary imperative, of divine blessing and election. This cannot be by-passed as easily as Walzer thinks.

Walzer is quite right to argue that we cannot assume that the critic is always to stand in the center of the public realm. Rather "criticism does not require us to step back from society as a whole but only to step away from certain sorts of power relationships within society. It is not connection but authority and domination from which we must distance ourselves."[75] It is opposition, not detachment, that is the fundamental quality of social and political criticism. This opposition can indeed lead to exile, alienation, or marginalization, but the experience is always of ambiguous connection to society.[76] For Walzer, marginality is "not a condition that makes for disinterest, dispassion, open-mindedness, or objectivity." Social criticism is an internal argument conducted through an act of interpretation of principles internal to existence itself.[77] The minimal code presented in a universal thin description of morality is

---

73. For more on the nature and role of prophecy in the Church, see Hill, *New Testament Prophecy*; Panagopoulos, *Prophetic Vocation in the New Testament and Today*. For exposition of the prophetic role of Jesus, see Hooker, *Signs of a Prophet*, and Wright, *Jesus and the Victory of God*, especially 145–472.

74. O'Donovan, *DN*, 188.

75. Walzer, *Interpretation and Social Criticism*, 60.

76. Ibid., 38, 60.

77. Ibid., 21, 37–38.

insufficient, on its own, for social criticism.[78] Social criticism is best seen, argues Walzer, as a by-product of a larger social activity of cultural elaboration and affirmation. Prophets do not "constitute a permanently subversive 'new class' [and are not] carriers of an adversary culture."[79] Rather they function in reference to a pre-history, for criticism is partly a reflexive activity that implies common possession of, though obviously not agreement on, the tradition.[80]

In our shift towards a non-relativistic, non-foundational and largely, though not finally, historicist theology of social criticism, it is also important to note a shift in Walzer's own conception of moral discourse. In earlier works such as *Spheres of Justice* and *Interpretation and Social Criticism*, Walzer conceives of morality along the lines of a core of basic universal principles that are then elaborated according to the specificities of different cultures. However in *Thick and Thin,* he realizes that his presumption of a universal starting point is inadequate, for "morality is thick from the beginning . . . and reveals itself thinly only on special occasions."[81] This recognition brings him close to a postmodern disavowal of epistemological foundationalism.

Walzer claims it is only on "special occasions" that morality reveals itself thinly. Yet is this not merely a residual universalism? It appears that Walzer's commitment to "thin" communication is unable to give an account of "conceptual identity." That is to say, when moral language does become thin, it is unclear on what basis he can assume that divergent moralities mean the same thing, even at the thinnest level, by terms like "good" or "justice."[82] For MacIntyre's "tradition-constituted enquiry," and, as we shall see, for the theology of John Howard Yoder, there is no such thing as "thin" encounters. Rather, both view inter-communal discourse as a concatenation of encounters between equally thick particulars. Against any universalist enterprise these encounters represent the only "public" possible—i.e., what we might call a series of "mini-publics."

Even this occasional account of "thin" communication may undermine Walzer's commitment to the critical role of thick particulars. That

78. Ibid., 25.
79. Ibid., 40.
80. Ibid., 32, 70f.
81. Walzer, *Thick and Thin*, 4.
82. On Walzer's failure on the question of conceptual identity, see Plant, *Politics, Theology and History*, 353–59.

is to say, he does not fully escape the twin dangers of a foundationalist appeal to universality on the one hand, and the historicist collapse of true uniqueness on the other. In order to do so, I suggest, he would need to reconsider his rejection of "messianic" forms of eschatology. This is not to say that Walzer is lacking in something recognizably eschatological to Christian ears—for he argues for the centrality of hope and an orientation to the future as central to the critical enterprise.[83] However, Walzer identifies messianism with the kind of utopianism that has an inherent tendency to overextend itself in an idealistic attempt to transcend historical contingency and prematurely resolve the "problem" of diversity.[84] In order to maintain this objection, Walzer is forced to introduce a historically anachronistic dichotomy between the prophetic tradition of ancient Israel and the messianism of early Christianity.[85] This, I suggest, is entirely inimical to the politically radical messianic eschatology I shall develop, which rejects any such attempt to master the contingent and control history. I argue then that messianism is not an ethics of foreclosure, nor a rationality of utopian ends justifying illiberal means; it is the refusal of all foreclosures and the real valuation of the particular.

This is akin, in this regard at least, to messianism as famously described by Walter Benjamin.[86] Here the prohibition placed upon the Jews against the magical speculations and future predictions of the soothsayers guards them from the evacuation of the significance of historicity.

> This stripped the future of its magic, to which all those succumb who turn to soothsayers for enlightenment. This does not imply, however, that for the Jews the future turned into homogenous, empty time. For every second of time was the strait gate through which the Messiah might enter.[87]

In this way too the Christian account of the Kingdom of God refuses futurism in favor of a participatory and inaugurated eschatology. That is to say, the messianic complexion of the moment of the now, *tō nun kairō*[88]

---

83. Walzer, *Company of Critics*, 17.

84. Walzer, *Exodus and Revolution*.

85. Walzer's point is more rhetorical than real—he is fully aware of the historical lineage of messianism in the prophets—cf. ibid., 116–19.

86. See especially Benjamin, "Theological-Political Fragment," and "Theses on the Philosophy of History."

87. Benjamin, "Theses on the Philosophy of History," 255.

88. Author's translation.

(Rom 3:26, 8:18, 11:15), exceeds, confers meaning upon, and brings to completion the otherwise vacuous formality of simple chronological progression.[89] The particularity of historicity proper interrupts and transforms (*kairos*) the endless play of historicism (*chronos*). It may do so only as the anticipation and remembrance in the present of the messianic and missionary incursion of a nonviolent and patient God.

Theological Transformations 2: MacIntyre and Ecclesiology

We have seen Walzer affirm the process of social criticism to be an integral part of the critical argument that constitutes a process of cultural affirmation and development. In this regard his work bears resemblance to MacIntyre's insistence that traditions are partly constituted by such critical argument. MacIntyre is able to do more justice than Walzer to the multiplicity of traditions inhabited by any one person. Such a realization is imperative if, as our theology of social and political criticism must, the process of ad hoc cultural discernment is to move beyond a naïve bipolarity that asserts either the wholesale translatability of thick particularity into thin publicity or the utter incommensurability of the gospel and the secular. The ecclesiological and eschatological moments mentioned above are also necessary here. MacIntyre may be subjected to more explicit theological transformations in a variety of ways. Alongside MacIntyre's work I will consider John Milbank's impressive attempt to radicalize (that is to say, theologize) MacIntyre through a disavowal of dialectics in favor of the rhetorical triumph of the Christian *mythos* over the nihilism of the secular narrative. In so doing I hope to mark out some initial points of contrast and commonality between both of these authors and the vision of Christian political critique defended here. This vision is, as we shall see, indebted to the ways in which the theology of John Howard Yoder conceives of the public truth of the gospel. The task of a more detailed comparison of Milbank and Yoder awaits us in chapter 4.

In responding to the broad trends of postmodernity, John Milbank rightly draws attention to the presence of a significant number of religious subtexts within even the most explicitly "non-religious" content of postmodern discourse.[90] Most fundamentally, for Milbank, what occurs

---

89. The political significance of this notion, with a different emphasis to that given here, is expounded in both Taubes, *Political Theology of Paul*, and Agamben, *Time that Remains*.

90. Milbank, "Problematizing the Secular," and "End of Enlightenment."

in the move to modernity is not the exclusion of religious concerns, but their forcible subjectivizing and immanentizing into a "univocal" humanistic horizon. For example, the assertion of the autonomy of "science" construes its object as "immanently" comprehensible. This, in turn, renders a God entirely beyond nature, who cannot but become increasingly redundant.[91] However, such a move, claims Milbank, is not the abolition of religious themes, but springs itself from a theological mistake. Milbank follows a line of thought expressed most originally in the work of Hans Urs von Balthasar. For Balthasar, the roots of modernity lie further back than Cartesian thought. They are to be traced to the thought of Joannes Duns Scotus (ca. 1265–1308) in the fourteenth century. In asserting that the notion of "being" is univocally attributed to both God and man, Duns Scotus collapsed the Thomistic notion of analogy and thus dissolved God's ontological transcendence.[92] This then provides the metaphysical seedbed in which the foundationalism and the pursuit of certainty characteristic of modernity flourished.

If modernity is thereby based on a theological error, then the crumbling of its own zenith—the Enlightenment project—was inevitable not, as MacIntyre has it, because of a loss of teleology and tradition-constituted enquiry, but, more fundamentally, because its foundationalism and quest for certainty imbibed anti-theological denials of the basis of all that "is" in notions of analogy, transcendence, and gift. Milbank criticizes the elements of MacIntyre's argument that imply a defense of tradition-constituted enquiry and appeal for a recovery of virtue in general. Such a general appeal remains foundationalist in its commitment to dialectics as the mode of enquiry into truth. This is a metaphysical mistake that begins not with Descartes, but with Plato.[93] By contrast, Milbank suggests that the nihilistic tendencies and "religious" subtexts remaining in modern and postmodern discourse alike may be countered only by rhetorical outnarration. One cannot escape foundationalism by reinscribing dialectical adjudication within traditions. Rather it is the specific content of Christian virtue—"its promotion of charity, forgiveness, patience

91. Here the debate surrounding nature and super-nature in the work of Henri de Lubac looms large. See de Lubac, *Drama of Atheist Humanism*, and *Mystery of the Supernatural*. For Milbank's reading of this important theme see Milbank, *Suspended Middle*.

92. Balthasar, *Glory of the Lord*; Milbank, *TST*, 302–6; and Pickstock, *After Writing*, 121–41. For an account of the relation of Milbank et al. to Balthasar's reading of modernity, see Hyman, *Predicament of Postmodern Theology*, 31–52.

93. Milbank, *TST*, 331.

etc"—which is alone capable of standing against the encroaching tide of postmodern nihilism.[94]

Milbank is right to say that for one to endorse the concept of traditioned reason *in general* implies precisely the kind of detachment that MacIntyre denies is possible.[95] MacIntyre locates epistemological crisis at the point of the breakdown of the internal argument that constitutes that tradition, and therefore provides the only ground for a commensurability of traditions. In his criticism of MacIntyre at this point Milbank exposes his own susceptibility to charges of perspectivism and a loss of publicity. He argues that

> . . . if criteria are still in full force, and if, as MacIntyre says, all criteria are tradition-specific, then how can we really talk of a rational switch in tradition? If a tradition has *really* collapsed, then this must mean that its criteria. . . have split asunder. . . . Hence there is a *questionableness* about every switch of tradition, which escapes dialectical adjudication. What triumphs is simply the persuasive power of a new narrative . . .[96]

For MacIntyre, only in times of radical crisis and challenge do adherents examine the fundamental tenets ("first principles") of their tradition. Such a strong assertion of inescapable particularity has been accused of a perspectivism that allows no grounds for realist interpretations of moral assertions. This accusation misses its target. In fact what MacIntyre attempts is a postmodern form of the weak correspondence theory of truth. While mundane issues may be resolved by reference to the internal coherence of the tradition (what MacIntyre, like Richard Rorty and other more strongly relativist thinkers, call the principle of "warranted assertability"[97]), epistemological crisis leads to an examination of the value of coherence itself, which can only be justified in reference to a realist, correspondence theory of truth.[98] That is not to say, of

94. Ibid., 332.
95. Ibid., 326–79.
96. Ibid., 346. For the charge of perspectivism, see Fergusson, *Community*, 134. See also Herbert, "Getting By in Babylon."
97. MacIntyre, *Whose Justice*, 363.
98. MacIntyre, in contrast to Milbank, denies that his view of tradition-constituted enquiry disallows the potential for inter-traditional communication. Disputants "can only vindicate the rational superiority of their theses and arguments, if and in so far as they can provide within their own language in use an adequate representation of the claims that they reject." MacIntyre, "Partial Response," 296.

course, that MacIntyre contradicts himself in positing a final access to "things-as-they-are-in-themselves" (strong correspondence theory), but rather that the possibility of translation between traditions implies the prospect of discovering untranslatable elements. The rational superiority of one's tradition is demonstrated in its ability to explain that which a rival tradition cannot, in relation to its central claims to truth.

Traditions are neither monolithic and immutable nor entirely incommensurate. Argumentation is essential to the life of the tradition: "when a tradition is in good order it is always partially constituted by an argument about the goods the pursuit of which gives to that tradition its particular point and purpose."[99] Not all traditions are in good order. MacIntyre is clear that they can "decay, disintegrate and disappear." The causes of such decay appear twofold: the failure to practice the virtues of the tradition, for the virtues sustain both the individual and the tradition which they inhabit;[100] and through encounter with a (presumably both diachronic and synchronic) plurality of traditions.[101] Thus, in a move reminiscent of Kuhnian paradigm shifts (where a crisis is generated by excess ad hoc justifications of a dying paradigm), MacIntyre is able to claim that an old tradition can be rejected when a newer tradition exhibits greater explanatory power.

The synchronic commensurability of traditions does not necessarily imply tradition-transcendent criteria for the synthesis of previously divergent traditions. In a move that does some justice to the fact that individuals inhabit multifarious communities, with different levels of commitment to and engagement with each, MacIntyre asserts that a native of one tradition, by means of full orientation in its thickness of life and imaginative inhabitation of the context, may come to speak the language of another tradition.

Michael Banner and John Milbank both accuse MacIntyre of a failure to escape the foundationalist epistemology and the precepts of the Enlightenment project that he explicitly disavows.[102] This continued affinity to the Enlightenment is located, says Banner, in MacIntyre's assumption that a realist morality must be capable of exhibiting its argumentative

---

99. MacIntyre, *After Virtue*, 222.
100. Ibid., 223f.
101. See Markham, *Plurality and Christian Ethics*, 225.
102. Banner, *Christian Ethics*, 42–44; Milbank, *TST*, 330–31.

superiority to its rivals.[103] In contrast, Banner's form of Barthian dogmatic ethics, like Milbank's "postmodern critical Augustinianism," claims not to require dialectical adjudication; for knowledge of good and evil is graciously given in revelation. The basic theological axiom of human finitude means that Christian ethics is not located within the apologetic task of locating revelation within the constraints of secular morality. "There is no place within this world from which Christianity can speak; but because Christianity cannot speak from within this world, it does not follow that Christianity cannot speak to it."[104]

The position I defend has a great deal of sympathy with these views. However, it diverges in two important ways: first, regarding the relation of rhetoric to dialectics, and second, regarding the tactics used in relation to secular ethical discourse. For Milbank any prospect for dialectical adjudication remains both universalist and foundationalist. However, MacIntyre's commitment to dialectics is, as David Fergusson puts it, "a corollary of his realism."[105] That is to say, the correspondence theory of truth does not, finally, for MacIntyre, lead to foundationalism, but more minimally appeals to dialectics in order to explain the possibility of any claim to rational superiority of the Christian story. In distinguishing so strongly between rhetoric and dialectics, Milbank criticizes MacIntyre for associating the former exclusively with an emergent individualism.[106] As we have seen, for Milbank the Christian mythos is not said to be rationally superior to nihilism, but rhetorically more persuasive. But need rhetoric be so divided from dialectics?

Certainly one needs to be cautious of locating Christian publicity within universalist accounts of rationality and the Kantian conception of reason. It is perhaps more satisfactory to view rhetoric, with Aristotle, as the counterpart to dialectics.[107] That is to say that rhetoric is more suitable to practical matters of politics and ethics, where the theoretical inquiry to which dialectics is suited remains insufficient. Rational adjudication is thereby subordinated to rhetoric, but not in such a way as to allow the Milbankian division to stand. If moral realism is to escape

---

103. See especially MacIntyre, "Moral Relativism, Truth and Justification."
104. Banner, *Christian Ethics*, 44.
105. Fergusson, *Community*, 133.
106. Milbank, *TST*, 328, referring to MacIntyre, *Whose Justice*, 55–56.
107. Aristotle *Rhetoric* 1354a1. In this I follow David Cunningham's excellent discussion of rhetoric and dialectical method in Cunningham, *Faithful Persuasion*, 12–17.

connotations of either perspectivism or foundationalism then the *final* rational superiority of the Christian story cannot be divorced from its rhetorical persuasiveness. Indeed the fledgling theological account one finds in MacIntyre has, as yet, taken insufficient account of eschatology in relation to the possibility of a rational validation of Christian teleology. Without descending into fideism, Christian political critique must flow from the apparently counter-factual lordship of Christ. One must question whether the Christian story can be rationally vindicated in its entirety before the coming of the Kingdom. I shall show in chapter 3 how the claims of Christian eschatology are "realist" in such a way as to avoid either fideism or sectarianism and provide the basis for Christian engagement in social transformation.

Yoder on the Gospel

Given this more complimentary relation of validation to persuasion I come to Yoder in order to contend that an ad hoc engagement with secular moral and political discourse denotes a faithful, and yet public, account of Christian particularity. Yoder was rarely interested in questions of method for their own sake. We might speculate that he would echo Jeffrey Stout's dictum that a "preoccupation with method is like clearing your throat: it can go on for only so long before you lose your audience."[108] But there is more to Yoder's approach than mere impatience with methodological abstraction. We saw above his concern that commitment to incommensurability on a priori methodological grounds itself participates in a covert and retrograde form of foundationalism. The fact that Yoder preferred to write short papers and conducted much of his prolific writing activities through the circulation of an enormous quantity of memoranda is evidence of his conviction that his vocation as a theologian involved him in a dialogical process of response to the needs of the Christian community. In relation to issues of translatability, incommensurability, and particularity, his "methodological" starting point, if indeed it may be described as such, may be summarized by his pointed invocation of the Quaker poet Kenneth Boulding's law—"if something has happened, it is possible."[109]

---

108. Stout, *Ethics After Babel*, 163.

109. Boulding cited in Yoder, "Absolute Philosophical Relativism is an Oxymoron."

The broadly methodological (though not "methodologistic" in his terms) aspects of his theology marks an attempt to understand how the mission of the Church, and the genre of "gospel," can be understood in relation to the regnant pluralism of contemporary moral debate. By pointing to the innate publicity of the notion of *evangel*—the good news of the one lordship of Christ, the proclamation of the arrival of "another king"—Yoder sought to show how the dialogical nature of theological discourse is implicated in the wider pattern of vulnerability and contextual contingency that characterizes the Church's mission.

The divergence between Yoder and Milbank is attributable to the latter's more ontologically dualistic forms of distinction between Christian and secular morality. The form of distinction employed by the two authors differs both in the constituent elements of its division (where it is located) and its mode of operation (the philosophical dynamics through which it is maintained). Briefly stated, this is to say that for Yoder, the distinction that is most fruitfully employed is not secular/sacred, or general/revealed, although these have some use, but rather church/world. The permeability of this division, which for Yoder is conceived as a duality of responses to the gospel, a division between faith and unbelief, is in marked contrast to Milbank.[110] Milbank's preference for rhetorical triumph over and against MacIntyrian dialectics establishes a somewhat monolithic account of the "secular" as irredeemably nihilistic. So also, for example, Michael Banner's use of Barth's image of the annexation of general ethics by Christian dogmatics attempts to display the inherent otherness of an ethics derived from and lived through the Christian narrative.[111] However, for Yoder this otherness has its proper object not in its opposition to "culture," or to "the secular" in Milbank's sense, but to the

---

110. Yoder, *CWS*, 32.

111. The image of the annexation of other modes of moral discourse is used by Barth in discussing the relation of theological ethics to "general ethics"—which is perhaps a more appropriate mode in relation to a falsely de-particularised attempt at public ethics, than is Milbank's dismissal of "nihilistic" social theory. "Dogmatic ethics can relate to the general conception of ethics only in a way which ... means an annexation of the kind that took place ... on the entry of the Children of Israel into Palestine. ... On no account had the Israelites to adopt or take part in their cultus or culture." However, Barth goes on to clarify that, while no apologetic move to mitigate the offence generated in the face of the proclamation of God's command is permissible, "theological ethics can and must establish a continuous relationship of its thinking and speaking with the human ethical problem as a whole." See Barth, *CD* II/2, 509–51.

"world" in the specific sense of those aspects of fallen creation, which, in continued rebellion to the lordship of Christ, remain unredeemed.

We shall explore at greater length in the third and fourth chapters of this book how the truth of the universal lordship of Christ is made public in communal nonviolent opposition to the rebellion of the worldly powers. Such resistance requires an ecclesiology begun in God's declaration of the fundamental goodness of creation, and is thus attendant upon a hermeneutical practice of discernment between the proper glory of creation and the parasitic perversion of that goodness. There is no simple equation for this calculation. For Yoder, methodological constructions of moral reasoning are subordinated to the complexity and particularity of Christian life—a life that in contemporary Western receptor cultures engenders a particular, public response to the "postmodern conditions" of plurality, alterity, and violence.

In common with MacIntyre, Yoder is critical of foundationalist epistemology: the methodological move to a prior, higher, or more fundamental basis for truth claims, over and above traditioned particularity. Whereas inadequate perspectivist readings of MacIntyre's vision of tradition-constituted enquiry, or of George Lindbeck's "postliberal" cultural-linguistic construal of doctrine, risk viewing particular truths as incommensurable on a priori epistemological grounds, Yoder refuses to allow *evangel* to be seen in such esoteric terms. The desire for certainty and the drive to master contingency are theological errors based in the false eschatology of "Constantinianism." The notion of Constantinianism, to which we shall return in detail in chapter 3, is paradigmatic for much of Yoder's social thought. It is to be linked here with foundationalism because it denotes, amongst other things, the attempt to reify contingency in order, in Yoder's characterization, to get a "handle" on history.[112] It therefore includes the desire to "start from scratch" in our moral and political engagements, in order to thereby discover some foundation for mastering particularity. There is, says Yoder, "no scratch from which to start."[113]

The truth of the gospel proclamation of the lordship of Christ is not maintained at a level of universalizable abstraction, but is true only insofar as it remains the lived particularity of the Christian community. The Church is that "royal priesthood" who, through its agents of memory, of direction, of "linguistic self-consciousness" and of "order and due

---

112. Yoder, *PJ*, 228.
113. Yoder, *FTN*, 10.

process" together ensure that the community works as a hermeneutical process, which is, at every stage, primary to theoretical, methodological abstraction about how "ideas" work.[114] Insofar as this represents an anti-theoretical pragmatic view of specific moral discernment, it is possible to see how Yoder goes on to maintain that the Christian life is too complex to be constrained by any one particular methodological construal of ethical theory.[115]

Most prevalent ethical theories are decisionist—they privilege the importance of the individual's choice; and "quandryist"—subordinating the dilemmas of everyday life to the most contrived and extreme of situations. Everyday practices and virtues are virtually ignored. For Yoder, as for Stanley Hauerwas's more explicit move to understandings of virtue and character within Christian ethics, an ecclesiological emphasis is not simply an abstract counterbalance to decisionist and quandryist theory. It is an anti-Constantinian move. To cling on to foundationalist moral epistemology is to subordinate necessarily particular practice to universalizing abstraction. The community is thus secondary to, and constrained by, a priori commitments to individualistic accounts of ethical method. This naturally partakes of the modern privatizing and individualizing tendencies of secularization, which militate against particular public presence.

To put it bluntly, in asserting that the concrete community of the church precedes moral epistemology, Yoder maintains the particularity of the community of the Jewish Jesus Christ against the Constantinian *Christus Pantocrator*. Equally, although this is not his explicit target, he thereby safeguards the community from the secularizing processes of enforced generalization and privatization characteristic of liberal denigration of public particularity. The scandal of particularity is that Christian ethics is for Christians[116]—it is not a universal (i.e., non-confessional) theory of the good life, but a call to, and condition of, discipleship. That is most emphatically not to deny that the Christian vision is anything other than universal in its scope and claim. Moral theology (indeed all theology) is not "a meta-level discipline that is concerned primarily with

114. Yoder, "Hermeneutics of Peoplehood," in *PK*, 15–45, esp. 27–35.

115. The relation of Yoder to both the philosophical school of ethical "anti-theory," and to the thought of both MacIntyre and Milbank, is usefully explored in Chris Huebner's doctoral dissertation: Huebner, "Unhandling History."

116. Yoder, "Why Ecclesiology is Social Ethics: Gospel Ethics Versus the Wider Wisdom," the Stone Lectures and the Morgan Lectures, revised version appears in *RP*, 102–26; 116f.

the question of the proper elucidation of and logical interrelationship between certain central concepts or loci."[117] When theology becomes reduced to, or constrained by, any abstract method or theory, it can no longer function to guide the life of the church. This is not to say that philosophical considerations of morality are inadmissible in Yoder's theology, but rather that such considerations are subordinate to the more concrete matters of the practice of everyday life. They form but one part of the constant hermeneutical process of communal existence.

Yoder's non-foundationalist, anti-theoretical theology thus combats any a priori construal of incommensurability or untranslatability of gospel truth. The question of translatability is not solved by prior methodological or linguistic moves, but is "a question of empirical history, resolved by real contacts between communities."[118] This, of course, is not the same thing as saying that gospel truth is public truth. Perhaps the most common understanding of "public"—as universal nonparticular accessibility or verifiability—is subject to a particularist critique of foundationalism. Yet Yoder strongly asserts that the gospel truth is a public truth, and the Bible a public document. Yoder's anti-theoretical stance is not, therefore, a denial of the importance of validation, or an appeal to arbitrary cultural linguistic preferences.

The primordiality of the hermeneutic function of the community, because of the missionary nature of *evangel* (the sending of the Church as part of the move of God to "his" creation), requires it to find an "interworld transformational grammar." Just as the New Testament writers were the first "transcultural reconceptualizers," the hermeneutical task of the Christian community is the emulation of their missionary exercise.[119] To affirm the importance, indeed the inevitability, of a transcultural hermeneutic process is not to circumvent the difficulties, conflicts, and misunderstandings that accompany any process of inculturation.[120] It is,

---

117. Yoder, "Walk and Word." See also Huebner, "Can a Gift be Commanded?" 482–83.

118. Yoder, "To Serve Our God and Rule the World," in *RP*, 127–40, at 137.

119. Yoder, *PK*, 56.

120. Note this is "inculturation", not "enculturation." Enculturation denotes the processes of socialization and the formation of all persons by their culture. Inculturation is a missiological notion on the bi-directional interplay of enculturation and gospel proclamation. Thus, John Paul II's encyclical *Redemptoris Missio* defines it thus: "The process of the Church's insertion into peoples' cultures is a lengthy one. It is not a matter of purely external adaptation, for inculturation "means the intimate transformation of authentic cultural values through their integration in Christianity and the insertion of Christianity

rather, to refuse to allow such difficulties epistemological privilege over the embodied practice of the community.

Richard Hays notes that Yoder "finds within history the hermeneutical point of contact with human reason that Barth steadfastly refused to acknowledge." For Yoder, "scripture creates a symbolic world which subordinates reason and history."[121] The transcultural and evangelistic nature of the truth of which the Bible speaks remains a public truth. It is not rendered public through foundational linguistic moves that deracinate the Jewishness of Jesus, making Christ an exemplar or idealist deserving our admiration. Rather, publicness arrives with the demand for the obedience named discipleship. That is to say, validation and publicity come through, rather than in spite of, difference and particularity. Indeed, for Yoder, it is because God is both nonviolent and patient that a theology of validation should be characterized by a peaceable and dialogical epistemology.

Diversity, and hence particularity, are created goods. It is only the hegemonic totalizing thrust of Constantinian foundationalism that cannot cope with otherness. This foundationalism is an attempt to escape the uncertainty attendant upon the fact of the Other. It aims to "bypass my becoming vulnerable to your world in your otherness."[122] By contrast Yoder's nonviolence, itself understandable only "within the Christologically determined symbolic universe of the New Testament texts,"[123] is both a *political* stance and an *epistemological* openness to the other. Gospel is a unique genre in that, because of its renunciation of coercion, assent is not required, but freely entered into.[124] The gospel is public in that it has "no secret formula, no memorized passwords; open reading, room for debate about its meaning, translatability."[125]

Epistemological nonviolence implies a "patient" method of moral reasoning, letting the public truth of the gospel speak for itself, not

---

in the various human cultures." The process is thus a profound and all-embracing one, which involves the Christian message and also the Church's reflection and practice. But at the same time it is a difficult process, for it must in no way compromise the distinctiveness and integrity of the Christian faith." John Paul II, *Redemptoris Missio*, para 52. The internal reference is to Extraordinary Assembly of 1985, *Final Report*, II D 4.

121. Hays, *Moral Vision*, 251–52.
122. Yoder, *MAB*, 134.
123. Hays, *Moral Vision*, 250.
124. Yoder, *MAB*, 134 n. 22.
125. Ibid., 137.

perverting it by seeking means of coercing assent.[126] Such a stance requires that one should adopt the subversive position paradigmatically exemplified in the Jeremianic mandate to "seek the peace of the city." Such a stance is pragmatic, and, in appearance, variegated.

> To "rule the world" in fellowship with the living Lamb, will sometimes mean humbly building a grassroots culture with Jeremiah. Sometimes (as with Joseph and Daniel) it will mean helping the pagan king solve one problem at a time. Sometimes (again with Daniel and his friends) it will mean disobeying the King's imperative of idolatry, refusing to be bamboozled by the claims made for the Emperor's new robe or his fiery furnace.[127]

The Return to Athens

Now that we have been to Babel—to a discussion of pluralism—it is time to return to Athens. The location of Christian political criticism within the proclamation of the gospel has been shown to provide ample ground for a theological response to our situation of pluralistic moral discourse. The "transcultural reconceptualizers" of which Yoder spoke always aimed to place the affirmation of the lordship of Christ within the cosmologies of the worlds they encountered. This is not apologetics in the sense that Barth rejected.[128] For the challenge facing Christian mission, and the theologians who serve it, is to emulate the exercise of these defenders of the faith who sought the grammar to proclaim aright the "strange things" heard in the streets of Thessalonica and the Athenian marketplace. The aim is not to master the tides of pluralism. It is more ad hoc than that. As Yoder has it:

> What we are looking for . . . is not a way to keep dry above the waves of relativity, but a way to stay within our bark, barely afloat and sometimes awash amidst those waves, yet neither dissolving into them nor being carried only where they want to push it.[129]

---

126. Yoder, *PMMR*, 24–42.

127. Yoder, *RP*, 135.

128. It is more akin to the ad hoc apologetics identified by William Wepehowski in his "Ad Hoc Apologetics."

129. Yoder, *PK*, 58.

The ubiquity of pluralist-relativist language threatens both the drive to totalization and the shift to apologetics in the Barthian sense. The first is found in "establishment epistemology" with its concern to back up a desire for "monocultural unity" with the power of political authority. The latter is characteristic of much mainstream Protestantism and represents the strategy to "define a kind of solid ground no longer subject to the reproach of others or to self-doubt as being vitiated by any kind of particularity."[130] Insofar as these are theological errors to be questioned, the Christian theologian can find a "tactical ally" in the pluralist questioning of prevailing orthodoxies.

Nevertheless the proclamation of the lordship of Christ turns this pluralist world upside down, much as it did the Hellenist world. There is no pluralist or relativist concession in Paul's use of the "unknown God" in Acts 17; no syncretism or appeasement in the use of the language of Christ's pre-existence in John 1, Hebrews 1, and Colossians 1. All of these moves represent the "appropriate missionary way to state the priority of Christ over the preoccupations of pagan faith."[131] Thus, for example, Yoder argues that the Johannine prologue subverts a proto-gnostic cosmology by affirming the coevality of the Logos with God and yet also asserting that it has truly become mortal flesh. The prior cosmological language "has been seized and used for a different message. No longer does the concept of Logos solve a problem of religion, reconciling the eternal with the temporal: it carries a proclamation of Incarnation drawing all who believe into the power of Sonship."[132] Likewise the task before those attempting to articulate a "public" theology is to demonstrate how the church can faithfully relate to contemporary understandings of the public sphere, of validation and moral discourse, and of concerns for "justice," "emancipation," and the like; and in doing all of that come to confess that it is under the lordship of Christ that the cosmos finds its true coherence and meaning.

---

130. Ibid., 60.

131. Yoder, *PT*, 130.

132. Yoder, "That Household We Are," 4. See also *PT* for an extended account of the historical impact of a theology built on christological foundations.

CHAPTER 2

Political Criticism and the Vulnerability of the Particular

"Accidental truths of history can never become the proof of necessary truths of reason.... That... is the ugly, broad ditch which I cannot get across..."[1]

—Gotthold Ephraim Lessing

"For our world it will be in his ordinariness as villager, as rabbi, as king on a donkey, and as liberator on a cross that we shall be able to express the claims which the apostolic proclaimers to Hellenism expressed in the language of preexistence and condescension.... This is the low road to general validity.... It thereby frees us to use any language, to enter any world in which people eat bread and pursue debtors, hope for power and execute subversives. The ordinariness of the humanness of Jesus is the warrant for the generalizability of his reconciliation.... The particularity of the incarnation is the universality of the good. There is no road but the low road. The truth has come to our side of the ditch."[2]

—John Howard Yoder

"Critique is the movement by which the subject gives itself the right to question truth on its effects of power and to question power on its discourses of truth... in a word, the politics of truth."[3]

—Michel Foucault

---

1. Lessing, *Theological Writings*, 53, 55. Cited in Yoder, *PK*, 46.
2. Yoder, *PK*, 62.
3. Foucault, "What is Critique," in *Politics of Truth*, 32.

Public(s) and Universal(s)

To affirm the situatedness and particularity of moral and political critique, as I have done, will immediately evoke a number of questions. How are those of different traditions to agree on some shared objectives? Surely, it will be suggested, agreement on the direction of social development, not to mention an acceptable account of whether actions can be described as right or wrong, just or unjust, must require the possibility of consensus? If agreement and, in some circumstances, agreeing to disagree, are not possible, then the factionalism and fragmentation of contemporary life will devour us all. Even if diversity really is as deep and intractable as the postmodernists insist, can we not rescue some of the hopes of modernity? Even if notions of individual autonomy and rationality are deeply suspect, are we not obliged to keep our focus on notions of equality, emancipation, freedom, and justice? Such is the pervasiveness of modernist presumptions in accounts of the public sphere that these latter values, in some form, are deemed to provide the deepest and most basic framework for common life. Even if we may dispute a particular construal of equality or justice, who could possibly disagree that the emancipation of the oppressed and excluded is a good idea? Well, I suspect, not many would do so. Even so, it is substantially more questionable whether the politics of liberal modernity are capable of delivering true emancipation, freedom, or justice.

If more substantive (e.g., theological) accounts need to be heard in public, how can they participate? For many theories of liberal democracy, especially those that dominate our understanding of publicness, the answer is simple—they cannot. Religion remains pejoratively associated with the pre-modern world in which, supposedly, it served to legitimate state power rather than critique it. Any emphasis on particularity smacks of obscurantism, fideism, and a lack of intelligibility. Even a critic of modernity like Richard Rorty insists that the relegation of religion to the private sphere is essential to the maintenance of democracy.[4] In order to demonstrate the public nature of theological social criticism, we began in the introductory chapter to articulate the publicness of the categories of mission and witness. In these next two chapters I will explore how

---

4. Rorty, "Religion as a Conversation Stopper," in *Philosophy and Social Hope*, 168–74. See also the engagement between Rorty and Nicholas Wolterstorff. Wolterstorff, "Engagement With Rorty," and Rorty, "Religion in the Public Square."

these theological categories place the modern construal of the relation of universal to particular in question. In the current chapter I will examine how theologians might respond to the concerns for intelligibility, publicity, and consensus as they appear in modern political theory. In the next chapter, I will then explore the theological, specifically the christological and eschatological, basis for a realism that re-orients the modernist account of publicity, particularity and universality.

Enormous amounts of theologians' time and effort, not to mention ink, have been spent on examining the way in which theology may be described as a public discourse. In doing so, one common, and largely helpful (though inevitably simplistic), division arises between revisionist and postliberal theologies. Revisionism may be simply described as the concern to render theological discourse public through the use of explanations understandable outside of the commitment and confession of the religious community. Postliberals, as William Placher writes,

> note *ad hoc* conjunctions and analogies with the questions and beliefs of non-Christians, but their primary concern is to preserve the Christian vision free of distortion, and they mistrust systematic efforts to correlate Christian beliefs with more general claims about human experience, which seem to them always to risk constraining and distorting the Christian "answers" to fit the "questions" posed by some aspect of contemporary culture.[5]

Over twenty years ago, when articulating the division between revisionism and postliberalism, Placher provided an account of three different senses of the term "public." That which dominates revisionism is close to that which I noted in our introduction to be the most prevalent in contemporary idiom—universal nonparticular accessibility or verifiability.[6] That which befits postliberal approaches directs its aim against the enforced privatizing aspects of liberal polities—"it understands a religion as fundamentally a public, communal activity, not a matter of the individual's experience."[7] The third sense does not necessarily apply more to one or other of these options. Either form of theological discourse is public, in this sense, in so far as it "effectively addresses political and social issues." It should already be clear that John Howard Yoder's theology

---

5. Placher, *Unapologetic Theology*, 154.

6. Placher defines this as "appeals to warrants available to any intelligent, reasonable, responsible person." Placher, "Revisionist and Postliberal Theologies," 407.

7. Ibid.

is, in this loosest of senses, thoroughly postliberal.[8] The question before us in this chapter is how theology may be public in this third sense.

I prefer the terms revisionist and postliberal to the alternatives of correlational versus confessional, or universal versus particular. These latter options obscure significant aspects of the debate. So-called "correlational" theologians do not simply eschew the validity of religious confession, although they generally circumscribe its publicity in various ways. Importantly for our present discussion, particularist accounts are not simply relativist. Many, in fact most, do claim that some property, faculty, or condition is universal—whether it is reason, communication, or, more theologically, natural law, or Christ himself. The question then, is which universal?

The critical moment of this chapter contends that insofar as theology attempts to render itself public through reference to a putative universal outside of Christian confession, it participates in an abstractive enterprise which, ironically, undermines its emancipatory and egalitarian intent. I shall show that the use of Jürgen Habermas by "public theologians" applies a theological gloss to the liberal moral question of the legitimate ordering of co-existing forms of life. This basic concern is pressing, but it requires more of theology than just a Christian answer to the liberal question; it requires a deeper questioning (similar to the mode of Foucault) of the means by which the subjugation inherent in modern claims to inclusion may be exposed and overcome.

Nevertheless, the constructive moment of the chapter notes the importance of a thoroughly hermeneutical conception of Christian publicity, which a completely historicist account simply cannot furnish. To that end, I shall explore how Yoder's theological ethics provide a christocentric redefinition of the tension between universal and particular that, in its account of the hermeneutical functioning of the Christian community, understands the public truth of the gospel as both the gift and calling of true emancipation, equality, freedom, and justice.

---

8. Although Yoder would have been rightly cautious of aligning himself with any theological school of thought. There are also significant differences between Yoder and some postliberal theologians (the term unites a diverse range of opinions). For example, Yoder's christocentrism yields a stronger and clearer form of realism than might be found in George Lindbeck's cultural-linguistic theory.

The Intolerant Tolerance of Justificatory Liberalism

One of the most influential approaches to resolving the problem of religion in public is that of what, following Christopher Eberle, we can name "justificatory liberalism."[9] The term refers generally to any philosopher, of any political persuasion, who would hold it appropriate to deny religious conviction any determinitive role in the justification of a particular policy, at least insofar as no more generalizable "public" justification can be given. The most obvious candidate here is John Rawls. Rawls's argument is well known. I will merely restate it, and significant theological objections to it, in the briefest of terms, before moving on to a form of justificatory liberalism that is both more explicitly critical and reformist in intent, and potentially more "open" to religion—that of Jürgen Habermas. Rawlsian liberalism rejects any attempt to establish a single common vision of the good, in favor of establishing a social unity solely on the procedures that may preserve our rights to pursue without interference the various goods and values found in our religious or secular "comprehensive doctrines."

In his original metaphysical account of liberalism, Rawls proposed his famous contractarian thought experiment, of an "original position" behind a "veil of ignorance," which will lead all reasonable people to support a notion of justice as fairness.[10] In later accounts Rawls sought to give a less metaphysical, more political account of liberalism—an account that gave explicit recognition of a pluralism of incompatible yet reasonable comprehensive doctrines.[11] Throughout his writings Rawls remains committed to the exclusion of explicitly religious reasoning from a determinative place in the public sphere. A commitment to intelligibility and rationality mean that when democratic societies undertake discussions about political policy or ethical issues, no appeal can be made to any special authority. All moral reasoning must be accessible and understandable to all people. In order to treat one's fellow citizens

---

9. The term "justificatory liberalism" is used by Christopher J. Eberle of all those who, on various grounds, deny religious conviction any determinitive role in the justification of a particular policy; at least insofar as no more generalizable "public" justification can be given. Eberle, *Religious Conviction*. Eberle is particularly interested in the more restricted case of the support or opposition of a coercive law on the sole basis of a religious rationale. "Justificatory liberals" would therefore include John Rawls, Robert Audi, Amy Gutmann, and Thomas Nagel. The term would also fit for Habermas.

10. Rawls, *Theory of Justice*.

11. Rawls, *Political Liberalism*.

properly, it seems logical that one is required to provide understandable reasons for one's own support of a particular policy or ethical view. Rawls then claims that not only should arguments be provided to justify any view held, but that these should be arguments that appeal only to ideals and principles that no reasonable person could possibly reject.

This is not to deny the formative influence of comprehensive doctrines (including religious views) on opinion formation. Rawls argues that all that political liberalism requires is an "overlapping consensus" between these comprehensive doctrines. Because religious views are not shared by all citizens, such views cannot provide the basis on which we may all reason in common. To introduce religious claims into such discussions will thereby immediately compromise the universality, and hence the legitimacy, of any agreement arising. Rawls thus operates with a clear and robust form of the modern division of private from public, locating religion solely within the former territory.

For his critics this imperative to exclude from public discussion even the forms of religious reasoning that may be acknowledged by Rawls to be a *rational* comprehensive doctrine may ironically compromise the norms of democratic participation. Nicholas Wolterstorff puts it strongly when he objects:

> given that it is of the very essence of liberal democracy that citizens enjoy equal freedom in law to live out their lives as they see fit, how can it be compatible with liberal democracy for its citizens to be *morally restrained* from deciding and discussing political issues as they see fit.... It belongs to the religious convictions of a good many religious people in our society that *they ought to base* their decisions concerning fundamental issues of justice *on* their religious convictions. They do not view it as an option whether or not to do it.[12]

This type of objection led Rawls to modify his position so that all comprehensive doctrines, including religious ones, "may be introduced in public reason at any time, provided that in due course public reasons, given by a reasonable political conception, are presented sufficient to support whatever the comprehensive doctrines are introduced to support."[13] So he is giving what seems to be a proviso—that it is acceptable to speak

---

12. Audi and Wolterstorff, *Religion in the Public Square*, 94, 105; See also Weithman, *Religion and Contemporary Liberalism*; and Cooke, "Secular State."

13. See "Introduction to the Paperback Edition," in Rawls *Political Liberalism*, li–lii; and "Idea of Public Reason," in *Law of Peoples*, 129–80.

of God in our ethical deliberation. But he does so only, as Jeffrey Stout puts it, by viewing religious reasons as IOUs that promise a more reasonable currency in the near future. Stout points out one obvious problem with this notion—it simply isn't how public debate works. He says of Rawls's view:

> It makes a bit more room for such instances of exemplary democratic reasoning as the religiously based oratory of the Abolitionists and of Martin Luther King Jr. But Rawls confesses that he does not know whether these orators "ever fulfilled the proviso" by eventually offering reasons of his officially approved sort. So, strictly speaking, from a Rawlsian point of view the jury is still out on these cases.[14]

I take such objections to be sufficient to reject the Rawlsian approach. If my wider contention in this chapter—that the vulnerable particularity of Christian witness is itself sufficiently public—is to hold, then we must consider the arguments of a figure who combines justificatory liberalism with a strong critique of the pathologies of modernity, and an increasing attention to the potential public role of religious conviction.

Habermas on Religion and Critical Social Theory

The German critical theorist Jürgen Habermas provides one of the most influential, expansive, and impressive theorizations of social criticism. Habermas's wide-ranging critical social theory is oriented to a normative account of communicative action. Communicative action is held to provide the space for the functioning of the public sphere along the lines of a model of deliberative democracy. His early work on *The Structural Transformation of the Public Sphere* highlights the problematic nature of claiming any assertion as authentically "public." For Habermas, the eighteenth-century model of a bourgeois public sphere, where public policy was subjected to sustained critical assessment, has become perverted. In its place we find a thoroughly mediatized public, manipulated through the modern practices of "publicity." In such circumstances (referred to as a "refeudalization" of the public sphere) any claim to universality is compromised.

> Here organizations strive for political compromises with the state and with one another, as much as possible to the exclusion of the

14. Stout, *Democracy and Tradition*, 68–69.

public; in this process, however, they have to procure plebiscitary agreement from a mediatized public by means of a display of staged or manipulated publicity.[15]

Unlike the extreme postmodernist celebration of such mediatizing as the annihilation of "reality" (Baudrillard), Habermas seeks to recover an authentic universality—i.e., a public.[16] Lastly and most importantly this has been attempted through a dialogical renovation of the Kantian tradition. From a basis in the Frankfurt school, Habermas moved beyond Horkheimer and Adorno towards a commitment to the continuation of the Enlightenment project.[17] The differentiation of modern culture into what Weber denoted the three autonomous spheres of science, morality, and art goes largely unquestioned. For Habermas, pace Adorno, the emancipatory intent of modernity cannot be realized through the privileging of any one of these spheres (as aesthetics was for Adorno). Instead, the potential for emancipatory change must be found in something universal to the whole lifeworld. Habermas turns to this dialogical renovation in order to demonstrate the potential for change inherent in "communicative" or "discursive" rationality. Thus the monological conception of the categorical imperative (attained by the unencumbered reflecting subject) is rejected in favor of a community of discourse universalizing moral norms, based upon common assent achieved through (noncoercive and inclusive) public discourse.

Habermas disavows the immediate (i.e., unmediated) provincialism of religious (and other "mythic") traditions, in favor of a reconstruction of those universal factors of human communication that alone can provide grounds for a truly noncoercive public consensus. Religious discourse claims a privileged access to truth (e.g., claims to revelation), which, for Habermas, cannot but insulate them from critique and thus drive them toward a coercive form of politics.[18] Instead, in somewhat reactionary

15. Habermas, *Structural Transformation*, 231–35.

16. The pessimism regarding the future of democracy that characterized *Structural Transformation* is replaced in later works with a stronger constructive moment in the account of communicative rationality operating in relation to the functioning of economic and state systems within the lifeworld. The basic concern for the recovery of conditions of publicity remains paramount.

17. Habermas, "Modernity."

18. Of course, Habermas's understanding of religious discourse as closed to critique bears little resemblance to the way in which the vast majority of theological reflection is undertaken. In addition to the critique offered below, a number of authors have objected to Habermas at this point. Habermas's stress on the value of reasoned argument sits ill

48 SEEK THE PEACE OF THE CITY

tones, Habermas presses for a "post-metaphysical" form of thought that necessarily operates with a "methodological atheism."[19] This entirely procedural focus on the establishment of "valid knowledge" of moral norms prohibits any appeal to norms and values as they are born out of the thickness of communal life. This "discourse ethics" contrasts a "normative consensus" (established on the basis of existing norms and traditions) from a "communicatively achieved consensus," where all affected parties achieve agreement in a free and open dialogue. The latter is said to be undetermined a priori by traditions, and is oriented towards the inclusive and non-coercive context of the "ideal speech situation." Thus Habermas describes communicative rationality as carrying with it

> connotations based ultimately on the central experience of the unconstrained, unifying, consensus-bringing force of argumentative speech, in which different participants overcome their merely subjective views and, owing to the mutuality of rationally motivated conviction, assure themselves of both the unity of the objective world and the intersubjectivity of their lifeworld.[20]

This, in turn, requires Habermas to reject those forms of linguistic interaction (speech acts) that are labeled "strategic." Strategic forms of communication distort communicative reason and constrict the possibility of pure intersubjectivity through their orientation to success rather than the attainment of understanding. There is an inescapable and undesirable element of coercion inherent in strategic communication. Habermas is aware, of course, that any actual speech act tends to possess a mixture of various "pure types" of communication.[21] His goal, therefore, is to recover the conditions for undistorted communication that alone can lead to the realization of the emancipatory thrust of modernity. Incongruously Habermas's own idiom is characterized by immense abstraction and pervasive jargon. His constructive proposals are shot through with the kind of strategic rhetorical invocations that his own system disavows.

---

with his pejorative picture here. Among many accounts of the reflexivity of theological discourse in refutation of Habermas, see Dillon, "Authority of the Holy."

19. Habermas, *Justification and Application*, 133–46. For a useful brief account of these moves, see Lalonde, *Critical Theology*, 25–42.
20. Habermas, *Theory of Communicative Action*, 1:110ff.
21. Ibid.

Modern philosophy's preoccupation, since Descartes, with the knowing subject is, says Habermas, insufficient for engendering the conditions necessary for the realization of the Enlightenment project.[22] For Habermas, contra subject-centerd reason, the formation of the individuated subject occurs within processes of discursive will formation. Unlike liberals less critical of modernity, he does not deny the situatedness of the self. The presuppositions of undistorted communication are historical and context-dependent and yet transcend that context in their universality. The rational adjudication of norms begins within concrete forms of life, but must necessarily move beyond them if the process is to escape parochialism and vulnerability to prejudice.[23] "The transcendental moment of *universal* validity bursts every provinciality asunder."[24] In place of this "philosophy of the subject" with its center on the self as knower, Habermas provides us with a conception of the self as communicator. The task of a critical theory of society is to "decenter" the subject and expose the pathologies of modernity in order to restore an authentic intersubjectivity.[25]

Habermas's procedural account of moral norms is characterized by two equally important principles. The principle of universalization (U) is designed to ensure impartiality. Norms are deemed valid only when submitted to a thought experiment in which all those affected by an action are imagined to be able to accept the consequences and side effects of the *general* observance of that norm. "The principle of universalization is intended to compel the *universal exchange of roles*."[26] This thought

---

22. Habermas, *Philosophical Discourse*, 294–326.

23. "Practical discourses are always related to the concrete point of departure of a disturbed normative agreement. These antecedent disruptions determine the topics that are up for discussion. This procedure, then, is not formal in the sense that it abstracts from content. Quite the contrary, in its openness, practical discourse is dependent upon contingent content being fed into it from outside. In discourse this is subjected to a process in which particular values are ultimately discarded as being not susceptible to consensus." Habermas, *Moral Consciousness*, 103.

24. Habermas, *Philosophical Discourse*, 322.

25. This recovery of the emancipatory concerns of the enlightenment through a retrieval of communicative rationality marks the significant divergence from Horkheimer and Adorno, who both viewed the enlightenment as irrevocably captivated by instrumental rationality. See most famously Adorno and Horkheimer, *Dialectic of Enlightenment*; for Habermas's critique, see Habermas, *Philosophical Discourse*, and *Theory of Communicative Action*, 2:383ff.

26. Habermas, *Moral Consciousness*, 65–66.

experiment is then grounded in concrete dialogue through the principle of discourse ethics (D). Norms are valid then, only when they meet the approval of all affected participants engaged in a *practical* discourse. The situatedness of the self means that these practical discourses are always related to concrete issues or moral crises that have "disturbed normative agreement." The procedural conditions are not formal in any sense that abstracts them from the specific content at issue. But, in that case the question remains, does the appealing description of intersubjective moral discourse (D) require the bracketing of the specificity of one's particular form of life (U)?

It is far from clear that Habermas is successful in pursuing a "universal pragmatics" by which the universal features of communicative competence are rediscovered a posteriori.[27] Habermas seems unable to demonstrate that the self as communicator provides a "universality" substantially less exclusionary than the "universal" of individual reason. Seyla Benhabib has provided a sensitive critique of Habermas's form of universalism at this point. She criticizes John Rawls for positing the abstract disembodied self as the archetypal harbinger of justice, thereby covertly privileging a "nostalgic ideal of the autonomous male ego."[28] Naturally, Habermas's decenterd self does not fit so easily here. Nevertheless the principle of universalization, as it operates in Habermas, can only truly be said to provide for consensus. But, contra Habermas, consensus, in and of itself, is neither a sufficient criterion of truth nor a demonstration of moral validity. It is the inclusion of all affected parties in public discourse, and not the insistence on universalization, which may prove most useful in Habermas's schema. And the two may be distinguished without any loss of the critical import of Habermas's work.[29]

However, Benhabib remains committed to a communicative mode of ethical deliberation that is unable to conceive of tradition as possessing, in and of itself, sufficient critical resources. She accepts the traditioned nature of the substantive presuppositions that motivate assent to the guiding principles of universal moral respect and egalitarian reciprocity. However, she goes on to argue that an ability to distance oneself from those traditions is indispensable, in order to allow for the self-critical practices essential for public ethical debate. As we noted in the previous

---

27. See Thompson, "Universal Pragmatics," in Thompson and Held, *Habermas*, 116–33.
28. Benhabib, *Situating the Self*, 3.
29. Ibid., 37.

chapter, Benhabib claims that without such distance communitarians will be unable to discern where the emphasis on formative tradition diverges from "an endorsement of social conformism, authoritarianism, and . . . patriarchalism."[30] The "universal" of actual discourse with the concrete other still requires an abstractive moment inadequately distanced from Habermas's U principle.

The specificity and focus of Michel Foucault's genealogical approach to social criticism provides an excellent contrast to Habermasian proceduralism. For Foucault, Habermas's decenterd subject, despite his best intentions, remains inadequately critical.[31] The abstract character of such an approach purchases its universality at the price of a higher degree of critical effectiveness. Foucault's genealogy, by contrast, acquires its critical bite at the cost of a certain tension between his preference for specific subjugated groups and his claim that genealogical method is fundamentally anti-normative.[32] Foucault finds the critical moment of the Enlightenment not, as Habermas does, in its shift from coercive particularity to universals, but precisely in its questioning of what really is universal. Foucault rejects any pretense of having discerned an ahistorical universal, be it reason, freedom, or communication. Genealogy enacts a politics of local critique, which alone, he says, can truly expose the processes of subjugation occurring through the disciplinary nature of knowledge and power. Importantly, critical theory and the genealogical exposure of subjugated knowledge share a fundamental emancipatory intent. But the Habermasian imperative for consensus may run the risk of pressing discourse toward a false peace.[33] By contrast, as David Owen puts it,

> By locating our activity of self-transformation within historically contingent relations of intersubjectivity, Foucault may be read as claiming that our becoming-in-the-world is always already a becoming-with-others. Indeed Foucault's concern with the hegemony of humanist structures of recognition may be located in part as a concern with humanism's desire to impose the law of the Same, that is, to institute a closure of our capacity for self-

30. Ibid., 74.

31. Notably, Foucault's own work returned to a focus on the self, and even, surprisingly for some critics, an account of autonomy. See Foucault, "What is Enlightenment?" in Rabinow, *Foucault Reader*, 32–50. See also Moss, "Foucault, Rawls and Public Reason."

32. Kelly, *Critique and Power*; Ashenden and Owen, *Foucault Contra Habermas*.

33. Coles, "Communicative Action."

transformation through the elimination of alterity (i.e., its reduction to normality).[34]

With regard to this liberative concern, one of the questions facing theologians is the way in which Christian particularity achieves its critical edge. I suggest that insofar as theologians introduce a Habermasian form of universalism into their accounts of the social-critical function of Christian participation in the public sphere, they also import a problematic understanding of Christian particularity. Because Habermas locates effective criticism within an abstractive universalism, particularity cannot be seen, in and of itself, as performing a social-critical function. By contrast, I contend that the critical edge of Christian particularity is characterized by an eschatological imagination that, as an exploration of Yoder's theology in the following chapters will show, can alone place the Church's social mission on firm ground.

The utopian dimension of the concept of the ideal speech situation cannot come to realization independent of the interpretive and dialogic functions of particular groups. But Habermas's account of religion militates against just this sort of realization. One cannot simply talk of Habermas as irredeemably secular, for latterly he has afforded some functional value to religious discourse. We shall explore this in more detail shortly. For now it is sufficient to note that, for the majority of Habermas's career, the value accorded to religion was measured solely in instrumental terms. The role of religious worldviews will eventually be superseded.[35] Without translation by the secularizing force of philosophy, religion would remain ineffective in the face of secular politics. Religion remains ineradicable insofar as it continues to provide what philosophy cannot—existential consolation, myth, symbol, and the semantic practices necessary for criticism.[36] "God" here functions as little more than a cipher for the unactualized potential of humanity. Habermas detects a "drive to universalization" internal to religious discourse. He claims this drive itself undermines the particularity of religious belief in a thrust towards the universality of philosophy. Religion, in many respects,

---

34. Owen, *Maturity and Modernity*, 205.

35. The charge of instrumentalism here is only sustainable in the light of the second charge of a secular supersessionism. Religion is currently ineradicable, however Habermas's overriding commitment to secularization will not allow him to concede the value of religion unmediated by the caustic translation of philosophy.

36. See Mendieta, "Introduction."

remains a coercive and authoritarian rationality. Indeed, the overriding commitment to universalization requires Habermas to conclude that the requisite philosophical transformation must appropriate the normative contents of religion. "[N]either science nor art can inherit the mantle of religion; only a morality, set communicatively aflow and developed into a discourse ethics, can replace the authority of the sacred."[37]

By contrast, some theologians have emphasized the distinctiveness of Christianity in such a way that any dialogic element to Christian social criticism appears impossible. Under such circumstances critique can appear to represent precisely the coercive rationality that Habermas seeks to avoid. Nevertheless I shall argue that a christocentric understanding of the relationship between universal and particular allows for a less problematic account of Christian social criticism. The term "christocentric," in and of itself, can mean many things. In the next chapter, I shall return to the work of the Mennonite theologian John Howard Yoder to clarify the specific complexion of the christocentrism most suited to our task. For Yoder's most famous work, *The Politics of Jesus*, the relevance of the peaceable way of Jesus for Christian ethics has been relativized by various attempts to dismiss or dilute the costly claims made upon the disciple by Christ's exemplary nonviolent life.[38] Yoder affirms the normativity of Jesus's nonviolent life and his death on the cross in the strongest possible terms. It is in this sense that I speak of a christocentric understanding of the relation between universal and particular.

We shall see that for Yoder particularity is inescapable. How then is the Christian to escape the connotation of coercion, as it is understood in Habermas's disavowal of strategic communication? For Yoder, the particularity of Christ shows the way. Christianity's is a vulnerable form of particularity. This vulnerability leads to a patient method of moral reasoning that, without bracketing its own particularity, refuses to encroach upon the freedom of the concrete other.[39] It is openness and vulnerability that render the Church a community of social critique. The Church can only fulfill this calling in full, frank, and repentant recognition of its own peccability.[40] As we saw in the previous chapter, because particularity is inescapable, dialogue is construed as a concatenation

37. Habermas, *Theory of Communicative Action*, 2:92; and *Religion and Rationality*, 24.
38. Yoder, *PJ*, 5–21.
39. Yoder, *PMMR*, 24–42.
40. Yoder, *PK*, 5.

of encounters between equally thick particulars. Particularity is always excessive of any putative universal. There is not a singular primordial universality more basic than traditioned particularity; but nor is there a range of free-floating atomistic particulars awaiting universalization. Publicness then becomes the ad hoc negotiation of "concrete convergences and divergences arising from relations between particulars."[41] Against any universalist enterprise, these encounters may appear as a series of "mini-publics." Nevertheless, no grander scale of publicity exists. It is, ironically, Enlightenment universalism that proceeds on the basis of a covert and pernicious coercion. Despite attempts to distance himself from foundationalism, Habermas's appeal to the "unforced force of the better argument" is compromised by his universalism.[42] This is, therefore, one example of the sort of appeal to universal foundations that Yoder's christocentric and nonviolent understanding of particularity places in question. For Yoder,

> the foundational appeal remains, after all, a mental power play to avoid my being dependent on your voluntary assent, to bypass my becoming vulnerable to your world in your otherness.[43]

From this perspective the Habermasian attempt to locate universals may be seen paradoxically to remain within a fundamentally Cartesian structure. The universality of the self as communicator may be discerned as it has emerged in history,[44] but, in order to render it more patently universal, that history is read with insufficient regard to its discontinuous and tragic elements. In the search for universals, as Barry Harvey expresses it, "[t]he particularity and contingency, the irreducibility and irreversibility, of *history* are reconfigured as the manageable pluralism of *historicity.*"[45] History, like religion, is reified in order to confine it to its deemed "proper function"—the self-contained, abstracted realm of the ideal, juxtaposed from the pragmatic "reality" of the will to power. This is close to Milbank's understanding of the sociological policing of the

---

41. Barber, "Particularity of Jesus," 82.
42. Habermas, *Theory of Communicative Action. Vol. 2.*
43. Yoder, *MAB*, 134.
44. Recently Habermas has conceded the need for an element of fallibilism in order to safeguard the a posteriori character of the "discovery" of this universal. See Kelly, "Foucault, Habermas," 388–89.
45. Harvey, "Insanity, Theocracy, and the Public Realm," 36.

sublime.[46] This reification of history, when understood in the light of Yoder's axiomatic identification of the Constantinian temptation (to which we shall return), occurs through the misplaced attempts to "make history come out right." Such strategies try to escape contingency, or at least to control it, and thus minimize its uncertainty.[47] The appeal to universals thereby reduces the vulnerability at the heart of both a truly non-coercive intersubjectivity and practices of local criticism.

The Theological Appropriation of Habermas

Theologians sympathetic to Habermas's critical modernism contend that discourse ethics requires a concept of prophetic agency in order to counteract any residue of ahistorical liberal optimism within the goal of the "ideal speech situation." While theological critics have endorsed the utopian character of this central tenet of discourse ethics, they have often been inadequately critical regarding the potential within the Habermasian schema to move towards its emancipatory goal.[48] Let us, then, enter into a series of brief expositions in order to explore the ways in which various "public theologians" have appropriated Habermas's schema. In the course of doing so we will begin to get a picture of how Yoder's nonviolent and dialogic particularism offers a more theologically satisfactory account of Christian social criticism.

Habermas's earlier vision of the role of religion sits ill with any attempt by theologians to assert the social-critical role of theological discourse. Nevertheless Habermas's understanding of communicative action, his diagnosis of the colonization of the lifeworld by the pernicious

---

46. Milbank, *TST*, 101–43. Harvey's account owes a great deal to Milbank's massive analysis.

47. Yoder, *PJ*, 228.

48. This is to say, not only that the counter-factual situation of the ideal speech situation points to "a prophetic factor" Rogerson et al., *Bible in Ethics*, 25, but that it is far from clear that Habermas sufficiently guards against the ideal trading on a liberal optimism regarding historical progress which is itself exclusionary. It is not my intention here to enter into a full examination of the prospects of Habermas's discourse ethics, his concept of communicative action, or his rather uncritically positive view of the role of civil society in relation to the colonization of the lifeworld by the systems of economy and state. What is under scrutiny here is the theological (most particularly ethical and ecclesiological) losses entailed in a univocal conflation of Enlightenment universality with the Christian affirmation of the universal lordship of Christ.

instrumental logics of the twin systems of a capitalist economy (money) and an administrative state (power)—and, more importantly for the purposes of this chapter, his universalist construal of social criticism—have all provided theological ethics with food for thought.[49]

The Restoration of Symbols—David Tracy

What then of the social-critical and utopian (in a positive sense) element of Christian truth claims? Certainly the founders of the Frankfurt school provided highly provocative reflections on the utopian dimension of Jewish messianism.[50] For one of the most astute "public" theologians, David Tracy, it is precisely here that the continued relevance of religion to public discourse may be demonstrated. Tracy criticizes Habermas's use of a simplistic division of cognitive realms, which denudes both religion and aesthetics of their public character. He asserts that if theology can see its task within a communicative (more specifically, dialogical) mode of reason, then it may be freed from captivity to cultural particularities, whilst remaining faithful to them.[51] This relationship of the particular to the public has been central to correlationalist views of theology from Tillich onwards.[52] Tracy argues that

> Insofar as the public realm is public and not, paradoxically, another private "reservation of the spirit" for the publicly spirited, only a critical social theory like Habermas' could free any public theology or public philosophy from purely culturalist and, at the limit, idealist analyses or merely impressionistic commentaries on the problems of the public realm.[53]

---

49. I do not claim to provide here any conclusive resolution to tensions between correlationalist and confessional theological method; nor do I entertain any hope of adjudicating between modern and postmodern understandings of social criticism. Such tasks would require far more nuanced criterion of assessment than can be offered here. I do not even claim that concern for the "universal" is an inappropriate way to conceive of theology's public calling. I merely propose to show that Habermasian universalism is inadequate for grounding a specifically Christian form of social criticism.

50. Habermas, *Religion and Rationality*, 4–5, 37–59.

51. Tracy, *Plurality and Ambiguity*, 25–27. For some clarification and critique of Tracy's use of the ideal speech situation as a regulative ideal, see Lash "Conversation in Gethsemane."

52. Tillich's own relation to the Frankfurt school is explored in Simpson, *Critical Social Theory*, 27–52.

53. Tracy, "Theology, Critical Social Theory," 31.

The innate social-critical moment of Christian eschatology provides grounds for its persistence as "public." Apocalyptic provides an ever-present reminder of the "explosive intensification and negations needed within all other genres."[54] Political discourse remains ineradicably symbolic. The correlation of the "classics" of the Christian tradition to its various "publics" requires a programmatic retrieval of traditional symbolic modes of naming God and reality which may attempt to reintroduce into a secularized modernity the full liberative and shocking disclosive power of the images Christian theology.[55] Tracy claims that religious symbols should be allowed their proper public function insofar as:

> The prophetic and eschatological symbols and the symbols descriptive of dangerous memories of the suffering of the oppressed serve as disclosures of a genuine utopian possibility for a better life for all in our society.[56]

For Tracy, Habermas's communicative rationality provides an essential means by which the correlationalist theologian can present the disclosive symbols of the "classics" of a tradition to the public sphere. The communicative presentation of such symbols makes known the fundamental existential issues, i.e., what Tracy names as "limit questions," inherent within theological discourse. Thus Tracy can assert that "the addressee of the theologian's reflections . . . by the very nature of the question as fundamental for any authentically human existence, [is] any fellow human being."[57] Publicness entails a grounding of specific, particular, religious claims within the requirements imposed by the need for a disclosive response to these limit questions.[58]

Theology is related to three different "publics"—academy, church, and society—to which the subdisciplines of fundamental, systematic, and practical theology respectively, though not exclusively, are addressed.[59] It is to his credit that through these distinctions Tracy can provide a singularly nuanced account of how religious traditions manifest and intensify

54. Tracy, *Analogical Imagination*, 265.
55. Martinez, *Confronting the Mystery of God*, 177.
56. Tracy, "Theology, Critical Social Theory," 39.
57. Tracy, *Analogical Imagination*, 4.
58. Martinez, *Confronting the Mystery of God*, 188; Tracy, *Blessed Rage for Order*.
59. Nevertheless the divisions imply a distinctness of logic and modes of discourse that cannot really obtain in relation to contemporary universities, churches, or society (wherever that may be found).

important dimensions of "human experience."[60] Even so, significantly, the preconditions for a disclosive response remain based in the pattern of generalization characteristic of justificatory liberalism. Discursive justification occurs through the use of warrants verifiable on grounds available to all rational persons, and based in a (both descriptive and normative account of) general human experience.

Significantly, the dialogic pluralism, which is to be taken to be determinative of publicity, disappears at this very point. The public accessibility of such signs, and the character of "general human experience," are based in very particular theological commitments. Here we can see the influence of Karl Rahner's transcendental anthropology upon Tracy's early methodological position.[61] Habermas's own account of such symbolic disclosure remains strongly indebted to Karl Jaspers's attempt to treat "metaphysical and religious doctrines as so many encodings of fundamental experiences which are inaccessible to conceptual explanation."[62] It is not at all clear that such a view is compatible with a Rahnerian theological anthropology. The unity of all humanity in the "religious root of our being" may be, as Ronald Thiemann says:

> a powerfully attractive sentiment, and it may even be a claim Christians are compelled to make on the basis of our doctrine of Creation. But it is decidedly not a claim that can be successfully argued, as Tracy, Ogden and others believe, as a necessarily true proposition on general philosophical grounds.[63]

More significantly, like Barth and Yoder, the christological realism I will develop in the next chapter places in question any such a search for a more universal or general theology of the context of intelligibility, prior to the actuality of the Trinitarian act of revelation.

---

60. For a useful account of how Tracy thereby improves on previous methods of correlation see Fiorenza, *Foundational Theology*, 282–84.

61. More recently Tracy seems to have moved away from the strictures imposed by this existential—transcendental theoretical edifice. Insofar as that is true, his theology escapes easy criticism as foundationalist. See Higton, "Hans Frei and David Tracy."

62. Habermas, *Liberating Power of Symbols*, 37.

63. Thiemann, *Constructing a Public Theology*, 91–92.

Memory and Eschatology: Helmut Peukert

In contrast to Tracy's anthropological universalism, it is a problematic eschatology that besets Helmut Peukert's attempt to locate an emancipatory theology on Habermasian grounds. Drawing on Walter Benjamin's *Theses on the Philosophy of History*, Peukert maintains that the concept of the ideal speech situation requires not only the inclusion of all those presently subjugated, oppressed, or excluded, but also, in the same moment of inclusion, the dead, and most particularly past victims of injustice. The Christian conception of the resurrection of the dead provides a foundation for what Peukert calls "anamnestic solidarity"—"a solidarity confirmed in an empathetic memory, in the recollection of the dead and the downtrodden."[64]

Peukert is suspicious of critical theory's importation of the detemporalized analytical tools characteristic of the empirical sciences. Without the resurrection of the dead, he says, an account of historical action is undermined by the paucity of a logic of time. This critical aporia in the theory of communicative action poses a fundamentally theological question—"the question of a reality witnessed for the other in the face of his death by acting in solidarity with him."[65] The eschatological foundation of solidarity and inclusion is indeed a clear way in which theological claims force critical theory to re-examine its own limitations and extend its concerns. However, it is less than clear that such claims represent a *supplementation* of critical theory, as Peukert implies, rather than placing its universalistic enterprise per se in question.

John Milbank rightly highlights the essentially Kantian structure of Peukert's question. He claims, "Peukert thinks that he has here finally placed theology on firm 'foundations,' in discovering the prior prepared site for religious understanding and practice which Christianity . . . most perfectly fulfils."[66] For Milbank, all such attempts must fail due to the "essentially self-sufficient nature" of this putative "eternal present" moment of inclusion. This is somewhat opaque terminology, but I take Milbank to mean that Peukert's conception of history not as a science, but as the form of empathetic memory remains constrained in a modernist imagining of temporality. Such a conception can only construe the past through

---

64. Peukert, *Science, Action and Fundamental Theology*, 202–10.
65. Ibid., 214.
66. Milbank, *TST*, 239–40.

a homogenizing logic of inevitable progress that cannot fully account for the transient, the discontinuous, or the tragic.[67] The production of such a reified homogeneity is exactly what abstractive universals do to history.

By contrast, we can follow Stanley Hauerwas's argument that in creating the church God has:

> storied the world, as now we have everything necessary to know the time in which we live. For God saves by making possible the existence of a people who are formed by God's time so that the world can know that we are creatures of a good creator, formed by God's time.[68]

In this sense, it has been said that Hauerwas's theological project involves "*the reconfiguration of time* in relation to (the narratives of) human existence made possible by the life, ministry, death, and resurrection of Jesus of Nazareth."[69] Time is not, then, the value-neutral organizing structure supplied by the mind that Kant believed it to be. Teleology, or more properly, eschatology, is determinative of a Christian understanding of what constitutes a "public" truth. I will discuss the importance of eschatology for moral realism in the next chapter.

The problem is, then, that Peukert is unable to re-temporalize Habermas in a manner sufficiently consonant with a frank account of the discontinuous and tragic, and therefore with the final, yet-to-be-completed redemption of such that is the basis of Christian hope. The ideal speech situation cannot accurately be said to provide a staging post on the way to the Kingdom, but only an attenuated eschatology. The full ethical importance of salvation (including themes of pacifism, sanctification, character, etc.) is thus circumscribed in reconfiguring the resurrection of Christ as an answer to a liberal question.[70] Peukert's eschatology is

---

67. See Bauckham and Hart, "Shape of Time." On the role of imagination in the construction of temporality, see Anderson, *Imagined Communities*, 22–26. Ironically the optimism of the modernist conception of linear progress was itself undercut by the negative slant of Horkheimer and Adorno's *Dialectic of Enlightenment*, and Adorno's *Negative Dialectics*. Romand Coles provides useful comparative reflections on this in "Identity and Difference."

68. Hauerwas, "Church as God's New Language," in *CET*, 47–65.

69. Cartwright, "Afterword," 654. Emphasis in original. For a discussion of how greater reflection on eschatology might clarify Hauerwas's thought, see Wells, *Transforming Fate into Destiny*.

70. Habermas's own discussion of anamnesis also displays the explicit correlation between the motivating and normative potential of memory in the drive to emancipation

attenuated insofar as the tension between the aeons (the already/not yet of the coming Kingdom) collapses into an abstractive anamnesis.

A more substantive eschatology may be more cautious about co-opting the Habermasian form of universal to its own logic of consummation. Here, Yoder's eschatology demonstrates an alternative way of proceeding. His is a partially realized inaugurated eschatology that provides the framework for both missiology and ecclesiology. The Church, as the foretaste of the Kingdom, bears witness to the universal lordship of Christ. That is the only universal one can claim as primary for Christian practices of local critique. Through its diverse practices of witness, the Christian community is called to an ad hoc and pragmatic form of social-critical engagement. As Yoder says in the last book published before his death:

> *the order of the faith community constitutes a public offer to the entire society.* To participate in the transforming process of becoming the faith community *is itself* to speak the prophetic word, *is itself* the beginning of the transformation of the cosmos.[71]

Both Tracy and Peukert highlight important aspects of the truly public nature of Christian theological discourse. The disclosive and liberative power of Christian symbols, and the hopeful eschatological account of memory and solidarity are both essential to an account of the social-critical potential of Christian life. But both accounts are insufficiently critical regarding the confluence of the universality to which Habermas's schema is normatively oriented, and the universality claimed in the Christian proclamation that "Christ is Lord." Despite the somewhat anti-dialogic construal found in his work, Milbank is suggestive when he pronounces that the universality of Christ

> transcends the universality of enlightenment in so far as it is not content with mere mutual toleration and non-interference with the liberties of others. It seeks in addition a work of freedom which is none other than perfect social harmony, a perfect consensus in which every natural and cultural difference finds its agreed place within the successions of space and time.[72]

---

with the continued claims of enlightenment universalism. Habermas, "Israel or Athens" in *Religion and Rationality*, 129–38.

71. Yoder, *FTN*, 27–28. Emphasis in original.

72. Milbank, *WMS*, 154.

In coming chapters I will explore further the need for a christocentric account of the relation between universal and particular. Before doing so we must turn to recent developments in Habermas's engagement with religion.

Habermas on the Translation of Religion

In recent years Habermas appears to have moved to a more amenable account of the public role of religion. As far back as 1991, Habermas had acknowledged the criticisms of theologians (most particularly Tracy and Peukert) that religion does not function solely to legitimate governmental authority, but may also empower protest movements and resistance of the pathological trends of modern power. In this way he recognizes that he had

> subsumed rather too hastily the development of religion in modernity with Max Weber under the "privatization of the powers of faith" and suggested too quickly an affirmative answer to the question as to "whether then from religious truths, after the religious world views have collapsed, nothing more and nothing other than the secular principles of a universalist ethics of responsibility can be salvaged . . ."[73]

It has become clearer to Habermas that religious belief cannot be discarded blithely as cognitively regressive or placed within a simple linear history of rationalization as secularization. Religions continue to possess encrypted semantic potential that must be rendered public by means of a reflexive and discursive appropriation of their legacy. It is only such publicly accessible reasons that possess the ability to move beyond the particularism of a specific community of faith. Thus, following Kant, Habermas argues that "the *critique* of religion is bound up with the motive of a *saving* appropriation." Nonetheless, the object of Kant's ire is no longer the dominant problem. The emphasis of the agenda must change:

> the project of *incorporating* central contents of the Bible into a rational faith has become more interesting than combating priestcraft and obscurantism. Pure practical reason can no longer be so confident in its ability to counteract a modernization spinning out of control armed solely with the insights of a theory of justice. The latter lacks the creativity of linguistic world-disclosure that

---

73. Habermas, *Religion and Rationality*, 79.

a normative consciousness afflicted with accelerating decline requires in order to regenerate itself.[74]

It is clear that there is indeed a development in Habermas's thought here, but it is insufficient. He has moved from a *rationalist* account that assumes, but does not demonstrate,[75] that the normative and semantic potential of Christian theology is subsumed within the march of idealist philosophy (Habermas's account of Hegel); to a *dialogical* approach, associated with Karl Jaspers, which "adopts a critical attitude toward religious traditions while at the same time being open to *learning* from them."[76] In this way he hopes both to move beyond Kant's pyrrhic victory over a "positivistically abridged concept of religion" and to avoid the pitfalls of Hegel's apparent radicalization of Kantian rationalism, in which philosophy must retreat again into metaphysics in order to maintain "the unequal marriage into which the philosophical embrace ultimately forces an overwhelmed religion."[77] Perhaps due to the influence of Kierkegaard, Habermas then sounds a thoroughly Barthian note in his objection to the Culture Protestantism emerging from Schleiermacher:

> Schleiermacher has to pay for this elegant reconciliation of religion and modernity, faith, and knowledge. The integration of the Church into society and the privatization of faith rob the religious relation to transcendence of its disruptive power within the world.[78]

Kantian philosophy of religion over-reached in that it "wanted to rob religion of more substance than practical reason can in all seriousness endure." Modernity has been deprived of precisely those resources that may remedy the "dwindling sensitivity to social pathologies" evident in contemporary Western society. Thus the dialogical approach to religious semantic potential requires that democratic societies not exclude such content that remains "capable of exercising an inspirational force on society *as a whole* as soon as they divulge their profane truth contents."[79] In doing so, however, it must remain agnostic, and insist on a division

---

74. Habermas, *Between Naturalism and Religion*, 211.
75. Adams, *Habermas and Theology*, 166.
76. Habermas, *Between Naturalism and Religion*, 245.
77. Ibid., 230.
78. Ibid., 234.
79. Ibid., 142.

between certainties of faith on the one hand and publicly criticizable validity claims on the other.[80]

Habermas here seeks to give a fuller account of how philosophy may "assimilate the semantic legacy of religious traditions without effacing the boundary between the universes of faith and knowledge."[81] There is a greater sensitivity to the putative integrity and irreducibility of religious traditions here. His approach

> eschews the rationalist presumption that it can itself decide which aspects of religious doctrines are rational and which irrational. The contents that reason appropriates through translation must not be lost for faith. . . . at best, philosophy *circumscribes* the opaque core of religious experience when it reflects on the specific character of religious language and on the intrinsic meaning of faith. This core remains as profoundly alien to discursive thought as the hermetic core of aesthetic experience, which likewise can be at best circumscribed, but not penetrated, by philosophical reflection."[82]

Unlike the earlier Rawlsian attempt at privatization of comprehensive doctrines, Habermas advocates a clear role for theological claims in the public processes of opinion formation. However, Habermas makes a clear distinction between the informal public realm of civil society—which is essentially a fluid and diverse network of "weak" publics—and the formal public sphere of legislative and judicial processes.[83] It is only in the former that religious content is permissible. In the latter all such content must be translated into generally intelligible language. There is no greater burden on the religious believer here, not least because Habermas places the burden of translation equally on secular citizens who are required to demonstrate openness and willingness to engage in the cooperative endeavor of translation.[84]

Crucially, Habermas's previous commitment to the transformative and dynamic nature of the process of discourse is undone by his separation of publics that then requires accessibility to be demonstrated prior to public deliberation, rather than as part of the process. Indeed,

---

80. Ibid., 143.
81. Ibid., 211.
82. Ibid., 143.
83. Habermas, *Between Facts and Norms*, 304–8.
84. Habermas, *Between Naturalism and Religion*, 5.

as Maeve Cooke demonstrates, there is a significant equivocation in Habermas's account of translation—is it a requirement or a regulative ideal? If Habermas's account is of a requirement, it can only be based on an account of the legitimacy of legal and political decisions, which requires all participants to provide precisely the same generally accessible reasons for deeming a decision valid—which seems unworkable and renders democratic legitimacy impossible.

Alternatively and more minimally, Habermas would have to claim that his notion of translation is a regulative ideal rather than a precondition of legitimacy.[85] If this is the case, then it seems advisable for the translation ideal to go the way of the other regulative ideal in Habermas's account—the ideal speech situation. For this ideal requires too much of religious claims in their seeking to meet modern conditions of publicity. I suggest that the precondition for legitimacy should not be described as "general accessibility" but as "intelligibility." Intelligibility is never determined a priori. It is a function of communication—if intelligibility happens, it is possible! This, of course, is a far more minimal account of the conditions of intelligibility than that emerging within the Kantian norm of autonomous reason. Milbank has shown persuasively how modernity has itself "privatized, spiritualized and transcendentalized the sacred, and concurrently reimagined nature, human action and society as a sphere of autonomous, sheerly formal power."[86] Habermas's concessions to public religion remain conditioned by this covertly metaphysical "postmetaphysical" view of publicity, accessibility, and verification. We shall see in the next two chapters how a robust theological realism provides an alternative account of publicity and critique.

Habermas's apparent softening with regard to theology is not clearly consistent and should not be seized upon too readily by theologians eager to endorse the powerfully appealing rhetoric of a sustained role for religion. Austin Harrington rightly cautions that there is an unreconciled tension between Habermas's Kantian emphasis on a critical application of reason to religious inheritances on the one hand, and "the proposition that reason depends genetically and genealogically on religious sources" on the other.

---

85. Cooke, "Secular State for a Postsecular Society?" 229. See also Cooke, "Salvaging and Secularising."

86. Milbank, *TST*, 9.

> In Habermas' conception it seems that while philosophy can "learn from" and pay its respects to religion, and to some extent reform itself in the light of what it has "learned," it still starts out from, and returns to, an essentially separate position in conceptual space.[87]

Habermas is critical of the extent to which Kant remained bound by an expectation of a "progressive replacement of positive religion by the belief in pure reason." Despite some modifications, Habermas's insistence that religious claims are to be expressed in a "more universal" language remains essentially Kantian in his attempt to identify and extract from religious inheritances that content which can hold its own in the face of reason. The Kantian salvage operation only exhumed partial remains—Christology became "a life well pleasing to God"; and the eschatological reign of God was reduced to a republic under laws of virtue. Habermas learns from Hegel to question this ahistorical reflexive assimilation of religious content that "strips religious traditions of their inherent substance." But in their place religion is permitted only a slightly expanded role that affirms the historical development and inherent plurality of its content. Religion, so understood, may re-enliven our dwindling normative consciousness and sensitivity to social pathologies only by eschewing any apologetic intent. It must relinquish any final commitment to the truthfulness of its own view and can no longer seek to insulate itself against the imperative for rational argumentative adjudication by means of a viciously circular apologetics. Habermas fails to appreciate how theologians have sought to render intelligible the central claims of the Christian faith in a diverse, critical, and dialogical manner. Indeed, Yoder's vision of the vulnerability of the particular, combined with his critique of foundationalism, goes further in this direction than does Habermas's own account of discourse—and does so without any need to suspend claims about "truth."

Even here, then, it seems that Habermas's avowed post-metaphysical methodological atheism continues to conceal thoroughly metaphysical and axiological commitments. Ironically, given one of the areas of contemporary concern where Habermas discerns a role for the resources gleaned from religious views,[88] I suggest that the best image for Habermas's initiative is not the linguistic metaphor of translation, but the biological

---

87. Harrington, "Habermas' Theological Turn," 50.
88. Habermas, *Future of Human Nature*.

metaphor of cloning. More specifically a metaphor of intra-cytoplasmic hybrids—entities or beings created solely for some temporary function (the "farming" of either stem cells or "semantic potential") that while remaining predominantly, though not exclusively, human at a genetic level, are not permitted full life. Just as with Kantian reductions, so here we may suspect that what is left is not quite Christian.

Three Rival Versions of Interpretive Mediation

The crux of the problem, then, is the interpretive mediation of universal and particular. We shall see this through a comparison of Yoder with three other approaches to the task of public theology. Robert Gascoigne attempts to transpose the particular into the universal; Francis Schüssler Fiorenza attempts a dialectical mediation between the two; and John Reader outlines a "local theology" responsive to local stories and specific experiences of engagement. We shall find that Yoder is closest to Reader's "local" vision of public discourse, while eschewing any methodological universal in favor of a vulnerable and dialogical particularity whose only universal is the proclamation "Christ is Lord."

Transposition and Universal Experience: Robert Gascoigne

Robert Gascoigne asserts a Rahnerian view of general human experience, which may allow for the direct and almost total transposition of values from the Christian community to the secular realm. Let us take his example in order to examine how a theology of interpretive mediation must, *pace* Gascoigne, be both communal and thoroughly christocentric (in the sense defined above). From a more postliberal stance, Ronald Thiemann has claimed that the parable of the Good Samaritan, as "a powerful evocation of love of neighbor as love of anyone in need," allows for a resonance with democratic values of justice and social care.[89] In response to this Gascoigne reconceives the basis for the recognition of such resonance. He asserts:

---

89. In designating Thiemann a postliberal I am working against his own self-description. He is rightly cautious that such easy categorization courts a largely reactionary impression. Thiemann, *Constructing a Public Theology*, 23. These concerns do not prohibit the use of the term in this discussion. I only align his nonfoundational theology with the broad conception of publicity designated "postliberal" at the start of the chapter.

it is difficult to see how a principle which draws on the Christian value of love of neighbour, evoked by Christian narrative, can resonate with a value familiar to all citizens, unless some appeal can be made to general human experience.[90]

Importantly, Gascoigne's use of the term "general human experience" is not purely descriptive, but includes an anthropologically normative sense. In so doing he remains vulnerable to narrativist and postmodern criticisms of foundationalism. Equally, there is some ethical reductionism here. While it is important to affirm that neighbor love translates to the public maxim of "care for anyone in need," the communicability emphasized by Gascoigne is achieved through an undialectical form of near-total transcultural translation. This translatability is purchased at the price of the depth of Christian witness.

That is to say, the reduction of the good Samaritan from enemy love to neighbor love (absent the christological redefinition of the enemy as neighbor) does not give sufficient attention to the divergent levels of duty implied in the distinction, so important to Yoder's account, between the agent within and the agent outside the church.[91] The central importance of the "otherness" of the church to Yoder's schema is best explicated in reference to the wider christocentric and eschatological themes of his theology. We turn to this task in the next two chapters. For now it is sufficient to note that this distinction does not conform to the Lutheran doctrine of the two Kingdoms. There the use of the notion of "vocation" functions as a "buffer against the critical impact of the specificity of the call of Jesus."[92] Something of the graciousness and radicality of the call to enemy love is lost if the narrative of the Good Samaritan can be sufficiently contained in the universal maxim to care for other people.

There is, for Yoder, always a partiality and tension inherent in public communication, rather than a translation without remainder. This is a tension that Gascoigne largely seeks to avoid. Which is to say, while Yoder affirms some translatability, something non-negotiable remains. In his later writings, Yoder frequently employed images (normatively) derived from Jewish patterns of thought. This is seen, for example, when

---

90. Gascoigne, *Public Forum and Christian Ethics*, 113–27.

91. On this, see especially Yoder, *CWS*.

92. See Yoder, "Why Ecclesiology is Social Ethics," in *RP*, 102–26, 113–14. For a clear explanation of how Yoder differs from Lutheran conceptions of Church and State, see his *CWS*, 60–73. For Luther, agape and justice remain utterly separate principles.

he sought to provide his critical conception of a Christian citizenship "for the nations." Here Yoder talks of the way that diaspora Jews "not only kept their subculture alive; Jews in fact contributed mightily to making the Gentile world viable." What then remains untranslatable? The confession that:

> there is no other God. The rejection not only of pagan cult but also of every way of putting their own YHWH/Lord in the same frame of reference with pagan deities, even not speaking the divine NAME as others would, was tied for the Jews in Babylon with the proclamation of his sovereignty over creation and history. *There is no setting into which that deconstructing, disenchanting proclamation cannot be translated, [and] none which can encompass it.*[93]

No translation without remainder here, but the disquieting, revolutionary confession of the otherness of God. Witness, most particularly witness to the way of God revealed in Christ, is the Christian mode of publicity.

It may be suggestive to consider how Gascoigne's account of the incarnation affects his construal of the mediation between universal and particular. While affirming that revelation is "self-*grounding*" he denies that it must, on that basis, be:

> self-*contained* in any sense that obscures or denies the relationship between the Christ event and the presence of the Spirit in human history as a whole. A tradition which accepts that the Spirit is present in creation and in human history must seek to speak of God in ways which take account of the fruits of the Spirit wherever and whenever they are found.[94]

Gascoigne's intention to place claims to revelation within a wider and more open theological framework are clear. But this short paragraph displays two important, but related, failures. First, it is exegetically problematic to assert that the Spirit is present in human history "as a whole" (at least as such categories illegitimately separate the ecclesiological context of the Pentecost narratives from earlier motifs of the pneumatological process of creation). On the contrary, the affirmation of the presence of the Spirit *extra muros ecclesiae* is dependent upon the nature of the paraclete as gift to the Church. Second, behind such assertions lies a

---

93. Yoder, *FTN*, 76–77. Emphasis mine.
94. Gascoigne, *Public Forum and Christian Ethics*, 137.

tacit (i.e., underdeveloped) pneumatology that remains undetermined by Christology.[95] Gascoigne continues:

> The unique revelatory significance of these events [the life, death and resurrection of Jesus] makes them different from all others, yet their reality as events in human history, as the incarnation of God in a human being, gives them—at the same time—a continuity with all human history.[96]

Any account of the incarnation has to strike a balance between continuity and revelatory uniqueness; however, by locating intelligibility and thus public verification in a "general human experience" occurring in "human history," the incarnation becomes a unique revelatory vehicle for a truth knowable, in the Spirit, by means other than Christ. The intelligibility of the incarnation is thus related to its *continuity* with human history. Where here is the radical imperative to repentance, the irruptive character of God's renewal of creation? For Gascoigne, though it is revelatory (in unspecified ways), the incarnation is an occurrence within the singular movement from creation through history—in the modernist sense of time as progressive. That is, the particular participates in the universal, of which the incarnation is only one, albeit the most revelatory, episode.

An alternative christocentric reading, based in a distinction of human and divine histories, would allow us to see creation and eschaton, and with them the fundamental historical interruption of the incarnation, in the light of the coming peaceable Kingdom.[97] Such a move is provided by Yoder, for whom, in contrast to less christocentric readings of history, the incarnation does not mean:

> that God took all of human nature as it was, put his seal of approval on it, and thereby ratified nature as revelation. The point is the opposite, that God broke through the borders of our standard definition of what is human, and gave a new formative definition in Jesus.[98]

---

95. By contrast, one can see in relation to Yoder's discussion of the doctrine of the Trinity in H. R. Niebuhr, that this sort of division is ethically problematic and rhetorically spurious. Yoder, "How H. Richard Niebuhr Reasoned," in *AT*, 31–89.

96. Gascoigne, *Public Forum and Christian Ethics*, 138.

97. A similar move is made by James McClendon, who insists that creation, salvation and eschaton be viewed in mutual interaction and support, as in fulfilment of the rule of God. McClendon, *Doctrine*, 146–89.

98. Yoder, *PJ*, 99.

For Yoder it is in the life, death, and resurrection of Jesus Christ that God's universal salvific will is manifest. By "manifest," I mean not merely "signified" or "mediated," but begun, achieved, and yet to be completed. Yoder ensures the uniqueness of the incarnation not through Christ's divinity, but in how this is seen in his radical humanness.[99] The element of continuity in this approach is, of course, not oriented to some general human history, but to the divine economy—history expressed in terms of election, covenant, and Kingdom. Like Barth, Yoder rejects Christian "apologetics"—in the sense of rendering Christ "credible" to non-Jewish culture in a way that transposes Christianity "into an ahistorical moral monotheism with no particular peoplehood and no defenses against acculturation."[100]

Gascoigne's attempt to relate universal and particular is appealing. He argues that the

> Christian narrative has a universal ethical meaning, a meaning in ethical and social practice which finds its ultimate cognitive "home" in Christian faith, but yet has its own practical self-evidence in its power to liberate and do justice.[101]

Nevertheless the lack of an ecclesiological focus in Gascoigne's account undermines his project. For him the goal remains the union of universal relevance and particular content within the communicative competence of the individual believer.

Yoder does not entirely disavow the importance of propositional translation, as his continued advocacy of "translatability" and the use of "middle axioms" in his earlier writings fully attests. A disavowal of foundationalist epistemology denies the possibility of accurate propositional generalization, i.e., total translatability. The ethical content of Christian

---

99. No docetic tendencies can therefore be admitted. Yoder could, perhaps, have made more explicit use of this distinction, in order to mitigate criticisms like that made by Nigel Wright, of "ecclesiological docetism." For Wright, Yoder is insufficiently attentive to the dependence of the church upon its environment, and its solidarity with it. N. G. Wright, *Disavowing Constantine*, 74. There is significant ambiguity in Wright's appeal for "solidarity" and a recognition of "dependence." Because the otherness of the church is not fundamentally ontological, but related to agents, both "dependence" and "solidarity" require a pneumatological base (on which the Church truly is "dependent"—in an absolute, rather than contextually relative, sense) and a significant degree of discernment—which Yoder, *pace* Wright, is able to provide through his conception of the hermeneutics of peoplehood.

100. Yoder, *JCSR*, 152.

101. Gascoigne, *Public Forum and Christian Ethics*, 153.

moral practices is not rendered public by a process of departicularized generalization, but rather through the hermeneutic function of the life of the Christian community. Translation occurs through a transcultural re-conceptualization. No wholesale transliteration is possible but bi-lingual communication is common.[102]

Dialectical Mediation and the Interpretive Community: Francis Schüssler Fiorenza

Gascoigne's approach fails due to its collapsing of particular into universal. Francis Schüssler Fiorenza provides a theological appropriation of Habermas that endeavors to overcome this tension through a dialectical mediation between universal and particular. In perpetuating a division of the "right" from the "good" Habermas excludes the latter from discursive justification. Fiorenza argues that Habermas is unable to eliminate either religion or the question of the good from the public side of the division between public and private spheres. A thin conception of the good must emerge. To the extent that this conception remains hidden, it impoverishes the publicity of discourse ethics. For Fiorenza, churches function as a particular ground for the interpretation through which a thick conception of the good is mediated. This is essential in order to maintain the affective support that is otherwise lacking in a de-contextualized universalist morality.[103] That is to say, churches are numbered among the few loci where, in Habermas's terminology, the lifeworld has not been colonized by the instrumental rationality of the capitalist sub-system.

The Kantian heritage of Habermas leads to a thoroughly universalist approach to verification of ethical prescriptions. Fiorenza modifies a Rawlsian conception in order to allow for a dialectical mediation of universalism and historicism. Such mediation entails "a broad reflective equilibrium between hermeneutic reconstructions of normative traditions and the discursive attempt to obtain reasoned agreement in regard to justice."[104] The specificities of a tradition form an essential part of

---

102. Yoder's use of the language of just-war logic, and even the acceptance (in specific dialogical instances) of the term "sectarian," intimate that such linguistic openness characterizes inner Christian dialogue as well. See Pfeil, "Yoder's Pedagogical Approach."

103. Fiorenza, "Church as a Community."

104. Ibid., 81. Rawls outlines the idea of reflective equilibrium in *Theory of Justice*, 42–45. This becomes one of the factors for his differentiation with Habermas; see "Reply to Habermas" as it is reproduced in paperback edition of *Political Liberalism*, esp. 381–85.

coming to this broad reflective equilibrium. The "narrow equilibrium" of what is normative in a tradition (which, following MacIntyre, we can suppose is known in part by internal discourse) is in a reciprocal critical relationship with what is taken to be publicly normative.[105] Public normativity is only known to be such, if it is not to be coercive and authoritarian, through the full assent of all participants.

Fiorenza can assert "the church [as a community of interpretation] keeps alive the utopian dimension that has been central to critical theory."[106] The flaw in Fiorenza's argument lies in the role afforded to universalism—the putative "universal" remains valuable primarily because of its ability to afford criticism of de facto customs and practices.[107] Yet it does not follow that such universalism allows for critical distance. Equally it is unclear that de facto values of equal regard, non-coercive conversation and emancipatory concern require a de jure universalist structure, as opposed to being the presumed, but rarely achieved, virtues of liberal politics.[108] In that sense it remains to be seen how the self as "communicator," any more than the self as "knower," can provide a basis for a theological account of a truly inclusive publicity.

By locating criticism solely on the side of objective universality Fiorenza's dialectical relation of universalism and historicism fails to allow for the local and immanent nature of theological critique. Ultimately such a form of theological universalism cannot escape the problematic anthropology and attenuated eschatology required to maintain a bi-polar scheme where intelligibility and identity are considered as incompatible alternatives in a zero-sum context.[109]

Local Criticism and the Universal Lordship of Christ: John Reader

The procedural concern for appropriate "frameworks" is not necessarily to be distinguished from the diverse experience of local critical engage-

105. Fiorenza, *Foundational Theology*, 301–11.
106. Fiorenza, "Church as a Community," 87.
107. Ibid., 80.
108. In this regard, Arne Rasmusson provides an interesting comparison of Hauerwas with the account of liberal virtues provided by William Galston's *Liberal Purposes*, in Rasmusson, *Church as Polis*, 277–81.
109. The image of a zero-sum game, somewhat over-used in recent discussions of third-way politics, redistribution of wealth, etc., seems to fit well here. It is used by Yoder in "On Not Being Ashamed of the Gospel."

ment. In advancing an account of a local dynamic process of theological reflection, John Reader utilizes Habermas's integrating framework for non-judgmental discourse in order to provide his own mediating framework to address the fragmentation of modern life. This framework allows a four-fold dialogue between local stories, contemporary analytical structures, Christian sources, and specific experiences of engagement with the issues facing local people.[110] Reader correctly asserts that churches offer the space within which others can share their stories, without thereby entering into conflict. However, he remains convinced of the need to be willing to "bracket" the major narratives of one's identity in order to listen to others. Even if such bracketing were possible, it is far from obvious that, for Christianity at least, such suspension is necessary for authentic and noncoercive practices of listening. Yoder provides us with a way of construing dialogical openness to the other which maintains the inescapable narrative constitution of human identity. Yoder's approach allows the "discovery of resonances" between the story and sources of the Christian community and the contemporary situation that Reader calls for.[111] Indeed such discernment is at the heart of the hermeneutic function of the church.

Yoder insists on the political import of both universal ministry and radical egalitarianism of "the Rule of Paul" (the procedure of meeting in the power of the Spirit, as seen in 1 Corinthians 14).[112] Such an emphasis is characteristic of Yoder's focus on the practices of the Christian community as significant public signs. It is these practices, not the departicularized "autonomy" of enlightenment rationalism (even in its decenterd Habermasian form), which can afford the most inclusive form of politics. That politics is not merely an intangible invocation of a vague principle of equality, but a radical social critique. So, for example, the Eucharist enacts a life of economic solidarity that impels the believer to further

110. Reader, *Local Theology*.

111. Ibid., 130.

112. On these see Yoder, "Sacrament as Social Process: Christ the transformer of Culture," in *RP*, 360–73, see also *BP* and *FC*. Yoder explains away the apparent contradiction in 1 Cor 14:34–35, which instructs women to be silent, by speculating that it refers to back-row chattering and the de-limiting of the proportion of the agenda given over to clarification, rather than disallowing legitimate participation, which would be contrary to the Pauline principle of universal ministry. *BP*, 61–62. A similar argument is made by Ben Witherington, who claims that the intent is to correct an abuse, not revoke a woman's right to speak, established in chapter 11. Witherington, *Conflict and Community in Corinth*, 287–88.

practices of reconciliatory activism—which in turn is supported through the ecclesial practice of fraternal admonition.[113] Yoder's programmatic essay "The Hermeneutics of Peoplehood" demonstrates how these public practical signs both require and engender a dialogic vulnerability and an eschatological patience:

> If we cannot transcend the vulnerability of belief by positing as accessible a nonparticular "natural," might we then celebrate confessionally that light and truth have taken on the vulnerability of the particular? That would then call for and empower *a missionary ethic of incarnation.*
>
> The challenge will still remain to find ways to translate and to work at a reciprocal adjudication of the varieties both of perception and of evaluation, where one provincial vision clashes and overlaps with another. But the way to do that is not to imagine or proclaim or seek or discover some "neutral" or "common" or "higher ground, but to work realistically at every concrete experience of overlap and conflict.[114]

The local and practical approach demonstrates how Yoder can insist that the Bible is a public document. Its texts bespeak a world in many ways like our own; a place of uncertainty, powerlessness, and hunger; of desire, ambition, and idolatry. In relation to such ubiquitous factors, the vulnerability of the particular shows the Christian community in its anticipatory role as both the gift and calling of true emancipation. The inclusive, hospitable, reconciliatory, and nonviolent life of the Church is inherently oriented to the prophetic role necessary for the inclusion of inchoate critiques from the excluded and subjugated into public discourse. This requires a crucial qualification to Milbank's critique of the Enlightenment. For the public theology we have begun to outline, it is only insofar as the Church embodies this critical and anticipatory stance that the universality of Christ *graciously* exceeds the universality of the Enlightenment.

---

113. Yoder, *BP*, see also "Binding and Loosing," in *RP*, 325–58; "Sacrament as Social Process: Christ the Transformer of Culture," in *RP*, 360–73.

114. Yoder, "Hermeneutics of Peoplehood," in *PK*, 15–45, quote from 44. Emphasis original.

Democracy, Tradition, and the Basis of Hope

We have seen in the above discussion that systematic attempts at securing democratic publicity through the circumscription or exclusion of religious claims are ill-founded, counter-productive, and theologically suspect. I have insisted that intelligibility and publicity occur only in a fragmentary, ad hoc way. For this reason, I contend, Jeffrey Stout's otherwise highly appealing account of public reason also fails. In his rightly acclaimed *Democracy and Tradition,* Stout insists that religious believers are not *morally* restrained from introducing religious reasons into public ethical debate; nor, as for Richard Rorty, are they always *pragmatically* restrained: but they are frequently *prudentially* restrained, because theological reason-giving is either redundant or simply doesn't work to secure public consensus.[115] Here Stout is combining two objections. The first claim, that religious reason giving may go beyond the discursive requirements of mundane political decisions, seems to me entirely right. Christians don't need to publicly assert the basic tenets of creedal orthodoxy in order to contribute to a local or municipal government's decision of which road to pave first.[116] Of course discursive prudence and effectiveness require us to refrain from excessively detailed reason giving for uncontroversial decisions. Pompous wind-bags, of whatever religious or non-religious conviction, frustrate the authenticity and efficiency of everyday deliberations. In cases where conclusions can be reached without significant recourse to deep explorations of religious or philosophical differences, there is no real restriction implied in the pragmatic attempt to resolve debate without such explorations.

The second form of imprudence relates more specifically to particular forms of theological argumentation. In genuinely controversial debates, theological conceptions are in no way prohibited from participation, so long as resentment of secularism and diversity does not raise its ugly head. But this is far more questionable. Stout's target here is the excessively rhetorical anti-secular and anti-liberal forms of religious reason giving characteristic of the "theologians of resentment" from Milbank to Hauerwas and Yoder (eliding, for these purposes, the significant differences between these figures, not least on precisely these issues). Such forms of theological argumentation are deemed imprudent given the religiously

---

115. Stout, *Democracy and Tradition*, 98–99.
116. Stout, "Survivors of the Nations," 216.

diverse nature of modern Western societies. Stout gives an account of a form of secularization that religious believers should not resent. This is a form of post-Christendom Western secularization emerging only once increasing theological and exegetical diversity eliminated the public role of the Bible as a reliable and clear arbiter. Thus, Stout claims:

> The mark of secularization, as I use the term, is rather the fact that participants in a given discursive practice are not in a position to take for granted that their interlocutors are making the same religious assumptions they are....
>
> Notice that secularization in this sense does not reflect a commitment to secularism, secular liberalism, or any other ideology. It is true that modern democratic discourse tends not to be "framed by a theological perspective" but this does not prevent any of the individuals participating in it from adopting a theological perspective.[117]

This is clearly preferable to Habermasian or Rawlsian schemes, for it does not commit participants to engage in the uncomfortable mental and religious contortionism required to accommodate believers' democratic practices to "secular reasoning" or an endorsement of a "secular" or "postmetaphysical" state. However, it is questionable whether this rather minimal account of the meaning of "secularization" is as useful as Stout thinks. Neither first-century Athens, nor sixteenth-century Zurich, for example, were religiously homogenous. Indeed, significant public debates revolved precisely around questions of the nature, existence, and will of God—and, consequently, of the obligations, limitations, and roles appropriate to citizens attendant upon these claims. We have already seen that there is a significant public role to be played by the statement of convictions that one cannot reasonably expect to attain widespread acceptance. The vitality of discursive practices requires those who will seek to contest dominant frameworks and assumptions, unsettle the status quo, and complicate the whole process.[118] That public ethical discourse tends then not to presuppose agreement on such issues does not necessarily lead us to the conclusion that the introduction of such explicitly theological premises will be imprudent. It is difficult to see how Stout arrives at the judgment of imprudence. Either this is a strong and uniform prohibition,

---

117. Stout, *Democracy and Tradition*, 97.

118. For an account of theological participation in ethical debate congenial to this argument, see Meilander "Against Consensus."

or, more minimally, it is an endorsement of the virtues that may sustain a non-authoritarian and vulnerable model of dialogue. In the former case, Rawls sneaks back in by the back door. Stout would have to be read as seeking to provide an a priori and systematic pre-condition to prudential decisions. There would be something rather odd about a desire to provide such general prohibitions to the discursive effectiveness and intelligibility of putatively pragmatic, and therefore necessarily ad hoc, judgments. Although at moments Stout appears to be making rule-like statements, this idiom is not central to his point. Such a reading would not take account of his repeated encouragement to all citizens to "love justice, cultivate the virtues of civility, and then say what you please."[119]

If, on the other hand, all Stout wants to say is that the strongly rhetorical anti-liberalism accompanying "new traditionalists'" approach to theological publicity proceeds by way of a resentment of plurality, then the evidence must be presented. In fact, as we shall see in more detail in the fourth chapter of this book, those Stout names "theologians of resentment" have diverse and sincerely held valuations of plurality and dialogue. In dealing with both Milbank and Hauerwas, Stout points to the excessive rhetoric that may undermine the impact these writers have in seeking to demonstrate the publicity of theology. His reading of Milbank is selective here, though we shall see later that I share some of his concerns. I suggest, though, that Stout has less grounds for concern with Hauerwas, and, indeed, that Stout needs Yoder more than he realizes. Stout locates his disagreement with Stanley Hauerwas at two points. First, that the unfair and almost entirely negative account of liberalism and justice in Hauerwas's work has militated against the formation of appropriately public forms of discourse and has thus allowed the pessimism of MacIntyre's diagnosis of modernity in *After Virtue* to become a self-fulfilling prophecy. Second, that the anti-modernism of MacIntyre has prevented Hauerwas from moving Yoder to the more positive account of politics that he had initially desired. But Yoder's account of the church/world division is never quite what Stout thinks it is. Stout does not sufficiently recognize that Yoder repeatedly stresses the vulnerability of witness. This is significant because it is the vulnerability of witness that chastens Hauerwas's synthesis of Yoder with the anti-liberalism of MacIntyre. It is true that Hauerwas has not always given voice to this chastening vulnerability and the consequent permeability of any

119. Stout, "Survivors of the Nations," 220.

church/world duality; though it lies just under the surface in his specific engagements with liberal institutions and issues.[120] Nonetheless, Hauerwas has recently begun to remedy this. Drawing on this rich motif, he is able to declare in defense of a radical democratic engagement that:

> politics names for me the practices required for the formation of a people in the virtues necessary for conversations and conflicts to take place if goods in common are to be discovered. These goods are not abstract but draw on the stories of failures and successes that make a people recognizable to one another. Vulnerability must be at the heart of such a politics just to the extent that living well requires readiness to learn from the stranger. I should like to think that vulnerability is at the heart of what it means to be Christians, because through worship we are trained to have our lives disrupted by that strangest of strangers—God.[121]

I suspect Stout would be encouraged by such statements—but they are achieved *because* rather than *in spite* of Hauerwas's union of a strong critique of modernity with Yoder's understanding of the relation of church to world. In recent years, Hauerwas has been explicit about the influence of Sheldon Wolin's prescient account of the evisceration of contemporary democracy on his critique of modernity. For his part, Stout also endorses much of Wolin's account, but finds that the bleakness of the diagnosis may itself increase the likelihood of failure in attempts to revive democratic practices.[122] Stout worries that both MacIntyre and Wolin, in different ways, place their hope only in the local level, and thus undermine the capacity of democratic citizens to hold national and global power to account (not least by their loss of hope in representative mechanisms of accountability).[123] This, for Stout, is a failure to balance the two aspects essential to the vocation of the social critic. The critic must both "draw attention to dangers," as Foucault amply demonstrated, and must also "enliven hope."[124] As we shall see in our discussion of Yoder and Foucault in chapter 6, this second aspect is substantially more

---

120. Hauerwas often defends himself against charges of sectarianism precisely on the grounds that he has offered accounts of why Christians can support significant aspects of liberal society—from the medical and legal professions, to issues of justice, war, and interreligious relations. See, for example, *CET*, 7.

121. Hauerwas and Coles, *Christianity, Democracy, and the Radical Ordinary*, 112.

122. Stout, "Spirit of Democracy," 19.

123 Ibid., 18.

124. Ibid., 7.

appealing than other common, restrictive and patrician readings of the social-critical enterprise as requiring both criticism and the provision of viable alternative policies. His reservation regarding Hauerwas and Yoder relates to the rigid codification of the boundary between church and world as a dualism of Christian virtue and liberal vice.[125] It will become evident that I do not agree that such an account is present in either Yoder or Hauerwas (though until recently, Hauerwas's rhetoric has given grounds for such a concern).[126] But, I suggest, despite his objections, Stout may find in a theology like Yoder's grounds to reconcile his own pessimistic and optimistic moments and provide a chastened hope in democracy. Yoder's theological realism bases the practice of critique in the character of a nonviolent, patient, forgiving, and reconciling God.[127] We turn to an exploration of the shape of Yoder's theological and moral realism in order to show how Christian political critique must be realist if it is to remain public.

---

125. Stout, *Democracy and Tradition*, 154.

126. This, of course, is also to disagree with Hauerwas's initial reading of the division of aeons in Yoder in "Nonresistant Church," in *VV*, 197–221.

127. Stout has expressed some reservations regarding the exegetical basis for this view; and of Yoder's consistency in defending it. Stout, "Spirit of Democracy," 14–16. The objections emerge from the expectation of a level of completeness and explicitness in the texts well beyond that which Yoder would claim was available.

CHAPTER 3

The Cruciformity of the Cosmos:
The Christological and Eschatological Basis for Realism

"The name of Jesus Christ is the very essence and source of all reality."[1]

—Karl Barth

"The eschatological is not one element of Christianity, but it is the medium of Christian faith as such, the key in which everything is set, the glow that suffuses everything here in the dawn of an expected new day. . . . the eschatological outlook is characteristic of all Christian proclamation, of every Christian existence, and of the whole Church."[2]

—Jürgen Moltmann

Realism(s) and the Theological Task

Previous chapters have shown something of the need to ground the public presence of the Church within the doctrines of eschatology and Christology. They have done so via a dialectical and comparative exploration of the fruits for Christian social criticism yielded by various public theologies. More specifically, we have begun to see how Yoder's commitment to a nonviolent God provides the foundation and source

1. Barth, *CD* I/2, 348.
2. Moltmann, *Theology of Hope*, 16.

for his ethical thought. In the next two chapters I will show that an eschatological-analogical pattern is central to a theologically adequate affirmation of the "realism" of moral language in general, and of political-critical discourse in particular. In this current chapter I shall delineate the contours of Yoder's eschatological and christological claims, and outline their importance for theological realism. It is as well to distinguish four senses of the term "realism" as they come to be used in this and subsequent chapters.

1. *Biblical* realism is a commitment to the normative value of Scripture. It is no simple biblicism. It is rather a faith commitment that, through detailed historical-critical methods, a basic movement and meaning will become apparent—a meaning undetermined by a higher authority of contemporary hermeneutical frameworks.[3] In Yoder's work the term does not imply an a priori attribution of authority to the canon as a whole, but rather, more minimally, that "[w]ithout debating whether the Bible is authoritative in principle, the realist reads and interprets it with the best skill available, and finds it saying something with authority."[4] It is an openness not just to reading the bible, but, individually and corporately, to *being read by it*.[5]

2. *Theological* realism in a minimal sense merely denotes the claim that language describing the "reality" of God displays a significant degree of correspondence to the way things really are. This is not a crude form of the correspondence theory of truth, but rather, as we shall see, responds to the analysis of postmodernity with a commitment to the truth contained in Christian confession. It is therefore to be distinguished from the forms of "radical theology," "anti-realism," or "non-realism" which in theological guise produce what Jeffrey Stout somewhat

---

3. Yoder therefore describes his view of the bible as "post-" not "pre-critical." See Yoder, "Politics of Jesus Revisited." For more detailed discussion of biblical realism, see *THW*, and on Yoder's "sophisticated interaction with historical-critical scholarship," see Hays, *Moral Vision*.

4. Yoder, *THW*, 128.

5. The title "How to Be Read By the Bible" was given to an earlier unpublished form of *THW*. Yoder finally rejected the title because of implications of subjectivism and the dangers of implying that "what God is interested in 'is reading me.'" Cf. publisher's foreword, ibid., 8.

acerbically refers to as "atheism in drag."[6] We shall explore the term in a maximal sense, claiming that not only is theological truth *real* truth, but it is more true, more fundamental, than any other truth. Which is to say, all other truths, insofar as they are "true," are so purely in analogical relation to theological reality. Of course, such a claim is not always demonstrable, nor indeed is it always particularly interesting. For example, it may be difficult to see quite how the truth claim "John is driving his car," which is verifiable on relatively simple empirical grounds, is (excluding ecological concerns) anything other than theologically inconsequential. This, of course, is not the case with moral language.

3. *Moral* realism refers to the cognitive status (objectivity) of moral assertions. At its basic level it is seen in the commonsensical view that, contrary to emotivistic reductions, moral statements mean what they say when they claim "x is wrong" or "it is your duty to do y." More significantly, as a form of metaethics, moral realism involves both metaphysical and epistemological claims.[7] Therefore moral realism cannot be refuted simply by the existence of disagreement, however vociferous and deeply rooted. I contend in this chapter that moral realism requires theological realism. Moreover the basis of moral realism in a specifically Christian, rather than simply theistic, theological realism has important consequences for the nature and practice of Christian ethics. As Oliver O'Donovan puts it "[t]rue knowledge of the moral order is knowledge 'in Christ.'"[8] It is ultimately the christological basis of moral realism that determines the specific normative content of Christian moral discourse.

4. *Ethical and political* realisms refer, in this book, primarily to the normative implications drawn from one's reading of the most salient characteristics of a present situation or dilemma.

---

6. Stout, *Ethics After Babel*, 301. For fuller critical accounts of the theological problems associated with this school of thought, most particularly their most trenchant apologist Don Cupitt, see Hyman, *Predicament of Postmodern Theology*, and Crowder, *God and Reality*.

7. For a clear discussion of the metaethical debates surrounding moral realism, see Brink, *Moral Realism*. However Brink's attempt to remain "metaphysically neutral" limits the scope of the work to a relatively abstract plane.

8. O'Donovan, *RMO*, 85.

"Realism" in this sense is the self-designation of those who seek a practicable and empirically accurate idiom for moral and theological discourse. The "reality" to which they refer is, however, not always as self-evident as it might appear. "Realism" often provides a partisan banner for those who would wish to dismiss dangerously idealistic counter-propositions. It is also often the preserve of those who either founded a particular mode of discourse (those who got there first) or the representatives of its status quo (those who set the agenda). What is "real" is determined by metaphysical, which is to say theological, commitments that may be, on occasion, somewhat dishonestly covered over with a palimpsest of pragmatism and "common sense." None of this critical definition should be taken as a counsel for idealism or a denial of the tragic and morally ambiguous elements of everyday life. This fourth sense will occupy us in more detail in chapter 5, in our discussion of the Christian realism of Reinhold Niebuhr.

Biblical and Theological Realisms in Yoder's Christology

We have seen that Yoder was largely suspicious of systematizing or "methodologistic" approaches to the theological task. Nonetheless his project rests on a distinctive reading of the central concerns of what would often be called "systematic theology." That is not to say his was a systematic approach in the narrowest sense of theologizing through an architectonic program seeking quasi-scientific comprehensiveness. Rather it is to say, in a Barthian vein, that dogmatics *is* ethics.[9] Although Yoder is by no means unique in such an approach, it is important to note that those, from Jürgen Moltmann to James McClendon, who would name eschatology or ethics as the starting point of a theological enterprise, do so in contradistinction to previously regnant procedure.[10]

---

9. Barth, *CD* I/2, 782–96.

10. McClendon, *Systematic Theology*, 3 vols. Another attempt to reorder systematics around eschatology from a "believer's church" stance in order to unite the emphases of kerygmatic (revelation, transcendence) and contextual (relevance, applicability) modes of theologizing may be found in Finger, *Christian Theology*, 2 vols., esp. vol. 1, 99–133.

Universalism and Jesulogical Christocentrism

For Yoder, most explicitly, these two starting points—the ethical and the eschatological—are united and indivisible. Moreover, they come together only in the person and work of Jesus, for it is in Christ that a new social reality has been inaugurated. The life of discipleship, of obedience to the normativity of Christ's nonviolence, indeed, "Christian ethics" itself, is only possible because of the fully public life, cross and resurrection of the Nazarene carpenter. This is the "reality" that finally halts the historicist train in its tracks. It is also why the accusations leveled against Yoder of being reductionist (degrading the gospel solely to "ethics") and "anti-metaphysical" or "anti-ontological" per se (i.e., as reflecting a low Christology unable to support the theological and ethical freight placed upon it) are significantly overplayed.[11] Rather, Yoder's preference for ethical and pragmatic categories is based in a commitment to an extremely high Christology, which nevertheless refuses to concede the particularity and normativity of Jesus.[12] In this vein he wrote of the centrality of a high Christology for the renewal of the believers' church.

> Only such a Christ has anything to say above the melee of a pluralism in which every sect has equal time and the truth question cannot be put. Only if the call of Jesus is ontologically founded, connected to the arc from creation to apocalypse, can it give us the leverage to challenge our conformity to our own age. This fulcrum from beyond the system is what the author to the Hebrews called the "confidence and pride of our hope."[13]

Such an insistence upon an ontological connection between the call of discipleship and the divine economy of reconciliation, redemption and restoration locates Yoder's Christology in the lineage of Barthian christocentrism. Barth's mature dogmatic realism countered the putative universality common to nineteenth- and twentieth-century theological tropes of culture, nature, and common grace by exposing these as inadequate attempts to displace theology from its origin, center, meaning,

---

11. Alain Epp Weaver rightly castigates Jim Reimer for this excessive critique. See A. E. Weaver, "Missionary Christology," 436–37. Reimer, "Theological Orthodoxy." The essay also appears with other critical engagements with Yoder's work in Reimer, *Mennonites and Classical Theology*.

12. For a clear discussion of the creedal nature of Yoder's "High Christology," see Carter, *Politics of the Cross*, 113–36; and A. E. Weaver, "Missionary Christology."

13. Yoder, "That Household We Are," 7.

and goal in Christ (Ephesians 1, Colossians 1, etc.). Thus Barth famously views Christ as the linchpin by which motifs of creation and covenant are held together.[14]

> He, Jesus Christ, is the man whose existence was necessary for the perfecting of the earth; for the redemption of its aridity, barrenness and death; for the meaningful fulfillment of its God-given hope; and especially for the realisation of the hope of Israel. He is the man who, taken from all creation, all humanity and all Israel, and yet belonging to them and a victim of their curse, was in that direct, personal and special immediacy to God to him a creature, man, the seed of Abraham and the Son of David. He is the man whose confidence and hope was God alone but really God; who is what He is for all, for all Israel, all humanity, and even the whole world; who in the deepest humility and fear of God gave up himself wholly to the fate of the creature, man and Israel and in this way was decisively exalted and reigns over all creatures, the King of Israel and Saviour of the world, triumphing over all their weakness.[15]

For Barth, the general only exists for the sake of the particular, and finds its meaning in it.[16] Barth therefore rightly provides an innovative reordering of the doctrine of election such that Christ himself is both the God who elects and the only elect human being. Creation and redemption are then both works of the elective God. From all eternity God willed to bear the name

> the Father of our Lord Jesus Christ, the Son of the Father, the Holy Spirit of the Father and the Son.... We are not thinking or speaking rightly of God Himself if we do not take as our starting-point the fact which could be both "first and last": that from all eternity God elected to bear this name. Over against all that is really outside God, Jesus Christ is the eternal will of God, the eternal decree of God and the eternal beginning of God.[17]

These two facets of Barthian Christology, namely the integral linking of Christ to both elect community and, only thus, to all of creation, and the identification of the elect and electing Jesus Christ as the "divine freedom

---

14. Barth, *CD* III/1, §41, 242–329.
15. Ibid., 239.
16. Barth, *CD* II/2, 8.
17. Ibid., 99.

itself in its operation *ad extra*" are essential, I suggest, to an appropriate theological account of the relation of particular and universal.

Thus, for example, the otherwise highly suggestive neo-Paulinism of some contemporary postmodern Marxist ontology proves inadequate. Alain Badiou's account of universalism and "the event" may be compromised by its separation of the formal pattern of Pauline universalism from the specific content of God's Abrahamic election.[18] Badiou is entirely correct, in my view, to assert that the Pauline corpus gives voice to the first full universalism, and as such to "a new era of truth."[19] This universalism is neither the possessive and territorial particularism of some variants of the theology of election, which he mistakenly associates with Judaism *in toto*;[20] nor the discourse of a "Greek" static natural totality, which attempts universality through philosophical mastery. Likewise, we might add that Pauline universalism marks a radical breach with modern inversions of these—the latter as a liberal procedural mastery of contingency and diversity; the former in the loathing of universalism given expression in Nietzsche's aristocratic transvaluation of value. Nevertheless, Badiou goes too far in claiming that this is essentially a Pauline innovation. The Old Testament never permits the universal and the particular to be seen as mutually exclusive. Quite the opposite—the particular is that which is moving, or moved by God, to the universal. Badiou is wrong to claim then that the antinomy of Jew and Greek is exhaustive of Pauline accounts of the unification of *ethnē*.[21] That Badiou limits himself to those texts that he deems incontrovertibly Pauline leads him to ignore Colossians. He misses out on the important implications of the claim that: "[i]n that renewal there is no longer Greek and Jew, circumcised and uncircumcised, *barbarian, Scythian*, slave and free; but Christ is all in all" (Col 3:11, emphasis mine). This provides an extra dimension to the New Testament account of universal and particular—namely that the elective movement from Abraham to the peoples of the earth (Gen 12:3, 18:18; Gal 3:8–9), from Israel to the Nations, is the

---

18. Badiou, *Saint Paul*. A far fuller account of the notion of event is found in Badiou's seminal *Being and Event*. Some excellent theological reflections on the promise of such notions for a renewed political theology are to be found in Davis, et al *Theology and the Political*.

19. Badiou, *Saint Paul*, 60.

20. We shall see in chapter 6 why this possessive reading of the politics of election is anything but synonymous with Judaism, conceived as a singular particular.

21. Badiou, *Saint Paul*, 40.

means by which the nations will come to recognize Israel's God as the God of all nations; the rule of Zion extends to the ends of the earth.[22] This is no minor exegetical oversight, for it is precisely in reference to such a universal vision, adopted and adapted by Paul's own Christology, that Badiou's account of the eruptive "evental grace" is found to be abstract and formless. I argue then that Colossians 1 asserts the supremacy of Christ as both creator and redeemer, and only thus may we declare him the world's true sovereign, its one non-homogenizing particular.

There is, of course, no crass division of Old and New Testament here. Alas, while Badiou is caustic in his denunciation of Marcion,[23] he achieves his separation of form from content, of *being* from *truth effects*,[24] in part by a series of equally problematic exaggerated canonical and theological divisions. He overplays the lack of significant reflection on the details of Jesus's public ministry in the writings of Paul, to dismiss these as "not the reality of the conviction but [that which] encumbers and even falsifies it."[25] Badiou regards Jesus's "exceptional singularity," including all miracles, teachings, and symbolic enactments, as theological detritus. At this point Badiou's refusal to engage with biblical scholarship (despite some evident awareness of major debates) cannot be ignored. Even the most cursory familiarity with New Testament scholarship would demonstrate that such "exploits" are anything but "the trusted staples of religious thaumaturgy and charlatanism."[26] They are pivotal to the inaugurated and collaborative eschatology proclaimed by the entire New Testament, and thus to the foundation of theological realism.[27] This then provides the foundation for two further questionable distinctions: a primary theological division between the resurrection of Christ (as that "fable" which alone founds the "event") and all prior public enactments, miracles, and teachings in the ministry of Jesus, thus excluding the latter from any significance in the "new era of truth"; and a secondary canonical division between Pauline sources and the rest of the New Testament.

---

22. There is no need here to recite the presence of such a theme in the Old Testament—the references are legion. An excellent and readable survey may be found in Bauckham, *Bible and Mission*.

23. Badiou, *Saint Paul*, 34–36.

24. Ibid., 23.

25. Ibid., 33.

26. Ibid., 32.

27. On collaborative eschatology and the resurrection, see Stewart, *Resurrection of Jesus*.

The synoptic Gospels appear largely as a lamentable recurrence of homogenizing particulars, and thus the domestication of Paul by the powers of priestcraft diagnosed by Nietzsche.[28] Indeed, this is a Paul shorn of the alleged obscurantism of "Church dialect"—"all this 'faith'! 'charity'! 'Holy Spirit'! What an extravagant waste of energy!"[29] If the Paul of the Marcionite canon was stripped of all Jewish reference and continuity, Badiou's Paul is scarcely less supercessionist.[30] Badiou is right to identify a particular affinity between Paul and the figure of Abraham—and there is significant mitigation to a bald accusation of Marcionitism in the assertion that the rupture between Pauline Christianity and Judaism is "a militant, not an ontological thesis."[31] This is clearly of a piece with Badiou's stated intent to escape, and liberate "Paul's" universalism, from theological captivity. In so doing though, we are presented with a militancy without content, without norm, and without hope. In Milbank's phrase, it may "sustain very well an ontology of *revolution*, but not an ontology of socialism."[32] I object to Badiou in such strident terms simply because, as much as his work holds out enormously promising conceptual resources for the formation of Christian ontology, the loss of a full focus on the canonical depiction of the details of the life and public ministry of Jesus of Nazareth evacuates any such ontology of a valuation of the material conditions and contingencies of Christology and thus debilitates any meaningful ethic. This is clear in Badiou's own assertion of an "eventalgrace" in which Jesus "becomes like an anonymous variable . . . entirely absorbed by his resurrection."[33]

> What the particular individual named Jesus said and did is only the contingent material seized upon by the event in view of an

---

28. Badiou, *Saint Paul*, 36. Indeed, Badiou is particularly dismissive of Lukan sources as being essentially "Roman" and socially and politically reactionary and conservative. He does so despite reliance upon Acts at various points—e.g., his repeated assertion of Paul's Roman citizenship. Such a reading of Luke-Acts is common enough, but lacks precision and is insufficiently attentive to the pressing political and social critique of Rome still present in those texts.

29. Ibid., 28.

30. ". . . the only continuity between the Good News according to Paul and prophetic Judaism is the equation Jesus = Christ. . . . the new universality bears no privileged relation to the Jewish community" (ibid., 20, 23).

31. Ibid., 35.

32. Milbank, "Materialism and Transcendence," 404.

33. Badiou, *Saint Paul*, 63.

entirely different destiny. In this sense, Jesus is neither a master nor an example. He is the name for what happens to us universally.

. . . Christ is not a master; disciples are out of the question. . . . The relation between lord and servant differs absolutely from that between master and disciple."[34]

A brief contrast between Badiou and Dietrich Bonhoeffer will be instructive here. Both wish to assert a basic theological contemporaneity—for Badiou a contemporaneity of Paul as the first theorizer of the universalism of the event; for Bonhoeffer the contemporaneity of Christ who is our center, even when at the periphery of our consciousness.[35] Bonhoeffer's Christology refused the liberal division of the Jesus of history from the Christ of faith and in so doing also disallowed the separation of discipleship from truth.[36] What appears to concern Badiou in relation to discipleship is the same Nietzschean critique given voice in both his rejection of the Gospels and his pejorative account of Jewish election—the domestication and inversion of the event through priestcraft, obscurantism, and the enclosed "religious" community. Bonhoeffer's Christology emphasized the direct, personal address of Jesus to believer and community, the historicity of the revelation of Christ, the inadmissible and impertinent nature of theological abstraction, and thus the nature of the Church as an end to possessive self-enclosure.

The being of the Crucified and Risen One is not to be separated from the truth effects of the event. As far back as *Act and Being* Bonhoeffer provides a socio-ontological account of revelation in which God's freedom is "a free choice to be bound to historical human beings."[37] The God who is free for humanity, not free from humanity, is knowable not in the abstract, but only *pro me* and *pro nobis*.[38] It is this "man for others,"

---

34. Ibid., 60, 63.

35. Bonhoeffer, *Christology*, 62.

36. See especially Bonhoeffer's essay "What is meant by Telling the Truth?" in *Ethics*, 358–67. See also Hauerwas, "Bonhoeffer on Truth and Politics," in *PF*, 55–72.

37. Bonhoeffer, *Act and Being*, 90. I owe this translation, and the notion of a "socio-ontological" account of revelation and divine freedom, to the excellent discussion of such themes in Green, *Bonhoeffer*, 86.

38. Bonhoeffer, *Christology*, 43–67. The rejection of abstraction is pivotal in Bonhoeffer's christocentric theological method. "If we speak of Jesus Christ as God, we may not say of him that he is the representative of an idea of God, which possesses the characteristics of omniscience and omnipotence (there is no such thing as this abstract divine nature!);

as Bonhoeffer would later describe Jesus in his prison correspondence,[39] who is the only basis for theological realism. "[O]nly the God-Man Jesus Christ is real, and only through Him will the world be preserved until it is ripe for its end."[40] It is on such a theological realism, that Christian moral realism may be founded.

> ... Good is the real itself. It is not the real in the abstract, the real which is detached from the reality of God, but the real which possesses reality only in God. There is no good without the real, for the good is not a general formula, and the real is impossible without the good.
> ... Henceforth one can speak neither of God nor of the world without speaking of Jesus. All concepts of reality which do not take account of Him are abstractions.[41]

For Bonhoeffer, Christ is the counter-logos to the idolatrous human logos, the self-enclosed exercise of an autonomous and self-established power. The human logos seeks to make of Christ a mere idea, something universally accessible, some timeless non-particular truth. But the counter-logos is not an idea, but an address, a "truth spoken in the concrete moment."[42] "Truth is not something static in and for itself, but an event between two persons. Truth happens only in community."[43] Thus the incarnate God moves us from self-imprisonment to a new humanity with its center in Christ—an existing for others; from an idolatrous assertion of humanity *sicut deus* to true creaturehood.[44] Christ himself "mediates" this transformative event to us at existential, historical, and natural levels. He is therefore present not only *in* but *as* Word, sacrament, and community.[45]

By this simple "as" Bonhoeffer clearly is not guilty of the kind of mediatorial Christology to which Badiou rightly objects:

---

rather, we must speak of his weakness, his manger, his cross. This man is no abstract God." *Christology*, 104.

39. Bonhoeffer, *Letters and Papers from Prison*.
40. Bonhoeffer, *Ethics*, 128.
41. Ibid., 188, 192.
42. Bonhoeffer, *Christology*, 50–51.
43. Ibid., 51.
44. Bonhoeffer, *Creation and Fall*.
45. Bonhoeffer, *Christology*, 62.

> With Paul, we notice a complete absence of the theme of mediation. Christ is not a mediation; he is not that through which we *know* God. Jesus Christ is the pure event, and as such is not a function, even were it to be a function of knowledge, or revelation.
>
> ... this question ran through the entire epoch of revolutionary politics. For many of those faithful to it, the revolution is not what arrives, but what must arrive so that there can be something else; it is communism's mediation . . . For Paul, by contrast, just as for those who think a revolution is a self-sufficient sequence of political truth, Christ is *a coming* [*une venue*]; he is what interrupts the previous regime of discourses. Christ is, in himself and for himself, *what happens to us*.[46]

Badiou is also right to deny Christology any legal mediatorial transaction external or secondary to the event itself. Such mediation "enters into composition with wisdom."[47] Likewise Barth objects to forms of mediatorial Christology that focus on Jesus only as a means, channel, or instrument of some general gift, some object of hope other than Christ himself. To do so is to compromise the irruptive nature of the event through the application of a christological superscription to a more general anthropology or ontology.[48] Barth utterly refuses any attempt to regard the name of Jesus "in a purely 'nominalistic' way, as a formal symbolical or historical sign of the event of atonement."[49] Here Badiou's account of the event is compromised by his avowed focus on the "general conditions for a new truth"[50] achieved through a refusal of substantive content of the truth-event. This is no reactionary attempt to re-inscribe a more theological Paul into contemporary political thought, and thus carve out a niche for belief. Badiou's preference for the endless anarchic interplay of the "many" is an unsustainable basis for the long and hard work of resisting global capitalism.[51] It is the substantive nature of the Christ event, in its non-homogenizing particularity, that makes possible truly realistic social transformation.

---

46. Badiou, *Saint Paul*, 48. Nonetheless, Milbank diagnoses a return of a Platonic mediation in Badiou's work. See Milbank, "Return of Mediation."

47. Ibid., 49.

48. Barth, *CD* IV/1, 116.

49. Ibid., 122–23.

50. Miller, "Universal Truths," 38.

51. For a similar argument see Bell, "Badiou's Faith and Paul's Gospel."

Without a more robust, high Christology, political theory following Badiou's conception of an interruptive and disruptive occurrence of the event can only become an emaciated ersatz imitation of the defense of a christocentric kairotic realism begun in the Barthian reading of Romans with its trope of *krisis*,[52] and elaborated diversely in Bonhoeffer and the later Barth. However, if the biblical realism found in these thinkers is itself to remain sufficiently christocentric, and the underlying account of divine character, love, and freedom is to escape from any capricious arbitrariness, then a stronger emphasis on the nonviolent reconciling economy of God is necessary. Here we must return to Yoder. To affirm that Christology is the wellspring from which the Christian moral life flows is, by itself, insufficient. Without specific content faithfully discerned in Scripture, it would be empty rhetoric. "Our criteria" says Yoder "must be not merely 'Christological' in some vague, cosmic sense, but 'Jesulogical.'"[53] That is not to deny the validity of a "cosmic" sense of Christology, but quite the opposite, to demand the more radical theological task of allowing the particular narrative of the life, death, and resurrection of Jesus of Nazareth to reveal the cosmic, metaphysical truth about God.[54]

Specifically, Yoder's christocentrism focuses on the centrality of Jesus's nonviolence as normative in a way that his itinerancy or his celibacy, for example, are not.[55] The difference boils down simply to this—Christ's nonviolence, unlike these other characteristics, is a revelation of the way that God *is*; and thus of the way that he is reconciling the world to

52. Barth, *Epistle to the Romans*.

53. Yoder, *FTN*, 241.

54. In expressing it in these terms I hope to show how, despite repeated use of a disjunction between the Hebraic emphasis on particularity and the Hellenistic predilection for the general, Yoder's Christology is not reliant on the accuracy of such a monolithic construction. The use of this bald dichotomy now appears dated. Unfortunately, Yoder's use of the distinction extends beyond a heuristic purpose in the undergraduate lectures that make up *Preface to Theology*, appearing even in works produced toward the end of his life; cf. Stanley Hauerwas and Alex Sider's comments in their introduction to *PT*, 22–24. Of course Yoder was aware of the limitations of the schema: cf. *THW*, 136–39. Nevertheless the emphasis of particularity in opposition to generalizing tendencies remains important, even if its blanket association with distinct ethnic or cultural groups is anachronistic.

55. *PJ*, 95. This is why Nigel Biggar's description of the "Anabaptist" view of discipleship as an *imitatio Christi*, which is said to include a simplistic and legalistic method of extrapolating directives from single points in the biblical narrative, would certainly not apply to Yoder. Bigger, *Hastening that Waits*, 108. Craig Carter makes a similar point in his comparison of Yoder and Barth. Carter, *Politics of the Cross*, 76–78.

himself. Indeed, it is "our participation in Christ's very being" that enables us to follow him.[56] It is the christocentrism of Yoder's theology that unites biblical realism with theological realism. God's reconciliatory and redemptive purposes are worked out on a hill at Calvary. They are achieved through the nonviolent agapeic absorption of human hostility. Through the miracle of the resurrection and the exaltation of Christ at God's right hand God transforms the apparent defeat of the cross into victory.

> This death reveals how God deals with evil; here is the only valid starting point for Christian pacifism or nonresistance. The cross is the extreme demonstration that *agape* seeks neither effectiveness nor justice, and is willing to suffer any loss or seeming defeat for the sake of obedience.
>
> But the cross is not defeat.... Effectiveness and success had been sacrificed for the sake of love, but this sacrifice was turned by God into a victory which vindicated to the utmost the apparent impotence of love.[57]

The selection of nonviolence as particularly normative is not an arbitrary elevation of one aspect of Jesus's ministry to exemplary moral status. His nonviolence is central to the fulfillment of the messianic promise. In Yoder's later work the normativity of Christian nonviolence is increasingly expressed in terms of the full particularity, especially the Jewishness, of Jesus's mission. It is in relation to this particularity that we see the ethical importance of the relationship between Christology and ecclesiology. For Yoder, it is not mere coincidence that "it was in the process of becoming non-Jewish that Christianity also became non-pacifist."[58]

Of course the "Jewishness" of Jesus's mission is hardly a univocal or simple attribution. Inevitably, Yoder's reading of both the Jewish context of Jesus's mission, and the consonance of his nonviolence with a pacifistic interpretation of later rabbinic Judaism, are contentious.[59] A full arbitration between complex readings of the character of Judaism, past and present, is well beyond the scope of our current discussion. Instead let us

---

56. Yoder, *DPR*, 61.
57. Yoder, *OR*, 59–60.
58. Yoder, *JCSR*, 72.

59. Yoder's understanding of the pacifism of the *Galut* (Diaspora) situation of Rabbinic Judaism was strongly influenced by his correspondence with the Jewish pacifist Rabbi Steven S. Schwarzchild, whose work included an exploration of the Talmudic roots of Jewish pacifism. See Cartwright and Ochs, "Editor's Introduction" to *JCSR*, 1–29, especially 12–19.

examine perhaps the most obvious objection to the twin assertions of the "Jewishness" and the pacifism of Jesus—the biblical narratives concerning Israel's holy wars.

Dependence on God—Biblical Realism and the War of YHWH

The importance of understanding both Jesus and Paul in greater relation to a context of Jewish messianic expectations is now subject to almost total consensus among biblical scholars. However, Yoder's commitment to "biblical realism" places a more significant burden on the relationship between the Jewishness of his normative Christology and his affirmation of the basic unity of the biblical message. Rather than concluding that the tradition of holy war, paradigmatically identified with Israel's conquest of the Canaanites, are simple ideological justifications of genocide, Yoder attempts to find in such passages a theology consistent with the christological fulcrum of his biblical realism.[60] In so doing, through reflection on the complexity and diversity of biblical traditions, he delineates two broad patterns of Jewish identity (and therefore of ecclesial identity). As Craig Carter helpfully summarizes it

> Yoder believes that the Jesus movement of the early 30s of the first century had far more in common with the Jeremianic vision of Diaspora, synagogue, and pacifism, which became the shape of rabbinic Judaism, than the Maccabean vision of nation, monarchy and war. In fact, Yoder sees the church as the final step in the development of an alternative to a racially based, militaristic, violent, worldly people of God.[61]

Yoder begins by insisting that it would be anachronistic to read contemporary understandings of the morality of killing into texts like those of Joshuanic war or the planned sacrifice of Isaac. One can no more equate this early tradition of "YHWH war" with the Crusades, for example, than one would view the story of Sarah giving her servant Hagar to her husband Abraham "as a wife" (Genesis 16) as equivalent with the modern notion of so-called "open marriage." Differences of

---

60. Yoder remarks on "the unsuspected value of the more objectionable patterns of thought in locating distinctive dimensions" as one beneficial facet of biblical realism, *THW*, 130.

61. See Carter, *Politics of the Cross*, 152–53; cf. also *JCSR*; *PK*, 9–12; and "Jewishness of Early Christian Pacifism" and "Non-violence of Judaism" compiled as chapters 2 and 3 of *CHRN*.

context, intention, and reception of such narratives preclude such a method. What would have struck the first readers or hearers, and what the author is likely to have intended in these stories of war and sacrifice, is the importance of utter dependence on God.[62]

Nevertheless it is difficult not to read as misplaced hyperbole the assertion that "[f]ar from constituting an embarrassment for those who follow Jesus's nonviolence, Hebrew holy war is the historical foundation for the same."[63] It is certainly questionable that such accounts can support, in themselves, an understanding of the nonviolent redemptive action of God that is normative for Yoder. Nor may they be viewed as a legitimation of human violence.[64] It seems unnecessary and somewhat disingenuous to imply, as one recent critical account has, that Yoder's argument is nothing more than a regrettable consequence of a (stereotypical) Barthian view of Scripture and a personal failure of integrity and moral courage in the face of a conservative Mennonite community.[65]

Significantly, the piecemeal approach of Yoder's engagements with the problematic tradition of YHWH war themselves highlight the most serious error of such criticisms. Biblical realism denies the possibility of proceeding along the lines of a systematic a priori expectation of finding pre-formed dogmatic formulae within complex conditioned narratives. "The Bible does not present a systematic theology; a *systematic* preface is therefore *not* a preface to *it*. The task is thus made impossible by the very character of the Biblical point of view."[66] In these fragmentary efforts

---

62. Yoder, *PJ*, 76–92; cf. "Wrath of God," "To Your Tents, Oh Israel," and "Introduction" to Lind, *Yahweh Is a Warrior*.

63. Yoder, *FTN*, 85 n. 11.

64. Thus Brueggemann writes "while the image of Yahweh as warrior presents the material and seeming justification for "macho" violence in the world, such *human* violence is not text-sponsored or text-based. To be sure, the image of Yahweh as warrior lives at the edge of such violence. But to step over that edge, as has often been done in the service of ideological reading, goes well beyond the text. It is likely that the violence assigned to Yahweh is to be understood as counterviolence, which functions primarily as the central principle in order to undermine or destabilize other violence." Brueggemann, *Theology of the Old Testament*, 241–44.

65. This is the conclusion of Ray Gingerich. Gingerich simply fails to account for Yoder's dynamic engagement with biblical criticism and his often outspoken criticisms of conservative tendencies in the Mennonite church and beyond. Gingerich, "Theological Foundations." A significantly more balanced engagement, that also includes excellent discussions of the issue in relation to contemporary Zionism, is to be found in A. E. Weaver's *Constantinianism, Zionism, Diaspora*.

66. Yoder, *THW*, 131.

Yoder is not attempting to read a detailed understanding of the nonviolent nature of God directly from these texts. That would be to expect too much. The task is simply to examine how texts that have so often been a source of embarrassment for Christians, especially those committed to nonviolence, may in fact reveal important points of theological consistency with the christological foundation of "biblical realism."

To that extent there is a strong correspondence between Yoder's work and the notion of "narrative theology." Nonetheless that correspondence must not be read, for example, as an identification of Yoder with the narrative aspects of Stanley Hauerwas's project.[67] Yoder is concerned that the corrective potential of narrative theology can shift towards a new form of "methodologism."

> Only from within the community of resurrection confession is the cruciformity of the cosmos a key rather than a scandal. Therefore the particular narrative is prior to the general idea of narrativeness.[68]

Once the more modest nature of Yoder's exegetical task is accepted, it remains for us to discern how the overriding message of utter dependence on YHWH in the narratives of Israel making war is to fit with the normativity of Christ's nonviolence? Here, Yoder did not provide a single comprehensive exegesis, but a series of reflections, hints, and hermeneutical moves designed to identify in broad strokes a christocentric biblical realism. The distinctiveness of the tradition of holy war is to be seen in relation to the role of Israel among the nations. From its very beginnings in being called from the world of the Gentiles, the people of Abraham is constituted by a refusal of the necessity of violence.

---

67. Yoder is critical of Hauerwas for what he sees as an overplayed emphasis on narrative and character. "One reason Hauerwas does not do text-based Bible study is that he is overawed by the notion of community-dependency and underawed by the objective reality of salvation history. Also underawed by the study of real (unsaved) history. He would rather read novels." Yoder, "Absolute Philosophical Relativism is an Oxymoron." This is somewhat unfair to the nature of Hauerwas's realism in relation to "the objective reality of salvation history," which surely cannot be in doubt (Hauerwas is more Barthian than such a picture would imply). Nevertheless, it is an important counter-emphasis and corrective to common perceptions of narrative projects. Of course, in his recent work, when Hauerwas wants to express this realism, he often turns to Yoder in order to do so—e.g., *WGU*.

68. Yoder, *PK*, 36. Thus he says "One will welcome the creative imagination of structuralists who protect narration from reduction to 'truths' and 'concepts,' yet an equal vigilance is needed to defend the particularity of Abraham, Samuel, Jeremiah and Jesus from reduction to mere specimens of a new kind of universal, namely narrative forms lying deeper than the ordering events and sufficient to explain them."

> What begins in Abraham, and crests in Jesus, is not merely a different set of ideas about the world or about morality; it is a new definition of God. A God enters into relations with people who does not fit into the designs of human communities and their rulers. He is a God who saves, but not by reinforcing the selfishness and living up to the appetites of his people: who may save other people, other peoples as well, and who may even ask his people to love their enemies.[69]

In this way, the people of Abraham are constituted solely by their dependency upon God's own provision. Yoder points to the Aqedah (Genesis 22) not so much as the suspension of the ethical in obedience to a capricious sovereign's command to kill Isaac, and thus end the very promise of posterity God had himself made to Abraham; but as precisely that which demonstrates his continued trust in God for his survival.[70] Going beyond Yoder's exegesis, we might add that this foundational event represents not just a gesture of dependence, but a dramatically enacted subversion of a residual idolization of death as the means of bringing life, a refutation of divine violence, and a subversion of child sacrifice.[71]

In accepting that YHWH is their warrior and king, Israel rejected the forms of kingship common to their neighbors—not for Israel, then, the technology of the standing army and the attendant idolatry of self-determination. The Joshuanic conquest of Canaan certainly counts as one of the most starkly violent and repulsive to the modern mind in the whole of the Old Testament. Nonetheless, here, as in the "military"

---

69. Yoder, *JCSR*, 243

70. Yoder, *OR*, 102–4. Yoder delineates this view in contrast to "the protestant sermonizing à la Kierkegaard or à la Bonhoeffer which have tried to make this ancient story a proof that God is sovereignly unaccountable, or irrationally self-contradictory, or that His power is most clearly seen where our good sense and our sensitivity are summoned to bow blindly before Him," 102. It is unclear why Yoder associates such a view with Bonhoeffer. I suspect the root of this somewhat misplaced accusation resides in the fact that both Bonhoeffer and Barth seem to posit a sovereign and free remainder to God's ethical command sufficient to issue in occasional suspension of any normative strictures derived from God's nonviolent character as revealed in Christ. Barth is rightly criticized for this in his concept of the *grenzfall*—see Yoder, *KBPW*. What is unsettled in the Aqedah is not our ability to know that God *really* is what Jesus reveals him to be, and is so all the way down; but that obedience and dependence upon God trump our own expectations of success arising from familiar enclosed systems of cause and effect—whether in the mechanism of child sacrifice, or the broader scale death of innocent young in modern warfare.

71. See Levenson, *Death and Resurrection of the Beloved Son*.

encounters with other nations during the exodus, it is YHWH who fights for his people; it is not their own military might that ensures victory (Exod 14:13). The conquest of Canaan may variously be interpreted as a sacrificial consecration of the land,[72] or as an act of liberative undermining of the Bronze Age fortress in which the aristocratic god Baal once kept the ruling class in perpetuity over the exploited majority residing outside of the city walls.[73] Either way these events are to be subjected to a retrospective hermeneutic that reads them in the light of God's more clearly miraculous deliverances, given sacramental recognition in the parade around Jericho or the wars of Gideon. This is no anachronistic selectivity. The New Testament itself clearly appropriates, reformulates, and transforms the motif of the divine warrior (1 Thess 5, Eph 6) such that the warrior of love conquers the hostile powers of death through "the militant exercise of faith, love, and the hope of salvation."[74] Christ himself engages in an eschatological remaking of Israel, a new "reading" of the world, and hence a reordering of politics and morality, which come together as a new vision of the real.[75]

Yoder's biblical realism privileges the anti-royal and egalitarian prophetic writings as precursory to Jesus's own perception of his mission. Israel's kingship experiment therefore fails precisely in its inability to keep the people focused on their covenant with YHWH as the source of their identity. It is unable to keep the conditions for kingship conceded by YHWH in Deut 17:14-20. The Davidic pattern is repeated in both "Sadducean accommodation and Zealot insurrection."[76] By contrast the new covenant announced by Jeremiah both looks back to pre-Davidic patterns and forward to John the Baptist's annunciation of the coming of Christ. Importantly, the reason Jesus rejects the option of revolutionary violence referred to as "the Zealot option" is that it is unable to truly reconstitute the identity of Israel.[77]

72. Yoder, *PJ*, 78–79 n. 4; *OR*, 104–7.
73. Brubacher, "Just War and the New Community."
74. Yoder Neufeld, *Put on the Armor of God*, 154.
75. This notion of Christ's "reading" of the world grounding a new, transgressive, and dispossessive vision of the real is elaborated in great complexity and detail in the recent work of Oliver Davies. See *Theology of Compassion* and *Creativity of God*.
76. Yoder, *JCSR*, 80.
77. It might be debatable whether the "zealots" as an identifiable group were present during the life of Jesus. However this hardly constitutes a refutation of Yoder's point that the rejection of a distinctive form of armed revolutionary zeal was central to Jesus's

> What is wrong with the Zealot path for Jesus is not that it produces its new order by use of illegitimate instruments, but that the order it produces cannot be new. An order created by the sword is at the heart still not the new peoplehood Jesus announces.[78]

Jesus's Normativity as the Focal Point of both Biblical and Theological Realism

There is, one could say, a coherence of theological and social vision between the strand of Mosaic anti-royal Judaism in Samuel's warning against Israel's call for "a king to govern them like all the other nations" (1 Samuel 8, see also Deuteronomy 17 and Judges 9) and Jesus's response to James and John in an imperative mode—"It shall not be so among you" (Mark 10:35–45).[79] Here also is the link between Jesus's rejection both of kingship and of the Zealot attempt to restore it on the one hand, and the obedience of Christ as suffering servant on the other.[80] Christ enacts and achieves the reconciliation of the world to God through his obedience to God's will, "to the point of death—even death on a cross" (Phil 2:8). Likewise, the imperative of obedience to Jesus's nonviolence does not spring from legalism or simple mimicry. The demand for obedience flows directly from the logic and reality of God.

> We do not, ultimately, love our neighbor because Jesus told us to. We love our neighbor because God is like that. It is not because Jesus told us that we love even beyond the limits of reason and justice, even to the point of refusing to kill and being willing to suffer—but because God is like that too.[81]

In the Philippian hymn the association of obedience with the incarnational motif of *kenosis* is an example of the transcultural missionary move exposited in the first chapter of this book. More importantly for our present purposes, it functions simultaneously as a cosmic theological

---

approach to his mission; cf. *PJ*, 56–59; see also Klassen, "Jesus and the Zealot Option." For an excellent account of how Jesus's mission is to be seen as the reconstitution of Israel around himself, see Wright, *Jesus and the Victory of God*.

78. Yoder, *OR*, 24.

79. On the deconstructive and delegitimizing polemical function of 1 Samuel 8 and other texts, see Brueggemann, *Old Testament Theology*, 235–51; and, more briefly Brueggemann, *Theology of the Old Testament*, 238–41.

80. Yoder, *FTN*, 60; *JCSR*, 187–88 and *passim*.

81. Yoder, *OR*, 52.

exploration and as a specific appeal for unity in the church at Philippi. The church must live in the new social reality made possible in Christ. Just as the prophet Jeremiah calls Israel back to a pre-kingship covenantal identity, so Paul calls the Philippian church to the model of servanthood and obedience shown in Christ to be the pattern of the outworking of grace. Without repudiating apologetic concerns for the affirmation of Christ's pre-existence, Yoder highlights the ethical and normative importance of the Philippian "Hymn of the Servant Lord." In his obedience Christ does not "think being like God a thing to be seized" (Phil 2:6) and thus succeeds where Adam failed.[82] It is in the imitation of this obedient pattern that the Church participates in the victory of Christ and, in an evocative and important turn of phrase, moves "with the grain of the universe."[83]

Yoder's claim that "[o]nly from within the community of resurrection confession is the cruciformity of the cosmos a key rather than a scandal" is therefore a claim to theological realism groundable only within the normativity of Jesus's nonviolence and obedience. Such affirmations do not represent fideism—or at least, are no more dependent upon particular faith commitments than any other religious or "secular" stance. Paul writes to the Colossians "He himself is before all things, and in him all things hold together" (Col 1:17). What is truly and foundationally "real" is revealed in Christ. Christ, to use Bruce Marshall's phrase, is the "epistemic trump" that grounds all theological truth.[84] In outlining a Trinitarian account of Christian claims to truth, Marshall argues:

> That the Father sees all things in the enfleshed Word does not mean that Jesus himself is all things, but rather that all things have their reality and particular character in virtue of their relation and ordering to him. . . . Only that can be whose existence and attributes fit with his; even that in creation which comes to oppose him must be wholly capable of being redeemed by him.[85]

---

82. This is Yoder's own translation; cf. *PT*, 79–88.

83. Yoder, *AE*. Charles T. Mathewes claims that Yoder "never gets around to offering a vision of existence during the world as sacramental or proleptic participation in the coming kingdom" and that, to the contrary, for Yoder any "attempts to realise justice in this world [are viewed as] impious attempts to usurp God's power." Mathewes, *Theology of Public Life*, 240–41. Mathewes's book is a finely-written appeal for an Augustinian theology of public life. There is, alas, no way of avoiding the conclusion that Mathewes's reading of Yoder is just plain wrong.

84. Marshall, *Trinity and Truth*, 108–40

85. Ibid., 112, 116.

Yoder's focus on nonviolence as the character of God leads him to say that Christ is only to be imitated at one point—the cross.[86] This is so because the cross of Christ is "the price of his social nonconformity"; it is "the political alternative to both insurrection and quietism."[87] Those who reject the normativity of Jesus for ethics may do so for a number of reasons. It is worth expositing at length one of the most famous examples of Yoder's predilection for listing the variety of manifestations of what he deemed to be basic theological errors.[88] In the first edition of *The Politics of Jesus* he notes the normativity of Jesus is commonly rejected because:

1. The ethic of Jesus is an ethic for an (probably brief) "Interim" period. The ethics of this "apocalyptic Sermonizer . . . are not permanent and generalizable attitudes towards social values."

2. Jesus was "a simple rural figure. . . . his radical personalization of all ethical problems is only possible in a village sociology." Jesus did not intend to "speak substantially to the problems of complex organizations, of institutions and offices, cliques and power and crowds."

3. Jesus and his followers had no control over their world. "[T]hey could not conceive of the exercise of social responsibility in any form other than that of simply *being* a faithful witnessing minority. The individual Christian, or all Christians together, must accept responsibilities that were inconceivable in Jesus's situation."[89]

4. "By definition" Jesus's message was ahistorical, spiritual, and existential. "What he proclaimed was not a social change but a new self-understanding, not obedience but atonement."

5. Jesus, like H. Richard Niebuhr, was really a "radical monotheist" directing people's attention to the discontinuity between God and humanity that relativizes all human values. Thus,

---

86. Yoder, *PJ*, 95.
87. Ibid., 36, 96.
88. Ibid., 1–20.

89. Paul Ramsey provides Yoder with an example of a contemporary theological ethicist who combines 2 and 3 here. In discussing a basis for a "multilateral ethics of protection" (3) he says "Jesus deals only with the simplest moral situation in which blows may be struck, the case of one person in relation to but one other" (2). Cf. Ramsey, *Basic Christian Ethics*, 167.

because the substance of all ethics is finite, God's will is not to be identified with any human value.

6. Jesus's work of justification and atonement should not be correlated with ethics. "How the death of Jesus works our justification is a divine miracle and mystery; how he died, or the kind of life which led to the kind of death he died, is therefore ethically immaterial."

This list was published in 1972. In relation to the intervening decades the currency of these options has waxed and waned. We can say that some of these remain pertinent to contemporary scholarship (3 most particularly), and others have receded from view (e.g., 4). In the second edition Yoder adds the following:

7. "There is historical-critical skepticism about whether the text says anything clear enough to guide us in the moral life, assuming we would want to follow Jesus."

8. The diversity of authorship and readership in the canon prohibits one single coherent revelation upon which to base a normative ethical stance.[90]

9. Historical and particular understandings of Jesus should be balanced against more ahistorical and generalizable construals of Jesus as sage or incarnate Wisdom.[91]

10. In the interests of systematic trinitarian coherence the radicality of Jesus's ethic needs to be balanced against, for example, a more conservative ethic found in reflection on the nature of the Father as creator.[92]

---

90. For Yoder this diversity mitigates only against fundamentalist views of a propositionally seamless biblical revelation. It does not offer a decisive challenge to the postcritical (biblical realist) approach of narrative understandings, where the unity in contextual diversity speaks more strongly for, rather than against, the importance of Christ.

91. For Yoder this reflects a questionable bias against particularity, which we have already seen in previous chapters is highly problematic. Equally Yoder is correct to note that such ahistorical readings do not necessarily yield a less political Jesus, or bring into question the essential normativity of that politics. For example, both Marcus Borg and John Dominic Crossan provide an account of Jesus as the teacher of an alternative social vision. Nevertheless what the "Jesus Seminar" does disallow, on a circuitous methodological basis, is a Jesus of Jewish apocalyptic eschatology. Cf. Hays, "Why Do You Stand?"

92. This highly modalist construal is found in H. Richard Niebuhr and is substantively critiqued in Yoder's "How H. Richard Niebuhr Reasoned: A Critique of *Christ and Culture*," in *AT*, 31–89.

11. "Jesus did not come to teach a way of life; most of his guidance is not original. His role is that of Savior."[93]

Against these claims Yoder's affirmation of the reality of Jesulogical norms may best be seen as an affirmation of creedal orthodoxy. The intention of the discernment of orthodoxy from heresy was not, at Nicea, simply the means for Constantine to stamp his authority on the Church. Despite the "dirty politics" involved in the formation of the creeds, we still find there a broad set of parameters, or fences around acceptable diversity, which attempt to safeguard in new linguistic settings the normativity of the historical Christ. The creeds would not, however, function for Yoder as timeless definitional statements. They are worth affirming and debating over, but not fighting and killing for. They are but some (highly influential) instances of the ecclesial hermeneutics, the "transcultural reconceptualization," in which the Holy Spirit leads the Church.[94]

By contrast, to eschew the normativity of Christ's nonviolent life is, Yoder suggests, to get caught in ever-renewing forms of ancient christological heresies. To set aside the normativity of Christ because of the contextual, and therefore supposedly limited, nature of his message (as in 1–5 and 9 above) is to see Jesus "through ebionitic eyes." Conversely, a concern for the cosmic Christ of faith as divorced from the Jesus of history (as may be seen in especially in 6, 10, and 11) falls foul of a docetic form of Christology.[95] What Yoder appeals for is not, then, a stripping away of christological traditions (in the MacIntyrean sense) in favor of a bare "plain sense" of the gospel.

> I ask rather that the implications of what the church has always said about Jesus as Word of the Father, as true God and true Man, be taken more seriously, as relevant to our social problems, than ever before.[96]

---

93. There is an element of hair-splitting, and even repetition, in the presentation of this list. It is unclear, for example, how 11 differs in substance from 6.

94. Yoder, *PT*, 223. For more on the creedal orthodoxy of Yoder's theology, see both A. E. Weaver, "Missionary Christology," and Carter, *Politics of the Cross*, 113–36.

95. Yoder, *PJ*, 93–111.

96. Ibid., 102.

The Importance of Theological Realism for Ethics

The imperative to imitate Christ "only" at the cross is not to be taken as a division of Christian ethics into two camps, those derived directly from normative Christology—nonviolence (somatically understood) and those imperatives derived inferentially, and thus with a greater degree of ambiguity, e.g., sexual ethics, etc. Rather the "only" is both a response to the heretical exclusions of the ethical normativity of the cross and an affirmation that the entire Christian moral life here finds its core. That is perhaps the difference between the early Yoder's use of "middle axioms" and the standard account by Oldham and Visser T'Hooft.[97] The latter are concerned almost exclusively with the translatability and relevance of theological-moral utterance. Middle axioms were to operate at a mid-range level between banal generalities and simplistically derived specific prescriptions. While much of this mid-range limitation still features in Yoder's account, the derivation of specific programs direct from literalistic biblical warrant is precluded on christological grounds. The important point of contrast is that for Yoder the use of "pagan" language to express moral truths does not imply that those maxims have any "reality," or metaphysical value, outside of Christ.[98] Their reality is not predicated on the existence of some supra-theological, or non-christocentric principle.

Moral truth is, we might say, related to an eschatological distinction, based in Article 6 of the Schleitheim confession (one of the foundational documents of Anabaptism) between those inside or outside of the perfection of Christ.[99] This does not then impute a second normative standard for those outside of the church. Nor is it to imply that those within the Church are, by their own merits, ethically superior. Rather it is to maintain the importance of the Spirit-empowered sociology of the Church, and the formative and performative practices of that community, in the life of discipleship conformed to Jesus's nonviolence.

---

97. Visser't Hooft and Oldham, *Church and its Function*.

98. Yoder, *CWS*, 72.

99. Importantly for our later discussion, the distinction here stems from concerns regarding the fittingness of Christian participation in government. "The sword is an ordering of God outside the perfection of Christ. . . . But within the perfection of Christ only the ban is used for the admonition and exclusion of one who has sinned, without the death of the flesh, simply the warning and the command to sin no more." *Schleitheim Confession*, Article 6.

Significantly, Yoder soon dropped the term "middle axiom." Indeed it does have serious shortcomings: it begs serious questions regarding ethical validation by those outside this perfection of Christ; stultifies the Christian condemnation or support of specific practices and policies; and connotes a primarily propositional account of ethical communication. It is, that is to say, highly susceptible to Yoder's own critique of methodologism. Nevertheless the concept of a single normative standard, and the refusal to allow the world an autonomous ethic, remain centrally based in the simple but revolutionary proclamation that "Christ is Lord." It is in this simple proclamation then that theological realism and moral realism meet.[100]

Theological and Moral Realisms in Yoder's Eschatology

In discussing the relation of the Christian life to the normativity of Jesus's nonviolence, we have seen that Yoder establishes the ethical life firmly in how God is reconciling the world to himself. We have seen that, to put it simply, Christ not only reveals God's plan, he *is* God's plan. This plan is underway, its success assured. The victory won in Christ is a victory achieved but yet to be completed. Thus the coming of the Kingdom of God, that central motif of the gospel, cannot be constructed or brought about by political machination, nor can it be dismissed, in the interim, as of little bearing "until he comes." It is the fundamental reality in the light of which we can know what the Church is for. This in turn characterizes the Christian life as an eschatological existence. The theological realism founded on Christ leads to a partially realized or inaugurated eschatology that focuses the ethical around categories of witness, patience, forgiveness, and nonviolence.

---

100. For this reason Robin Lovin is erroneous in his claim that Barth and Hauerwas are theological realists, but not moral realists. See Lovin, *Christian Realism*. It is true that Barth differs from Bonhoeffer in locating moral realism more squarely in the doctrine of reconciliation than Bonhoeffer's doctrine of the mandates would seem to allow. The variation of Barth's and Bonhoeffer's account of creation and eschatology is important, of course, but Lovin seeks to mark out far too great a divergence here. The gap between Barth and Bonhoeffer here is not a breach that compromises the former's moral realism. David Haddorff has rightly suggested that the difference between Lovin and Barth is that Lovin retains a Kantian ontology with an essentially modern account of moral realism (Christian ethics as a subspecies of precisely the general ethics that Barth rejects), whereas Barth's account of *solus Christus* grounds a particular, inclusive, and postmodern moral realism. See Haddorff, "Postmodern Realism," 282.

Eschatology, Resurrection, and Political Critique

In 1906 Albert Schweitzer's groundbreaking study of Jesus in reference to late Jewish apocalyptic furnished renewed attention on the eschatological dimension of Jesus's mission.[101] Since then many theologians have, unlike Schweitzer himself, found in eschatology the very roots of a social-critical Christian theology.[102] We need not engage in a laborious comparative exercise in order to see some important parallels between Yoder's eschatology and that found in more systematic detail in the likes of Barth and Moltmann. The Kingdom, says Yoder, is a social order that allows for the sabbatical politics of Jubilee—an order of equality, forgiveness, liberation, and nonviolence.[103] Following our account of the christocentric nature of theological realism, it seems clear that, like Barth, Yoder's eschatological realism does not point to a reality external to the person of Christ, abstractable from his being. For Christ is the *Eschatos*—in him the Kingdom of God comes.[104] This is to concur with Barth's account of "the revelation of God as the abolition of religion" when he asserts that "[t]he name of Jesus Christ is the very essence and source of all reality."[105]

Theology is a truthful discipline in so far as it refers not simply (though not in total disjunction) to the "reality" of empirical experience, but to Christ, the *Eschatos*, as its "most concrete reality."[106] In order to demonstrate how this may obtain ontologically, Barth explores the doctrine of the hypostatic union.[107] Ingolf Dalferth expresses this well when he describes this reality as

---

101. Schweitzer, *Quest of the Historical Jesus*. The first translation into English appeared in 1910.

102. A useful summary of scholarly understandings of apocalyptic, including a brief critique of Schweitzer, is found in Wright, *New Testament and the People of God*, 280–338. On the political meaning of apocalyptic, see also O'Donovan, "Political Thought."

103. Yoder's use of the ethical importance of the concept of Jubilee, itself dependent on the work of André Trocmé, significantly predates contemporary uses in the theology of economics and international debt. See *PJ*, 60–75. The importance of Jubilee for the ethical implications of eschatology is not undermined by a negative answer to the question of whether Israel ever enacted the practice. The point is that Jesus declares it as part of his message about the Kingdom.

104. McDowell, *Hope in Barth's Eschatology*, 135.

105. Barth, *CD* I/2, 348.

106. Dalferth, "Barth's Eschatological Realism," 29.

107. Barth, *CD* II/1, 69f.

> [n]either God's immanence in the world nor a deification of the world but the eschatological assumption of the world into God. . . . In short, our world of common experience is an enhypostatic reality which exists only in so far as it is incorporated into the concrete reality of God's saving self-realisation in Christ.[108]

This is a reality, which, as founded in the *bodily* resurrection of Christ, cannot but represent a challenge to the political order.[109] To shortcircuit the gospel narrative by moving straight from cross to ascension, without the uncomfortable fact of the resurrection, may furnish the happy ending the modern consumer individual has been groomed to expect from religion. Likewise, a spiritualized or nonbodily view of the resurrection avoids the strangeness of the language of miracles only by evacuating the narrative of its social-critical power. It is in the bodily resurrection that God vindicates Jesus's nonviolent messianism, for it is here that death, the power of the tyrant, is overcome. As N. T. Wright writes in his study of the resurrection:

> No tyrant is threatened by Jesus going to heaven, leaving his body in a tomb. No governments face the authentic Christian challenge when the church's social preaching tries to base itself on Jesus' teaching, detached from the central and energizing fact of his resurrection (or when, for that matter, the resurrection is affirmed simply as an example of a supernatural "happy ending" which guarantees post-mortem bliss).
> . . . The resurrection constitutes Jesus as the world's true sovereign, the "son of god" who claims absolute allegiance from everyone and everything within creation. He is the start of the creator's new world: its pilot project, indeed its pilot.[110]

Likewise, any contemporary discomfort with the dramatic language of apocalyptic can easily slide into a stoic acceptance and complicity with the imperial domination that biblical apocalyptic sought to resist. From Daniel's nonviolent resistance of the Seleucid empire, to Pauline

---

108. Dalferth, "Barth's Eschatological Realism," 29.

109. It is important to proceed with caution here. A common criticism of *Politics of Jesus* is that it fails to focus sufficiently on the resurrection, thereby leaving the cross standing alone as the symbol of low Christology. We have already seen that such a designation ill-fits Yoder's work; nevertheless Yoder was less than candid in his account of the resurrection in that particular book. It cannot be stressed strongly enough, however, that the reality of the resurrection infuses every fiber of Yoder's theology.

110. Wright, *Resurrection of the Son of God*, 730–31.

anti-imperialism, and on into the critique of Rome found in the vision of John of Patmos, apocalyptic eschatology is no yearning for escape into another world.[111] Rather, it is a way of living in this world, of loving this time.[112] As Bonhoeffer puts it

> Ethical thinking in terms of spheres, then, is invalidated by faith in the revelation [apocalypse] of the ultimate reality in Jesus Christ, and this means that there is no real possibility of being Christian outside the reality of the world and that there is no real worldly existence outside the reality of Jesus Christ.[113]

Eschatology and the Charge of Reductionism

Yoder's general theological bias towards the social and political implications of the gospel is a corrective against spiritualizing and internalizing tendencies. As a consequence of such remedial intent he has been criticized for underplaying "the existential-sacramental power of Jesus's message—that part having to do with divine grace, the personal forgiveness of sin, the inner renewal of the spirit, and the individual's stance before God."[114] There is some truth to this criticism, in so far as individual "spiritual" aspects rarely appear in Yoder's writings. It is less true of sacramental concerns per se. His focus on the sacramental does not yield a high conception of individual sacramental spirituality, but, in keeping with his concerns, maintains in the strongest possible terms the communal importance of sacraments to the social-critical life of the Church.[115] However, it would be inaccurate to see this as a concession to

---

111. The references for such a reading of apocalyptic as anti-imperial are legion. See for example Howard-Brook and Gwyther, *Unveiling Empire*; Kovacs and Rowland, *Revelation Through the Centuries*; Rowland, *Open Heaven*; Horsley, *Paul and Empire*; Horsley and Silberman *Message and the Kingdom*; Horsley, *Jesus and Empire*; Horsley, *Paul and the Roman Imperial Order*; Elliott, *Liberating Paul*; Rieger, *Christ and Empire*; Swartley *Covenant of Peace*.

112. I owe this way of stating the case to Daniel Barber's excellent "Particularity of Jesus."

113. Bonhoeffer, *Ethics*, 198. Identifying Bonhoeffer's ethical account of revelation as "apocalyptic" is disputed. In doing so, I agree with Ziegler "Dietrich Bonhoeffer."

114. Reimer, "Mennonites, Christ, and Culture." Similar comments come from Cartwright, "Sharing the House of God," especially 604–5.

115. E.g., Yoder, *BP*; "Binding and Loosing," in *RP*, 325–58; "Sacrament as Social Process: Christ the Transformer of Culture," in *RP*, 360–73. We shall return to this in greater detail over the forthcoming chapters.

the charge of reductionism. The reasons why the charge of reductionism is unfair are themselves consummately theological—they derive from the dogmatic content of Yoder's project. Specifically they concern, first, the nature of dogmatics and the theological vocation itself, and second, the ethical implications of eschatology.

Mitigation appears in the form of his view of the ad hoc, responsive, and corrective vocation of the theologian.[116] Yoder's starting point for the necessity and status of theological reflection is the missionary needs of the Church. "There had to be theology because there was action in the church, and because there was the danger of false, unbalanced, or improper doctrine."[117] The theologian, especially the theological ethicist "has no independent merit." The theologian is in the service of the Church, most importantly, because that individual is not, in herself, the "agent of moral discernment." That appellation belongs to the Holy Spirit alone.[118] The doctrinal task of the theological ethicist is here seen in striking parallel to what Barth calls "irregular dogmatics." Irregular dogmatics eschews systematic comprehensiveness in favor of the discussion of a particular problem facing the Church.[119] In doing so, however, it does not thereby bring into question the proper role to be played by "regular dogmatics." In relation to our present concern, it is true that Yoder was usually asked to speak around issues of the political aspects of the gospel. Yoder perceived his task in relation to the need for a corrective

---

116. See for example Yoder, *FTN*, 9–11.

117. Yoder, *PT*, 127.

118. This is conceived in accordance with Yoder's believer's church ecclesiology. Thus "[t]he agent of moral discernment is not a theologian, a bishop, or a pollster, but the Holy Spirit, discerned as the unity of the entire body." *RP*, 139. In this presidential address for the Society of Christian Ethics (Duke University, 1988) Yoder employs the fascinating image of the theologian as the "lymphocyte" of the immune system. "The lifeblood of that body is language. When the ability of human blood to carry its freight is threatened by an antigen, the type B lymphocytes produce antibodies to fit that specific invader. The lymphocytes' function has no independent merit. While the body is healthy they are not needed. There is no use for the antibodies before the antigen invades, although their traces stay in the system after the disease is over. Our guild's vocation is vigilance against the abuse of words or the logic of the discerning community. We are neither the umpires nor the examiners, the bishops nor the catechists, the evangelists nor the moderators. We are the immune system of the language flow that keeps the body going."

119. Barth, *CD* I/1, 316–20. Eugene Rogers provides an excellent example of the commonality between "irregular dogmatics" and the Roman Catholic conception of the ecclesial vocation of the theologian in relation to the issues surrounding homosexuality. Rogers, *Sexuality and the Christian Body*, 5–8.

to spiritualizing tendencies. Therefore his work does not represent a wholesale rejection of the "individual" and "spiritual" elements of the gospel, but condemns the narrowing of Christian life to such a level as a betrayal of the gospel. Again such a narrowing represents a docetic reduction, for it denies that "the newness of the gospel can take on flesh."[120] The charge against him cannot be one of reductionism. For that claim to be sustained he would have needed to claim, or at least strongly imply, that not only was the gospel political to the core, but that it was nothing else. That he did not claim.[121]

In addition to this pneumatological-ecclesiological response to the charge of reductionism, an eschatological point follows. Eschatology, as Moltmann correctly notes, inevitably brings together the "personal," the "historical," and the "cosmic."[122] Without entering complex discussions of, for example, the relation of time to eternity, which feature more in the writings of Moltmann than would ever have befitted Yoder's method, it is possible to see then, that the critics are mistaken.[123] There is a realism implied in the logic of eschatology itself, which places the separation of the political, the "existential," and the cosmic under threat of erasure. That realism is based in the proclamation of the Church—Christ is Lord. It is the hope that springs from that kerygmatic moment that makes the recovery of a form of ecclesial politics consonant with the contours of eschatological reality an imperative task. Thus Yoder can claim that

> The vision of the lordship of Christ over the powers made it possible for the first Christians to see even tragic events as having positive potential, like the cross itself. . . . This is then the immediate political pertinence, in the situation of frustration, of confessing with the Creed that it is Jesus who for us and who for our liberation was made human. This is the New Testament refutation of the definition of Jesus as apolitical. Gustavo Gutierrez

---

120. Yoder, *FTN*, 82.

121. For his responses to the charge of reductionism in relation to this corrective role, see Yoder, *PJ*, 226–27; and *FTN*, 82–84.

122. Moltmann, *Coming of God*.

123. E.g., ibid., 279–95. For critical reflections on these issues, see for example Bauckham, "Time and Eternity." Even here little attention is given to the possible ethical implications of such complex matters. A useful general comparative study of Moltmann and Yoder is found in N. G. Wright, *Disavowing Constantine*.

says this by denouncing the "distinction of the planes." I said it simply by calling Jesus "political."[124]

Eschatology and Moral Realism

Indeed, I shall show below that it is in taking account of the moral realism implied in the claims of eschatology that Yoder is able to turn the tables on his critics. The rest of this chapter will thereby demonstrate that a realist political eschatology is the only way to escape both ethical reductionism and the common accusation of "sectarianism." We have noted already the importance of Christology and eschatology to Yoder's theological realism. Correlative to this "eschatological realism" is a form of radical political critique. Tim Gorringe reflects on the radical politics found in both Barth and Moltmann as a result of their eschatological commitments. Gorringe's description of the role of eschatology in these theologians strikes a resonant chord with Yoder's theological vision. So, Gorringe says

> The cross casts a shadow on all "healthy" humanity, where our most secure standing place is shattered, set ablaze and finally dissolved. . . . What the eschatology of these theologians offers us is not just the courage of despair but the courage of faith in the God who raised Jesus from the dead. The task of the church, they teach us, in an increasingly apocalyptic scenario, is to live by the messianic politics of resistance and hope.[125]

Of course it is not enough to say that eschatology leads to radical political critique, for the movement is ambiguous and contingent. Eschatology may just as easily result in a conservative impulse.[126] Radical critique all too frequently degenerates into naïve utopianism or, as Hannah Arendt famously notes, revolutions end by devouring their own children.[127] It is, therefore, only the beginning to say, with Barth, that eschatology should not lead to flight from this life, but orients us to the world and to history.[128] Importantly for our present concern Yoder's

---

124. Yoder, *FTN*, 138.
125. Gorringe, "Eschatology and Political Radicalism," 97, 114.
126. On this, see Moltmann, "Liberation of the Future."
127. Arendt, *On Revolution*; see also Lehmann, *Transfiguration of Politics*.
128. "The Christian hope does not lead us away from this life; it is rather the uncovering of the truth in which God sees our life. It is the conquest of death, but not a flight into

eschatology proceeded to reflect on the continued importance of apocalyptic as a genre which reveals the cruciform politics of apparent powerlessness. Thus he notes, "Let it therefore not be wrongly thought that only underdogs used the idioms of apocalypse. So did Constantine and Charlemagne. So did Ronald Reagan." The point is that the centrality of the nonviolent Christ is what ensures the truthfulness of eschatology. Just as a failure to take seriously the Jesulogical complexion of truth issues in heretical Christologies, so theologically deficient political visions flow from eschatological heresies. Thus, Yoder continues,

> It is not false when people who call themselves "realists," from Machiavelli to Klausewitz to Reinhold Niebuhr, tell us that power comes from the barrel of a gun. That is one kind of power; but the alternative is not weakness but other kinds of power. It is not that the seers compensate for their being in fact incapacitated, by dreaming vindictively about cosmic catastrophe; it is that to be disarmed after the mode of Christ is to be endowed with the power of truth-telling . . . and community-building, for which the metaphors of cosmic conflict are most apt because they break the frame of normalcy.[129]

This christocentric model of powerlessness is not simply some *post factum* justification that seeks to make a theological virtue out of a sociological necessity.[130] It is, rather, a central ethical motif of life lived in the present and future reality of the Kingdom. In Jesus, God has inaugurated a new social order. That is the *Original Revolution* of which Yoder speaks. God has acted decisively in order to redeem, not simply to "complete" history. But that redemptive action has not yet been fully realized. We live then in a time of eschatological tension, between the already and the not-yet. The kingdom of the Son precedes the kingdom of the Father (1 Corinthians 15).[131] Thus Yoder defines eschatology simply as "a hope

---

the Beyond. The reality of this life is involved. Eschatology, rightly understood, is the most practical thing that can be thought." Barth, *Dogmatics in Outline*, 154.

129. Yoder, "Ethics and Eschatology," 124.

130. Stephen Sykes, for example, accuses Moltmann of such a *post factum* justification of the loss of political influence, and indicts him for a misunderstanding of the Pauline theology of the cross. Sykes, *Identity of Christianity*, 75. Even if Sykes is correct to note problems with the notion of powerlessness advocated in *Crucified God*, it would surely be a gross misrepresentation of the gospel to imply that invocations of powerlessness throughout Christianity's history can be reduced to a pragmatic rear-guard action against encroaching forms of secularization.

131. Yoder, *CWS*, 12.

that, defying present frustration, defines a present position in terms of a yet unseen goal that gives it meaning."[132]

Yoder employs the image used by Oscar Cullmann of D-Day, the event of the subjugation of the old aeon, and V-Day, the consummation of victory.[133] Here we need to be clear. Moltmann accuses Cullmann's linear conception of time of a deistic determinism that reduces eschatological tension to pure temporality.[134] This is similar, he implies, to the secular eschatologies of the nineteenth-century idea of history. The failure of this vision of completion was, says Moltmann, that it took up only one side of the eschatological expectation. It seized upon the millenarian hope for the fulfillment of the *telos* of history, but failed to account for the apocalyptic hope for the *finis*, the rupture of historical movement.[135] Whether or not that is fair to Cullmann we can certainly say that Yoder's eschatology is not mere futurology. The promise of the kingdom is not simply "more of the same."[136] What Moltmann would refer to as *Adventus*, and the early Barth would have named as *krisis*, is found, for Yoder, in apocalyptic.[137] Apocalyptic

> ... redefines the cosmos in a way prerequisite to the moral independence which it takes to speak truth to power and to persevere in living against the stream when no reward is in sight.[138]

---

132. Yoder, *RP*, 145, *OR*, 56.

133. Yoder, *RP*, 150; *OR*, 63–64; *CWS*, 9, etc. Cf. Cullmann, *Christ and Time*, 144–74. The usefulness of this metaphor is not predicated upon the historical accuracy of the implication of inevitability in the interregnum between D-Day and V-Day.

134. Moltmann, *Coming of God*, 10–13.

135. Ibid., 131–34.

136. For Yoder's comments on the pseudo-science of futurology, see, for example, Yoder, "Karl Barth, Post-Christendom Theologian."

137. David Michael Hughes is wrong, therefore, to cite Yoder's comment that "The unforeseeable future is farther along in the same direction as the foreseeable future for which we are responsible" (*PJ*, 241) in defense of the view that Yoder was not inclined toward the apocalyptic view of history "wherein the new age is radically different from the age we now live in." Hughes, "Ethical Use of Power," 126. The entire section is a defense of apocalyptic, not an eschewal of it. The point Yoder is quite clearly making is that first-century apocalyptic literature is not susceptible to later modern characterizations of eschatology as "pie in the sky bye and bye." Yoder is therefore criticizing the anachronistic reading of modern divisions between "this-worldly" and "other-worldly" into the genre. In no way is this a denial of the novelty found in the eschatological rupture. Hughes's careless remark can only appear incredible in the light of the pervasiveness of apocalyptic in Yoder's writings.

138. Yoder, *AE*.

The danger facing the Church is therefore the same danger that faced Israel in its move to kingship—the loss of dependence upon God as the basis for the life of the community. An apocalyptic eschatology does not furnish the community with an escape route from contingency. "[T]he new world or the new regime under which we live is not" according to Yoder "a simple alternative to present experience but rather a renewed way of living within the present."[139] It is life in the light of the reality of the lordship of Christ. "It does not assume that time will end tomorrow; it reveals why it is meaningful that history should go on at all."[140]

To attempt to master the contingency of life, to gain control over the "movement of history," is to collapse eschatological tension. We have seen that the nonviolence of Christ is normative for Yoder not because of any extrinsic principle of imitation, but because of the truth of God. Truthful living, and therefore an account of moral realism, requires nonviolent practice. That is what Stanley Hauerwas means when he proclaims with typical hyperbole that only pacifists can truly understand the Bible.[141] Here Yoder's thought fits well with the "postliberal" conception of intratextuality. As Lindbeck describes it,

> Intratextual theology redescribes reality within the scriptural framework rather than translating Scripture into extrascriptural categories. It is the text, so to speak, which absorbs the world, rather than the world the text.[142]

The intelligibility and applicability of the eschatological pattern does not require the mediation and mitigation of the strangeness of apocalyptic.[143] Rather it is in the light of that strangeness that the Christian life participates in the reality of the lordship of Christ. This is not a counsel for fideism, for it does not enclose the believer, or more properly the believing community, within a hermetic "biblical" world outside of the "normal" world.[144] Rather, the notion of intratextuality is realist in a

---

139. Yoder, *PJ*, 185.
140. Ibid., 105.
141. Hauerwas, *US*, 8, 153.
142. Lindbeck, *Nature of Doctrine*, 118.
143. On the importance of an "intratextual" view of apocalyptic see Hays, "Why Do You Stand Looking Up Toward Heaven?"
144. For useful discussion on this point see Tilley, "Incommensurability." See also Sue Patterson's comment that "If Christianity absorbs the world, it does so according to a christo-typology which begins as intratextual but immediately involves the reader and the reader's world." Patterson, *Realist Christian*, 64.

thoroughly eschatological sense. What is most true for the Church, the lordship of Christ, is also true for the world. Thus it is that Yoder can declare that the Church "precedes the world epistemologically" and, therefore, "axiologically."[145] Put simply, the commitment to theological realism requires a specifically christocentric form of moral realism because "the people of God are called to be today what the world is called to be ultimately."[146]

Moral and Ethical Realism in Yoder's Account of Constantinianism

Given this eschatological-ecclesiological texture to moral reality in Yoder, we can consider how the collapse of eschatological tension can lead to heretical forms of ecclesial-political vision. In so doing we presage the link between moral realism and ethical realism. In this section we discuss this in relation to Yoder's typological identification of "Constantinianism." We shall examine in more detail how this fundamental eschatological error affects the "realism" of Reinhold Niebuhr in our discussion, in chapter 6, of the possibility of nonviolent forms of liberative political praxis in the Christian life.

The "disavowal of Constantine" is central to the schematic through which Yoder expressed his generally critical account of the way that Christian social ethics has been undertaken. The term "Constantinian" does not refer simply to the person of the Emperor Constantine any more than "Pelagianism" merely refers to the originator of that particular heretical move.[147] Like Pelagianism, Constantinianism is a heretical move based on a faulty account of human agency in relation to divine grace. It is the archetypal attempt to seize the reins of historical movement. Constantinianism is the cipher referring to the shift in the basis of the Church's political life that occurs when the coming of the Kingdom is located with the projects of violent "power."

---

145. Yoder, *PK*, 11. Bonhoeffer's eschatology provides a similar emphasis, and a correction to what became standard Lutheran account, when he argues that the penultimate does not possess an autonomous existence separate from the ultimate. Bonhoeffer, *Ethics*, 120–85.

146. Yoder, *BP*, ix.

147. See Yoder, *RP*, 245. Another polemical reading of the Constantinian shift as the triumph of imperial ideology over Christianity is provided by Alastair Kee in *Constantine versus Christ*. For useful introductory works on Constantine, see Drake, *Constantine and the Bishops*, and Lieu and Montserrat, *Constantine*.

It would be a mistake to read into this notion a blanket denial of the importance and efficacy of all purposive social action. There is no counsel for passivity in this pacifism. Indeed, we shall see later that an adequate theology of social change requires just such a cautionary note. The point is that, in its literally "ungracious" optimism in human agency, the Constantinian schema compresses and re-orders the linear aspect of eschatology. Yoder expresses it thus—"the purpose of exterminating, rather than subduing, evil, is shifted from the endtime to the present."[148] And yet, simultaneously, this foreshortened linear aspect (Moltmann's *futurum*) is elevated well above the interruptive (Moltmann's *Adventus*). It is, to borrow a phrase from Jacques Ellul, the "false presence of the kingdom."[149] In such a realized or presentist eschatology "[a]ll that God can possibly have in store for a future victory is more of what has already been won."[150] Its anthropology is based on the sort of construal of moral agency and the controllability of history that the genre of apocalyptic has split asunder. It has failed to take to heart the importance of the message of the gospel narratives that

> ... the calculating link between our obedience and ultimate efficacy has been broken, since the triumph of God comes through resurrection and not through effective sovereignty or assured survival.[151]

The Constantinian temptation does not (always) approach the Church as the naked *libido dominandi*, or the Nietzschean "will to power," but is clothed in the seductive attire of the desire to render its mission effective. Now, of course, "effectiveness" is not in itself an inappropriate goal. What Yoder seeks to ascertain is how human action may be seen as truly "effective" in a way consonant with the nonviolent lordship of Christ. That involved him in a typological and historiographical exercise. Historiography is conceived in this case as that activity of conceptual archaeology through which the movement of the Holy Spirit is discerned in some practices of nonviolent politics. It is to re-read history in order to see that, in Yoder's words, "*at certain points* there is specifiable good news about the human condition, the goodness or the newness of which

---

148. Yoder, *OR*, 66.
149. See Ellul, *False Presence of the Kingdom*.
150. Yoder, *PK*, 137.
151. Yoder, *PJ*, 239.

those who hitherto have been controlling the storytelling ha[ve] not yet appropriated."[152]

There is a danger with all typological analysis that in seeking neat divisions and hidden patterns one rides roughshod over the diversity and nuance of historical experience. Yoder, in his more polemical moments, was certainly not immune from this; but the point of his historiographical efforts is precisely to unsettle what he called "the frame of normalcy."[153] That is, to upset those ways of seeing moral questions which blind the church to the truth to which it is to bear witness. But this is more than a corrective heuristic device, for it is based in the conviction that true historical movement is seen more with the peaceable ones and the underdog, than with the shifting tides of imperial power.

Yoder's schema is an attempt to name a basic theological error, which is nonetheless manifest in pluriform ways. He identifies five forms of "Constantinianism," moving somewhat inelegantly to "neo-neo-neo-neo-Constantinianism."[154] Thus, for example, with the rise of the nation-state neo-Constantinianism identifies the Church with the fate of particular states, rather than the Holy Roman Empire. Equally, the Constantinian temptation may arise in supposedly secular situations when Christians make common cause with nongovernmental projects in ways insufficiently attentive to the otherness of the nonviolent Church. The historiographic discernment, stemming back to Yoder's narration of the Jeremianic diaspora pattern, leads him to identify, during these times, the faithful practice of witnessing minorities.[155]

---

152. Yoder, "Burden and Discipline," 22.

153. For example, his description of the Constantinian synthesis as "that fusion of church and society of which Constantine was the architect, Eusebius the priest, Augustine the apologete, and the Crusades and Inquisition the culmination" (Yoder, *RP*, 89) is a triumph of polemic over historical discipline which is far too dismissive of the diversity between, for example, the "priest" and the "apologete." A more generous version is found in comments like this: "Ambrose and Augustine did the best they could. They did not mean to sell out, but they did buy into a system [the Just War tradition] whose inherent dynamism they could no longer control" (Yoder, *PK*, 75–76).

154. Yoder, *OR*, 148–85; *RP*, 194–218. Whilst this more nuanced typology mitigates criticisms of simplistic historiography (for example, from LeMasters *Import of Eschatology*) it remains true that Yoder's polemical remarks against, for example, the establishment of the Church of England, bear little resemblance to the ways in which "establishment" currently functions. See Avis, *Church, State and Establishment*.

155. Yoder's historical writings are far too numerous to list here. Yoder's doctoral dissertation *Täufertum und Reformation in der Schweiz: Vol. 1. De Gespräch zwischen Täufern und Reformatoren 1523–1538* and the second volume *Täufertum und Reformation im*

It may be useful to distinguish, in a way Yoder did not, the temptation of Constantinianism from the epoch of Christendom. New and subtle forms of the Constantinian shift occurred throughout the era of "Christendom," but they also occur in our "post-Christendom" situation. I do not doubt that the intention of Christendom theologians was not simply a defense of a particular political configuration, but rather, in many cases, was also an attempt to discern in those situations the faithful mission of the Church. In that sense I agree with Oliver O'Donovan's description of Christendom as a "*response* to mission."[156] The problem is that evil consequences may be attendant on beneficent and faithful intentions. Thus the important division is between a "minority-missionary" ecclesiology as opposed to the "established-pedagogical" view.[157]

Constantinianism is likened to a false prophecy whereby, in the words of Jeremiah, "They have treated the wound of my people carelessly, saying, 'Peace, peace' when there is no peace." (Jer 6:13–15; 8:7–14) In so doing there occurs a fusion of the two aeons that combines "the providential purpose of the state, that of achieving a 'tolerable balance of egoisms' . . . and the redemptive purpose of the church, [which is] the rejection of egoism in the commitment to discipleship. This confusion leads" says Yoder "to the paganization of the church and the demonization [i.e., idolatry] of the state."[158] That is the danger of preaching a peace without eschatology. Constantinianism is constitutionally incapable of making Christ's lordship known. Yoder is unequivocal—without eschatology the object of faith must be found within the world as it now is, and the Church as witnessing community sinks into the quagmire of Constantinianism.

> Previously Christians had known as a fact of experience that the Church existed but had to believe against appearances that Christ ruled over the world. After Constantine one knew as a fact of experience that Christ was ruling over the world but had to believe against the evidence that there existed "a believing church." Thus

---

Gespräche zwischen Schweizerischen Täufern und Reformatoren have recently been published together in English as Yoder, *ARS*. Also worthy of special mention are his specific studies of individual Anabaptist figures such as *The Legacy of Michael Sattler*; and with Pipkin, *Balthasar Hubmaier*; as well as his translation of the foundational document, *The Schleitheim Confession*. In addition, his vast teaching materials on historical theology include *CAW* and *CHRN*.

156. O'Donovan, *DN*, 195.
157. Yoder, "Free Church Perspective," in *RP*, 277–88, 283.
158. Yoder, *RP*, 153.

the order of redemption was subordinated to that of preservation, and the Christian hope turned inside out.[159]

Contrary to his critics, Yoder's account of Constantinianism is not merely a rejection of all power and all politics. It is not a shibboleth for all that is misguided or tragic in the history of the Church. The basic flaw, from which the pluriform faults of Constantinianism flow, is the collapse of eschatology that occurs when the "otherness of the Church" is lost.[160] The scandal of particularity returns here as the ironic reversal of the frequent accusation of sectarianism. To affirm the otherness of the Church is, then, to find in christocentric eschatology the realism that ultimately assuages the scandal of particularity.

It is Constantinianism that is the true sectarianism. More than this, the way the notion of sectarianism is often employed requires the sort of understanding of ethical or political "reality" which, from Constantine through to Troeltsch and beyond, has functioned to police the dangerous nature of the gospel proclamation.[161] The Troeltschean description of the Church type and the Sect type continues to hold descriptive force.[162] But it is increasingly recognized that the sociological description cannot escape damaging normative implications.[163] The charge of sectarianism is often accompanied by attempts to broaden the basis of the Christian life beyond the strictures of christocentrism. This often takes the form of accusations of a failure to take doctrines of creation or the Trinity seriously. It would be more accurate to argue that Yoder's project reflects a remedial intention to highlight the problems that arise when Christian ethics works with a notion of creation divorced from the specificity of Christology. We shall return to the doctrine of the Trinity in the next chapter.[164] For now it is enough to note that such charges often mitigate

159. Ibid., 57.
160. Ibid., 109.
161. Thus Hauerwas notes "I have emphasized the importance of a recovery of the integrity of the Church as an alternative political community. That I have done so, however, does not commit me to a sectarian ecclesiology, unless it is assumed that the secular state has the right to determine what will and will not count as political." Hauerwas, *CET*, 1–19; see also *DF* on "Democratic Policing of Christianity."
162. Cf. Troeltsch, *Social Teaching of the Christian Churches*, 328–83.
163. For example, Arne Rasmusson provides a useful brief genealogy, and summarizes the responses of Hauerwas and Milbank along these lines, in Rasmusson, *Church as Polis*, 231–47.
164. Oliver O'Donovan seems to me to strike the right note when he notes the inadequacy of schemes which juxtapose an ethics of creation to an ethics of the kingdom.

the costliness of the Christian life by relegating radical witness to a non-normative role of pricking the conscience of those who bear the burden of social responsibility. In so doing they appeal to the inevitable provinciality of the sort of view advanced by Yoder.

But it is in relation to that provinciality that Yoder reverses the sectarian charge. If what we have said about the truthfulness of theological and moral discourse holds, then it follows that both the pluralism of a radical historicism and the quest for a universal ground to truth go awry in their failure to take God in Christ as the foundation of truthfulness. Constantinianism claims to locate the movement or telos of history, the true coming universal, with its own social projects. In allying itself with such false (and often exclusionary) universals, the Church takes leave of what is truly universal—or more appropriately, what is truly "catholic." Constantine did not really rule the entire world, still less do individual nation-states, social movements, or even, as we shall see later, global capitalism—but Christ does.[165] Crucially, this "progressive abandonment of catholicity" circumscribes the social-critical ability of the Church. There is, therefore, an integral link between the otherness of the Church and the christological and eschatological texture of realism in all four forms identified here.

The only true public is based upon the one who was first raised up for "public" ridicule on the cross, only to unmask the empire and its reverence of death by being raised up again in the newness of life. Contrary to the false publics founded on Constantinian sectarianism, the Church's anticipatory life maintains a fragile but genuine publicity. That the crucified and risen one now governs at the right hand of the Father creates for us a public space of witness—constituted both by his presence and his absence.[166] We now turn to the exploration of how christological and eschatological realism yields a socially critical ecclesiology.

"For the very act of God which ushers in his kingdom is the resurrection of Christ from the dead, the reaffirmation of his creation." This, of course, leaves plenty of ground for diverse moral and theological opinions. O'Donovan continues: "ethics which starts from this point may sometimes emphasize the newness, sometimes the primitiveness of the order that is there affirmed. But it will not be tempted to overthrow or deny either in the name of the other." *RMO*, 15.

165. Yoder, *RP*, 200.

166. On the political and ecclesiological significance of the ascension as both presence and absence of Christ, see Douglas Farrow's now classic treatment in *Ascension and Ecclesia*.

CHAPTER 4

The Ecclesiology of Nonviolent Witness

"The church does communicate to the world what God plans to do, because it shows that God is beginning to do it."[1]

—John Howard Yoder

Continuing the Pattern: Analogy and Witness

The previous chapter demonstrated the importance of maintaining a theologically realist basis for social and political critique. We now turn to explore how the christological and eschatological complexion of theological reality determines Yoder's account of the mission of the Church. I shall argue that the motifs of analogy and participation best express the way in which theological realism is made present in the life of discipleship. We shall begin with a brief exploration of the role of analogy in theological ethics, after which I shall explore some key aspects of Yoder's ecclesiology. In so doing I hope to demonstrate how diverse aspects of Yoder's ecclesiological reflections spring from a commitment to an "eschatological-analogical" pattern. We have already noted central motifs of ecclesial "otherness" and witnessing practices in Yoder's ecclesiology. I will show how these, along with other aspects of his reflections on the Church, such as the recovery of Anabaptist identity, restitutionism, and even his ecumenical engagements, mould his theology of social change.

1. Yoder, *RP*, 126.

As befits his occasional and responsive theological method, Yoder never found it necessary to undertake any systematic examination of the functioning of the analogical and participative motifs that I detect in his thought. It will therefore be instructive to undertake a comparative exercise in which Yoder's ecclesiology of witness is placed alongside two other largely analogical accounts of ecclesiology. I therefore engage in a discussion of Miroslav Volf's understanding of the church as the image of the Trinity, before concluding with a thematic comparison of Yoder with John Milbank's ontology of gift.

In recent years there has been something of a resurgence in the understanding of the importance of analogical forms of thought for theological truth claims. Whether it be through increased attention to the *analogia entis* detected in the thought of Thomas Aquinas, or in the Barthian corrective of the *analogia fidei*, analogy has once more become central to descriptions of God and the world.[2] While it will not be possible to engage in any in-depth discussion of the epistemological and ontological consequences of this emphasis, it is important to note how the tenets of Yoder's theological realism inform his ecclesiology, and therefore his social ethics, in a broadly analogical manner. I take analogy here to be the operative category in characterizing both the resemblance and elements of dissimilarity of present practices and structures with an originary (in this case, the eschatological lordship of Christ) in which, in some way, they may be said to participate.

---

2. Radical Orthodoxy's juxtaposition of Scotist univocity with Thomist analogical being is perhaps the most prominent and systematic example. However, from von Balthasar to David Tracy, analogy is in vogue. Alister McGrath has provided an interesting synthetic attempt to mitigate the polemical excesses of Barth's critique of the *analogia entis*, which also grounds analogy within a commitment to theological realism. Thus he argues: "The *analogia entis* affirms the theoretical capacity of any aspect of the created order—including events and entitites—to mirror their creator; the *analogia fidei* identifies those aspects that have been authorized to act in this manner—whether or not they correspond to human preconceptions of their suitability for this purpose." McGrath, *Scientific Theology*, 116. In relation to social ethics, I suspect that many aspects of the way the theology of analogy works out in Radical Orthodoxy will demonstrate a substantial degree of consonance with Yoder's theology of witness. See especially Ward, *Cities of God*, on analogy in this context. However, the neo-platonic metaphysics that Milbank and others in Radical Orthodoxy rely upon to give their account of materiality, participation, and analogy marks a significant divergence from the account I offer. There is not scope for a thoroughgoing analysis of a non-platonic notion of participation in this current work. For a critique of this element of Radical Orthodoxy, see Smith, "Will the Real Plato Please Stand Up?"

In previous chapters we have noted briefly how, for Yoder, central aspects of ecclesial life, including baptism, Eucharist, and fraternal admonition, are described as exemplary prefigurations of the eschatological community. Yoder moves in a direction similar to Barth, when the latter advocated a series of analogies between the church and the world.[3] In *The Christian Community and the Civil Community*, Barth outlines a rather idiosyncratic list of "analogies" between the nature of God, the Kingdom, and the Church on the one hand, and the normative practices outlined for the civil community on the other. The analogical relation between church and world is fundamentally a matter of exemplary witness. For both Yoder and Barth, true church law is "exemplary" law.[4]

For Yoder, however, the notion of analogy cannot simply be a matter of noting a certain parallelism in norms; but reveals, more significantly, the character of the way God has elected to reconcile the world to himself. "The church does communicate to the world what God plans to do, because it shows that God is beginning to do it."[5] It may be instructive, in this regard, to note the difference between metaphor and analogy. To note some commonality between ecclesial and civil practices, in and of itself, does not attribute any common ontological source or derivative relationship between the two practices. In that sense such comments would qualify only as metaphors or similes. It is the attribution of an ontological, or, in a more biblical idiom, a participatory (e.g., 1 Cor 10:16; Heb 3:14, etc.) relation that we move from metaphor to analogy. Yoder engaged in an enormous range of ecclesiological reflections, ranging through methodological, historical, ethical and ecumenical concerns. I suggest that it is the understanding of an analogical embodiment of eschatological and christological realism that knits together the apparently disparate fibers of such wide-ranging engagements.

The Marks of Yoder's Church

Before examining the ethical consequences of Yoder's ecclesiology it is as well to sketch the contours of his normative understanding of the

---

3. Barth does this primarily in *Christian Community and Civil Community* and in *CD* IV/2, 719ff. For Yoder, Barth's use of analogy is somewhat imprecise, exploratory and even whimsical. *RP*, 125, and also his "Karl Barth, Post-Christendom Theologian."

4. Barth, *CD* IV/2, 719. Yoder diverges from Bromiley's translation of Barth's *Recht* as "law," preferring "exemplary *order*." Yoder, *FTN*, 24. See also *RP*, 103–26.

5. Yoder, *RP*, 126.

Church. Yoder's vision of the Church combines a focus on discipleship derived from his Anabaptism, with a critically ecumenical openness. From his own Anabaptist heritage Yoder provides an ecclesiology that is radical, restitutionist, and focused on the "otherness" of the Church. Yet, his account of ecumenism bears witness to his own critical relationship to Mennonitism. Yoder's view will not counsel the separationist formation of mini-Constantinian sects.[6] Rather, the egalitarian vision of ecclesial peoplehood provides the hermeneutical context for the discernment and development of Christian witness in relation to contemporary culture. By viewing the Church as made possible only through the gracious empowerment of a new sociality, Yoder provides an ecclesiology that is capable of grounding a truly transformational Christian life.

The Recovery of the Anabaptist Vision

Around the time of his doctoral studies in Basel, Yoder became involved in what was to become known as the "Concern" group, which grew out of a series of conferences of American Mennonites living in Europe.[7] Sharing a concern for renewed attention to the history and identity of Anabaptism, the Concern movement was strongly influenced by the historiographical work of an earlier generation of scholars and historians who sought "the recovery of the Anabaptist vision." Harold S. Bender, a leading light of this earlier stage, presented Anabaptist identity as the evangelical form of Protestantism, which sought to "recreate without compromise the original New Testament church, the vision of Christ and the apostles."[8] The character of this vision focused on the notion of a voluntary, non-resistant, and egalitarian community of discipleship. The Concern movement brought renewed fervor and a sharper critical edge to this earlier historiographical enterprise. So, for example, Yoder was

---

6. See Yoder, "Anabaptist Vision."

7. It is beyond the scope of the current discussion to elaborate the details of Yoder's account of the Anabaptist vision—though we should note clearly that the importance and validity of such scholarship for Yoder's own theological oeuvre is oriented to continued faithful discernment. Excellent discussions of Yoder's involvement in the renewal of Anabaptist self-understanding include Craig Carter's chapter "Yoder and the Recovery of the Anabaptist Vision," in *Politics of the Cross*, 31–59; Nation, *John Howard Yoder*, 31–75; and the more detailed explication of Yoder's role in the "Concern" movement in Toews, "Concern Movement." Yoder's own account of the themes prominent in the concern group are found in Yoder, "What Are our Concerns?"

8. Bender, *Anabaptist Vision*, 13.

critical of Bender's acceptance of the shift in Mennonite identity towards a denominational self-conception that compromised the missionary thrust of the Anabaptist vision.[9]

For the Concern movement the recovery of Anabaptist identity was part and parcel of the search for a form of "social responsibility" consonant with the demands of discipleship.[10] Far from yielding isolationism, this greater focus on the theological importance of discipleship can provide an appropriate grounding for collaborative effort. So, for Yoder, unlike the earlier generation of Mennonite theologians seeking to re-enliven their sense of identity, the total rejection of Christian participation in nonviolent social action was insufficient to understand the concept of non-resistance. Yoder criticized his predecessors for an anti-ecumenical spirit that denies the "inherent close relations Mennonites could well have to peace movements."[11] Despite these comments Yoder remains in line with Bender and Guy Herschberger insofar as his positive outlook on nonviolent action does not extend to many tactics characteristic of that approach. As we shall see in more detail in the next chapter, just as a just-war thinker would not sanction all violence, neither does Yoder sanction all nonviolent strategies.

Restitutionism and History

The internal recovery of Anabaptist identity has been accompanied by increasingly wide interest in the importance of the radical wing of the Reformation. Variously described as the churches of the "radical reformation," the "free church," or, with Max Weber, the "believers' church," the diverse traditions on the left wing of the reformation display important common aspects.[12] For Yoder these include congregationalism, voluntary membership, religious liberty (often, though not necessarily, manifesting itself in a separation of Church and state), and nonviolence.[13] In sharing most, though not necessarily all of these, the diverse visions of those grouped together as the "Anabaptists" are implicated in a "restitutionist" claim for the Church. James McClendon expresses the restitutionist heart

---

9. Carter, *Politics of the Cross*, 37.
10. Yoder, "Anabaptist Dissent."
11. Yoder, *NS*, 113.
12. An excellent survey is found in Durnbaugh, *Believers' Church*.
13. Yoder, *JCSR*, 136–37.

of what he names as the "baptist" (in a non-denominational sense) vision when he offers the following hermeneutical principle:

> [The baptist vision is] shared awareness of the present Christian community as the primitive community and the eschatological community. In other words, the church now is the primitive church and the church on the day of judgment is the church now; the obedience and liberty of the followers of Jesus of Nazareth is our liberty, our obedience.[14]

Of course the ambiguity of the "is" is central to the full explication of this motif. The "is" represents something akin to the eucharistic "this *is* my body." That is to say, following our earlier distinction, it may be appropriately located somewhere around the interstice of metaphorical and analogical senses of the verb. To understand the "is" we need to pay greater attention to the very beginning of his maxim. It is in describing his ecclesiology as derived from this *hermeneutical* principle that McClendon's phrase is most important. The church *is* a hermeneutical community. Its self-understanding is marked by this apparently simple verb in such a way as to place all ecclesial history in question. In this "is" we find the truth of eschatology impinging upon all other claims to knowledge. If only the first half of McClendon's phrase were taken (the church now is the primitive church), then restitutionism would indeed be arcane, naïve, and romantic. However, here, I suggest, McClendon, like Yoder, demonstrates an eschatological sense of reality.[15] That basic pattern shows how the importance of a restitutionist ecclesiology lies in its empowering of the Church to live faithfully in the present, the messy middle.

The task of the Church in the present is not the recovery of a pristine primitive church order, as the caricature of restitutionism or sectarianism often has it.[16] The task is one of discernment and avoidance of unfaithfulness—present, past, and future. It therefore involves the Church in an ongoing process of historiographical discernment. We saw in the previous chapter how the diagnosis of forms of Constantinianism is part of this. For Yoder this means that restitutionism requires the Church to take the exigencies and ambiguities of history and the peccability of the

---

14. McClendon, *Ethics*, 27–34.

15. For their joint defense of restitutionism, see Yoder and McClendon, "Christian Identity."

16. See Yoder, "Primitivism."

Church more seriously than most mainstream accounts allow.[17] This is the heart of his complaint against the imprecise or generalistic invocation of the indefectibility of the church. Yoder proposes a strongly eschatological alternative to the Constantinian metaphysical dualism of the invisible and indefectible true church subsisting within the mass of nominally "Christian" citizenry. The Church, as the paradigmatic "aftertaste of God's loving triumph on the cross and foretaste of His ultimate loving triumph in His kingdom,"[18] is a community of obedience to the nonviolent way of Jesus Christ: i.e., discipleship.

Yoder's anti-Constantinian historiography consistently attempts to discern the faithful nonviolence of the minority church. This does not yield a punctiliar ecclesiology, attempting to discern and recover some idealized instantiation of the Church within Anabaptist history. Yoder is always more critical than that! For example, he asserts that the experiences of the sixteenth-century radical reformers produced "an especially strong polar judgment upon the past establishment of Christianity. When taken alone, that example provides a too negative picture of the potential for constructive social change."[19] The models of the historic radical reformation hold a prototypical and paradigmatic role, but do not function to provide a denominationally apologetic or proselytizing strategy.[20] "What is meant by the label "Anabaptist" Yoder tells us "is not a century but a hermeneutic."[21]

This, of course, is the crux of Samuel Taylor Coleridge's oft-used aphorism that "He who begins by loving Christianity better than Truth will proceed by loving his own sect or church better than Christianity, and end by loving himself better than all."[22] The costliness of the life of discipleship, bound up, as it is for Yoder, with practices of nonviolence, is not just the calling of those within the Church with a specific, more stringent, vocation. Discipleship is exemplary in relation to the world, but definitive of the Church.

17. Yoder, *PK*, 123–34.
18. Yoder, *CWS*, 10.
19. Yoder, *PK*, 4–5.
20. For explicit denial of primitivism and denominational apologetics, see *BP*, 10; and *PK*, 4, respectively.
21. Yoder, "Anabaptist Vision," 5.
22. Coleridge, *Aids to Reflection*, 107.

This can be seen most clearly if we take account of Yoder's view of the Church as an unfinished social project. That is, we might say, the interplay of the traditional mark of catholicity and the ongoing nature of the reformation—*ecclesia semper reformanda*.[23] One could say that Yoder's is an ecclesiology of a "becoming church"—the Church is only the bearer of the meaning of history insofar as it is faithful to its calling. As Yoder's own conception of the theological task attests, the *ecclesia viatorum* requires a fragmentary, or "irregular," form of teaching.[24] It therefore needs to continue "looping back" to Scripture and tradition in order to navigate the course of fidelity.[25] The capacity for this "midcourse correction" is pneumatological. Therefore, I suggest, it is exhibited in both the congregational focus and the transformative impact of Yoder's ecclesiology. What Yoder names as "the hermeneutics of peoplehood" begins by insisting on the ongoing nature of the Reformation.[26] Following Paul's notion of the universality of charisma (1 Cor 12) Yoder locates the possibility for continued reformation in congregational processes of discernment.[27] The hermeneutical processes of the Church include, amongst others, the role of "agents of memory" whose task is the renewed and flexible application of the traditions and history of the Church.[28] This task, as we have already seen, implicates the entire Church in an anti-Constantinian form

23. The "catholicity" of Yoder's vision is exposited well by both Nation and Cartwright. Nation, "John Howard Yoder," and *John Howard Yoder*; and Cartwright, "Radical Reform." For Yoder's insistence that the reformation is not over, see *RP*, 301–20.

24. Yoder, *RP*, 121.

25. Yoder, *PK*, 69ff. See also Yoder's contention that this hermeneutical role of the community is primordial, though not exclusive of outside voices. "If Scripture were a systematized compendium of final answers, to be applied with compelling deductive logic to all future settings, then the person to do it would be the most learned master of the texts, or of deductive logic. If however our guide is a repertory of more or less pertinent paradigms, needing to be selected and transformed transculturally in ever new settings, no one person can monopolize that process. It must be carried by the entire believing community, joining complementarily those who are most authentically part of the local setting with those who best represent the worldwide community and the canonical memories." Yoder, *FTN*, 92–93.

26. The failure of the magisterial reformers to stay practically committed to the slogan *ecclesia reformata, semper reformanda* is, according to Yoder, a result of the shift away from the pneumatological and congregational processes of reform, whereby civil government becomes the instrument of reformation. Yoder, *PK*, 23–24.

27. Ibid., 28–34. For a fuller exposition of "the rule of Paul" in Yoder's theology see *BP*, 61–70, and *FC*.

28. Yoder, *PK*, 30–32.

of historiography. For Yoder, the ecclesial tasks of reformation, discernment and social transformation come together in the eschatological logic of the gospel.

Part of the witness of the becoming church, as eschatological firstfruits, is, therefore, its commitment to social transformation, properly understood. Following Tolstoy, Yoder asserts that true progress in history is borne by the underdogs.[29] Thus the notion of the Church as an "unfinished project" ties in with its own social mission, or what liberation theologians have named "the preferential option for the poor." Importantly, in this regard, Yoder's ecclesiocentrism does not lead to hermeticism. God is active beyond the Church. God's activity must be discerned through specifically "Jesulogical" criteria: God is active in history through suffering servanthood, not pedagogic statecraft. God's activity outside of the Church is not a secondary or additional locus of the Spirit, but rather represents a judgment on the Church and call for its faithfulness. It is, therefore, a serious misunderstanding to assert, as some critics have, that Yoder does not recognize Christ's lordship outside of the Church.[30] Rather, as the community of those who acknowledge Christ's lordship not only over themselves but over history, the Church is the means by which witness is borne to this present, but hidden, lordship. The lordship of Christ is wider than his headship of the Church, but both belong to the order of grace. Indeed, this relation between the lordship and headship of Christ is pivotal for the realism in which Yoder's analogical vision of ecclesial ethics can be maintained.

The becoming church is open to the possibility of radical criticism. In contrast to affirmations of the indefectibility of the invisible church, the recognition of the fallibility of the becoming church is substantially more than a grudging epistemological concession. "[I]n contrast to other views of the church, this is one which holds more strongly than others to a positive doctrine of fallibility. Any existing church is not only fallible but in fact peccable."[31]

---

29. Yoder, "To Serve Our God," 3–14, reproduced in *RP*, 127–40, 137. It is important to note that Yoder is critical of Tolstoy's "elite purism." He is also critical of H. R. Niebuhr's conflation of Tolstoy's position with the radical reformation experience of nonviolence, within his "Christ against Culture" model. Niebuhr, *Christ and Culture*. See *RP*, 136; see also "How H. Richard Niebuhr Reasoned."

30. E.g., Fitz-Gibbon, *In the World*, 86–87. Contrary to such dismissive critiques, Yoder consistently asserts Christ's Lordship over the principalities and powers, and over history; e.g., *CWS*, 8–14; *PJ*, 157ff.; *FTN*, 24; *ARS*, 281–82.

31. Yoder, *PK*, 5.

This realization includes, for Yoder, a full and frank account of how the schism between messianic Judaism (early Christianity) and other forms of Judaism was a contingent, not a necessary, development.[32] We shall return to this in chapter 6. More significantly for our present purpose, the possibility of radical social criticism and the imperative to dialogue are direct correlates of the "otherness" of the Church to the world.

The Otherness of the Church as Grounds for its Public Presence

Yoder argues that the non-coercive nature of the gospel implies a "specific" (modifying the previously dominant term "distinctive"[33]) stance in relation to its surrounding culture. We have already found this stance to be pragmatic and variegated although normatively obedient to the nonviolence of Christ. In his construal of dialogue and patience, Yoder differs from those theologies that would outline a strategy for the rhetorical or theocratic triumph over secularity.

> We must abandon the chimerical vision of a set of semantic or definitional moves which would transcend the limits of one's own identity, rationally coercing assent, without taking account of a particular interlocutor or a specific dialogical setting. We must relinquish the dream of a set of social moves which would find or construct a "world" so big as to enclose everyone else. . . . Evangel has to submit—wants to submit—vulnerably to the conditions of meaning of the receptor culture.[34]

The posture of the Church in relation to its receptor culture and, more particularly, the state, is not one of systematic withdrawal or of absorption or assimilation but of "revolutionary subordination" (Romans

---

32. Yoder, *JCSR*, 43–66 and passim.

33. Yoder uses the term "specific," to modify a previously dominant term "distinctive." Thus he says, "To make 'distinctiveness' a value criterion is to measure the truth value of a meaning system A in terms of other systems that happen to be around, from which [it] is supposed to differ. That is a method mistake. Some of the neighbouring systems may be very much like it. Some of them may be historically derived from it, which is true of most of the post-Christian value systems in the West. To ask that Christian thought be *unique* is nonsense. What we should ask of Christian statements is that they be *specifically* or *specifiably* Christian, i.e., true to kind, authentically representing their species." Yoder, "On Not Being Ashamed," 295. See also Yoder, "People in the World," in *RP*, 81 n. 19, and "How H. Richard Niebuhr Reasoned," in *AT*, 31–89 and esp. 282 n. 113.

34. Ibid., 290–91.

12–14).[35] Subordination is neither subjection nor submission,[36] but the relinquishing of the will to power. Revolutionary subordination is an inherently subversive stance, for it is the faithful nonviolent Church, not the inherently violent state, which is the bearer of the meaning of history.[37] The particularity of Christian practice, i.e., the specificity of the Church, is related to the otherness of its stance within the world. Yoder uses the term "world" (*aion houtos* in Paul, *kosmos* in John) not as synonymous with creation, or nature itself, but their fallen form—that which is no longer conformed to the creative intent.[38] As we noted at the outset of the book, this division is conceived as a duality of responses to the gospel—a division between faith and unbelief. I agree with Stanley Hauerwas that this represents a division not of ontology, aeons, or discrete realms, but a "difference between agents." Hauerwas's use of the term "agent" should not be taken to imply an identification of Yoder with the use of the category of agency as it is often used in liberal defenses of the self. Rather, he says, Yoder's location of the church/world distinction with agents:

> makes clear (1) that the distinction between church and world runs through every agent and thus there is no basis for self-righteousness on the part of those who explicitly identify with the church; and (2) that the "necessities" many claim must be accepted as part and parcel of being "world," such as violence, are such only because of our unfaithfulness. Thus the world, when it is true to its nature as God's redeemed subject, can be ordered and governed without resort to violence.[39]

The otherness of the Church is central to the discernment through which the Christian community becomes the analogical embodiment of eschatological reality. Whilst the distinctiveness of the Church to its receptor culture is dependent on the character of that culture, the "otherness of the church" to the world is an essential *notum* of its specificity. This otherness is grounded in the nonviolence of Christ. As Christ refused the

---

35. Yoder, *PJ*, 162–92. Yoder's use of the concept of "revolutionary subordination," especially as it is found in the *haustafeln* of Col 3:18—4:1, Eph 5:21—6:9, 1 Pet 2:13—3:7, etc., must be said to be, at the very least, somewhat optimistic. The use of such texts as the theological basis for subjugation and defense of patriarchial hierarchy immediately raises concerns over the precision with which such a phrase must be used.

36. Ibid., 172.

37. Yoder, *CWS*, 13.

38. Yoder, "Otherness of the Church," 286–96, as it appears in *RP*, 53–64, 55. *ARS*, 264.

39. Hauerwas, *TPK*, 166 n. 3.

zealot option, so those who participate in his victory must likewise refuse the moral logic of a Constantinian schema, which juxtaposes nonviolent fidelity with the "necessary violence" of effectiveness. The practice of nonviolent open sociality stems from the Church's faith that it need not seek to rule the world by its own means. It cannot make history come out right. That history will "come out right" is known only because Christ is Lord. Christians can only be said to imitate and participate in the cross in so far as they (inevitably) suffer as a result of "representing to an unwilling world the Order to come."[40]

> Because, therefore, our hope is in Christ, the prophetic originality that the church must represent in the world is not simply that the church has a more sacred cause for the sake of which it can worthily push people around. It is rather that the church has a cause that dispenses it—enjoins it—from pushing people around in unworthy ways.[41]

The Church's renunciation of the violent will to power is only possible because of its participation in Christ. The new creation inaugurated in Christ is restorative; a personal (though not merely individual) regeneration placed within an eschatological vision embodied in a community, the Church. Thus the concept of justification by faith applies not simply to the ontology of the individual but is the transformation "of the perspective of one who has accepted Christ as his context."[42] Justification is the solidarity of Christ with regenerate believers, and *as such*, as we shall see, it implies a social process of reconciliation between peoples.[43] The Church is the first fruits of eschatological reconciliation. The being and the message of the community are indivisible.

Sacrament as Social Practice

The constitutive practices of the Christian community *are* a prophetic and public "word." "Worship is the communal cultivation of an alternative

---

40. Yoder, *PJ*, 95–96; see also *RP*, 87f.
41. Yoder, "Let the Church Be the Church," in *OR*, 113–31, 126.
42. Yoder, *PJ*, 223. It is a matter of some contention how far Yoder's lack of an existential account of justification leads to an excessively instrumental reading of the sacraments. See Reimer, "Mennonites, Christ, and Culture," and Cartwright, "Sharing the House of God," 604–5.
43. Ibid., 224.

construction of society and of history."[44] Table fellowship is paradigmatic of the evangelistic invitation to the Kingdom of God—the embrace of the other as other; it enacts the inclusion of the excluded not within the system from which they were previously expelled, but in the new creation in Christ. More particularly, the Eucharist is a practice of economic solidarity. Baptism engenders an egalitarian community, it inducts the believer into a new humanity. The communal process of fraternal admonition (the binding and loosing of Matt 18:15–20), which provides the practical and theological foundation for the centrality of the local congregation in Yoder's "believer's church" ecclesiology, functions to orient moral discernment towards reconciliatory practice.[45] These practices are founded on the recognition of the lordship of Christ.

> The first word in the reaffirmation of the human dignity of the oppressed is thus to constitute in their celebrative life the coming Rule of God and a new construal of the cosmos under God. To sing "The Lamb is Worthy to Receive Power," as did the early communities whose hymnody is reflected in the first vision of John, is not mere poetry. It is performative proclamation. It redefines the cosmos in a way prerequisite to the moral independence which it takes to speak truth to power and to persevere in living against the stream when no reward is in sight.[46]

The divinely empowered sociology of the Christian community is, in its particularity, a public sign of the coming Kingdom. As a sociality grounded in redemption, it witnesses to the "world," by virtue of its participation in Christ, that the meaning of history is not one yet to be determined within a closed system of violence, but is already achieved in the victory of Christ over the powers. Against epistemological theories of the incommensurability of communally particular truths, Yoder asserts that, based in the Jewish experience of diaspora citizenship, the Christian community's practices are not esoteric but fully public. That is to say, they are public not only in their accessibility but also in their impact. Yoder's view of particularity, his non-foundationalist epistemology, and consequently his view of the hermeneutical function of Christian peoplehood are integrally related to a view of public truth and agency

---

44. Yoder, *PK*, 43.
45. Yoder, *BP*; *RP*, 325–58, and 360–73.
46. Yoder, *AE*, 53.

exemplified in the model of the sixth-century prophets.[47] The stance of "revolutionary subordination" alluded to above is thus linked with the Jeremianic mandate to "seek the welfare of the city where I have sent you into exile, and pray to the Lord on its behalf, for in its welfare you will find your welfare" (Jer 29:7). The issue is how to "seek the welfare of the city" without committing the fundamental error of Constantinianism—confusing the goals, orientation, and history of, for example, a particular nation with the eschatological vision.

This will become clearer if we compare Yoder to Ronald Preston. In the ecumenical social ethics of Ronald Preston, we find a strong blend of Niebuhrian "realism" and the Christian socialism of F. D. Maurice and William Temple. For Preston, the primary function of the Christian community in public moral debate is to seek for the common good. Preston argues that the task of the Church is to hold society together by the creation of "fellow-feeling and co-operation": "the first political task of the church is to strengthen the sense of a common morality in the community, the moral virtues or basic human decencies that Adam Smith presupposed."[48]

By contrast, for Yoder, as for Hauerwas, the primary social responsibility of the Church is to *be* the Church. The Church is an embodiment of an alternate sociology. It displays a quality of non-conformed involvement in society.[49] This is not to say that the Church will not have the effect of engendering common moral goals and conduct; rather it is, in line with Yoder's anti-Constantinian ecclesiocentrism, to say that such effects are to be seen as a consequence of the Church's fidelity to its mission.

Yoder argues that

> [t]he church is not fundamentally a source of moral stimulus to encourage the development of a better society—though a faithful church should also have this effect—it is for the sake of the church's own work that society continues to function.[50]

---

47. On similar grounds Hauerwas contrasts his own view with that of Jeffrey Stout's "modest pragmatism." He claims that the resources of such a pragmatism cannot be rendered intelligible when they continue to abstracted from the memories of particular communities of virtue. Hauerwas, and Kenneson, Phillip, "Flight from Foundationalism, or Things Aren't as Bad as They Seem," in *WW*, 97–110.

48. Preston et al., *Church and Society*, 19; and *Religion and the Persistence*, 132–33.

49. Yoder, *PJ*, 39.

50. Yoder, *CWS*, 13.

This contrast allows us to see that Preston, like Niebuhr—as many critics have noted—subordinates Christology and ecclesiology to anthropology and the doctrine of (fallen) creation.[51] Furthermore, underlying these moves is a Constantinian form of eschatology through which the Church becomes the facilitator of the conditions of moral consensus under which the state can, by its own means, build the Kingdom. That is to say, the way in which the Church may most appropriately "seek the peace of the city" is through attentiveness to that "reality" in which it is able to exist. Social transformation and ecclesial existence both require the same analogical and participative relation to eschatological reality.

Yoder's Ecumenical Openness

The Church's participation in the transformation of the cosmos can only occur when, through its constant "looping back," the Christian community reflects the divine nature. Recall Yoder's insistence that "we do not, ultimately, love our neighbor because Jesus told us to. We love our neighbor because God is like that."[52] In an introduction to the posthumous publication of his lectures on Christology, Stanley Hauerwas and Alex Sider clearly show that Yoder's understanding of salvation as the obedient life of discipleship disallows strong distinctions between justification and sanctification and "forced us to abandon a distinction between objective and subjective accounts of Christ's work. We quite literally become through the work of the Holy Spirit participants in Christ's reconciliation of the world."[53]

The analogical and participative motifs, by which this division of the subjective from objective works of Christ is blurred, also allow Yoder to maintain that ecclesiology *is* ethics. In both ecclesiology and ethics Yoder's guiding category was "witness." "Witness" names those diverse practices of ecclesial and ethical life which can only ever be meaningful when understood as empowered by, and participating in, christological and eschatological reality. This will become clearer if we briefly examine Yoder's ecumenical theology. In common with much twentieth-century

---

51. For Yoder's criticism of Reinhold Niebuhr, see, for example, "Reinhold Niebuhr," and "Peace without Eschatology," reproduced in *RP*, 143–67. Yoder also appears to have Niebuhr in mind in his defense of the continued relevance of the figure of Jesus to ethics in *PJ*, 1–20. See also Long, *Divine Economy*, 57ff.

52. Yoder, *OR*, 52.

53. Hauerwas and Sider, "Introduction," in Yoder, *PT*, 21–22.

ecumenical theology, Yoder locates the importance of ecumenical effort in the credibility of witness. It is only when the participative aspect of Christian unity is paramount that witness reflects divine truth, and thus achieves credibility.

The calling to unity is, of course, a christological imperative.[54] This scriptural imperative has historically provided the major motivational impulse for ecumenical efforts (hence the frequency of the citation of Jesus's high priestly prayer in ecumenical documents). The fourth Gospel has Christ pray for his disciples and:

> ... on behalf of those who will believe in me through their word, that they may all be one. As You, Father, are in me and I am in you, may they also be in us, so that the world may believe that you have sent me. The glory that you have given me I have given them, so that they may be one, as we are one. (John 17:20–22)

Yoder points to the ecumenical importance of this participative motif:

> The function of the unity of the future believers is, therefore, to make credible the fundamental claim ("that the world might believe," said twice) and to reflect the nature of the unity between the Son and the Father, to render that credible witness substantial.[55]

Participation in the Triune God, who is reconciling the world to himself, requires of initiatives for Christian unity that they too engage in wider reconciling practices. The primary imperative is not, therefore, full visible unity, or any other structural conception of unity, but a unity in which the nature of God is analogically embodied in the world. It is not simply for efficient or bureaucratic reasons (the merger of small businesses to achieve a "critical mass" of market share) nor a protective strategy (the huddling together of the beleaguered religious for protection against the cold wind of secularization) that such efforts are made; but for the very realization of Church as Church—the eternally reforming and ever reconciling community of the coming Kingdom.

As a representative for the historic peace churches in many international ecumenical efforts, as Michael Cartwright correctly notes, Yoder's witness to that tradition "takes shape *within* a consistently articulated belief that the unity of the church is a gift of God's Holy Spirit, which

---

54. Yoder, "The Imperative of Christian Unity," in *RP*, 290–99.
55. Ibid., 291.

enables Christians to embody God's *shalom* in the world."[56] This belief in turn led in Yoder's thought to a call for the reorientation of large-scale ecumenical councils away from concern for structural unity toward a unity in mission seen through the articulation and embodiment of the "wholeness shalom demands."[57] Structural reconciliation should not, then, be the primary goal of ecumenical conversation. Here again we encounter the importance of discernment and continual reformation of the believing community. This is no denigration of structural or doctrinal issues. It is a call for ecumenical effort to hold in view the potential for apostasy at all stages of the move from doctrine to practice.[58] Yoder points to concrete examples of the ethical locus of apostasy—the accumulation of wealth, the loss of the feminist thrust of the Gospels, colonialism, the Inquisition, and, of course, the legitimation of war.[59] Equally, Yoder's vision of the exemplary sociality of the witnessing community is predicated on a particular vision of human sociality. The claim, against the assertion of the powers, is that "your definition of polis, of the social, of the wholeness of being human socially, is perverted."[60] Thus we can see that Yoder's concern, both in ecumenical discussions and in his ethical thought, is to foster cruciform forms of dialogic, discerning, and dissenting Christian community.

The hermeneutical and congregational conception of the Church combines with a strongly restitutionist thrust to press for forms of dialogue that yield something more than a false peace. It is the task of those so gifted within the Church to facilitate a critical awareness of necessary

---

56. Cartwright, "Radical Reform," 3. In this sense Cartwright correctly links Yoder's ecumenism to his work with the Fellowship of Reconcilliation. Most notably this link is seen in Gwyn et al., *Declaration of Peace*.

57. Yoder, "Peace." See also "Catholicity in Search of Location," in *RP*, 300–320. "The logical alternative to someone else's design for merger is not my design for merger; it is rather a search for modes of dialogue that does not begin by asking which structures are right" (309).

58. "The issue is (as Jesus said it) the traditions of men versus the commandment of God. That rough word of Jesus introduces seriousness that ecumenical politeness had hidden. Not all varieties of vision—or of ethics—can fit together within a tolerant pluralism. What we need is tools to identify and denounce error, while welcoming variety and celebrating complimentarity." *PK*, 76. "The lazy solution of pluralism reinforces the false view that unity is based on agreement, so that every dispute calls for division. As a matter of fact, disagreement calls not for dividing but for reconciling people." *RP*, 292.

59. Yoder, *PK*, 72–74. See also Koontz, "Confessional Theology," esp. 148–64.

60. Yoder, *PJ*, 106–7.

conflict and divergence, both within the Church itself and between the Church and the world. Thus it is that the ecumenical, catholic, and radical aspects of ecclesiology can only come together (and thus can only then be truly ecumenical, catholic, and radical) in the unfinished social project of the witnessing community.

> Catholicity is not "looking for a home" in the sense of a vagabond who "once lodged will no longer roam"; it is a lived reality that will have its place or "location" wherever all comers participate, in the power of the Triune God, in proclaiming to all nations (beginning where they are) all that Jesus taught. Only if the avowed agenda is that broad and that open can we claim the promises of the Lord who pledged that he would accompany us to the end of the age.[61]

Trinity, Participation, and Analogy in the Church's Social Program

Despite the richness of Yoder's ecumenical and ecclesiological reflections, he did not examine in any systematic way the nature of the interplay of participative and analogical motifs. This may be seen in the relative rarity of substantive systematic expositions of trinitarian theology in his writings.[62] I suggest some exploration of such themes may aid our discussion of the analogical relation of the Church's social mission to the reconciliatory action of God. The trinitarian basis of the ecumenically popular theology of *koinonia* (here, I suggest, most usefully translated as

---

61. Yoder, *RP*, 320.

62. Of course, it does not follow that the lack of substantial explicit Trinitarian exposition in Yoder implies the "unitarianism of the son," of which he is sometimes accused. E.g., Wright, *Disavowing Constantine*, 163. Wright also notes the lack of sufficient reflection on the christological implications of Christ's creatorial involvement in Yoder's vision of discipleship. However, it is misleading to say that Yoder finds no role for the confession that Christ is the agent of creation (Col 1:16, 1 Cor 8:6, etc.). It would be closer to the mark to say that in employing this theme, in one of the few places where Trinitarian theology receives explicit attention, the focus remains the defense of the normativity of the nonviolence of Jesus Christ, as this reveals the nature of God. That Christ is the agent of creation therefore provides grounds for the identity *of the work* of the Father and the Son, and thus militates against claims for competing or contradictory revelatory mandates, whether they are based in creation (independent of redemption), pneumatology or logos Christology. See *AT*, 62. It is important to note that Yoder is fully aware that this modalist Trinitarianism functions, in H. R. Niebuhr, primarily as a symbol for "a concern for a balance between Christ and other moral authorities" and is not, therefore, to be seen as an essential doctrinal facet of his (Niebuhr's) view of moral imperatives and culture.

"reconciliatory solidarity") has become the focus of a number of recent systematic accounts of society.[63] For Leonardo Boff, for example, just as the *koinonia* of the three Trinitarian persons inevitably goes beyond itself into creation, so the Church, as a community of fellowship and solidarity, goes beyond itself to foster "more participatory and humanizing relationships" within society.[64] Indeed such normative reflection proceeds on the basic, and correct, understanding that, in some way, the inner life of the Christian community is a life of going out to the other. That is to say, it is a life of incessant diastolic and systolic rhythm.[65] Before tackling the account of social change implied here, the remainder of this chapter must explore how the claims made for theological and moral realism come together in the analogical understanding of the relationship between the nonviolent nature of God and the concomitant nature of the church.

However, no theme, no matter how appealing, can be applied as a panacea for all the injuries to ecclesial communion. The popular use of *koinonia* is no exception. In so far as the focus on the potential for convergence within the notion of *koinonia* has obscured the necessary role played by (peaceable) conflict in the discernment of apostasy, this imaging of the Trinity becomes inappropriately univocal.[66] The analogical move is made, thus, from the inner-life of the Triune God to the nature of the Church, and by extension (in various contestable ways) to the solidarity of the Church with the sufferings of the world. Moreover, this solidarity is based in the vision of human sociality seen in salvation

---

63. The theme of *koinonia*, variously translated as communion, community, fellowship etc., has provided a rare conceptual bridge in the striving for Christian unity. Cf. Best and Gassmann, *On the Way to Fuller Koinonia*, and Tillard, *Church of Churches*. The fellowship between Christians, as both gift and calling, is correctly located in the imaging of the inner life of the Triune God. As Nicholas Sagovsky puts it, "The Christian practice of *koinonia* is seen as a practical participation in the love of God, which can be entered upon only with repentance and is normally sustained within or by reference to confessional Christian communities. Only by the activity of the Spirit can we live, in its fullest sense, 'the common life.'" Sagovsky, *Ecumenism*, 17.

64. Boff, *Trinity and Society*, 149.

65. McClendon helpfully discusses the diastolic/systolic image in relation to the theology of culture in *Witness*, 418–20.

66. The importance, for ecumenical theology, of a robust understanding of the legitimate role of conflict is also noted in ibid., 8–9, 200–201; and Sykes, *Identity of Christianity*, 13–16. For Yoder's reflections on the "normalcy of the conflict process" in Church life, see his observation that where the word "church" is found on the lips of Christ, it is so in a context referring primarily to judgment—i.e., binding and loosing. *RP*, 323–58; *BP*; and "A Theological Point of Reference."

history. Witness the statement of one recent Anglican-Roman Catholic dialogue (ARCIC II): "Life in Christ is the gift and promise of new creation, the ground of community and the pattern of social relations. It is the shared inheritance of the Church and the hope of every believer."[67]

The pursuit of social justice, particularly in collaborative action, is commonly seen in ecumenical thought as a "*koinonia*-generating" activity.[68] Community, solidarity, and Christian unity are fostered within an ongoing cycle in which the Church is engaged in a dynamic process of becoming more truly itself. However, as the move is made from innertrinitarian *koinonia* to that of the Church, and thence to the relation of Church with world, great care must be taken to avoid any simple linear exposition that occludes significant areas of conflict, contrasting visions of the good, and divergent social and political programs.

It is important to begin an appraisal of such accounts with the recognition, following Craig Carter's reading, that there is a "practical Trinitarianism" in Yoder's thought that far exceeds the exploratory comments of his own published writings.[69] Without engaging in a painstaking and complex point-by-point comparison I shall explore something of the use of trinitarian themes in theological ethics. I shall then trace the relationship between God and his Church in John Milbank's developing theology of gift. By engaging with both Miroslav Volf and John Milbank I hope to flag up moments of correspondence and of tension that directly impinge upon the analogical conception of the social critical ecclesiology here exposited.

---

67. ARCIC II, *Life in Christ*, 3, para. 4.

68. WCC, "Costly Commitment," in Best and Robra, *Ecclesiology and Ethics*, 33.

69. Carter, *Politics of the Cross*, 125–26. Yoder comments on classical and contemporary readings of the trinity in *PT*, 180–209. Critics of Yoder who locate a disregard for creation in the paucity of significant trinitarian reflection seem to fall foul of a specifically ethical form of modalism. Nigel Goring Wright, for example, accuses Yoder of a "unitarianism of the son" that allows only a formal role for the Trinity and eclipses creation through inattention to the Father and Spirit. *Disavowing Constantine*, 163. These criticisms seem to conflate issues of explicit emphasis with misplaced concerns of heretical tendencies. Yoder's imbalanced attention away from substantial understandings of the Father and the Spirit is properly seen as a corrective emphasis, rather than a dogmatic disregard for the other two persons of the Trinity. There is something of the famous division between Barth and Brunner here, for Yoder castigates those who "play the Creator/Father off against the Redeemer/Son in such a way that the will of God as Father (known reliably by means of reason) counts for the social realm, as the words and example of the Son do not." *RP*, 370–71.

"The Trinity Is Our Social Program": Miroslav Volf

Miroslav Volf helpfully expounds a *koinonia* ecclesiology based on the priority of the gathered church and an egalitarian and accountable polity.[70] He provides a vision of "Catholic personhood," of authentic individuality within community. Like most theologies based on the notion of *koinonia*, Volf maintains that it would be a mistake to attempt to apply trinitarian concepts of "person," "relation," and "*perichoresis*" to the Church in anything but an analogous sense.[71] The use of analogy, as opposed to univocity, implies both a degree of correspondence and a degree of divergence and rupture. Aware of this, Volf states that to view the Church as a community of fully perichoretic sociality would lead to the dissolution of the legitimate, though both perverted and significantly overstated, insights of modernity—i.e., the integrity of individuality.[72] Personhood, like the peoplehood envisioned as Christian unity, is to be seen as, in some way, both gift and calling. More importantly for our purposes here, to image the Trinity in our sociality leads us to a practice of noncoercive inclusive "embrace" that, nonetheless, is based in (i.e., never in contradiction to) the particularity of Jesus. The Spirit (whose character and revelation are *sui generis* consonant with the nonviolent character of Christ) functions to de-center the self, to orient it towards the embrace of the other. In so doing the "catholic person" is seen to be an "evangelical person"—engaged in the transformation of the world.[73]

---

70. Volf, *After Our Likeness*.

71. Volf, "Trinity is our Social Program," 405. See also Looney, "*Koinonia* Ecclesiology," 162.

72. Something of this dissolution of the individual may be detected in the shift from "individual" as a category of "being" (substantial individuality) to one designating a mere "locutionary space." This is a move characteristic of some forms of the recent attempt to outline exclusively relational views of personhood. Such dissolution begins with the valuable and undeniable maxim that human identity is formed within relationship and encounter with the other. A person is, in the words of Alastair McFadyen, "[a] compounded sedimentation of a significant history of interaction." McFadyen, *Call to Personhood*, 317ff. See also Cunningham, *These Three are One*, 198–204. But what begins as a valuable insight is commonly sustained through an overplayed rhetorical division between relationality and ontology. That is to say, relational personhood is maintained only at the cost of either denying a realist understanding of the ontology of personhood, or by implying a hierarchy of degrees of personhood based on the particular quality of one's interpersonal relationships. For a useful critique along these lines, see H. Harris, "Should We Say?"

73. Volf, *Exclusion and Embrace*, 52f.

The "evangelical person" is formed in the "ecumenical community," thus the commitment to the one lordship of Christ must be seen alongside the need to maintain a "multicultural community of Christian churches." In order to avoid a tribalistic perversion of the lordship of Christ, the catholicity of the Church requires the cultivation of "the proper relation between distance from the culture and belonging to it."[74] This is no modernist agenda for "inclusion" thinly overwritten with banal theological rhetoric of the openness to "culture." The proper relation to culture is found in the prevenience of grace.[75] Jesus did not create a social order of liberal tolerance (which too often degenerates into apathy or indifference), but inaugurated a scandalous fellowship with the excluded and downtrodden. Volf is clear that it is not tolerance but grace that is the prime principle of Christian sociality. Such grace is found in the offer of forgiveness. For a culture of absolute individualism this offer of grace could only be read as condescending, especially when accompanied by an "intolerant" or judgmental demand for repentance. Equally, the grounding of such "catholic" and "evangelical" personhood is as much transcendent as individual. The Spirit is a gifting Spirit, a Spirit in whom, for the sake of the Kingdom, differentiation functions within universality.[76]

> The Spirit of communion opens up every person to others, so that every person can reflect something of the eschatological communion of the entire people of God with the triune God in a unique way through the relations in which that person lives.[77]

The evangelistic mission of the Church includes the analogical imaging of what Volf names as God's "reception of hostile humanity"— the movement from exclusion to embrace through a fourfold process of repentance, forgiveness, "making space in oneself for the other," and "healing memory."[78] It is in this way that the Church finds its identity as an image of the Trinity. Such an image implies the ecclesiological primacy of the congregation as the primary focus of the mutual interdependence that constitutes the divinely-willed form of inclusive sociality.

74. Ibid., 37, 53–55.

75. E.g., "the economy of undeserved grace has primacy over the economy of moral deserts." Or ". . . there is a profound 'injustice' about the God of the biblical tradition. It is called *grace*." Ibid., 85, and 221 respectively.

76. Moltmann, *Church in the Power of the Spirit*, 306.

77. Volf, *After Our Likeness*, 282.

78. Volf, *Exclusion and Embrace*, 100.

The catholicity of the Church is not derivative of a larger or purer form of ecclesial identity drawn from the universal or invisible Church, but is an anticipation of the "eschatological catholicity of the people of God in the totality of God's new creation."[79]

The correspondence here with Yoder's radical notion of catholicity, and the theological realism outlined in the previous chapter, are notable. Equally, Volf highlights themes consonant with, though not explicitly parallel to Yoder's concerns. For example, his construction of the analogical imaging of trinitarian self-donation does not assert the identity of that cycle with the love of enemies demanded of disciples. The latter represents the former form of love as it becomes engaged in the transformation of the world. It is a re-active suffering love, a love imaging the character of trinitarian self-donation only as it is revealed in the incarnation.

> The delight of love is transmuted into the agony of love—the agony of opposition to non-love, the agony of suffering at the hands of non-love, and the agony of sympathy with non-love's victims. Hence the cross of Christ.[80]

For Volf, the element of dissonance in the analogy between Trinity and Church is highlighted on the cross. The suffering inherent in the Church's Christlike stance is the point at which analogical embodiment of the harmony of inner-Trinitarian *perichoresis* is ruptured. But this rupture is important for an account of the social mission of the Church. Although it is not a move Volf performs, it is not a difficult leap of the imagination to move from incarnation to witness here. Recall Yoder's claim that in the incarnation "God broke through the borders of our standard definition of what is human, and gave a new formative definition in Jesus."[81] Thus the incarnation, that mysterious occurrence of Christ as wholly man and wholly God, contains the tension of analogy and rupture. We noted above that Yoder views analogy as an operative category within the notion of witness. Analogy is possible because it shows how God is reconciling the world to himself. We know, because of Jesus, that God's reconciliatory purpose is achieved through suffering servanthood. Furthermore, when shorn of any perverse masochistic instrumentality, openness to suffering

---

79. Volf, *After Our Likeness*, 272.
80. Volf, "Trinity is Our Social Program," 414.
81. Yoder, *PJ*, 99.

may become a *notum ecclesiae*.[82] Thus the degree of analogy and participation is proportional to the recognition of the reality of Christ's lordship. Any analogical embodiment is, therefore, subject to the agential duality of Church and world. It is in the costliness and offence of the nonviolent life of discipleship that the analogy with the Triune God is maintained. Only in this way, I suggest, may the Church be a true public.

The imperative for the Church in a world of violence is, therefore, not to withdraw but to participate in the opening-up of a nonviolent future. Paradigmatically, non-resistance is the means by which God, in Christ, "absorbs and nullifies human hostility and so restores communion."[83] Analagously, active non-resistance, or, perhaps more satisfactorily, taking note of a shift in Yoderian vocabulary away from traditional Mennonite categories, "nonviolent resistance,"[84] is the model for discipleship.[85] This may be said to exemplify a particular form of theodicy.[86] Embodying the analogy is the performative practice of hope. Living in the reality of divine forgiveness witnesses to the very nature of God. We shall examine the importance of such a witness for social change in the next chapter. For now, we can follow Hauerwas, writing on issues of "necessary violence," in describing the transformative potential of the mode of witness as:

> attempting one step at a time to make the world less war determined. We do that exactly by entering into the complex world of deterrence and disarmament strategy believing that a community nurtured on the habits of peace might be able to see new opportunities not otherwise present. For what creates new opportunities is being a kind of people who have been freed from the assumption that war is our fate.[87]

To express the analogical pattern according to the narrative moments of the divine economy, we could say that: creation establishes the

---

82. "The fact that it suffers is no justification for a church. But if a church is fundamentally incapable of suffering, then its claim to recognition is significantly weakened." Yoder, *ARS*, 292–95.

83. Wright, *Disavowing Constantine*, 84.

84. On the significance of this change for Yoder's view of acceptable Christian modes of action, see Zimbleman, "Contribution of John Howard Yoder," 388.

85. Yoder, *PT*, 229–30.

86. See Pinches, "Christian Pacifism." It is important to note that Yoder did not, in any way, view his work as providing a theodicy. Such an enterprise was not seen as important for his own discussions.

87. Hauerwas, *ATN*, 198.

pattern, the fall conceals and perverts it, the incarnation reveals it, the cross and resurrection restore it, and the Church witnesses to its coming as a Kingdom. The shape of reconciliation, that is, of redeemed sociality, is ecclesial. It is the incarnation that inaugurates this witnessing peoplehood, and the gifting Spirit that sustains it. We turn then to John Milbank's understanding of the Christian life as gift in order to trace further the ecclesial shape of forgiveness.

The Gift of a Strange Ethic: John Milbank

As with Volf's account of trinitarian analogy and Christian sociality, Milbank offers us an account of the relationship of the Church to God that is profoundly marked by the postmodern concern for plurality and difference. In a programmatic contrast to a nihilistic construal of alterity, Milbank counterposes a vision of human sociality as a divine gift, operating within the logic of analogy. His account begins, in *Theology and Social Theory*, by narrating a "counter-ethic" to the myth of necessary violence.[88] In a world whose moral vision is filtered through a prior commitment to the ontological priority of violence, Christian morality, Milbank says, "is a thing so strange, that it must be declared immoral or amoral according to all other human norms and codes of morality."[89]

Milbank's understanding of difference is pivotal for his ethics. Nihilism sees the world as a flux of perpetual conflict, whereby one rhetoric triumphs and becomes dominant, only to be displaced by the next. By contrast, Christianity pursues a "universalism which tried to subsume rather than merely abolish difference."[90] In an oft-used musical analogy, Christianity is likened to baroque music—the harmony, though stretched to the limit by pervasive dissonance, remains, in the end, unified.[91] This then yields a vision of sociality as "complex space," a socialism of the gift.[92] Ecclesial practice participates in the nature of the Triune God as

---

88. Milbank, *TST*, esp. 278–325, 380–438. Milbank links this counter-ethic with a counter-ontology affirming the ontological primacy of peace. Yoder tended to avoid explicit discussions of ontology. We shall see later that Milbank proceeds from a very different ecclesiological construal of public practice, language and open sociality.

89. Milbank, *WMS*, 219.

90. Milbank, "Postmodern Critical Augustinianism."

91. Milbank, *TST*, 430.

92. Milbank, "On Complex Space," in *WMS*, 268–92; "Socialism of the Gift." It should be noted that Milbank's language can sometimes appear more ambiguous than seems

transcendental peace, which, in contrast to nihilism, comes through differential relation. Only Christianity, with its ontology of peace, can overcome nihilism and thus reassert itself as a metanarrative capable of reconciling post-modern difference in a way that subsumes but does not destroy diversity. As we saw in the first chapter of this book, through his aesthetic turn Milbank claims that God cannot be arrived at by dialectical search for "truth," but can be known only through the rhetorical attractiveness of an ontology of difference. As such God is known as both "the 'speaking' of created difference, *and* as the inexhaustible plenitude of otherness."[93] This harmonic conception of difference has been undergirded by Milbank's development of the ontology of peace into a trinitarian ontology of gift.

Human selfhood is then reconfigured in contradistinction to the myth of absolute self-possession that has, since Descartes, dominated accounts of identity.[94] Nor is the self received in utter passivity.[95] "The Church begins as an exchange and not as a simple reception of a unilateral gift."[96] Because creation occurred *ex nihilo*, becoming is privileged over static being.[97] Subjectivity is that gift which occupies no space between giver and recipient, for no recipient, and therefore nothing known as "giver," can be said to exist prior to gift-exchange. Rather, creatures are themselves gift and as such are grounded in the intra-divine love that is constitutive of the Trinity. This is why Milbank can claim "the doctrine of the Trinity discovers the infinite God to include a radically 'external' relationality."[98]

---

helpful; e.g., his references to the "blending" of difference—e.g., "Name of Jesus," and "End of Dialogue," 187. The notion of blending is perhaps problematic in so far as it can be seen as an image of dilution or dissolution.

93. Milbank, *TST*, 430.

94. Milbank, "Soul of Reciprocity Part One," and "Soul of Reciprocity Part Two."

95. One can perhaps detect something of a purely passive constitution of personhood in figures like Eberhard Jüngel and Hans Urs von Balthasar. On Jüngel, see Spjuth, "Redemption Without Actuality," 505–22. Balthasar's ecclesiology of communion revolves around the Church imaging the solely receptive feminine (Marian) fiat, a "letting be" which characterizes the divine-human relationship as one of divine masculine activity and feminine receptivity respectively. David Schindler bases an otherwise constructive view of moral community on this Balthasarian theme. See Schindler, *Heart of the World*.

96. Milbank, "Can a Gift be Given?" 119–61, 150.

97. Milbank, "Postmodern Critical Augustinianism," 227–28.

98. Milbank, "Can a Gift be Given?" 135–36; see also "Can Morality Be Christian?" in *WMS*, 219–32.

In developing this scheme of the gift there are a number of important differences between Yoder and Milbank. Some, such as the latter's view of hierarchy and the nature of ecclesial authority, we need not examine.[99] Others, such as the Thomistic and neo-platonic strands of Milbank's thinking on participation and analogy may display themes that are, *prima facie*, inimical to Yoder's own views. The Thomistic vision of all creation as "engraced" may be one example. Yoder's own response to such themes is perhaps better read as having in view the sort of departicularizing moves characteristic of some neo-scholastics. In that case, the distance with Milbank is more apparent than real; for as Milbank, and others like Jean Porter, have amply demonstrated, such a move is in fact inimical to Thomism, properly understood.[100] Still other aspects such as the relation of the particularity of Jesus to the life of the Church, and the nature of dialogue and the possibility of nonviolence, have direct bearing on how the eschatological-analogical pattern can yield an account of social change and social criticism.

The Particularity of Jesus

Ironically, given his stringent concerns for ontology, Milbank's own theological realism comes under attack due to his inability to escape the speculative moment that he detects at the heart of doctrine.[101] Milbank insists that the basis of theological realism occurs at the point where the speculative idea returns to the concrete narrative level.[102] It is not, therefore, a realism based on the secular prioritization of being over becoming; not an "immanent reality cut off from the transcendent. Therefore, 'realism' in the usual secular sense is the *enemy* of theological realism."[103] The trinitarian extension of being as gift allows Milbank to assert one single christological-ecclesial narrative. That is to say, to take the example of the doctrine of the incarnation, in order to avoid a purely extrinsic notion of the work of Christ, the Church is said to perform a "non-identical repetition" of that work. However in seeking to advance a concept of incarnation and atonement that may become for us not "mere facts" but "characterisable modes of being," Milbank encloses

99. Milbank, *BR*.

100. For Porter on the danger of departicularizing nautral law in this way, see Porter, *Natural and Divine Law*.

101. Bauerschmidt, "Word Made Speculative?"

102. Milbank, *TST*, 385.

103. Milbank, "Intensities," 487.

himself in a process of necessary abstraction in which, despite his best efforts, the particularity of Jesus is lost—with deeply regrettable ethical consequences.[104] Milbank juxtaposes a purely christological and a wider ecclesiological reading of the incarnation. Only the latter, he claims, can do justice to both the particularity of Jesus *and* the coming of the Church that was always-already present in Jesus's actions. Jesus is then simply the founder, the first of many.[105] In order for the incarnation to escape mere extrinsic authority for the believer, the very effect of Jesus on his followers "in a certain, not really-to-be-regretted fashion, obscured him in favour of an 'idea.'"[106]

This is not a simple low-Christology, an invocation to platonic imitation of a transcendental original. Christ the logos is the very source, goal, and context of our action. Therefore Milbank claims, with typical rhetorical flourish, all that remains of Jesus's particularity, once the identification of Jesus with pre-existent logos is complete, is the proper name "Jesus."[107] Yet this is not, he claims, to evacuate Christ of humanity. Nonidentical repetition is not imitation of an idea, but the repetition of the structured transformation made known in the gospel narratives. Only in this way are the particularities of Jesus's life said to be indispensable. Milbank rightly seeks to deconstruct any arbitrary division between the figure of Christ and the life of the Church. However, he achieves this only through the unwarranted assertion that the Gospels "are not actually all that much concerned with Jesus as an individual."[108]

The abstraction by which logos-Christology was able to assert the priority of Christ over pagan metaphysics has shed too much along the way. The *totus Christus* of Jesus as the "realised collective character of the church" is maintained only because the concrete and particular participates of necessity in "the aspiration to provide universal normative contexts", which thereby renders the particular abstract.[109] This appears in marked contrast with the reading of the Johannine prologue found in Yoder, where logos-Christology functions primarily to safeguard the concrete and particular Jesus.

104. Milbank, "Name of Jesus," 314–15.
105. Ibid., 317.
106. Milbank, *TST*, 384f.
107. Milbank, "Name of Jesus," 316, 325.
108. Ibid., 179.
109. Ibid., 320.

Importantly, this abstractive method has been balanced more recently with a focus on the peculiarities of the Gospels.[110] Indeed Milbank contends of the Church:

> At the center of this new social and even "political" institution lies an absolute mystery: the insistence on Christ's specificity.... there is a real "affinity" to be constantly produced, discovered and enacted. Were this unnecessary, then Christ would be unnecessary; a mere command to "be reconciled" would do.... Of course we are to imitate Christ and to live ecstatically through exchange, losing our lives in order to gain them. But if *only* Christ reconciles us to each other . . . then this can only mean that the specific shape of Christ's body in his reconciled life and its continued renewal in the Church (where it is authentic, which must also be ceaselessly discerned) provides for us the true aesthetic example of our reshaping of our social existence.[111]

Evidently Milbank's trinitarian ontology claims to proceed from the particularity of Jesus. Through the continuity of Christ and Church in a single narrative, he avoids the concerns articulated by Yoder, in relation to H. R. Niebuhr, that an appeal to the Trinity relativizes the specificity of Christ.[112] Nevertheless those elements of Jesus's particularity that are perhaps most significant for Yoder—his Jewishness, his pacifism, his identification with the excluded—do not feature in any determinative or prominent sense for Milbank.

The particularity of Jesus assumes a role in Yoder that cannot be maintained within Milbank's abstractive enterprise. Milbank attempts to reconfigure theological realism along the lines of his rejection of Scotist univocity of being—becoming rather than being, gift not self-possession, ecclesiology as opposed to (extrinsicist) Christology. Ironically, as with Badiou's metaphysics of the event, Milbank's attempt to ground a participatory ontology in Christ ends up subsuming Jesus into a more general metaphysic of gift. It thereby compromises the very realism and vision of a counter-public Milbank defends. Yoder's realism, by contrast, does not allow any theoretical construct to take precedence over the normativity of Christ for Christian communal life.[113] The universality of the logos

---

110. E.g., Milbank's fascinating focus on the role of the mob in the trial of Jesus. *BR*, 79–93.
111. Ibid., 103.
112. Yoder, *AT*, 61–63.
113. Huebner, "Can a Gift be Commanded?"

is indivisible from the universal lordship of Christ, for which the particularities of Jesus's life are indispensable not merely because they are to be non-identically repeated (although the concept seems pregnant with possibility) but because they reveal something essential to the nature of that lordship. Equally, Yoder maintains a similar understanding of the giftedness of selfhood. Selfhood is a gift not just because it flows directly from inner-trinitarian perichoresis, but also because selfhood is indivisible from peoplehood, and peoplehood is, as for diaspora Judaism, an ever-renewed gift of covenant promise.[114]

The Possibility of Nonviolence

Nonviolence is not just an ethic about power, it is also "an epistemology about how to let truth speak for itself."[115] Yoder follows the Gandhian notion of life as a series of "experiments with truth."[116] His is an epistemology that stresses confession and grace rather than possession and technique.[117] The truth takes possession of us. Thus Yoder's invocation of the importance of dialogue is not a

> "polite relativism" seeking to "escape the reproach of the counter-question" . . . We do not have the truth; we confess a truth which has taken possession of us through no merit of our own. That truth, being the revelation of God's own vulnerability on the cross, cannot be otherwise commended than in the vulnerability of open encounter with the neighbour.[118]

Yoder's tone differs here from Milbank's understanding of dialogue. For example, Milbank is skeptical of inter-religious dialogue, viewing it as erecting a false genus of "religion" which is said to unite all "religions." It thereby construes them as a series of "beliefs" as opposed to a "social project." On such a basis, Milbank argues, any putative practical consensus between religions is only possible with the general acceptance of secularization and liberal values.[119] He suggests, therefore, that

> With an extreme degree of paradox, one must claim that it is only through insisting on the finality of the Christian reading of "what

---

114. See the conception of diaspora identity in Yoder, *FTN*, 51–77.
115. Ibid., *PMMR*, 27–28.
116. Ibid., *MAB*, 135.
117. Ibid., *THW*, 39.
118. Ibid., *JCSR*, 142.
119. Milbank, "End of Dialogue," 182.

there is" that one can both fulfill respect for the other and complete and secure this otherness as pure neighborly difference.[120]

Yoder would have been equally skeptical about inter-religious dialogue construed in those terms.[121] However, whereas Milbank is largely content to diagnose the disorder of this secularist "policing of the sublime," Yoder's understanding of the vulnerability inherent in Christian witness moves him to affirm that "mission and dialogue are not alternatives: each is valid only within the other, properly understood."[122] This vulnerability leads Romand Coles to characterize Yoder's patience as a "*wild patience*: love for the untamed entangled growings of heralding, listening, waiting."[123]

The notion of the vulnerability of witness highlights a dramatic difference between Milbank and Yoder on the nature of nonviolence. Despite his insistence on the basis of the Christian moral life in the ontology of peace, Milbank is finally unable to follow through to a commitment to nonviolence. He criticizes Hauerwas's ethics of virtue for privileging peaceableness over other Christian virtues (justice). He claims that in situations where one cannot evade tragic choices the persistence in non-coercion (understood as "a particular mode of action"[124]) lapses into a "deontological schematism." This is because an ethics of virtue cannot escape the standard account of morality as the management of moral luck.[125] The problematic of moral luck—that the virtuous life and the ethical pursuit of happiness are dependent upon secure social conditions—has, according to Milbank, determined Christian ethics to such a great degree that the ethical conception of grace as empowering gift has been lost.[126]

Yet Milbank is inconsistent with regard to the tragic—for he asserts somewhat confusingly that one can "hold out for a tragic refusal of the

---

120. Ibid., 189.

121. Yoder, "Disavowal of Constantine," in *RP*, 242–61.

122. Yoder, *RP*, 255.

123. Coles, "Wild Patience," 324.

124. This is not a designation Hauerwas or Yoder would accept. For both Hauerwas and Yoder "nonviolence" does not simply name a particular identifiable practice (e.g., the avoidance of killing), but the condition of living in a community of discipleship. C.f. *PF*, esp. chap. 7. "Explaining Christian Nonviolence," 169–84.

125. Milbank, "Between Purgation and Illumination," 191.

126. Milbank, "Midwinter Sacrifice."

pacifist position without denying that it is likely that any implication in violence is likely to prove futile in the long run."[127] He is emphatic in disclaiming a pacifist interpretation of his work.[128] Pivotal to this disavowal is his insistence that "Christianity has traditionally seen peace as the comprehensive eschatological goal, and *not* as the name of a virtue."[129] This arbitrary division between Kingdom and present virtue seems to cut across his own insistence on the radicality of giftedness.

For Milbank, other-regarding self-sacrifice cannot be said to be the essence of Christian morality, for not only is such an account too easily secularized, it also lapses into a "latent paradox," for self-possession is ironically maintained in the imperative to sacrifice. "What we 'own,' [is] the ethical," says Milbank "[which] is nothing other than radical self-dispossession."[130] What if, by contrast, Christian ethics is characterized by the reciprocity of trinitarian gift, so that one does not even possess one's own deed? Here again is the choice between nihilism and Christianity, for to escape from the illusion of self-possession is either to take leave of the ethical and submit to flux and fortune, or it is to realize that selfhood is gift and the ethical is conditional upon "utter exposure" to grace.[131] Of course, this is why "Christian morality is a thing so strange that it must be declared immoral or amoral according to all other human norms and codes of morality."[132]

While conceding that Hauerwas maintains that Christian virtues are themselves directed precisely to the transformation of the conditions of moral luck, Milbank refuses to allow the imaginative realization of a peaceable response to escape a fundamentally consequentialist axiology.[133] Tragic violence may be required, it is said, because "there must be

127. Milbank, "Between Purgation and Illumination," 191.

128. See Milbank, "Enclaves, or Where is the Church," 349; "Testing Pacifism"; and "Christian Peace."

129. Milbank, *TST*, 418.

130. Milbank, "Midwinter Sacrifice," 16.

131. Ibid., 23.

132. Milbank, "Can Morality be Christian?" in *WMS*, 219–32, 219.

133. Milbank's inability to see pacifism as anything but consequentialist slips into a pejorative accusation of insincerity—see his glib dismissal of the Anabaptist rejection of the sword as a mere self-concerned pragmatism. "Pacifism was for the radical church . . . a tactic of survival. It was safer, if you were going to be so radical and go your own way, to say that you were pacifist. That allowed people to leave you alone." Milbank, "Radical Orthodoxy and the Radical Reformation," 45–46.

cases where one practically knows that a sudden change of heart on the part of the violent and unjust is virtually impossible."[134] But, it follows from Yoder's analogical and participative logic that nonviolent *agape* is not simply a strategy for eliciting the correct response from a free agent (this would pervert witness into propaganda); rather it is the very condition of that freedom (including the freedom to reject God—albeit thereby paradoxically rejecting one's own existence).

In such comments Milbank is disingenuous to the pacifism of Hauerwas and, by extension, Yoder. Yoder's pacifism is not based on the commitment that nonviolence is an efficacious tactic, nor is it correctly described as "a particular mode of action." It stands or falls on grounds of Christ's lordship.[135] What is regrettable here is that while Milbank affirms that the peaceable way of life is "no more and no less 'imaginary' than existing social practices which always write violence into their scripts," he fails to see that christological pacifism is based within the same imaginative construction of reality as resurrection, gift, and the lordship of Christ.[136] As a consequence of this, Milbank is claimed as an ally by Hans Boersma in his recent problematic attempt to outline a vision of divine violence as redemptive.[137] Boersma's uncritical elision of materiality (the contingent need for the erection and enforcement of boundaries) and violence (the necessary means for safeguarding materiality so understood) would seem contrary to Milbank's disavowal of agonism. Alas Milbank's pejorative account of pacifism as a passive and unnatural refusal to value proximate goods cannot avoid a similar drift. Where Boersma seeks to encourage Milbank into an emboldened embrace of positive violence, we would seek a shift in the opposite direction.

Time and again Milbank provides insightful comments on the nature of ecclesial life in a world still deeply fissured with violence, suffering, and corruption, only to retreat from the logic of nonviolence through inordinately polemical and inaccurate portrayals of pacifism. His explicit account of Christian nonviolence as a peculiarly voyeuristic passivity that is thereby doubly complicit in the continuation of violence is a straw-man.[138] He has yet to engage, in any fair or substantial way, with

---

134. Milbank, "Between Purgation and Illumination," 191.
135. Yoder, *NS*.
136. Milbank, "Between Purgation and Illumination," 192.
137. Boersma, *Violence, Hospitality and the Cross*, and "Being Reconciled."
138. Milbank, *BR*, 26–43.

the claims of Yoder or Hauerwas that nonviolence follows from the logic of christological realism and thus enables a robust and nuanced account of social change. In persisting in this stereotype of pacifism, Milbank singularly fails to provide evidence for how his counter-ontology furnishes a counter-ethic.

Nonviolent Witness as True Public

In chapter 2 we noted Jeffrey Stout's reservations regarding the capacity of Yoder's theology to meet the conditions of social critique—to both "draw attention to dangers" and to "enliven hope." The argument of this book so far is that the eschatological-analogical pattern of the witness of the Church is its mode of publicity and critique. I have suggested that this fragile but genuine publicity may expose the false "publics" of "the world"—whether they be presented through a covert totalitarian dominance or an all-too-easy claim to consensus. True publicity, like Wolin's account of democracy, remains "fugitive." But this brittle fugitive publicity is not grounds for despair, for it is enlivened by (and thus brings forth) a properly eschatological hope.

The claim that the Church is a true public has a long but often neglected pedigree. It is this that lies behind the second definition of "public" given by William Placher—that religion is itself a public activity, and not simply a matter of individual preference and experience. It is given its strongest rhetorical force in Augustine's famous insistence that the *civitas dei* is the only true *res publica*, in contrast to the atomistic and disordered *civitas terrena*.[139] Contrary to the readings propounded by Hannah Arendt[140] and Robert Markus,[141] Rowan Williams has shown convincingly that Augustine is not here repudiating the public political realm of the *polis*, but is "engaged in a *redefinition* of the public itself, designed to show that it is life outside the Christian community which fails to be truly public, authentically political."[142] Despite Yoder's incautious and pejorative verdict on Augustine, it is clear that there is some significant

---

139. Most famously, of course, in *City of God*, Book XIX.
140. Arendt, *Human Condition*.
141. Markus, *Saeculum*.
142. Williams "Politics and the Soul," 58. This analysis is given far greater depth and nuance in Dodaro's *Christ and the Just Society*.

common ground here.[143] Augustine's account is then but one variant of the Christian eschatological unsettling of previously stable divisions and power relations. Just as the antinomy of *oikos* and *polis* in the ancient world is undone in Christ's *ekklesia*,[144] so contemporary formations of private religion and public secularity are also brought into question.[145]

Against the monolithic singular public of political liberalism, and the total claim of the singular society under a singular sovereign power in which it takes shape, the Church's own publicity declares, with the writer of Hebrews, that "here we have no lasting city" (Heb 13:14). Reinhard Hütter has argued convincingly that when the Church loses a sense of itself as public, it invariably defines itself by an alien logic and a deficient account of politics.[146] It may then only define itself as "political" and "public" through the adoption of an alternate, non-eschatological, telos that brings with it contestable and dangerous categories of national identity, state sovereignty, or the modalities of a singular civil society. For the remainder of this book I will seek to demonstrate how the public witness of the Church whose telos resides in the eschatological consummation of the redemptive purposes of a nonviolent God may itself bring into question precisely these categories and modalities. In chapter 6, I consider how this vision relates to contemporary concerns for sovereignty and legitimacy in and beyond the state. In chapter 7, I conclude with a reflection on the compatibility or otherwise of this witness with recent accounts of civil society. Prior to these discussions, however, I turn to an examination of the nature of social transformation.

---

143. We do not have space here to explore the potential synergies and critiques to be found between Yoder and Augustine. For some recent discussions, see A. E. Weaver, "Unjust Lies and Just Wars"; and Schlabach, "Christian Witness in the Earthly City." Doctoral theses from Charlie Collier and Justin Neufeld, amongst others, will advance this important dialogue. Robert Markus has also recently explored the relation between the two figures by emphasizing Augustine's sensitivity to the dangers Yoder identifies in Constantinianism, without thereby endorsing Yoder's own account. Markus, *Christianity and the Secular*.

144. See for example the rhetorical subversion in the mixed metaphors (both citizen and household) in Eph 2:19; and the intertwining of communal public activity and isolated private domesticity in Acts 4:32. Needless to say, the subversion of such antinomies is neither wholesale nor uniform in the New Testament. For excellent discussions of this, see Wannenwetsch, *Political Worship*, chap. 6, 117–206. See also Rasmussen, *Church as Polis*; and Long, *Goodness of God*.

145. In addition to Milbank, *TST*, see at a general level Asad, *Formations of the Secular*; and Taylor, *Secular Age*.

146. Hütter, *Suffering Divine Things*, 158–71.

CHAPTER 5

Doxology and Social Change:
The Subversive Citizenship of the Messianic Community

"The atmosphere of liberation is not compulsive management of events, not calculation of effects in proportion to effort, but wonderment and praise, doxology."[1]

—John Howard Yoder

"[T]he very presence of the church in a world ruled by the Powers is a superlatively positive and aggressive fact.... All resistance and every attack against the gods of this age will be unfruitful, unless the church herself is resistance and attack, unless she demonstrates in her life and fellowship how men can live freed from the Powers."[2]

—Hendrikus Berkhof

"... it is never a question of church or world. Rather it is a question of having a people so captured by the worship of God that they can be for the world what the world so desperately needs."[3]

—Stanley Hauerwas

---

1. Yoder, "Withdrawal and Diaspora," 84.
2. Berkhof, *Christ and the Powers*, 51.
3. Hauerwas and Coles, *Christianity*, 111–12.

Reimagining Social Change

We saw in the previous chapter that Milbank's account of the analogical relation between Christ and his Church is compromised by a disingenuous reading of Christian pacifism. I propose to show that the way in which Yoder bases his theological realism on the normativity of Jesus's nonviolence entails an understanding of social change that is pregnant with potential for many current social issues. I will provide a novel reading of Yoder's understanding of social change as a series of practices located within the life of praise. I suggest that the motif of doxology, while only appearing sporadically in his writings, actually undergirds Yoder's entire theology of social transformation.[4] I begin by using Yoder's account of fraternal admonition ("binding and loosing") to explore how a communal practice of reconciliation may impact on wider social practices of exclusion and punishment. I therefore examine aspects of Yoder's occasional writings on capital punishment and his more substantial, though as yet unpublished, writings on the theology of punishment.[5]

In so doing, like previous chapters, this will lead us to critique and expand a number of influential aspects of contemporary postmodern critical theory. Most particularly it will explore important themes arising from René Girard's conception of mimetic desire and scapegoating, and Michel de Certeau's understanding of "tactical" forms of social action. After conducting these discussions I aim to show how Yoder's thought

---

4. In addition to the epigram for this chapter, Yoder also chooses the motif in contrast to a quandaryist orientation. "The focus on dilemma is more useful pastorally than it is for guiding social choices. It is more helpful for purposes of analysis and critique than for building an alternative world. Without contesting the relative utility of those dilemma formulations, I suggest that a more rounded biblical perspective would talk about ethics in terms of doxology or proclamation, of koinonia or kingdom. These motifs have in common that they define Christian moral discourse by beginning with the answer rather than with the question." Yoder, "Church and Change," 8. See also "Theological Critique of Violence," and "Fuller Definition of Violence."

5. An earlier version of this chapter asserted that these writings have yet to be subject to any extensive academic analysis. That chapter was prepared before the publication of Hauerwas's *Performing the Faith*—chapter 8 of which is entitled "Punishing Christians," 185–200. Much of what I say here finds common cause with that essay. However, neither that essay nor this chapter move beyond a simple sketch some important constituent parts of a theological response to practices of punishment. Due to constraints of space, this chapter will restrict itself to brief indications of themes and practices pertinent to a theology of punishment. A fuller exploration of these themes will form the basis of another forthcoming book, currently in preparation under the working title of *Peace, Penance, and Punishment*.

provides us with a theology of social change that performs three important moves:

1. it *relocates* authentic social transformation within doxology;
2. it *redefines* effectiveness according to the divine economy—which is an economy of forgiveness and patience;
3. and it *reaffirms* a nuanced form of liberation theology that is peculiarly apposite to modern western culture.

We have already noted how Yoder's understanding of witness leads him to view the practices of the Christian community as significant public witness. We turn first to an exposition of one of these practices, fraternal admonition, in which is found the most elegant expression of the complex vision of human reconciliation and interdependence that will inform our discussion of social change.

Reconciliation and Communal Practice

For Yoder, the "becoming church" exists only where a vibrant practice of fraternal admonition is in operation. He observes, following Balthasar Hubmaier, that the Church is only fully present where "binding and loosing" take place.[6] In the Christian community the process of fraternal admonition orients all conflict towards a restorative or reintegrative goal. Whilst a variety of biblical texts are alluded to, Matt 18:15–20 is paradigmatic of the mutually constitutive practices of moral discernment and forgiveness. The more exclusionary, or at least more ambiguous, practice advocated by Paul in 1 Corinthians 5 is interpreted in this light.[7] The performative practice of fraternal admonition is the efficacious sign of our

---

6. Yoder argues that reference to binding and loosing occurs at the only places in the Gospels where the word "Church" is reported as used by Jesus (e.g., Matt 16:19, 18:18; John 29:23). See Yoder, "Binding and Loosing," 337.

7. There seems to be significant divergence on the primary intention behind exclusionary practice in the Corinthian community. Adela Collins argues that the function was primarily the maintenance of the holiness of the community, with little regard for the fate of the man "handed over." By contrast, Ben Witherington argues that the practice is undertaken in the hope that it will lead to repentance and restoration. As will be clear from the discussion below, both Yoder and myself are closer to Witherington on this point. Collins, "Function of Excommunication," esp. 259, 263. Witherington, *Conflict and Community*, 159.

living within the reality made possible by Christ's atoning work. That is to say, it is a gift of the Spirit and a precondition to authentic worship.[8]

Naturally enough, the practices that together constitute the embodiment of the eschatological-analogical pattern co-inhere logically as well as pragmatically. Thus Yoder takes his stance against pedobaptism on grounds of the nature of fraternal admonition. Yoder does not, as Oliver O'Donovan claims, assert that the issue is one of maintaining uncoerced voluntariety, thus conforming the Church to the model of a club or political party.[9] Rather the issue is that, through baptism, one submits to "the mutual obligation of giving and receiving counsel in the congregation; this is what a child cannot do."[10] Voluntariety, in the sense of the freedom of the individual utterly uncoerced and unconstrained by circumstance or context, is not what the practice of believers' baptism seeks to maintain. Such a view represents an extreme version of the modernist myth, which violates and contradicts the mutual interdependence of participants in the Christian community, subsequent to baptism. The defense of voluntariety in the criticism of paedobaptist practice therefore functions to safeguard the importance of an uncoerced, fully informed, public decision that is the precondition of the ecclesially-constitutive practice of fraternal admonition.

Voluntariety is essential to maintain the integrity of the mutually interdependent community in which individual guilt is never used as a basis for scapegoating; and where the responsibility and culpability of the community is always asserted alongside any recognition of individual fault.[11] Thus communal performative practices, particularly the process of fraternal admonition and excommunication, do not participate in a process of projecting guilt onto the (soon to be excluded) other; but rather demonstrate an alternative way of construing guilt, difference, and the integrity of the community.

---

8. Yoder, "Binding and Loosing." Yoder suggests that the gifts of the Spirit are more often spoken of in connection with discernment and forgiveness (e.g., Matt 18:19, 20) than in relation to witnessing (Acts 1:8). However it is perhaps better to see witness as founded on the constitutive practice of fraternal admonition, than to separate the two into divergent pneumatological activities.

9. O'Donovan, *DN*, 223–24.

10. Yoder, *RP*, 338.

11. See for example Yoder's (generally ethically conservative) discussion of second marriages within the Christian community, viewed as a failure of the community to offer the solidarity and familial setting requisite to sustain the person. *One Flesh Until Death*, 26.

Equally, such a conception goes some way to countering the common-place juxtaposition of divine forgiveness and human justice. Emmanuel Levinas famously objects that the Christian belief in a God who forgives sins becomes inhuman (i.e., radically unjust) in its failure to respect the victim as the primary forgiving agent.[12] The instigation of a procedure that requires a victimizer to turn in penitence toward their victim(s) may begin to mitigate this concern. Yet it may do so in full recognition of the prevenience of grace—for both penitence and reconciliation are undertaken within the empowering presence of the Holy Spirit.

The Church's witness to the reconciliation of humanity to God centers not on individual kerygmatic proclamations, but, says Yoder, on the (diaconal) "quality of personal relationships that even the outsider may observe."[13] What is required is not the avoidance of conflict at all costs, for the peaceable Kingdom remains a Kingdom of truth and justice, but a reconciling and nonviolent practice of conflict.[14] The Spirit does not empower members of the Christian community to bury grievances, leaving them to fester, but to resolve and redeem them. Discourses of power are not ignored; rather, through the practice of reconciling forgiveness, language is oriented to the sustenance of that community that is engendered in eucharistic fellowship and inaugurated in the rite of baptism.[15]

For Yoder the practice of "binding and loosing" enables a correct understanding of the ecclesiological priority of the congregation. The "bearing of one another's burdens" is primarily experienced in direct, personal, fraternal relations. Synodical government, collegiality, etc., may share in the nature of ecclesiality, but the primary focus of ecclesial identity is the gathered church. Indeed, it is important to note that, in a pre-Constantinian setting, the regrettable practice of excommunication is not to be seen as violently exclusionary. The excommunicant excludes him or herself through persistent unrepentant sin (Tit 3:11). The sin that most properly leads to excommunication is the denial of the lordship of Christ. Such a denial occurs through the refusal to practice forgiveness,

---

12. Jones, *Embodying Forgiveness*, 104–5, 126–27. For Levinas's criticism of the Christian view of forgiveness, see Levinas, *Difficult Freedom*, 20.

13. Yoder, *RP*, 352.

14. See Yoder, "Theological Point of Reference." For a similar point, see Hauerwas, "Peacmaking" in *CET*, 89–97.

15. Jones, *Embodying Forgiveness*, 190ff. I use sustenance in the sense of nourishment (the indispensable resource of growth and vitality) and not merely maintenance (which may imply conservative reluctance to change).

either by the failure to reciprocate forgiveness (Matt 18:23–35), or unrepentant persistence in a particular sinful behavior (1 Cor 5). Each of these represents the rejection of a life lived, by the power of the Spirit, in the light of the atonement achieved in Christ.[16]

Even the moment of excommunication remains oriented to the hope for the reintegration of the person—to be achieved through their recognition of the lordship of Christ. This concern is present even in the *prima facie* violently exclusionary exhortation of 1 Cor 5:5. The imperative to hand over the unrepentant man to Satan "for the destruction of the flesh" (*sarx*) is framed within the desire that, in doing so, the man's spirit "may be saved in the day of the Lord." It is not possible here to enter the complex exegetical discussion of the relation of flesh (*sarx*) to the law, or to salvation and the Day of the Lord; suffice it to say that the handing over to Satan (see also 1 Tim 1:20) does not validate, in the light of the consistent nonviolence implied on a Yoderian reading of fraternal admonition, any acceptance of pedagogic violence of the kind, for example, advocated by Augustine in his dispute with the Donatists.

For Augustine, the *usus* (a circumscribed utilization of fallen earthly means) of violence *pro ecclesia utilate* is not "peaceable," but may be "redeemed" by a retrospective acceptance by the person/s coerced, and thus may contribute to the final goal of peace. In *Theology and Social Theory*, Milbank argues, despite his own eventual equivocation on the subject of violence, that this represents a failure of Augustine to follow through the ontological distinctions on which he constructed his view of the *Civitas Dei*. In this way talk of a punishing God is inappropriate, for punishment, no matter what its motivation, always contains a moment of pure violence. The God who always remains true to (i.e., within) his nature cannot therefore punish, for "punishment is not an act of a real nature upon another nature." Milbank thus argues that the only punishment appropriate to sin is the "deleterious effect of sin itself upon nature, and the torment of knowing reality only in terms of one's estrangement from it."[17]

---

16. It should never go unsaid that this has only infrequently been the real reason for excommunication, as practiced in the Church. The complicity of the Church in violence, exclusion, and intolerance is, ultimately, a refusal to acknowledge the Lordship of Christ.

17. Milbank, *TST*, 418–20. Milbank has since modified this view, arguing more strongly in favour of the punitive practices of Augustine: "in *Theology and Social Theory* I did say that I don't think that Augustine had enough sense of the risk and ambiguity of punishment. Although I think now even more strongly he was right to see that as inescapable. You can tell that I have had children since I wrote *Theology and Social Theory*." Milbank,

Two points follow from this. First, the recovery of the full missiological potential of the practice of fraternal admonition itself requires an act of penitence begun through the application of Yoder's anti-Constantinain historiography. And second, only once the lessons of that process have been learnt can a robust theology of punishment point us towards a fuller theology of social change. We have already seen that Yoder's concern for the structural issues that occupied much ecumenical dialogue relate primarily to the nature and possibility of faithful witness. We can see in relation to the most extreme part of the practices of fraternal admonition, namely the procedures for excommunication, just how these structural issues may affect the content and social significance of the Church's witness.

The function of excommunication was radically altered through the Constantinian shift. The exclusion of the person here differs both in terms of primary agent and in terms of consequence. For the pre-Constantinian view the primary agent is the free individual, not the exclusionary community.[18] The emergence of more hierarchical and juridical structures of authority, which appear consonant with the broad characteristics of Constantinian Christianity, imply the priority of the conserving function of excommunication, serving to maintain the orthodoxy and the purity of the true, imperial Church. This is not to say that such conserving functions were not present within the pre-Constantinian practice, but that they were framed within the understanding of communal interpersonal responsibility mentioned above. Pardon and judgment remained, as Oliver O'Donovan's puts it, "complementary aspects of the way truth impinges on falsehood."[19]

Ecclesial authority came to be molded more on images of compulsion (that is, the exercise of ecclesial authority was derived from the coercive authority of the state) rather than on persuasion (the rhetorical exercise of authority, imaged on the Trinity that can recognize polyphony,

---

"Testing Pacifism," 204. He has yet to explore how such punishment is consistent with an ontology of peace.

18. In order to mitigate charges of simplistic and tendentious historiography, it should be noted that the characterizations of the pre-Constantinian and Constantinian views are functioning here rhetorically as ideal types. The susceptibility of the pre-Constantinian church to the exclusionary will-to-power seems undeniable; the difference I am aiming to clarify is between the understandings of excommunication which, broadly, emerge from divergent constructions of authority, the locus of ecclesial identity, and the relation of the Christian community to political and civil sanctions of wider society.

19. O'Donovan, *RMO*, 177.

communal interdependence, and particularity).[20] Equally, the consequence of exclusion from the Church, when that Church is associated with both the full means of sustaining life and the legal rights of citizenship, is to exclude the individual not only from ecclesial fellowship (and thus salvation[21]) but from civil, economic, and political society in general.[22]

Here we encounter the way in which, for good or bad, the understandings of punishment in wider society operate in ways strongly influenced by the dominant understanding of both the atoning work of Christ and the embodiment of that work in the life of the Church.[23] When, as Yoder insists, the Constantinian shift eroded the distinction between Church and world, it thereby collapsed the analogical tension within which social practices of punishment could be most properly related to ecclesial practices of reintegration. To some degree the proper analogies may still be discerned within the complex field of penology. The pre-Constantinian function of excommunication is perhaps best seen as akin to a concept of considerable currency within discussions of criminal justice—"reintegrative shaming." The deterrence implied in the concept of "reintegrative shaming," as it is articulated by John Braithwaite, does not create a class of outcasts. Any ceremonial means of degradation (excommunication) is to be counterbalanced by gestures of reacceptance (penance).[24]

Commentators like Braithwaite and, from an Anabaptist perspective, Howard Zehr, note that the cultural apparatus that routinized the

---

20. On the importance of a rhetorical, persuasive, and above all, trinitarian model of authority, see Cunningham, *These Three Are One*, 304–35.

21. To see a "violence" implied in the exclusion from salvation, would, by most definitions of violence, require that the exclusion is imposed from outside, presumably against the will of the excluded individual. It would not therefore be violent to affirm the exclusive nature of the deleterious effects of sin. It seems inappropriate to locate violence within the ideal type of pre-Constantinian excommunication.

22. The distinction of civil, economic, and political society is, of course, grounded within the context of modern nation-states, and would not, therefore, apply to most Constantinian settings. It does, however, reveal three interconnected elements of social existence within these settings. Especially from the time of what Yoder would name as "neo-Constantinianism," i.e., from the Middle Ages, where Churches become identified, not with the "universal" empire, but with particular emergent nation-states. For a discussion of the legal and civil impact of excommunication under the conditions of neo-Constantinianism, see Vodola, *Excommunication in the Middle Ages*, 70–102, and passim.

23. For a discussion on the relation of practices of punishment to various understandings of the atonement, see the study provided in Gorringe, *God's Just Vengeance*.

24. Braithwaite, *Crime, Shame and Reintegration*, 35f. For a theological examination of criminal justice and reintegrative shaming, see Gorringe, *God's Just Vengeance*, 255f.

repentant role within society have withered or disappeared in the West.[25] Duncan Forrester sounds a valuable cautionary note when he says that any recovery of such reintegrative practices, for example within the criminal justice system, must beware of the tendency for such agendas to authorize severely arbitrary and often coercive action.[26] The loss of such practices testifies to the significant element of fragmentation (in MacIntyre's sense) displayed in the public understanding of the social function of punishment. This unresolved fragmentation penetrates the formulation of penal policy, which often proceeds with scant reference to the wider purposes and processes within which it operates.[27] The use of the language of rehabilitation in justificatory discourse sits uncomfortably alongside societal practices that owe more to strongly retributive notions of "justice." The clamorous vindictiveness of a popular culture tutored by tabloid journalism is plain to see. Yet the same logic also occurs in a more covert, but equally vociferous, desire for vengeance throughout the echelons of contemporary Western culture.

Is it sufficient to dismiss this desire as the vestiges of an unsophisticated bloodlust, a morally uncouth failure of civility? I suggest not, for righteous indignation springs from deeper cultural wells. The desire to punish appears to follow all too "naturally" from any perceived offence, egregious injury, or impugned honor. Let us consider then the ways in which practices of punishment spring from these basic cultural impulses. Following the French cultural critic René Girard, and drawing on Yoder's unpublished writings on the issue, I shall show how a conception of social change that is grounded in the fundamental eschatological claims outlined previously may provide the beginnings of a desperately needed theology of punishment.

Redemption and Punitive Desire

Mimesis and Social Cohesion

Through a vigorous, if sometimes incautious, account of the primitive functions of myth within diverse cultures, René Girard expounds his

---

25. Braithwaite, *Crime, Shame and Reintegration*, 162.

26. Forrester, *Christian Justice*, 74.

27. Brief theological responses to this situation are found in Wood, *End of Punishment*, and Jones and Sedgwick, *Future of Criminal Justice*.

"mimetic" theory of practices of scapegoating.[28] Girard claims that human culture depends upon a primordial mechanism of ostracism for its cohesion. In the beginning was the desire for identity, and identity was established through imitation (*mimesis*) of the other. Yet in imitating the other a basic rivalry develops into the desire to exceed or even replace the object of imitation. That rivalry and the violence that proceeds from it erode social cohesion. For society to continue, for culture to exist, this mimetic desire must be satiated. It is in foundational acts of violence, of expulsion, that the balance is restored. Those parties who, like rutting deer, are otherwise locked in a perpetual cycle of self-assertion and counter-assertion, can unite in a single determinative act against an innocent party. By projecting their own social ills, their own frailties, onto this other, and then killing or expelling that other, peace may be restored.

In Girard's account foundational myths, indeed the very nature of religion, are based in the subsequent sacralizing of both the victim and the process by which society can continue to exist. Of course this is, at root, a functional account of religion of Durkheimean lineage.[29] It is in the theological implications Girard draws from this that we can find insights of great potential in our development of a theology of punishment. If religion is essentially sacrifice, then religion operates through the obfuscation of society's murderous foundations. By contrast, Girard claims that what is absolutely distinctive about biblical religion is that, from the beginning, it deconstructs and exposes this obfuscation. Israel traces its identity to Abel, the murdered brother. Biblical religion is the story of the God of the exiled people, the victims, the scapegoats. This, just like Yoder's, is a christocentric reading of the biblical message. It is Jesus who fully and finally unmasks the victimage mechanisms. Christ breaks the spiral of violence begetting violence and thus "reveals and uproots the structural matrix of all religion."[30]

---

28. My account here depends upon Girard, *Violence and the Sacred*, and *Things Hidden*.

29. Milbank is helpful in questioning this; see *TST*, 392–95, and "Stories of Sacrifice."

30. Girard, *Things Hidden*, 179. Despite Girard's positive reading of the Gospels it is possible to argue that the New Testament does not entirely escape mimetic desire. See, for example, the discussion of 1 Cor 5:3–5 in Duff, "René Girard in Corinth," especially 98–99. Of course, this reading of 1 Corinthians 5 would sit ill with that implied in our earlier discussion. Nevertheless, Girard is commonly and rightly criticized for concluding "[t]here is nothing in the Gospels to suggest that the death of Jesus is a sacrifice, whatever definition (expiation, substitution, etc) we may give for that sacrifice." Ibid., 180.

Yet the promise of Girard's analysis is let down by a view of atonement devoid of any participative or ontological character. Girard's is a fundamentally Pelagian conception of grace. "It has," he claims

> never been easier to change people's allegiance and to alter their behavior, since the vanity and stupidity of violence have never been more obvious. . . . For the first time, people are capable of escaping from the misunderstanding and ignorance that have surrounded mankind throughout its history.[31]

In such an exemplary theory of the atonement imitation returns anew, for it remains the only viable means of escaping the victimage mechanism. The Gospels may reveal the character of mimesis and thereby sound the death knell of its covert hegemony, but that revelation still comes to the believer as an external and largely propositional notion. Girard does not make it clear just how that externalized notion of imitation may escape degenerating into a formalism, which would reinstate mimetic rivalry within the body of Christ. The dangers he finds inherent in sacrificial notions of expiation are not expunged through the model of imitation as repetition. By contrast, we have seen that for Yoder the *imitatio Christi* is founded on ontological claims, which render the life of discipleship dynamic, imaginative, and peaceable.

Yoder's unpublished engagements with the Girardian system are broadly positive, although Yoder expresses a number of concerns both with its comprehensiveness at a theoretical level and its practical implications. He notes that Girard pays scant attention to the divergent forms of modern punitive behavior. So, for example, there is little in the Girardian corpus concerning pedagogic or paternal forms of punishment, which would be conceptually distinct from both the judicial actions of states and overtly retributive expressions of anger.[32] Equally, Yoder is concerned to point out the lacuna in Girard's account of the *covert* nature of mimetic violence. The most glaring exception to the sublimation of such desire occurs within contemporary debates concerning capital punishment.

Overt Violence: The Case of Capital Punishment

It is important to acknowledge the concerns and social functions that lead to the persistence of the death penalty (or calls for its reinstatement).

---

31. Girard, *Things Hidden*, 201.
32. Yoder, *YHIC*.

Those who would advocate capital punishment on biblical grounds regularly point to the *lex talionis* in their defense. Indeed in popular discussion the very phrase "an eye for an eye" is often taken as sufficient expression of the supposedly self-evident reading of justice (*suum cuique*) as simple reciprocity. To do so is exegetically misleading, but nonetheless provides strong evidence for the continued presence of an acceptable face of retributive desire.

The case against this reading of the *lex talionis* is widespread and increasingly well known. It is sufficient for our purposes to note that:

1. This rule for retaliation exists, in part, to hold in check the tendency of retribution to escalate *beyond* simple equivalence. It is a negative principle of restraint, and not, as the defenders of capital punishment may imply, a prescription.

2. Much of the biblical literature, including the *lex talionis*, are primarily oriented away from retribution, and towards the means by which *shalom* may be restored.[33]

3. Even where restitution appears impossible we see that, from the first, God's response is one of protection of the offender against retaliation (and not, therefore, an imperative for vengeance). For example, in response to Cain's fear that, in being driven "away from the soil" and becoming a fugitive, he will be subject to reprisal—"anyone who meets me may kill me"—YHWH places upon him a mark of protection (Gen 4:13–16).[34]

4. The one sense in which the rule was enforced with strict reciprocity (i.e., without substitution by other modes of recompense) was in the case of murder—"a life for a life."[35] Yet, even here its practice is rare, with restrictive evidentiary procedures (Deut 19:15) indicating a bias against its widespread use.[36]

We can identify two related concerns that often prove the most persuasive in the arsenal of the advocate of capital punishment: the notion of an imbalanced moral order, and, following on from that, an

33. See for example Marshall, *Beyond Retribution*, and Zehr, *Changing Lenses*.
34. Yoder, "Noah's Covenant," 430–31.
35. It is worth noting in this regard that the *lex talionis* also functioned to safeguard the concerns of the powerless, who may otherwise have received short-shrift in compensatory payments from the powerful. See Gorringe, *God's Just Vengeance*, 40–45.
36. Stassen, "Biblical Teaching on Capital Punishment."

understanding of the innate value of punishment.[37] These do indeed bear a striking resemblance to the Girardian understanding of the victimage mechanism, yet they operate in an entirely explicit arena. The apparent strength of the argument is derived from a strong sense that some offenses offend not only against the individual victim(s), but against society and "the moral order" itself. Thus, it is claimed, this moral order must again be set in balance. The ancient codes express this in their notions of purity. The shedding of blood requires a liturgical practice of purification and expiation (e.g., Num 35:30–34).[38] Yet the concept persists, often in forms that formally disavow the metaphysical basis of previous understandings. So, for example, Walter Berns claims that the reason we deem it appropriate to bring to trial war criminals from battles long since fought is that in so doing we demonstrate the existence of a moral order:

> By punishing them, we demonstrate that there are laws that bind men across generations . . . that we are not simply isolated individuals . . . it is right, morally right, to be angry with criminals and to express that anger publicly, officially, and in an appropriate manner, which may require the worst of them to be executed.[39]

This rhetoric again shows how modern defenses of capital punishment trade on a spurious claim to supposedly self-evident principles of justice. The ritual concept of expiation is predicated on the theological claim that blood, as the force of life, belongs to the creator of that life, God (Gen 9:4–6). In the absence of that foundation the function of retribution in relation to the moral order can only be seen as a positive gloss upon Durkheim's understanding of punishment as the formalized (indeed entirely ritualized) expression of collective sentiment. Yet it thus fails entirely to account for the sense of tragic futility in penal practice that Durkheim expressed alongside this understanding.[40]

---

37. Other common arguments, such as those of deterrence, or the specific demands of the victim, or family of the victim, are less convincing. The vast majority of empirical evidence speaks against the notion of deterrence. The notion of justice "for the victim" or victim's family, are questionable on two fronts—first it is by no means clear that even the majority of such parties desire a capital sentence, and second, it is entirely dubious that the judicial order exists to commute such demands.

38. Of course, the impurity resulting from the shedding of blood in murder is not easily or entirely separable from the impurity of the shedding of menstrual blood.

39. Berns, "The Morality of Anger."

40. For an excellent discussion of the nature and limitations of Durkheim's view, see Garland, *Punishment and Modern Society*, 23–81.

In actuality it is far from clear that the need to "bring to justice" criminals who committed crimes so long ago can only be based in retributive notions. The assumption is that retribution is the only way to reinstate the balance of the moral order. But that assumption can only hold if we, like Berns, juxtapose the widest and most generous conception of the effects of retributive justice with the straw man of a utilitarian and individualized notion of restorative justice. Contrary to Berns's assumptions, the restorative and reconciliatory function of such trials does not merely apply to the direct victims of an offense. They can and must also occur on a wider social and cultural plane. The function of such trials is at least as much a recognition of the need for truth-telling as a part of the long process of reconciliation—as the South African experience and other post-conflict processes readily attest.[41] Equally, the claim that the restoration of the moral order may, in some cases, require the "ultimate" or most extreme punishment simply begs the question. Indeed, the euphemistic language in which such claims are expressed may demonstrate an unwillingness to account for precisely how, in the absence of a theological understanding of God's claim on all lifeblood, capital punishment achieves a valid and effective satisfaction of this need.[42]

Christ, the Coming End of Punishment

It is disingenuous of advocates of capital punishment to accuse those who oppose them of a dereliction of moral order. To privilege motifs of restoration and reconciliation is not a refusal to take the guilt of the offender seriously. As Yoder puts it, "[t]he issue is not whether there is moral guilt. There is. The issue is what the Christian attitude toward the

---

41. See De Gruchy, *Reconciliation*, Biggar, *Burying the Past*, Tombs and Liechty, *Explorations in Reconciliation*.

42. Thus Yoder comments, "The killing of a killer is not a civil, nonreligious matter. It is a sacrificial act. The blood—i.e., the life—of every man and beast belongs to God. To respect this divine ownership means, in the case of animals, that the blood of a sacrificed victim is not to be consumed. For humans, it means that there shall be no killing. If there is killing, the offense is a cosmic, ritual, religious evil, demanding ceremonial compensation. It is not a moral matter: in morality a second wrong does not make a right. It is not a civil, legislative matter: it is originally stated in a setting where there is not government." Yoder, "Noah's Covenant," 435. The passage in question—the supposed mandate for capital punishment in the Noachic covenant in Genesis 9—is therefore insufficient grounds for advocacy of modern practices of capital punishment. Indeed the passage offers significantly stronger grounds for vegetarianism than death penalties enforced by the state.

guilty should be."[43] The matter requires a more substantial exploration of the remaining social functions of punishment than we can provide here. David Garland provides a helpful account in *Punishment and Modern Society*. Rather than reducing punishment to one particular aspect of its function, Garland seeks to understand it as

> . . . a distinctive social institution which, in its routine practices, somehow contrives to condense a whole web of social relations and cultural meanings.
>
> Punishment is, on the face of things, an apparatus for dealing with criminals—a circumscribed, discrete, legal-administrative entity. But it is also . . . an expression of state power, a statement of collective morality, a vehicle for emotional expression, an economically conditioned social policy, an embodiment of current sensibilities, and a set of symbols which display a cultural ethos and help create a social identity.[44]

To treat punishment as a "social institution" allows Garland to hold together these diverse functions in such a way as to allow each to critique and be critiqued by other functions. It is a descriptive vision of penal practice that disavows holding these separate functions as mutually exclusive. Durkheim, and, in a more normative vein, Girard, are largely correct to note the role played by punishment in social cohesion. Nevertheless to argue that punishment is an expressive form of moral action does not demonstrate the validity of what is expressed.

It is here that the differences between Girard and Yoder become most apparent. In Girard mimetic desire can continue largely because it remains covert. By exposing its arbitrary nature, Christ shows us that, as much as it may continue to dominate the social patterns of our lives, mimesis is fundamentally unjust and irrational. This rationalist understanding of Christ's exposure may be seen in Girard's description of a "non-sacrificial" reading of the Gospels. Christ "*perceives* both the threat and possibility of salvation" and therefore seeks to "*enlighten* men about what awaits them if they continue in the pathways they have taken before."[45] When Yoder objects that even overt violence continues to exert enormous influence in our social institutions, he is able to explain how retributive notions remain so prevalent, even when they appear to offer no substantial rational grounding.

43. Yoder, *CCP*, 22.
44. Garland, *Punishment and Modern Society*, 287.
45. Girard, *Things Hidden*, 206–7. Emphasis mine.

The danger is that, in presenting Christ's victory in solely rational terms, the time of eschatological transition becomes a procedure of progressive revelation. It is not enough for Christ to reveal that mimetic violence is irrational; he must, and indeed does, provide a way of living without violence. Girard does express something of this when he speaks of violence in highly hypostasized language.

> Violence is unable to bear the presence of a being that owes it nothing . . . Violence reveals its own game in such a way that its workings are compromised at their very source; the more it tries to conceal its ridiculous secret from now on, by forcing itself into action, the more it will succeed in revealing itself.[46]

Yet the victory Christ wins over the powers of violence comes to the believer in ways that are largely epiphanic.

By contrast it is the cosmic dimension of Christ's victory that moves Yoder's theology beyond the external and formal repetition that stereotypically characterizes radical protestant notions of imitation. The ontological claims of Christ's cosmic victory directly impinge upon the validity and practice of punishment. So it is that Yoder can claim that, rather than always having been morally uncouth and irrational, the ritual needs (i.e., not primarily moral or civil) previously expressed in expiatory requirements of the death penalty are fully and finally met in Christ.[47] Yoder's account therefore demonstrates a greater exegetical sensitivity; for, unlike Girard's dismissive rhetoric, it can make full use of the explicitly sacrificial language of the epistle to the Hebrews:[48]

> Instead of claiming for the Son of Adam his place just *beneath* the angels, however, Messiah is declared to be *above* them at the Lord's right hand, appointed Son, reflecting the stamp of the divine nature, upholding the universe. Yet this cosmic honor was no exemption from human limits. His perfection is not a timeless divine status but was *attained* through weakness with prayers and

---

46. Ibid., 209.

47. Yoder, *YHIC*, chapter 5. On this Yoder also draws on Barth, *CD* III/4, 437ff. Cf. Yoder, *CCP*, 13.

48. Girard views Hebrews as the source from which the pernicious sacrificial mythologizing of Christianity flows. See *Things Hidden*, 227–31. A number of attempts have been made recently to provide readings of Hebrews with substantially more consistence with Girard's account of the end of sacrifice. Schwager, *Jesus in the Drama of Salvation*, 182–91; Hardin, "Sacrificial Language"; Johns, "Better Sacrifice"; and Heim, *Saved From Sacrifice*, 156–60.

supplications, loud cries and tears. Fully assuming the priestly system, as both priest and victim, once for all he ends the claims of the sacrificial system to order the community of faith, putting in its place a new covenant, a new universalized priestly order, an unshakable kingdom.

Yet this cosmic sovereignty is not a simple possession. Our contribution to proving or bringing about this sovereignty is our faithfulness to Jesus.[49]

A solely rationalist account is insufficiently eschatological, and therefore must inevitably be disappointed when the hoped for change of mind fails to emerge. Further validation of the point may be found through an examination of the exegetical basis Yoder and others provide for the vision of social change that arises from this cosmic reading of the significance of Christ's work. We begin, of course, in Matt 5:38–42. "You have heard that it was said, 'An eye for an eye and a tooth for a tooth.' But I say to you, Do not resist an evildoer. But if anyone strikes you on the right cheek, turn the other also . . ." (Matt 5:38–39). Here Christ renders redundant the provisions of the *lex talionis*.[50] He also shows how forgiveness names a mode of social transformation that can allow continuing practices of punishment to be judged. Jesus calls his followers to true social change, which can occur only in obedience and imitation of the creative and redemptive love of God.[51] So it is that Christian Duquoc writes:

> The believer imitates the creative God when he exorcises the demands of legal justice and works at a new relationship with the one he has forgiven. This is the way in which forgiveness transforms human relationships and so possesses a capacity to reveal the original face of God.[52]

In reflecting this creative, transformative love of God, the plea for the Christian "not to resist the evildoer" is no mere call to supine passivity. Yoder states the point with characteristic elegance—"'subordination' is itself the Christian form of rebellion. It is the way we share in God's

---

49. Yoder, *PK*, 51.

50. I here follow Marshall, *Beyond Retribution*, 86–87, for whom Jesus does not so much "abrogate" or over rule previous provisions, as declare their functioning superfluous for his followers.

51. Cf. Wright, *Jesus and the Victory of God*, 507.

52. Duquoc, "Forgiveness of God," 42.

patience with a system we basically reject."[53] Indeed, both the Gospel text and Rom 12:17–19 apply the notion of non-resistance in a manner that refers specifically to either violent uprising or the seeking of full legal recompense. In neither of these cases would a total renunciation of the possibility of opposing evil have been envisaged.[54]

Walter Wink has provided an important reading of the Matthean text that supports this basic orientation. A back-handed blow to the right cheek (as pictured in Matt 5:39) would have represented a grave insult—a humiliating admonition of an inferior. Whereas the usual response in a situation of unequal power relations would have been to cower in shame, Jesus here explicitly affirms a course of action that radically questions the ability of the perpetrator to dehumanize the victim. The attacker's only options in seeking to strike again would be either to use his left hand, which, for a Jew at least, is deemed unclean and would have been subject to penalty on that basis; or to hit with a fist, which carried the connotation of a recognition of equal status. To turn the other cheek would be to assert one's equality with the man attempting to humiliate you.[55]

Yoder reads the household codes of Romans 13, Ephesians 5–6, etc., along similar lines—as a counsel for "revolutionary subordination." He offers an important distinction that emphasizes both the voluntariety and the eschatological basis of radical Christian politics:

> The term *hypotassesthai* is not best rendered by subjection, which carries a connotation of being thrown down and run over, nor by submission, with its connotation of passivity. Subordination means the acceptance of an order, as it exists, but with the new meaning given to it by the fact that one's acceptance of it is willing and meaningfully motivated.[56]

Unlike pre-existing stoic versions, Yoder claims these codes include, for the first time, an element of reciprocity and a privileged treatment of the subjected party as a full moral agent. They thereby display "a tactic for change in the light of the new Christological reality."[57] Undeniably this radical vision suffered at the hands of later patriarchal interests. Yoder is uncompromising in his condemnation of such readings. The failure

---

53. Yoder, *PJ*, 200 n. 10.
54. Ibid., 202 n. 14 (n.b. the text erroneously cites Rom 12:7).
55. Wink, "Neither Passivity Nor Violence," and *Engaging the Powers*, 175–77.
56. Yoder, *PJ*, 172.
57. Ibid., 192.

of later generations to focus on this emancipatory potential is not only a failure to recognize the appropriate missionary tactic. Because, for Yoder, the stance of subordination is authoritative (i.e., operates with the grain of the cosmos) on christological grounds, this loss also represents a false Christology—"a waning of the vision of the cross as ethical, and of Jesus as Servant."[58]

The understanding of social change that operates here derives its pragmatism, or, we might say, its "realism," from the tension inherent in eschatology. The principle of analogy and witness through which, as we have seen, Yoder articulates his ecclesiology, does not give us any means of escaping ambiguity. Nor can the kingship of Christ be used to claim authority for the imposition of a social program. We are not, as Walter Rauschenbach and the "social gospellers" proposed, to "Christianize" the social order. Rather, following the very nature of Christ's kingship, we are to follow Jesus's own example of subordination "because the new world or the new regime under which we live is not a simple alternative to present experience but rather a renewed way of living within the present."[59]

Theological reflection on the nature and possibility of social change must take its cues from the reality of this "new regime." The kingship of Christ relativizes the status and authority of the civil order. This is particularly the case with reference to the continued judicial functioning of the state. Jesus declares the *lex talionis* redundant for those who would follow him. Nonetheless, there is a continued role for the institutions of punishment. But the legitimacy of this role is to be claimed only to the extent that retributive and expiatory aspects are expunged from punitive practice. Thus, confident of Christ's victory, the Church can argue for creative and restorative forms of penal reform. Here, as elsewhere, it is the ontological bearing of Christ's atoning work that reveals the nature and possibility of social change:

> The resurrection and ascension of Christ guarantee that there is no situation in which nothing can be done. The world can be challenged, one point at a time, to take one step in the right direction, to move up one modest notch in the approximation of the righteousness of love.[60]

58. Ibid., 189–90. In locating the problem christologically as well as in terms of mission, Yoder goes further than Elizabeth Schüssler Fiorenza. See *In Memory of Her*, 251ff.

59. Yoder, *PJ*, 185.

60. Yoder, "Against the Death Penalty," 142. Cf. "Noah's Covenant," 440.

The Tactic of Forgiveness

The Meaningfulness of Eschatological Politics

Yoder's conception of "revolutionary subordination" allows him to open up the conception of "the political" to recognize the moral and political agency of the subordinate party, in their subordination. We have seen previously that James Scott attempts to articulate something of the political terrain occupied by those excluded from the mechanisms of public accountability through his conception of the "hidden transcript."[61]

> So long as we confine our conception of the political to activity that is openly declared we are driven to conclude that subordinate groups essentially lack a political life or that what political life they do have is restricted to those exceptional moments of popular explosion. To do so is to miss the immense political terrain that lies between quiescence and revolt.[62]

The consonance between Scott's notion of the hidden transcript and Yoder's insistence on the revolutionary nature of nonviolent resistance is striking. In his study of the politics of revolutionary subordination, David Toole suggests that Jesus, and with him the Church, may bridge the divide between public and hidden transcripts in a number of ways.[63] As well as fully public acts, such as political lobbying, protests, etc., and fully private acts, such as Jesus's private meetings with his disciples, there are a range of intermediate stances. If public acts take place center stage, and private acts fully offstage, then these intermediate "voicings of the hidden transcript" occur on the border between the two—stochastically stepping between the very edge of the stage and the wings. For Toole, it is in the liberating vision of Jesus's parabolic message that such intermediate breaches take place.[64] Finally, a more dramatic rupture can occur through acts of insubordination, such as martyrs praying *for* the emperor, which are ultimately public acts of defiance. While Toole places too strong a distinction between this final form of "insubordination" and Yoder's

---

61. Scott, *Domination,* and *Weapons of the Weak.*

62. Scott, *Domination,* 199.

63. Indeed Toole's *Waiting For Godot In Sarajevo* provides one of the only substantial published treatments of Yoder's motif of "revolutionary subordination."

64. See Toole, *Waiting For Godot In Sarajevo,* 235–41. For a fuller account of the political import of the parables of Christ, see Myers, *Binding the Strong Man.*

revolutionary subordination, he does note that all these actions subvert what Scott calls "the self-portrait of dominant elites."[65]

Toole's account attends well to the meaningfulness of such political practices. The significance and worth of such acts require interpretation within one of three frameworks—nihilism, tragedy, or apocalypse. Toole rightly notes that the clarity of such conceptual distinctions does not translate so easily in practice. The nihilistic countenancing of despair "simply bespeaks a world at war with itself, a world run amok with no bounds, no constraints, no guidance."[66] The tragic politics of Foucault, whilst originating in Nietzschean categories, by contrast, engenders a politics of resistance that asserts a tragic meaning to death. In affirming the "lyricism" of protest, be it from the "madman" or the poet, Foucault invokes a politics not based on the exclusionary confinement of the other. This remains a *tragic* politics, however, because precisely in its lamentations for the dead and the subjugated, the hope of ultimate vindication disappears. Even then, the meaningfulness of living in the face of suffering is affirmed in "physically committed actions in the face of domination, even though such actions hold out no promise of 'success.'"[67] It is in this loss of eschatological hope that such tragic politics differs from what Toole names as "apocalyptic."[68] In his account of "apocalyptic" politics, Toole turns to Yoder; and yet, as his engagements with Milbank will show, Toole himself fails to give sufficient account of the communal and doxological complexion that undergird Yoder's conception of Christian social action. Toole points to the ontological commitments that inform revolutionary subordination when he marks its contrast to nihilism with the claim that apocalyptic allows us "to imagine that history works according to a different logic."[69]

For Yoder the certainty with which ethicists presume to predict the outcome of a tragically necessary violent act rests upon the false "axiom

---

65. Such "insubordinate" acts correspond exactly with Yoder's defense of civil disobedience. Other concepts such as the Jeremianic vision of diaspora citizenship and the public nature of Christian particularity in general, which are fundamental to the reading of Yoder expounded here, are simply absent from Toole's account.

66. Toole, *Waiting for Godot in Sarajevo*, 51.

67. Ibid., 204.

68. In seeking for typological distinction I suspect that Toole underplays both Foucault's own activism and the inspirational and empowering effect he had on various other campaigns and forms of resistance—see for example McNay, *Foucault and Feminism*.

69. Toole, *Waiting for Godot in Sarajevo*, 216.

of systemic causal perspicuity [that] is part of the legacy of the enlightenment in its most sanguine phases."[70] The apocalyptic style that Yoder advocates strikes down "our confidence in system-immanent causal descriptions of how the future is sure to unfold from the choice we are now making."[71] This causal perspicuity has commonly been invoked in defense of social conservatism, i.e., in the appeal by those in power to explain that "the way things are" is the *only* way they can be. Apocalyptic imagination deconstructs this deferential assumption of the status quo, in such a way as to evoke the emancipatory potential of a life of revolutionary subordination. Yoder says:

> A community playing the victim role within a society needs first of all to know not what they would do differently if they were rulers, nor how to seize power, but that the present power constellation which oppresses them is not the last word.[72]

Yoder puts this in terms of his normative Christology, when he asserts that the

> causal link between obedience and efficacy has been broken. . . . the relationship between the obedience of God's people and the triumph of God's cause is not a relationship of cause and effect but one of cross and resurrection.[73]

Equally, we can see how it is that Milbank may assert that Christianity "is the total inversion of any heroic identity of virtue with strength, achievement or conquest."[74] Nonetheless, in a revealing remark Toole criticizes Milbank on the basis of his Christology:

> To speculate that conflict has no ontological purchase, although it may make for neat distinctions, does not allow us to account for the extent to which conflict captures and determines us.
> . . . Milbank's mistake finally, I think, is to stress the incarnation of the logos as the decisive moment and not to stress even more that the logos incarnate passed through the cross.[75]

---

70. Yoder, *AE*, 54. The recognition of the fallacious nature of the presumption of predictability in relation to justifications of the use of violence in self-defence is expounded by Yoder in *WWU*, 12–17.

71. Yoder, *Ethics and Eschatology*, 122.

72. Yoder, *AE*, 53.

73. Yoder, *PJ*, 239, 232.

74. Milbank, *TST*, 286.

75. Toole, *Waiting for Godot in Sarajevo*, 76.

However, perhaps because the notion of communal analogy is missing from his reading of Yoder, Toole does not manage to make the move from an eschatologically meaningful politics to what I shall describe as a truly doxological politics. In affirming what we might call the essential "messiness" of life in eschatological tension, Toole criticizes Milbank's invocation of the incarnation, but in so doing implicitly concedes too much to the Niebuhrian dichotomy of eschatological patience and social transformation. Toole asserts that it is the uncrucified logos that remains paradigmatic for what he takes to be Milbank's account of nonviolence.

> An incarnate but uncrucified logos all too easily flows as pure presence. Our participation in the incarnation alone suggests that we always have the power, as Milbank all too often says, to arrange and rearrange the flow of being into a nonviolent one. In fact, though, in between the cross and the eschaton, we participate in a slain logos that is always caught in violence and that does not provide us with the sort of transformative powers Milbank speaks of.[76]

I agree that Milbank's Christology is insufficient in its account of the cross. However, Milbank clearly does not give the almost Pelagian account of nonviolence that Toole supposes. For his part, Toole's analysis seems to cease at the passion, without taking sufficient theological account of the ethical, which is also to say ontological, importance of the resurrection of Christ as a reimagination of the political. That is, the doxological character of the rejoicing community, which is for Yoder the basis of its revolutionary subordination, is missing. Strikingly absent from Toole's otherwise appealing account of the politics of apocalyptic are precisely those aspects of Yoder's theology that we have determined to be essential to his vision of social and political critique—a description of revolutionary subordination as an alternative to variant forms of Constantinianism; an ad hoc and vulnerable modality expressed through the Jeremianic vision of diaspora citizenship; and a clear and nuanced demonstration of the public nature of Christian particularity.

Tactics and Theological Realism

The work of the French Jesuit cultural critic Michel de Certeau, while expressed in a more theoretical and abstract idiom than James Scott's,

---

76. Ibid., 77.

can help us to follow through the ways in which subjected parties may "use" the systems "imposed" upon them.[77] His famous distinction between "strategies" and "tactics" has been put to great use by Hauerwas in answering the recurrent charge of sectarianism.[78] However, my purpose here will be better served by using this distinction, along with a brief examination of other essential facets of Certeau's thought, in order to demonstrate something of how the practice of forgiveness may be seen as socially transformative.

Perhaps the most important distinction is between those forms of action that operate within a framework in which they are fully at home, i.e., strategies, and those practices of resistance that cannot claim their context as their own, i.e., tactics. Certeau's oft-cited and admirably clear definition deserves re-statement.

> I call a strategy the calculation (or manipulation) of power relationships that becomes possible as soon as a subject with will and power . . . can be isolated. It postulates a place that can be delimited as its own and serve as the base from which relations with an exteriority composed of targets or threats can be managed. . . . it is an effort to delimit one's own place in a world bewitched by the invisible powers of the Other.[79]

Indeed from this definition Certeau is able to identify certain characteristics of strategic logic that display an obvious kinship with Yoder's eschatological critique of modern technocratic notions of "systemic causal perspicuity." Strategic action represents the triumph of place over time and thereby is able to "transform the uncertainties of history into readable spaces."[80] In contrast to the *places* claimed by strategic action, tactical operations must be "calculated in the absence of a proper locus." These "arts of the weak" can only open up *spaces* within the frameworks defined by the strategist. Their impact is immediate and localized, their vision fragmented, even myopic by strategic standards. But, precisely as such, their enaction represents the triumph of time over place.

> [A] tactic is determined by the *absence of power* just as a strategy is organized by the postulation of power. . . . strategies pin their hopes on the resistance that the *establishment of a place* offers to

77. Certeau, *Practice of Everyday Life*, 18.
78. Hauerwas, AC, 15–18.
79. Certeau, *Practice of Everyday Life*, 35–36.
80. Ibid.

the erosion of time; tactics on a clever *utilization of time*, of the opportunities it presents and also of the play that it introduces into the foundations of power.[81]

In insisting that the Church acts tactically Hauerwas offers an important defense against the commonplace accusations of sectarianism. If the Church's acts are tactical then withdrawal is not an option—there is no possibility of a delineated place, in Certeau's sense, into which one may withdraw. Importantly, Certeau's own reflections on the presence of the Church also depend on these fundamental distinctions.[82] Sharply critical of the reformist stance taken by some influential Catholic theologians in response to an increasingly secularized modernity, Certeau asserted that the Church has become embroiled in an alien strategic rationality. It is now "easily manipulable by powers of another order."[83] The Church has been replaced by civil society "in the role of defining tasks and positions."[84] The production of social places is no longer the role of the Church.

Yet for Certeau this loss of the "ecclesial site" is not to be lamented, for it presents the Christian with the possibility of a more faithful appropriation of the theological moments of discipleship and repentance, of *nachfolge* and *metanoia*. In pointing to these two moments, Certeau characterizes Christianity not as a site, but as a direction, a movement to the outside—a "going beyond" toward the other. Yet unlike Derrida and much post-structuralist thought, it is not "the other" per se, as some abstracted notion of alterity, to which Certeau's Christianity is addressed. Just as for Yoder, it is only in particular experiences of concrete "others" that we can open up what Frederick Christian Bauerschmidt calls a "nonviolent discursive space."[85]

Equally, just as in Yoder, this orientation requires a commitment to explicit consideration of historiography. For Certeau it is the fragmented stories of the other, "heterologies," which can shed light on the strategic

---

81. Ibid., 38–39.

82. Interestingly, Hauerwas makes no explicit reference to Certeau's own theological discussions.

83. Certeau, "Weakness of Believing," 218.

84. Ibid., 227. It is worth noting that for Certeau this secular production of space begins as early as the thirteenth century, when the "hegemony of rationalism and scientism" emerges from a view of the world that "can no longer be read 'from the point of view of the divine.'" See Ward, "Michel de Certeau's 'Spiritual Spaces,'" esp. 429–30.

85. Bauerschmidt, "Abrahamic Voyage," 5.

operations that produce the "reality" we inhabit. The role of myth, fable, and story is central here. Certeau writes

> ... the "real" as represented by historiography does not correspond to the "real" that determines its production. It hides behind the picture of a past the present that produces and organizes it. ... this storytelling has a pragmatic efficacy. In pretending to recount the real, it manufactures it. It is performative. It renders believable what it says, and it generates appropriate action. ... the bewitching voices of the narration transform, reorient, and regulate the space of social relations.[86]

Certeau's constant drive towards "others" lead, both personally and intellectually, to a nomadic style that allows both critics and followers to identify a drift toward nihilism. This nomadic paradigm also impacts Certeau's reading of the relationship of the Christian to Christ. Jesus represents the "inaugurating rupture" that makes possible all further Christian praxis.[87] Yet it is the absence of the ascended Christ that makes room for the Christian movement. We encounter Christ only through texts. Yet in these texts "Jesus is the vanishing unknown factor." "The Bible passes by like a convoy of representations." The will to secure a singular timeless meaning in the texts is therefore deemed fetishistic. Certeau appeals for a diverse practice of reading that is based in the notion of writing as "a textual site of the non-site, it weaves alterities." [88]

Certeau appears to read the Constantinian role of the Church as the only possible continuation of a Christian communal space. The loss of such a role is therefore the demise of the ecclesial per se. This loss is itself deemed to be part of the (almost Hegelian) movement of the Spirit. For just as Christ "makes room" for the Spirit to found the Church, so the Church must "make room" for the Spirit to "go beyond" once more. Yet here Certeau appears almost tri-theistic. A more Trinitarian pneumatology would emphasize that in the moments of ascension and pentecost Christ *remains* present even as he is absent (cf. Matt 28:20). It is Christ's continued presence in the Spirit that is the ground of possibility for our participation in him. It is, contra Certeau, that participation, both individually and corporately, which constitutes the true ground for *tactical* Christian action.

86. Certeau, "History," 40–43.
87. Bauerschmidt, "Abrahamic Voyage," 12.
88. Certeau, "Weakness of Believing," 232–34.

Despite these shortcomings, Certeau provides us with a rich conceptual vocabulary in which to express the continued witness of the Church. It furnishes a notion of social action that can account for the true political import of Yoder's description of the "minority missionary" position. Fredrick Bauerschmidt summarizes this aspect of Certeau well:

> De Certeau's thinking is not so much utopian as it is *hetero*pian; it recognizes that there are within the arena defined by a societal grid, a multitude of *other* spaces constantly being produced by those who seize the incalculable opportunities offered by tiny deviation within a system of domination. What is *real* and what is possible cannot simply be defined by what falls within the panoptic gaze which defines a place. "Politics" for de Certeau must include not only the *polis* as defined by its planners and managers, but also the *polis* as it is "practiced" by its occupants.[89]

Doxology and the Tactical Performance of Forgiveness

By using this language we can express Yoder's vision of the Church as a community that opens up these heterological spaces as partial significations of the coming Kingdom. Indeed it is the presence of the Kingdom in Christ, and (through the continued presence of the Spirit) the Church's bearing witness to that presence, which provides the only "place" from which such spaces may be opened. As the atoning work of Christ reopened the space before the throne of God, so, in the Spirit, the Church is empowered to open spaces of witness to the cosmic importance of that work. I propose that it is in relation to the atoning work of Christ that we can bring together our considerations of how Yoder's theology goes beyond that of both Certeau and Girard. The rationalist limitations of Girard's account and the circumscription of ecclesial spaces in Certeau both arise from a failure to take seriously that which Yoder finds foundational—the ecclesial shape of present witness to the cosmic impact of Christ's work.

Yoder's refusal to treat witness and social change as separable and occasionally contradictory items on the Church's agenda is only sustainable if he is right about eschatology. The notion of "performative practices" with which we began this chapter can be happily combined with the categories of "tactic" and "space" in order to move beyond Girard's

---

89. Bauerschmidt, "Abrahamic Voayage," 9.

reading of the significance of Christ. In a culture still deeply ingrained with retributivist notions of punishment, the witness of the Church through reconciliatory practices is unlikely to have the effect of persuading sufficient numbers of people of the inappropriateness of expiatory demands. But, I suggest, forgiveness may better be seen as a *tactical subversion* of the hegemony of retribution. Indeed, as such it mirrors the claim made by Jesus in relation to the *lex talionis*. Forgiveness operates according to an innovative logic—a kenotic, gracious creativity, which opens up redemptive space within the balanced systems of equivalence and "just desserts."

The hope of social change is therefore a hope that waits upon and anticipates the inbreaking of the Kingdom. The partial prefiguring of that Kingdom must, it follows, proceed according to that gracious and creative logic found in Christ's atoning work. It is only in recognition of that pattern that the Church may both bear witness to the coming Kingdom, and participate in projects of social transformation. To extend a favored metaphor of Certeau's, that of the tactical as "poaching," to such basic theological categories, we can put the point thus: the poachers know a secret, albeit one that they persistently aim to disclose—that the landowner, the gentleman, is a usurper, for the land truly belongs to Christ, the master poacher. The tactical forays onto land governed through strategic logic represent the insurgency of the Kingdom—the eschatological in-breaking.

Eschatological patience is, for Yoder, a mode of action not an excuse for inaction. But that action is expressed not in strategic social programs, but in what I have described as tactical forays. Of course, Yoder would have been extremely cautious of the language of "tactic"—for any attempt to reduce the Church's ministry to such categories would carry with it precisely the sort of methodologistic restrictions he sought to avoid. Certeau's language is useful insofar as it demonstrates the way that what I have named "eschatological realism" may impact social programs. Nevertheless, Yoder's caution with regard to methodologistic absolutizing of any abstract modality is salutary in that it refuses the romanticizing valuation of the transgressive characteristic of Certeau's thought. Christ is, we might say, both the only order and the only transgression of the false orders of the principalities and powers. The supervenient category in Yoder's understanding of the place of the Church in relation to social change is, I suggest, not tactic, nor even "exile" (although this is extremely important as we shall see in the next chapter), but praise. The logic of social change is a logic of doxology.

As Dan Hardy and David Ford have shown, praise, as the responsive element of the ecology of blessing,

> is the comprehensive activity for man in relation to God.... It is through persisting simultaneously both in wholehearted praise ... and in the nurturing of human dignity that the most characteristic dynamics of Judaeo-Christian living are created and developed.... God's glory and his liberating action meet with our delighted surrender in love to him and to each other.[90]

They perceptively contrast a praise-centered vision of evangelism with a problem-centered approach, the latter being said to lack the "logic of overflow" that places "the problem" (in this case human sinfulness) in the wider perspective of the divine economy.[91] Remembering our discussion of Yoder's disavowal of quandaryism in ethical reflection, it seems fruitful to extend this contrast between "problem" and "praise" centered approaches to the issue of Christian social engagement. Hardy and Ford are perceptive in their identification of a pervasive stoicized Christianity that abstracts "freedom" from its basis in the joyful overflow of divine love and moralizes it into an abstract principle of human well-being, to be achieved by a stale and legalistic moral rectitude. The danger of this is clear.

> The nation-state is delighted to welcome a religion that is so timid and orderly, leaving the passions free for economics, war, and collective sport. In Britain today the civic religion might be described as a stoicism with Christian influence.[92]

To locate social transformation within doxology seems to provide a dramatically anti-stoic view. Indeed, it is from a stance of praise that those otherwise peculiar characteristics of radical Christian ethics are fully explicable. Once it is clear that the Christian life is responsive to a prior and prevenient divine initiative, then the complimentarity of the counsel for eschatological patience with supererogatory excess may be maintained—both "work" only in the economy of grace.

90. Hardy and Ford, *Jubilate*, 74, 77.
91. Ibid., 148ff.
92. Ibid., 144. This civic religion is, ironically, the reversal of the Troeltschean adoption of stoicism by the early church.

Doxology and the Re-Imagining of the Political

In what ways does the account of social transformation given above relate to other influential strands of theological reflection on politics? In order to assess this, we shall now briefly consider two important areas of modern political theology and social ethics: the "realism" associated with Reinhold Niebuhr, and the political radicalism collected around notions of theologies of liberation. Both deserve a more detailed and nuanced consideration than I can possibly give here. It will suffice for our present needs to consider each only in broad outline, and only in regard to aspects that directly impinge upon the account of social change given above.[93] I contend that in making doxology the supervenient category of a theology of social change Yoder is able to *redefine* notions of effectiveness in line with the economy of forgiveness and divine patience. Also, in focusing on notions of political action that privilege tactical modes, I suggest that Yoder's vision is able to offer a *reaffirmation* of central tenets of liberation theology.

Efficacy and Fidelity in the Constantinian Grid

Perhaps the easiest mistake to make in coming to an understanding of the doxological nature of Christian social transformation is to interpret it within the hermeneutical grid outlined in Weber, Troeltsch, and the Niebuhrs, which juxtaposes fidelity to the gospel with practical efficacy. Lamentably, such a move is common. It is based in a fundamentally different conception of power to that employed by Yoder. Real power, says Yoder, is power based in the lordship of Christ; it is diaconal and revolutionary. The locus of power is in obedience not dominion, "weakness" not coercion.[94] Such an assertion is central to our re-imagining of politics along christological lines, for such a re-imagined politics places

---

93. Excellent considerations of both schools are available. Langdon Gilkey's *On Niebuhr* and Robin Lovin's *Reinhold Niebuhr and Christian Realism* both provide a more positive and sympathetic reading than that given here. They are, however, perhaps overly-generous with regard to the weaknesses we are to note. One of Stanley Hauerwas's most sustained critiques of Niebuhr also repays close attention—*WGU*, 87–140. In relation to liberation theology I am sympathetic to the work of two of Hauerwas's pupils—Cavanaugh, *Torture and Eucharist*, and Bell, *Liberation Theology*. Needless to say, here as elsewhere, there is no replacement for sustained engagement with the primary texts themselves.

94. Yoder, *OR*, 166; cf. Hughes, "Ethical Use of Power."

both ruler and violent insurrectionist under the charge of perverse conceptions of power.

> To assume that "being politically relevant" is itself a univocal option so that in saying "yes" to it one knows where one is going, is to overestimate the capacity of "the nature of politics" to dictate its own direction. . . . Jesus's way is not less but more relevant to the question of how society moves than is the struggle for possession of the levers of command; . . . He refused to concede that those in power represent an ideal, a logically proper, or even an empirically acceptable definition of what it means to be political. He did not say (as some sectarian pacifists or some pietists might), "you can have your politics and I shall do something else more important"; he said, "your definition of polis, of the social, of the wholeness of being human socially, is perverted."[95]

This is not to say that concerns for effectiveness in ethical reasoning are inadmissible, for down that path lies the ivory tower! Rather, the predictive calculus on which patrician ethical deliberations rest is simply inadequate. As MacIntyre has shown, the concept of managerial effectiveness is a contemporary moral fiction, albeit a pervasive and broadly institutionalized one.[96] That is not to say it is entirely false, but rather that the degree of "effectiveness" claimed is both excessive and largely uncontested. The *modus operandi* of what Max Weber would have called "bureaucratic" or "legal-rational" authority has taken on an almost incontrovertible (even metaphysical) certainty. It is therefore only in those (ecclesial) communities where power is diaconal rather than bureaucratic and managerial in mode that the justification of moral authority is anything other than Weberian in form.[97]

The gracious work of the Spirit means that any description of politics that does not take some account of miraculous pneumatological empowering as pivotal to Christian moral agency and its relation to the politics of transformation is essentially sub-Christian.[98] To expect God to

---

95. Yoder, *PJ*, 106–7.
96. Macintyre, *After Virtue*, 88–108.
97. Ibid., 109.
98. Carter, *Politics of the Cross*, 162. Yoder's pneumatology exhibits the same paucity of detail and emphasis as much Western theology. However, his insistence on the consonance of the Spirit's acts with Jesus's nonviolence and his innovative refusal of any separation of justification and sanctification move in a direction that anticipates the strong valuation of the *material* work of the Spirit found in Eugene Rogers's excellent *After the Spirit*. I suggest it is precisely this refusal to separate justification and sanctification that prevents a

work through the ruler is, therefore, "to define what God wants by what it is possible for rulers to do."[99] In saying this Yoder is not advocating a pneumatological form of sectarian perfectionism. Yoder is not interested in providing an account of the possibility of a sinless Christian life, but rather in making an authentic Christian witness visible in history.[100]

It is here that we can finally begin to draw together some thematic strands from earlier chapters. It follows from our earlier discussion of "eschatological realism" that this visible witness provides the context for "ethical realism." The proper function of supposedly "utopian" visions is to bear witness to eschatological reality. Here we see once again Yoder's preference for the modes of praxis and witness over abstraction and apologetics.

> It is the function of minority communities to remember and to create utopian visions. There is no hope for society without an awareness of transcendence. Transcendence is kept alive not on the grounds of logical proof to the effect that there is a cosmos with a hereafter, but by the vitality of communities in which a different way of being keeps breaking in here and now.[101]

The restriction of Christian pacifism to the role of conscience-pricking idealism falls down precisely because it is unable or unwilling to view the cosmic claims made in eschatological realism as pertinent to ethical reasoning. The point is, one could say, related to fundamentally divergent understandings of divine providence. The Constantinian location of historical agency with the ruler (or, equally with the violent insurrectionist) fails to view the Kingdom as more than the sum of humanity's best historico-political insights, and thus fails to see God's self-revelatory act in Christ as offering a new account of history. At best, the eschatology behind such optimism is Hegelian inevitabilism. By contrast, for Yoder, the relationship of true social change, as based in diaconal authority, to

---

tritheistic inscription of sibling rivalry into the very being of God. The Spirit is not some irritating little sister hurrying along behind her brother and mimicking his actions. "The Spirit rests on material bodies in the economy, because she rests on the Son in the Trinity. . . . The Spirit's befriending of material bodies is her continual elaboration and crowning and consummation of the Incarnation, which is not the work of the Son only, but of the Father and the Spirit as well" (62).

99. Carter, *Politics of the Cross*, 161.

100. Yoder, "Anabaptist Dissent," esp. 58ff.

101. Yoder, *PK*, 94.

Doxology and Social Change

the coming of the Kingdom is characterized by the historical rupture inaugurated in Christ.

> The New Jerusalem is not produced by remodelling the Old in line with even the best contemporary insights. Our hope cannot be fully sublimated into affirmative expectations of the possibilities of the structure of society when properly used.[102]

For these reasons, I suggest that the account of the "multitude" proffered by Michael Hardt and Antonio Negri as the means for resisting "Empire" is insufficient.[103] Hardt and Negri's account runs parallel to that given here in numerous ways: the critique of the impoverished political imagination that conflates nation with community;[104] the isolation and privatization of public space, resulting in a hamstrung and enfeebled form of critical resistance;[105] the parasitic, indeed vampiric operation of Empire;[106] and the provision of an account of a transformative peoplehood arising in opposition to such predation.[107] Hardt and Negri are right, of course, to insist that "no effective blueprint [for a political alternative to Empire] will ever arise from a theoretical articulation such as [theirs]. It will arise only in practice."[108] The experimental emphasis is appealing,[109] but there is a reticence to describe even the basic complexion of such practices. Indeed the virtues and facets of this hoped-for resistance—a "being against" that is truly a "being for" love and community, the global citizenship of the free circulating multitude[110]—are conceived in such

---

102. Yoder, "Church and State," 287.
103. Hardt and Negri, *Empire*, and *Multitude*.
104. Hardt and Negri, *Empire*, 107.
105. Ibid., 188.
106. Ibid., 62. Hardt and Negri's account remains reductively bi-polar here. What they name as "Empire" would appear in the present analysis as one dominant modality of the rebellious principalities and powers.
107. I use the term "peoplehood" in order to make explicit the connection with Yoder's insistence on the need for a "particular peoplehood" in order to sustain witness without sliding into acculturation. *JCSR*, 152. In that sense it is far closer to Hardt and Negri's "universality of free and productive practices" named "multitude", than to the "organized [by Empire] particularity that defends established privileges and properties) denominated as a 'People.'" *Empire*, 316.
108. Hardt and Negri, *Empire*, 206.
109. Ibid., 411.
110. Ibid., 361–64.

amorphous language as to render them barely "practices" at all.[111] The rejection of teleology and substantive accounts of the "being for" results in an exclusive valorization of the negative moment in protest. While the rhetoric includes an impression of an advental, even kairotic emergence of the multitude, it is an event that is purely future—with no anticipatory or partial embodiment in contemporary practice. This rueful rhetoric in their critique of Empire is not the immanentized Augustinian alternative politics they claim it is; nor is it just, as Mitchell Cohen describes it, an "ontological tantrum"[112]; but also in fact a postmodern stoicism. Ironically perhaps, this is precisely the same failure exhibited in the "realism" of Niebuhr.[113]

Realism and Grace in Reinhold Niebuhr

Reinhold Niebuhr provided a naunced and forceful account of the relation of the coming Kingdom to social change. Yet I suggest that even Niebuhr's pessimistic anti-humanism eventually becomes, at key points, an unreconstructed liberal optimism. In order to demonstrate this it is necessary to examine the way that categories of tension and paradox determine Niebuhr's thought. In so doing we shall consider criticisms of Niebuhr made by both Yoder and Milbank. Despite its strengths, Milbank's account will be found wanting in ways that affect his own rejection of pacifism.

Simpler forms of Constantinian logic may be fundamentally mistaken in asserting a division between effectiveness and fidelity in the abstract, but this is a theological straw man. For both Niebuhr and Yoder there is no such thing as "effectiveness" or "fidelity" in the abstract. For both, fidelity is characterized by pacifism and powerlessness.[114] It is clear

---

111. The greater reflection on contemporary events and phenomena in *Multitude* does little to aid the substantiation of their account. Negri's *Politics of Subversion* provides further tantalizing hints, but never enough to gain a sense of the full flavor.

112. Cohen "An Empire of Cant." Ironically, Cohen's article strikes a somewhat exasperated tone. More significantly it proceeds, in part, from a far more sanguine account of the post-Westphalian nation-state than my account would wish to accommodate—see chapters 1 and 6.

113. It is noteworthy that both Niebuhr, and Hardt and Negri, turn to Augustine here. In actuality, I suspect, both are indebted to views in substantial variance with Augustine's intent—Niebuhr to Gelasian separations, and Hardt and Negri to an almost manichaeistic dualism.

114. It is to Yoder's credit that (unlike Milbank) he does not abstract methodological criticisms of the Niebuhrian juxtaposition from the context of Christian pacifism.

that Niebuhr, following Schweitzer, locates Jesus's pacifism within an imminent eschatological horizon and, in so doing, determines its impracticability for the construction of a cogent and efficacious Christian social ethic. Niebuhr affords a role to vocational pacifism as the presence of an idealistic critique, which is useful only as an ever-present corrective sign to the preferable mainstream just-war logic. The recognition of this role is based upon a prior concession by this pacifist minority of all claims to effectiveness.[115] It is this prior concession that Yoder simply cannot accept.

It is here that Niebuhr's Christology falls down. The cross itself, for Niebuhr, is a sign of the ineffectiveness of Jesus's messianic pacifism. In the cross we see "love triumphant in its own integrity," but this is not a triumph in the world or in society.[116] The cross is utterly ahistorical. Christ's victory over the powers does not yield a lordship in history. Indeed, Niebuhr provides a mythical reading of the resurrection that interprets the event as symbolic of the theological demand that "the superhistorical triumph of the good" must, in some way, "sublimate rather than annul" the processes of human history.[117] The consequences of this are dire. Niebuhr does not seem to be able to escape a docetic denial of Christ's humanity and thus cannot furnish an account of human moral action, which is graciously related to the divine economy.[118] Yoder expresses the problem thus:

> [Niebuhr] can consider forgiving grace as central in relation to our sinfulness, and enabling grace as only a temptation to pride. Whereas the Bible speaks of our "resurrection with Christ" as opening new ethical possibilities, grace is for Niebuhr primarily the way to have peace in spite of our continuing sin.[119]

With the recognition of the impossibility of nonviolent effectiveness comes the loss of discipleship.

Niebuhr's famous anthropological slant and his uncompromising rehabilitation of notions of original sin were undoubtedly apposite correctives to the liberal optimism of the Social Gospel. Nevertheless, the pattern of his thought may be characterized as a "hermeneutic of sinful reality" whose overarching categories (paradox, myth, and the impossible

---

115. Yoder, *CAW*, 350–51.
116. Yoder, "Reinhold Niebuhr," 109.
117. Niebuhr, *Nature and Destiny of Man*, 2:308. Cf. Gilkey, *On Niebuhr*, 217–22.
118. The docetism of Niebuhr is noted by Hays, *Moral Vision*, 218.
119. Yoder, "Reinhold Niebuhr," 115.

possibility) skew important theological themes. In particular this framework compromises much of the content of the theology of grace in which the doctrine of original sin finds its resolution. Niebuhr's separation of forgiveness and justice along the lines of an arbitrary division of the personal and the political is a case in point. His assertion that forgiveness represents one of many examples of the "impossible possibility" of Christian discipleship fails to follow the logic of reconciling grace wherein forgiveness is not only a therapy for individual guilt, but also aims at the healing of "the ruptured communion of original sin."[120]

Categories of paradox and tension abound in Niebuhr's writings. The tragic ambiguity of historical existence is based in the essential character of man as both free and, simultaneously, a slave to sin. The occasion for man's greatest possibilities resides in his creativity—yet it is also here that, in opposition to the purely positive reading of humanism, Niebuhr asserts this same human creativity as the occasion for the greatest sin.

> The fact that man can transcend Himself in infinite regression and cannot find the end of life except in God is the mark of his creativity and uniqueness; closely related to this capacity is his inclination to transmute his partial and finite self and his partial and finite values into the infinite good. Therein lies his sin.[121]

While human creativity is grounded in the transcendence of God, the hubristic tendencies of man nonetheless require that the resolution of original sin also depends largely on the historic mediation of grace. Arising from his anthropological bent, Niebuhr's construal of redeeming grace operates according to the same antinomy of fidelity and effectiveness, which he applies in his famous critique of pacifism.[122] There is, we might say, a privileging of common grace over special grace that relegates the latter to a peripheral and largely inconsequential role.

In order to see how this structure operates in Niebuhr, we begin with his notion of revelation. Unlike other supposedly "neo-orthodox" theologians, Niebuhr affirmed a strong and expansive notion of general

---

120. The phrase comes from Jones, *Embodying Forgiveness*, 267. For Niebuhr's explicit description of forgiveness along such lines, see Niebuhr, *Interpretation of Christian Ethics*, 233–47.

121. Niebuhr, *Nature and Destiny of Man*, 1:131.

122. The classic statement of this is, of course, Niebuhr, "Why the Christian Church Is Not Pacifist."

revelation.[123] He posits three universal elements to human experience: a sense of dependence on the ultimate source of being (note the parallels to the language of Schleiermacher and Tillich); a sense of moral obligation and personal unworthiness; and the longing for (though not the promise of) forgiveness. It is by dint of these persistent and universal experiences that we can know ourselves as creatures bound to sin yet dependent upon God (revealed as creator, judge, and redeemer, respectively). It is only through the special revelation of God in history, as expressed in biblical religion, that the assurance of forgiveness, and thus the completion of general revelation, can be obtained.[124]

Yet the division of general from special revelation runs, for Niebuhr, down the modernist fault line of private versus public.[125] The basic thesis of Niebuhr's *Moral Man and Immoral Society* also follows this pattern. For just as special revelation, when (in some way) operative in history, holds the key to the completion of general revelation, so that same sphere of operation—i.e., the public, historical, and political arena—displays the greatest opportunity for suasion to original sin. As we saw above in relation to the resurrection, Niebuhr's method for relating special to general revelation occurs through categories of myth and symbol.[126] Like Ernst Troeltsch before him, Niebuhr affirms the continued value of the mythic nature of religious language that is expressed in contradistinction to a naïve literalism. Religious myths are seen as the only way to convey within the limitations of human imagination, the otherwise inexpressible truths regarding the human condition that are the preserve of special revelation.[127]

It is in relation to Niebuhr's understanding of common grace that the antinomy of fidelity and effectiveness is fully inscribed into the substance

---

123. Gilkey gives an excellent account of this. Gilkey, *On Niebuhr*, 70–75.

124. Niebuhr, *Nature and Destiny of Man*, 1:154.

125. Ibid., 136.

126. Yet in his use of the terms Niebuhr exposes a contrast between the way this vocabulary functions in modern and postmodern idioms. Niebuhr's modern understanding is unlike the reading of those categories provided by the likes of Certeau, which largely maintains a connection, however vague, to the realist connotation of the narrative content of myth.

127. On Niebuhr's relation to Troeltsch on this point see Hauerwas, *WGU*, 108–10. Especially interesting is the speculation that the genealogy for such a notion runs through the dissertation produced on Troeltsch by Reinhold's brother H. Richard. Hauerwas does not connect the role of myth to the understanding of special and general revelation.

of ethical reality itself. The grace exhibited in common life corresponds to the form of consciousness of sin made available in general revelation. Common grace therefore refers to the providential orderings of history and social structure in which politics is able to pursue justice and achieve a "tolerable balance of egoisms." It is, then, not special grace but common grace that guarantees that the thesis of *Moral Man and Immoral Society* will not always hold true to the same degree. Divine providence can and does order the idolatry of self-love towards the common good.[128] By contrast, the special grace in which Jesus's ethic of non-resistance and forgiveness is based can only be mediated to the present by means of the suppression of its cosmic and ontological claims. Pacifism and accounts of forgiveness are vocational positions, charged with bearing witness to the symbols of the supra-historical triumph of the good. They are only admissible under the guise of idealistic and utopian banner of the "impossible possibility."

Yoder's position offers a stringent denial of this overarching antinomy. He contends that the ethics of responsibility renders grace as a "purely forensic justification by faith" that ratifies intentional compromises made because of our inability to be perfect. It is Bonhoeffer's cheap grace, Paul's "sinning that grace may abound."[129] Redemption, for Yoder, is ethical; it is related to a concept of forgiving, empowering grace. This notion of grace is manifest in a diaconal understanding of power, a refusal of violence as a justifiable means to a "good" end, and an understanding of Christian ethical agency as patient participation in the divine economy.[130] "The relation between our obedience and the achievement of God's purposes stands in analogy to the hidden lordship of Him who was crucified and raised."[131]

This is not, of course, to say that Yoder renders consequentialist reasoning a priori inadmissible in Christian morality. Rather he subordi-

---

128. Gilkey, *On Niebuhr*, 205–13.

129. Yoder, "Anabaptist Dissent," 60.

130. "That lordship is servanthood, that he who empties himself unto death is elevated to the right hand of the Father, is not a gnostic redemption cult historicized, it is the career of YHWH's Servant doxologized. It constitutes within real human history a concrete (civil!) alternative both to the world-dominating claims of Cyrus (or Ceasar) and the righteous zeal of the Maccabees. This is not political language being used metaphorically to describe spiritual transcendence or quietism. It is a concretely alternative way to be God's Servant, in both corporate and individual personhood." Yoder, *FTN*, 86.

131. Yoder, *OR*, 160.

nates such methods to the divine economy. I demonstrated in chapter 3 that the claims of Christology and eschatology are the "realities" that remain determinative for Christian ethics. For Yoder, what is "effective" is to be judged by those standards. We then saw how the Church participates in and bears witness to those realities by virtue of its analogical public practices. It is the Church that may demonstrate the anachronistic nature of Niebuhr's division of common and special grace. Niebuhr's lack of any substantive ecclesiology leaves him without any means to escape, or bring to an end, the tragic necessity of the coercive nation-state.[132] The doxological life of the Church is the setting within which the present workings of grace can be rendered intelligible (while remaining inscrutable).

> It is . . . a misperception when radicals, responding to the way issues have been put by Tolstoy and by Niebuhr, tend to concede that this ethic of "obedience" sacrifices "effectiveness." It does reject some ways of deriving ethics from effectiveness calculation, but it represents a commitment to and not against long and broad usefulness.[133]

A similar line of argument is pursued by John Milbank. In arguing that the "realities" that are normative for Niebuhr are determined by their own language and rhetoric, Milbank tacitly links Niebuhr with the fundamental error of Weberian sociology—a spurious promotion of the secular culture of modernity with its denial of the possibility of substantive norms that allow one to discriminate just from unjust power.[134] Here there is, for Milbank, a tendency for Niebuhrian "Christian realism" to shift from anti-liberalism to liberal optimism.[135] Because Niebuhr remains a child of the enlightenment rationalism that assumed a "reality" independent of theology, to which theological ethicists bring their insights, he ends up "betraying the entire Christian reading of history."[136]

---

132. Yoder claims that, in failing to consider the ethical importance of the Church, "the thesis of *Moral Man and Immoral Society* falls down in the crucial case, the only one which is really decisive for Christian ethics." "Reinhold Niebuhr and Christian Pacifism," 115.

133. Yoder, *PK*, 99.

134. Milbank, *TST*, 75–100.

135. A parallel argument, that Niebuhr remains individualistic in his theology, and takes insufficient account of the realities made possible by life in the Spirit, is advanced by Colin Gunton in "Reinhold Niebuhr."

136. Milbank, *WMS*, 250ff.

Niebuhr's anthropological slant takes for granted a pagan affirmation of original, permanent, and insoluble conflict. In this his Hobbesianism extends to his social anthropology. The alternative to this conflict is, as one would expect from Milbank, an Augustinian affirmation of fundamental created goodness that is able to see love as "the original law of human social being."[137]

In very different ways both Niebuhr and Milbank owe the structural oppositions around which their theologies are constructed to that basic division delineated by Augustine as the *civtas dei* and the *civitas terrena*. Niebuhr assembles his theology of social structures around a paradoxical and dialectical opposition of eternity and time, the transcendent God and his creation. Milbank constructs his theology of social structures around an ontological division of the two cities. If Yoder's insistence on the socially-transformative nature of the stance of doxological politics is to hold, then such a dualism must be replaced with a more dynamic reading of the state's relation to the lordship of Christ.[138] Yoder's own distinction between Church and world in terms of the eschatological horizon does not trade off rhetorical dichotomies of time from eternity, and visibility from invisibility on the one hand, or impossibility from possibility, love from justice, ideal from "real" on the other.

I suggest that Yoder's reading of eschatology, empowering grace, and the nature of social transformation is preferable to that present in either Milbank or Niebuhr. We have seen how Yoder's critique of Niebuhr proceeds on the basis of a more satisfactory theology of grace. I suggest that, precisely in the pacifism Milbank rejects, Yoder is able to furnish an account of the importance of historical action that better fits the biblical

---

137. Ibid., 237, 252 n. 10.

138. While Yoder's understanding of Augustine's intent is not always fair, he identifies a danger in Augustinain neo-platonism. In relation to the role of the Bible as a power for civil change, Yoder says of Augustine's neo-platonism, "the canonical-critical thrust is narrowed when, as we have done it in the West from Augustine through Luther and Pietism to Kierkegaard, Bultmann, and Billy Graham, its focus is upon a righteousness which is *coram Deo*, in 'the heart,' and not 'merely' civil. That narrowing is however, potentially, if not necessarily, a betrayal. When systematized, it sets up as a screen between us and the text the Neoplatonic scheme according to which the opposite of the city of God is the earthly city; i.e., God is located and works in an *other* world. . . . The narrowing of the Augustinian agenda may be of some use . . . . to warn against self-righteousness. . . . it may refine in a salutary way our expectations of direct relevance. Yet it becomes a betrayal when it denies that the newness of the gospel can take on flesh. . . . The Neoplatonic dualism between inner and outer or between spirit and matter usually serves to defend religious establishment against this-worldly criticism." Yoder, *FTN*, 79–93, 82–84.

understanding of eschatological patience.[139] To circumvent this dynamic, as Milbank does, through bi-polar ontological categories, renders his system insensitive to the interplay of old and new aeons found in the Pauline theology of the principalities and powers. It is not, in the end, the ontological distinction between earthly violence and heavenly peace *simpliciter* that imperils the practicability of Milbank's schema, but the unanimous identification of the secular with an ontology of violence, rather than a realm of *varying degrees of* (but not yet total) subjection to the lordship of Christ—i.e., a *saeculum*—that which is (in the process of) passing away. In Milbank there is little sense of the providential ordering of the principalities and powers in the time of eschatological tension. To rule out, a priori, on such grounds, the varying degrees of collaboration, prophetic critique, and intercommunal discourse available to the Church can only have a stultifying effect on the socially-transformative re-imagining of politics.

Reaffirming Liberation Theology

Before we turn to Yoder's theology of the state it is necessary to consider his relation to one other school of theological reflection on the poltical order—liberation theology. Just as we can best understand the "realism" of Niebuhr when we view it as a responsive moment set over against the liberal optimism of the "Social Gospel," so I propose that that broad and diverse range of theologies grouped together under the term "liberation theology" might also be most efficiently described, at least for our concerns, as responsive.[140] The orientation of liberation theologies toward praxis is well known. Indeed, this impatience with abstraction marks one of many clear parallels with Yoder's own work. A fuller comparative account would also point to the commonality between the two visions in their commitment to the contextual (ecclesial) vocation of the theologian; or to the development of liberationist reflection on Latin American "base communities" as representing a significant instantiation of, for want of a better term, a more "protestantized" notion of radical ecclesial exis-

---

139. On the essentially patient character of Yoder's schema, see *PMMR*.

140. In thus labeling these theologies "responsive" I mean no pejorative implication. Quite the converse, for, as I showed in relation to Yoder's conception of the ecclesial vocation of the theologian, the responsive (as opposed to the "reactionary") mode is not only fitting, but essential to the nature of theological discourse.

tence.[141] However, for the sake of brevity I shall begin by focusing on an area of divergence between liberation theology and the theology of social change advocated here. It is liberation theology's origins in response to what is often described as the theology of New Christendom that is most pertinent to our present purposes.

Faced with a series of disastrous alliances with confessional political parties at the beginning of the twentieth century, Pope Pius XI famously advocated a withdrawal of the Roman Catholic church from direct political involvement in favor of participation in the social sphere.[142] Through this "social Catholicism," especially seen in the development of the "Catholic Action" initiative, Pius XI hoped to reconstruct a Christian social order through the spiritual formation of Christian citizens.[143] The theological principles undergirding this were most strongly articulated by the French Catholic philosopher Jacques Maritain. For Maritain, the church is to exercise only "indirect" power, thereby respecting the autonomy of the temporal realm while simultaneously maintaining the superiority of the spiritual.[144] By eschewing the notion of direct power, and with it the model of Christendom, Maritain claimed to free Christianity from a purely instrumental view of the temporal. Politics, which is to be exclusively associated with the operations of the state, is finally recognized to possess an integrity for its own sake.

In the New Christendom, the role of the Church was largely "spiritual"—not in the ethereal, privatized, and individualized sense which dominates contemporary usage, but, more specifically as the supra-temporal space of ultimate values. These values impact "indirectly" upon the social. Thus Maritain's axiomatic distinction of the temporal and spiritual planes led him to make a further division between acting as a "Christian as such" engaged in Christ's church on the spiritual plane, and

141. "Protestantized" is Yoder's description here. See Yoder, "Wider Setting of Liberation Theology," 286. On this issue, see also Boff, *Ecclesiogenesis*. For other reflections on liberation theology, see Yoder, "Biblical Roots of Liberation Theology," "Withdrawal and Diaspora," and "Orientation in Midstream."

142. The enaction of concordats to that effect with first Mussolini in 1929, and then Hitler in 1933, are, of course, the subject of great notoriety. I will not comment here on the vexed questions and speculative historical moralizing that so often accompanies discussion of these unfortunate moves.

143. I am indebted to the excellent account of the history of Catholic Action provided in Cavanaugh, *Torture and Eucharist*, 123–50.

144. Maritain, *Things That Are Not Caesar's*; see also Cavanaugh, *Torture and Eucharist*, 155–99.

acting "as Christian" (but not as church) in order to infuse the temporal world with values.¹⁴⁵ The intention behind making such divisions explicit was to extricate the Church from the encumbrances of partisan alliances by affirming a dual role for the Church in relation to the social order; it is to evangelize and to inspire the temporal, but not to intervene.¹⁴⁶

Many genealogies of liberation theology correctly note the progressive impact that occurred in the development of Social Catholicism as it moved away from the previous endorsement of (usually rather conservative) politics.¹⁴⁷ Yet growing dissatisfaction arose as the reformist policies often advocated by New Christendom's adherents presided over dramatic increases in inequality. The moderacy engendered in the affirmation of the Church as the supra-temporal soul of human society could not accommodate the irruptive presence of greater consciousness of poverty and injustice, and the disquieting affirmation of a "preferential option" for the poor that followed from it. However, contrary to the less-than-favorable stereotype, the radicalism with which liberationists attempted to replace ineffective reformism was not commonly a counsel for armed insurrection. While some, like the Colombian guerrilla priest Camilo Torres, famously issued a call to armed revolutionary struggle, most liberation theologians do not advocate such measures. Torres is no more determinative for liberation theologians on this issue than Thomas Müntzer is for the Anabaptists. Yet it would be going too far to claim any explicit correspondence between liberation theology's variegated stance on the issue of revolutionary violence and Yoder's pacifism.

Nonetheless, in pointing to the circumscribed reaffirmation of liberation theology in his work I seek to avoid any dubious association of Yoder with the criticisms of Latin American liberation theology made by "the North Atlantic non-pacifist churchman, who is more critical of insurrectionist regimes than of colonial administrations and more critical of revolutionary minorities than of the national histories of their own countries."¹⁴⁸ Such an identification would be dramatically misleading.

---

145. Maritain, *Integral Humanism*, 294, as cited in Cavanaugh, *Torture and Eucharist*, 167.

146. Gutiérrez, *Theology of Liberation*, 64.

147. E.g., ibid., 52–61; Bell, *Liberation Theology*, 45–51; Sigmund, *Liberation Theology at the Crossroads*, 28–39.

148. Yoder, *CAW*, 534. It is questionable whether Yoder himself manages to fully escape such a bias. Joel Zimbleman accuses Yoder of insufficiently distancing himself from a strictly positivist formulation of legitimate government. Joel Zimbleman, "Theological

Yoder opposes "revolution" in the sense of violent insurrection, for it remains profoundly optimistic about a Constantinian method of incarnating the Kingdom in a political program. The term "revolution" in this sense remains, despite its semantic coincidence, the practical opposite of "revolutionary subordination." There is an important distinction to be made between theologies of revolution and theologies of liberation. The difference, for Yoder, permeates to the level of basic theological orientation:

> . . . focusing on the moral imperative of revolution is dysfunctional. It shifts attention from the realness to a possible extreme case, concluding that a violent insurrection should almost be the normal thing to plan for. . . . Why is "liberation" a better way to say "revolution"? It points to the broader values that you are concerned about, not only to a change of regime. It says that what you want is that people can be free, not simply that you get rid of the bad guy.[149]

Yet if we follow Gustavo Gutiérrez's critique of Maritain we can note an important divergence with the understanding of social change advocated here. That difference relates to the political nature of the Church. For Gutiérrez, at least in *A Theology of Liberation*, Maritain's schema is blighted by the continued presence of an "ecclesiastical narcissism."[150] The very same affirmation of a supra-temporal church, which for Maritain in the 1930s and 1940s had been an attempt to mobilize a less conservative form of Catholicism, had by the 1960s become a means of curbing more radical engagement.[151] The failure of Maritain is not found in his affirming the autonomy of the temporal too strongly, but rather in undermining this autonomy through a continued commitment to the Christianization of society.

Here Gutiérrez points to the progress of secularization in order to affirm the omnipresence of God's grace within the world. This in turn

---

Ethics," 288–89. It will become apparent in chapter 6 that Yoder, in disallowing any attack on a government's legitimacy, may appear to justify state coercion while ruling out revolutionary violence. Such a conclusion would, however, be rather too hasty. I am sympathetic to Zimbleman's concern, but suggest that, despite some ambiguity, Yoder does not privilege state violence over revolutionary violence in such a way as to render the overturning of a particular regime on Christian grounds impossible.

149. Yoder, *CAW*, 523.
150. Gutiérrez, *Theology of Liberation*, 55.
151. Ibid., 65.

leads to two emphases—one with which we can speculate Yoder would largely have concurred, and the other which is entirely inimical to the properly missiological ecclesiocentrism that pervades Yoder's theology. I suggest that both Gutiérrez (and other liberation theologians) and Yoder can accommodate within their ecclesiology the essential motif of the Christ's identification with the "underside of history." For Yoder, the "preferential option for the poor" would be a strong indication of God's providential act of calling his Church to greater faithfulness. Gutiérrez comes close to this in reflecting on the documents of the second Vatican council:

> The document issues a call for collaboration between believers and non-believers in the "just upbuilding of this world in which they live in common." It is a world that is different from, but that need not be hostile to, the church. It is a world in which Christ is present and active, and it is from outside itself, from the world, that he calls the Christian community, too, to the gospel.
> . . . what is ultimately important is not that the church be poor, but that the poor of this world be the people of God—that disquieting witness of a God who liberates.[152]

Here we see the valuable corrective element of Gutiérrez's identification of "ecclesiastical narcissism." The heart of the objection is that Maritain's distinction of the planes privileges Christ's headship of the Church to the exclusion of his lordship over history; the former thereby being regarded as the sole category of Christian social transformation. Behind the slogan of a "preferential option for the poor" lies a commitment to the fact that Christ's lordship over history is discernible only from the position of the outcast and the underdog. With this Yoder would have been in full agreement. Thus Yoder affirms that "no biblically-oriented theology can fail in some sense . . . to be a theology of liberation."[153]

Yet there is a danger of what we might call a "secularized supersessionism" in the language Gutiérrez's employs to make his point. That is to say, the identity of the poor *as such* as the "people of God" is expressed in language that implies a discrete election and promise independent of the mission of the Church. Thus Gutiérrez ends up operating with a twofold theology of grace that radically bisects the mutually inherent

---

152. Gutiérrez, *Power of the Poor*, 211. That the Church of the poor is the "true church" is expounded in greater sophistication in Sobrino, *The True Church*.
153. Yoder, "Biblical Roots of Liberation Theology," 68.

claims that Christ is head of the Church *and* lord of history. There is a fundamental collapse of the distinction between Church and world in which each, in its own special way, is fully graced. This, of course, Yoder would never accept.

Here Yoder would have much more in common with both John Milbank and the work of two commentators on liberation theology who have emerged from Hauerwas's tutelage—William Cavanaugh and Daniel Bell Jr. Milbank objects to Gutiérrez's reliance on the Rahnerian understanding of grace (which we encountered in our discussion of public theology in our second chapter), which thus attributes to the social sphere a form of grace that requires any theology of social change to be founded upon pre-theological sociology.[154] Equally, both Cavanaugh and Bell identify the importance for liberation theology to acknowledge the resources for social critique internal to ecclesial practices. Bell advocates a recovery of practices of penance as part of a wider rehabilitation of the "politics of forgiveness." Only such a politics can provide liberation theology with the resources it needs to counter the capitalist "technology of desire."[155]

In his reflections on the Church in Pinochet's Chile, William Cavanaugh sounds a thoroughly Yoderian note when he asserts:

> The church must see that its own disciplinary resources—Eucharist, penance, virtue, works of mercy, martyrdom—are not matters of the soul which may somehow "animate" the "real world" of bodies, but are rather body/soul disciplines meant to produce actions, practices, habits that are visible in the world.[156]

Cavanaugh goes on to explore the way in which the Eucharist represents a counter-politics to the torture of the Pinochet regime. Torture and Eucharist are, for Cavanaugh, read as opposing arcane disciplines: the former being "an anti-liturgy for the realization of the state's power on the bodies of others," while the latter is a "liturgical realization of Christ's suffering and redemptive body in the body of His followers."[157] The socially

---

154. Milbank, *TST*, 407–8.

155. Bell, *Liberation Theology*.

156. Cavanaugh, *Torture and Eucharist*, 197.

157. Ibid., 206. Cavanaugh does not refer to Bonhoeffer's discussion when designating both torture and Eucharist as *disciplinae arcanorum*. However, Bonhoeffer's sense of these practices as taking place in private—and of that privacy empowering those engaging in the practice to continue in the mission of their community—give an appropriate complexion

transformative nature of Eucharistic practice is seen in stark contrast to the practice of torture.

> Torture creates fearful and isolated bodies, bodies docile to the purposes of the regime; the Eucharist effects the body of Christ, a body marked by resistance to worldly power. Torture creates victims; Eucharist creates witnesses, martyrs. Isolation is overcome in the Eucharist by the building of a communal body which resists the state's attempts to disappear it.
>
> Perhaps most importantly, the eschatological imagination of the Eucharist overcomes the secular imagination of separate spiritual and temporal planes which abetted the regime's disciplining of the body politic.[158]

Cavanaugh emphasizes that the Eucharist is the imagination of the Church, not in the sense that Christians constitute the Church by their imaginative acts (for that surely is the work of the Spirit), but rather "[t]he Eucharist is God's imagination of the church; we participate in that imagination insofar as we are imagined by God, incorporated into the body of Christ through grace."[159] In Cavanaugh's account the Eucharist functions as the archetypal sacrament, the paradigm of doxological practice. The re-imagining of the political that takes place in the doxological life of the Christian community is part of that same imaginative apprehension of the divine that is the very nature of revelation.[160]

In his discussion of the imaginative nature of ecclesial politics Cavanaugh brings to expression an important element of what I describe as the doxological relocation of social transformation. Yet it is also important to stress that, for Yoder, non-ecclesial practices of protest and dissent may also disclose something of the way God is reconciling the world to himself. Certain kinds of protest and civil disobedience also operate "with the grain of the cosmos." Nevertheless, the degree to which Yoder

---

to the verb "scripting"—i.e., the movement from definitive practice to the definitive narrative implied in the rendering of persons as the object of the verb.

Insofar as Cavanaugh's recognition of torture as an anti-liturgy is, at least implicitly, able to accommodate the insight that such practices may be designated as rites of the idolatry of the principalities and powers, it is preferable to Catherine Pickstock's lamentation of early-modernity as the loss of doxology and liturgy in the realm of culture. See Pickstock, *After Writing*.

158. Cavanaugh, *Torture and Eucharist*, 206.

159. Ibid., 272–73.

160. For an account of how it is through the imagination that one is "brought into living contact with" God, see Avis, *God and the Creative Imagination*.

is able to justify such practices is ambiguous. Joel Zimbleman is right to highlight the shift in Yoder's vocabulary from the traditional Mennonite category of "non-resistance" to "nonviolent resistance." There is indeed a development in Yoder's thinking towards a greater diversity of means in which "the Christian might expansively express a life of redemptive engagement and witness."[161] Regrettably, the division of violence from coercion and of coercion from force are never fully explicated by Yoder.[162] Zimbleman rightly objects that these terminological differences are more than semantic.[163] The terminological shift (which, contra Zimbleman, was far from epochal, and never fully consistent) represents a willingness to admit that "coercion—short of violence, lethal or nonlethal—may be used by the Christian to effect a dynamic witness independent of the goal of attaining certain ends."[164]

For Yoder, activities such as strikes and demonstrations (insofar as they are intent on the disruption of the legitimate functioning of society or even the destruction of the fabric of society) are likened to a form of warfare, and are therefore to be rejected.[165] Yoder's advocacy of nonviolent action is determined by his critique of criteria of efficacy and his insistence that the relation of the Church to the world always involves ad hoc engagements as opposed to optimistic and programmatic strategies. Indeed, civil disobedience is emphatically not a "war without violence." Against what one could call a nonviolent version of Clausewitz, Yoder is quite clear that the definition of what constitutes proper civil disobedience must remain open:

> By the nature of the case, the concept of civil disobedience cannot be self-defining. It designates a response to a particular demand of a particular governmental authority, because the person who would ordinarily be willingly subject to that authority holds its dictates to be overruled by a higher power.[166]

---

161. Zimbleman, "Contribution of John Howard Yoder," 388.

162. There are specific attempts to define violence in appropriate fashions for ascertaining what it is about "violence" that requires theological critique—e.g., violence is wrong because "the majesty of the creator God is under attack," etc. See Yoder, "Theological Critique of Violence."

163. Zimbleman, "Theological Ethics," especially 300–314.

164. Zimbleman, "Contribution of John Howard Yoder," 388.

165. Yoder, *FTN*, 116–19. See also A. E. Weaver, "After Politics."

166. Yoder, "Foreword to 'Symposium on Civil Disobedience,'" 889. See also Shaffer, *Moral Memoranda*, 46–49.

Thus for Yoder the symbolic politics of civil disobedience is only the tip of the iceberg. The social impact of these apparently sporadic activities is largely dependent upon the "size of the hidden bloc below the surface." That is to say, it requires a principled, even a routinized, readiness to adopt a position of resistance. For Yoder, a pragmatic commitment to "effective" nonviolence is insufficient for this need, because it inscribes a problematic distinction between "moral" and "practical" rejections of violence. There must, therefore, be a discerning community able to sustain a nonviolent struggle for liberation through its willingness to suffer apparent defeat for the sake of its cause.[167] For, as we saw above, from the apparent defeat of the cross God, through the resurrection, vindicates Christ's peaceable mission. It is fundamental to Yoder's account that he distinguishes between subordination and obedience. Some forms of civil disobedience are permissible but subordination always remains a duty. In an unpublished paper Yoder outlines some preconditions for authentic protest. Protest is based in the revelation of the God of Israel (not the abstract god of the philosophers); it requires a committed community to sustain that protest in their life together; and it requires a non-sectarian mission to the wider world.[168] The conscientious objector remains subordinate to the state, insofar as in their refusal to participate in state-sanctioned violence they accept the penalties that the government imposes.

> The willingness to suffer is then not merely a test of our patience or a dead space of waiting; it is itself a participation in the character of God's victorious patience with the rebellious powers of his creation. We subject ourselves to government because it was in so doing that Jesus revealed and achieved God's victory.[169]

This leads to a fundamentally pragmatic and positive account of certain forms of protest. When action for social change is *relocated* in the horizon of doxology, authentic protest is possible. Practically there can be no distinction, at least no distinction of kind, between sacrament and political declaration.[170] Ultimately, fraternal admonition and the politics

---

167. Yoder, "Church and Change," 15–17. Yoder repeats the point elsewhere—e.g., "The believing community as an empirical social entity is a power for change. To band together in common dissidence provides a kind of social leverage that is not provided by any other social form." *PK*, 91.

168. Yoder, "Christianity and Protest in America."

169. Yoder, *PJ*, 209.

170. Yoder, "Sacrament as Social Process," in *RP*, 359–73.

of Martin Luther King Jr. are of the same type of action.[171] Both operate within the claims of Christ's lordship expressed in the worship of the Christian community. In both, we can detect both the *redefinition* of effectiveness according to the divine economy of patience, and the circumscribed *reaffirmation* of liberation theology that are described above. We now turn to a discussion of the consequences this central proclamation of the Church has for contemporary understandings of the nature of the state and the practices of government.

---

171. On Yoder's appreciation of Martin Luther King Jr., see for example "The Power Equation," in *FTN*, 125–47.

CHAPTER 6

Eschatology, Exile, and Election:
A Theology of Governmental Power With and Beyond Yoder

"On all sides pundits proclaim that the nation-state is in trouble. The truth is, it has been in trouble ever since Christ rose from the dead."

—Oliver O'Donovan[1]

"My point is not that everything is bad, but that everything is dangerous, which is not exactly the same as bad. If everything is dangerous, then we always have something to do. So my position leads not to apathy but to hyper- and pessimistic activism."

—Michel Foucault[2]

THREE MOMENTS IN A THEOLOGY OF GOVERNMENTAL POWER

In previous chapters I have demonstrated how practices of Christian dissent, in following an analogical pattern and affirming the concrete importance of the confession of Christ's lordship over history, are among the primary means of affirming the public nature of theological discourse. We now turn to perhaps the second most significant subject of properly Christian dissent (the first being the Church itself)—the exercise of

1. O'Donovan, *DN*, 241.
2. Foucault, *Ethics, Subjectivity and Truth*, 256.

governmental power. It is important to note at the very outset that the orientation of the prophetic community towards the exercise of governmental power is substantially broader than any theological reflection on the nature and role of the state.

We have begun to see how the "eschatological realism" outlined earlier impacts an understanding of social change. We have also noted how the language of diaspora citizenship became central to Yoder's expression of the public presence of the Church. I now suggest that these two facets of Yoder's theology, the eschatological and exilic motifs, denote two essential elements for our present reflections: two panels of a theological triptych of governmental power. I will then claim that Michel Foucault gives us resources for understanding what non-Constantinian forms of political critique might look like, before showing how Yoder intimates toward a third panel (which remained largely tacit)—election. But to merely exposit parallels between two "thinkers" is neither useful nor interesting—the thrust of the argument is not to explore the commonalities between Yoder's theology and Foucault's political thought,[3] but to show

3. A note of caution should begin this chapter. Both Yoder and Foucault defy easy categorization or summary; reading either is (or can be) a deeply unsettling experience; neither scholar was particularly interested in producing a systematized corpus of publications or saw their vocation as primarily or exclusively "academic." If by "academic" we mean to evoke the fully pejorative sense of the term—something oriented to the construction or refurbishment of ivory towers—the picture is, of course, a stereotype; but it may still be a useful fiction against which to set oneself. Foucault famously railed against the limitations of academic discourse: "I would like my books to be a kind of tool-box which others can rummage through to find a tool which they can use however they wish in their own area . . . I would like the little volume that I want to write on disciplinary systems to be useful to an educator, a warden, a magistrate, a conscientious objector. I don't write for an audience, I write for users, not readers." Foucault, "Prisons et asiles dans le mécanisme du pouvoir," in *Dits et Ecrits t.II*, 523–24. Yoder's strong sense of the ecclesial vocation of the theologian likewise led him to assert the "subservience [of theology] to particular issues and needs, which may make it a luxury to find time for elegance and roundness . . . the vision of the *ecclesia viatorum* does account properly for a permanently fragmentary quality in what needs to be done by the ministry of teaching." Yoder, *RP*, 121.

So let me be clear—I do not propose to undertake anything so daunting, or so contrary to the self-perception of Yoder or Foucault as a synthesis or a staged "dialogue." I merely wish to add one more brief contribution to the small number of scholarly engagements with these two figures that identify quite particular elements of common ground, or fruitful contrasts. It is nearly a decade since David Toole drew the fascinating contrast between the tragic politics of Foucault and the apocalyptic account in Yoder referred to in the last chapter. Other scholars have given us a useful comparison of Yoder's account of particularity in moral discourse with Foucault's work—e.g., Blum, "Foucault, Genealogy, Anabaptism"—or have engaged with Foucault's exploration of *parrhesia* (truthful speech) from Yoderian starting-points—e.g., Huebner, *Precarious Peace*; Hovey, "Free Christian

how Yoder and Foucault may both help the Church to be "more truly political . . . more properly ordered community, than is the state."[4] Thus I shall show how the three panels of this triptych impact the claims and concerns that orient contemporary political theory—thus eschatology will be shown to offer a critique of notions of legitimacy; exile brings into question excessive concerns with governmental sovereignty; and election contrasts with the pathological tendencies in modern Western notions of voluntariety as the key to popular sovereignty.[5]

In naming these three moments it should become clear how the account of governmental power given in this chapter requires and builds upon the arguments of previous chapters. Thus the eschatological realism defined in chapter 3 is seen here in its ability to "demythologize" our understanding of the nature and purpose of governmental claims to sovereignty. The ecclesiological moments of chapter 4—restitutionist historiography, a stress on the "otherness" of the Church, and the social critical role of ecclesial practices—come together in the motif of exilic (diaspora) citizenship. The exposition of the doctrine of election then builds upon the tactical and doxological character of social change outlined in the previous chapter.

Speech: Plundering Foucault." With these I am in broad agreement. However, I will argue that such parallels and contrasts must be supplemented by an analysis of the theology of witness and Christian political critique in a setting that Yoder might have described as neo-neo-neo-neo-neo-Constantinianism; and which Foucault, perhaps more elegantly, names the "era of governmentality." Of course, Yoder's own typology of ever variant forms of "Constantinianism" ran to four "neo's"; by adding a fifth I hope to show that Yoder's account of Constantinianism is applicable to Christian responses to exercises of governmental power other than the few forms he mentions. See Yoder, "Constantinian Sources," in *PK*, 135–47.

4. Yoder, *CWS*, 17.

5. Given Yoder's concern for the partial and fragmentary nature of theology, it may be as well for me to indicate that in outlining a threefold theology in response to three aspects of modern political theory I do not claim any completeness. Indeed the reason why I think a schema of eschatology, exile, and election is helpful is that these motifs all militate against false resolutions and completeness. Modern political theory seeks to contain politics within the three concerns mentioned—it locates legitimacy in the exercise of sovereign power in a way that flows from and itself enables the negative freedom of the self-possessing individual. Yoder's political theology isn't so much a competing schema as an unsettling of that putative completeness—in his words, "the new world or the new regime under which we live is not a simple alternative to present experience but rather a renewed way of living within the present." Yoder, *PJ*, 185.

Eschatology: The Crisis of Legitimation[6]

The central and, for our present purposes, the largest panel of our triptych relates to the ways that the reality expressed in the Church's earliest kerygmatic proclamation—that Christ is Lord—relativizes and demythologizes state sovereignty. By the latter term I do not mean a Bultmannian approach to theological speech about the state, but rather the deconstructive and critical tenor achieved by Pauline language in its dealings with governmental claims (myths) of sovereignty and right.

Desacralizing the Powers

In expressing the uncertainty of discerning the victory of God in the present, the author of the letter to the Hebrews states:

> In putting everything under him, God left nothing that is not subject to him. Yet at present we do not see everything subject to him. But we [do] see Jesus, who was made a little lower than the angels, now crowned with glory and honour because he suffered death, so that by the grace of God he might taste death for everyone. (Heb 2:8–9)

Christ is seated at the right hand of the Father. He is not simply intercessor or advocate, for his reign extends beyond the heart of the individual believer. To be seated beside the King is to take on the role of prime minister, the one who governs over the powers.[7] Yoder claims that God has not created, instituted, or ordained the powers in their fallen form, but has *ordered* them according to his providential purpose.[8] It is within this Pauline cosmological language of the "principalities and powers" (exousiology) that the claims of eschatology impinge upon the exercise of governmental power. The language of the powers provides an important means of analyzing the persistence of evil and the "spirituality" of social structures. Significantly, it is in employing this language that Yoder seeks

---

6. The term "legitimation crisis" relates to the dissonance that may be detected when a particular state or administration maintains legal authority to govern but does not, or at least does not demonstrate, that it functions in such a way as to fulfill its mandate. The term is popularized in the work of Jürgen Habermas—see Habermas, *Legitimation Crisis*.

7. Yoder, *PT*, 114–20.

8. Yoder, *PJ*, 201.

to deny any competing (non-pacifist) ethical norm locating the political in the order of natural law.[9]

The Politics of Jesus played a considerable role in the restoration of the language of the principalities and powers to theological and ethical currency, as did Yoder's efforts in translating and promoting Hendrikus Berkhof's classic *Christ and the Powers*. Naturally, the terms are open to significant diversity of interpretation. Certain elements of Pauline cosmology should be retained if the terms are to remain meaningful. While most references to the powers consider them in their fallen state, this should not be allowed to obscure their basis in the creative purposes of God (Col 1:15–17). Since the victory of Christ, the powers are subject to God's providential sovereignty. They, like all of creation, are caught in a time of eschatological tension. "The cosmic powers will not be destroyed, but they will be tamed, as they too will find their place in the new humanity."[10] For Yoder this implies two things: first that "we cannot live without them" (yet, because they harm and enslave us, we cannot fully live with them); and second, that it is not the duty of the Church to attack the powers, for "this Christ has done. The church concentrates upon not being seduced by them. By existing the church demonstrates that their rebellion has been vanquished."[11]

In order to apply such language to modern practices of social critique, some form of correspondence with contemporary phenomena must be discerned. For Yoder the correspondence is fundamentally analogical. The language of the powers is roughly equivalent to the modern conception of psychological and socio-political "structures."[12] This equivalence does not take the form of a complete identification, but of a structural analogy with contemporary phenomena. A stronger form of correspondence is found in Walter Wink's influential trilogy on the powers.[13] Further along that scale, Jacques Ellul's social criticism seems to conflate the powers entirely with specific phenomena of money, power, technology, media, etc.[14] Too close an identification would collapse the

9. Yoder, *CWS*, 33–34, *PJ*, 159, "Does Natural Law?"
10. Yoder, *HCPP*, 114.
11. Yoder, *PJ*, 150.
12. Yoder, *CWS*, 8.
13. Wink, *Naming the Powers*; *Unmasking the Powers*; and *Engaging the Powers*.
14. See, for example, Ellul, *False Presence*; *Technological Society*; *Violence*; *New Demons*; and *Ethics of Freedom*.

hermeneutic distance necessary for Yoder's vision of the Church as a community of moral discernment.[15] Unfortunately Yoder rarely provided any specific examination of how the language of the powers contributes to the task of Christian social criticism. Brief considerations of Wink and Ellul will allow us to see how the language of the powers may be employed in Christian practices of social criticism.

For Walter Wink, social and political structures have an inner and an outer aspect. In contrast to the prevalent materialistic worldview, for which matter and spirit are opposed in a dualism that relegates the latter to inconsequential margins, the language of power in the New Testament reconnects the two in one indivisible unity.

> *The Powers are simultaneously the outer and inner aspects of one and the same indivisible concretion of power.* "Spiritual" here means the inner dimension of the material, the "within" of things, the subjectivity of objective entities in the world.[16]

For Wink, the imprecision of the biblical language points to the apparent ubiquity of the phenomena. In naming this "indefinable something" as "the power of the air" (Eph 2:2) the author of Ephesians points to how the dominion of the powers occurs in

> the invisible but palpable environment of opinions, beliefs, propaganda, convictions, prejudices, hatreds, racial and class biases, taboos, and loyalties that condition our perception of the world long before we reach the age of choice, often before we reach the age of speech.[17]

Wink points to the manner in which language of the powers commonly designates a wider and more subtle constellation of power—of which the "state" forms only one part. In naming this "the domination system," Wink proceeds to expose how biblical language can unmask the violent underpinnings of many cultural formations. The myth of redemptive violence is in the very cultural air we breathe. Its currency in notions of pre-emptive attacks on "rogue states" (however deplorable

---

15. It is not possible here to examine in any great detail how these authors different construal of the relationship of powers language to contemporary phenomena affects their own social critical method. A good, if too critical, engagement with the issue comes from Andrew Lincoln in "Liberation from the Powers." See also the detailed critique provided in Dawn, "Concept of the Principalities and Powers."

16. Wink, *Naming the Powers*, 107.

17. Ibid., 82–84.

they may be) caught up in the rhetoric of a "war on terrorism" may be a particularly pernicious current example, but the tendrils of its logic extend far beyond such uninhibited assertions. As Wink says, "Christian moral discrimination tends to follow the flag, and few there are who, like Amos or Isaiah or Thoreau, can entertain the notion that God might not be on their nation's side."[18] Sounding a note one could easily imagine emanating from Yoder, he asserts that, in relation to the powers, the task of the church is

> to unmask their idolatrous pretensions, to identify their dehumanizing values, to strip from them the mantle of respectability, and to disenthrall their victims. It is uniquely equipped to help people unmask and die to the Powers.[19]

Jacques Ellul's prolific writings, both in theology and social criticism, have been shown to provide one of the most sustained uses of language of the principalities and powers in contemporary Western thought. For Ellul only the freedom given in Christ can liberate us from the necessity of the powers. Realism, in Christian perspective, is a stance that is not proven, first and foremost, by the exercise of reason, nor by what succeeds, but by what is consonant with this freedom from all other lordships.[20] It is this assertion of freedom that is the basis for the Church's engagements with the powers.[21]

Christian freedom is contrasted with what Ellul rather ambiguously terms "necessity"—the biological, psychological, cultural, social, and political conditionings that together represent the modern experience.[22] For Ellul the notion of a modern secularized world free of the mythic and the sacred is a dangerous fiction. In a "post-Christian" context there is a new and largely unrecognized "sacred."[23] For our purposes the equation of such "determinisms" with the powers is important, for the two dominant poles of this "new sacred" are technique on the one hand and the state on the other. Ellul claims

---

18. Wink, *Engaging the Powers*, 214.
19. Ibid., 164.
20. Dawn, "Concept of the Principalities and Powers," 33, 111.
21. See especially Ellul, *Ethics of Freedom*.
22. Dawn, "Concept of the Principalities and Powers," 86.
23. Ellul, *New Demons*.

[f]reedom is completely without meaning unless it is related to necessity, unless it represents victory over necessity. . . . In the modern world, the most dangerous form of determinism is the technological phenomenon. It is not a question of getting rid of it, but, by an act of freedom, of transcending it.[24]

The new myths of progressive history and the revelation of the sciences support a new, modern sacred. This sacred provides people with notions of meaning and authenticity fundamentally dependent on the constellation of "the social" known as the nation-state.[25] The technological society emerges in tandem with the nation-state. For Ellul, once technique develops past a certain point, it poses problems that only the state, with its apparatus of power and finance, can co-ordinate and therefore "resolve." This itself transforms and extends the role of the state. The state "considers itself the ordainer and preceptor of the nation. It takes charge of the national life and becomes the nation-state."[26] If the nation-state and technology represent the new sacred, then their converse, the profane, is revolution. But the profane is easily co-opted into the power of the new sacred. The revolutionary impulse aims to replace the ruling elite, but in so doing tends to provide an occasion, through the escalation of violence and the use of propaganda, for the greater expansion of the power of the sacred state.[27]

In relating the language of the principalities and powers to the contingent conditions of the development of the modern nation-state, one can follow Ellul and Wink in setting the full rhetorical force of biblical language against any pretense of the necessity or naturalness of state operations. Equally, the analogy must not collapse into identification—such that abstractions like "state," "sovereignty," or "legitimacy" are identified as necessary or permanent forms of the powers, or regnant structures seen as the only way things can be. By rejecting "natural law" as a basis

---

24. Ellul, *Technological Society*, xxxi. The notably individualistic language chosen by Ellul here renders Christian freedom inseparable from the notion of autonomy found in liberal accounts of the self. On Ellul's individualism, see Dawn, "Concept of the Principalities and Powers," 243; and Gill, *Word of God in the Ethics of Jacques Ellul*, 169. Indeed, I suggest Ellul here displays similarities with Girard—e.g., the optimistic and rationalistic account of the power of the will to affect substantial change.

25. Ellul, *New Demons*, 58–68.

26. Ellul, *Technological Society*, 228–318.

27. Gill, *Word of God*, 133; Dawn, "Concept of the Principalities and Powers," 227. The point is best made in Ellul, *Autopsy of Revolution*; and *Violence*.

for a theology of the state, Yoder provides a christological negation of early modern notions, from Bodin to Hobbes, of the nation-state as the natural product of social will. Such accounts perpetuate an idolatrous assertion of sovereign power as independent of eschatological claims.[28] For some critics, the separation from eschatological reality found in the notion of popular sovereignty provides the "necessary historical condition of modern political tyranny and totalitarianism."[29] The work of Benedict Anderson amply demonstrates the manner in which national identity, and its fabrication and molding for purposes of state formation, now dominate the constellation of imagined communities.[30] In the rise of nation-states, social space becomes unified. The complexities of diverse claims upon a person's loyalties are vitiated by the supervenient claims of state sovereignty.[31]

Indeed, contrary to some popular accounts, the multiple trends referred to by the term "globalization" may in fact enhance the claims of sovereign states over their citizens.[32] It is not simply that the rise of multinational corporations denotes the advent of rival bodies able to exercise power and influence equal to, or greater than, many nation-states— although that is, prima facie, indisputable. It has never really been the

28. Of course, the emergence of the notion of legitimacy based in natural law progresses from the relatively complex and robustly theological Thomist framework through to more naturalistic (i.e., less christocentric) accounts from the early seventeenth century. Hugo Grotius's attempts to place international order on the basis of a natural law, whose source remained God, but which proceeded by means of the emergence of a popular mandate—*De Iure Belli ac Pacis*, book 1. This may well have sewn the seeds for Hobbes's view of a *lex naturalis* no longer construed as the dictates of God, but with the prudential exercise of reason oriented to self-preservation in an agonistic setting and operating simply to discern universal abstract laws like "Seek for Peace" and "don't do to others what you don't want done to you." Hobbes, *Leviathan*, chap. 14. It is not clear that Yoder's sometimes rather monolithic dismissal of "natural law" is sufficiently attentive to the contingent and questionable nature of such developments.

29. Joan Lockwood O'Donovan associates the view with figures as diverse as Hannah Arendt and Pope Leo XIII—See "Nation, State and Civil Society," in *BI*, 276–95, 290. See also Oliver O'Donovan's comment that "[t]he doctrine that we set up political authority, as a device to secure our own essentially private, local and unpolitical purposes, has left the Western democracies in a state of pervasive moral debilitation, which, from time to time, inevitably throws up idolatrous and authoritarian reactions." *DN*, 49.

30. Anderson, *Imagined Communities*.

31. On the distinction of complex and simple forms of social space, see Milbank, *WMS*, 268–92; and Cavanaugh, "Killing for the Telephone Company."

32. For a clear and useful discussion of the central issues here, see Smith, Solinger, and Topik, *States and Sovereignty*.

case that the claimed sovereignty of the state indicated an uncontested authority to govern.[33] Rather, the emergence of this "post national constellation" places the possibility of democratic legitimation in question at precisely the same moment as states trade upon that legitimacy in order to strengthen their international authority.[34] The loss of direct state control does not necessarily correlate with a similar loss of claimed authority. Yet to claim, with the New Testament, that Christ is victorious over the powers is to introduce a circumscribing and relativizing ingredient into the mix. It is precisely Christ's independence from the claims of the powers that breaches the veil of their authority and ubiquity. Here is the man who refuses to live *sicut deus*,[35] who declines the false freedom offered in the rebellion of the powers. Saint Paul talks of the Christ event as disarming and rendering impotent (*apekdusamenos*) these rulers and authorities, fearlessly making of them a bold and public example (*edeigmatisen en parrhesia*) and triumphing (*thriambeusas*) over them.[36]

Towards a Functional Sense of Legitimacy

So how might Yoder's eschatology and exousiology relate to concerns for "legitimacy" in political theory? Despite some regrettable ambiguity, which in turn contributes to common misunderstandings of his work as excessively negative in regard to the state, Yoder's most important claim regarding "legitimacy" is stark: "Christian witness does not provide any foundations for government, either practically or philosophically, but . . . the Christian rather accepts the powers that be and speaks to them in a corrective way."[37] This is the political equivalent to Yoder's christologically circumscribed methodological historicism that clearly states that "there is no scratch from which to start."[38] Political witness, no less than debate with other interlocutors, must begin in the messy middle. Yoder was rightly impatient with theorizations and abstractions that aimed at prior "semantic or definitional moves," which ensured some

---

33. See Krasner, "Globalization and Sovereignty."

34. The term "postnational constellation" comes from Habermas, *Postnational Constellation*.

35. Bonhoeffer, *Creation and Fall*, 111–14.

36. Col 2:15—author's translation.

37. Yoder, *CWS*, 41.

38. Yoder, *FTN*, 10.

neutral or universal place to begin discussion.[39] For our purposes those abstractions would include "the state of nature," and the commonplace polarity of "anarchy" and "totalitarianism"—between which extremes some "legitimate" state would rest. That a "democracy" claims to sail us between these chimerical Scylla and Charybdis is not sufficient grounds for declaring it "legitimate."[40] Yoder says this more elegantly than I when he insists that "the witness to the state has never been *based on* a theory about what the state is and should be in itself, nor has it been rendered *for the sake of* the state 'in itself.'"[41] It is false, he claims, to assume

> that if one does not have a theory justifying the existence of government one has no grounds for criticizing governmental performance.... The state does not need to be theoretically justified in order to exist; it does exist. Whether our speaking to the state presupposes that we must have a theory of why the state exists will depend on the nature and ground of our critique.... Paul's acceptance of Roman rule makes no use of the idea... that standards for any state can be read out of Genesis.[42]

Thus Yoder's work provides an alternative to those forms of political theology that see their task in terms largely borrowed from the political dilemmas addressed by Hobbes, Locke, and other harbingers of the liberal tradition—i.e., the need to provide some thinly theologized grounds for sovereignty and the legitimacy of the nation-state. Equally, we should note a significant contrast with one of the most robust theological accounts of political judgment and the overplayed concern for "legitimacy"—that of Oliver O'Donovan, for whom the fundamental issue is the emergence of less theological (indeed actively de-theologizing) notions of legitimacy after Grotius. These notions then become idolatrous when straying beyond the bounds of Christ's "reauthorization" of the state's judgment.[43] The problem for Yoder is not simply that the state becomes idolatrous by straining at its eschatological leash. The fundamental error (heresy) occurs when eschatology is turned inside-out, and the state is said to

---

39. Yoder, "On Not Being Ashamed," 290–91.

40. In saying that "totalitarianism" is chimerical I do not deny that a state may, in actuality, exhibit such characteristics, and that such would impel resistance. Rather, I want to show that "democracy" is far from immune from sliding into many such traits.

41. Yoder, *CWS*, 77. Emphasis in original.

42. Ibid., 78 n. 5

43. See in particular O'Donovan, *DN* and *WJ*.

show forth Christ's sovereignty in its own actions in a way that is more truly "political" than the life of the believing community. Fourth-century panegyrics addressed by Eusebius and Lactantius to Constantine make this quite explicit. Lactantius praised Constantine as demonstrating that

> [t]he providence of the supreme Deity has raised thee to the imperial dignity, that thou mightest be able with true piety to rescind the injurious decrees of others, to correct faults, to provide with a father's clemency for the safety of men,—in short, to remove the wicked from the state, whom being cast down by preeminent piety, God has delivered into your hands, that it might be evident to all in what true majesty consists.[44]

This divine deputation of sovereignty to the emperor becomes, by the reign of James I in the early seventeenth century, a simple parallelism of the arbitrary and absolute power of God and King. It then devolves without critical resistance, from the absolutist monarch to the global conglomeration of sovereign selves named by Hardt and Negri as Empire.

At this juncture we note there remains an ambiguity in relation to the notion of "legitimacy," which in turn contributes to common misunderstandings of Yoder's work as excessively negative in regard to the state. I suggest this may be remedied by a more explicit location of "legitimacy" within the functional norms found in an eschatological framework. This is in marked contrast to dominant procedural concerns for mechanisms deemed to secure democratic legitimation—for which, as Oliver O'Donovan rightly objects, the test of legitimacy has lost any connection with the thick practices of political representation.[45] Yoder distinguishes his reading of Romans 13 from those who treat the text as the sole biblical basis for the discernment of a legitimate state.[46] There are a number of objections that Yoder raises to the notion of legitimacy. He contrasts two

---

44. Lactantius *Divine Institutes* VII, 26. I am indebted to Thomas Heilke's discussion of Lactantius here. Heilke uses Charles Cochrane's translation to provide a more direct, though perhaps anachronistic translation—using "sovereignty" in place of "majesty." Heilke, "Yoder's Idea of Constantinianism," 119 n. 41. The divergent translations reveal the beginnings of a gradual shift in political theology—that divine majesty is directly manifest in what we moderns would call political "sovereignty." That is far more explicit in the claims made by Jean Bodin regarding *majestas* as monarchical supremacy. Bodin, *Six Books of the Commonwealth*.

45. O'Donovan, *WJ*, 165. O'Donovan also rightly insists that this representation is, first and foremost, an account of "the relation of redeemed humanity to Christ" (157).

46. Yoder, *PJ*, 193–211.

customary readings of Romans 13—the "positivistic" and the "legitimistic" or normative view. The positivistic approach is characterized by an attempt to render an affirmative moral judgment on the existence of the current government by virtue of its very occurrence. "If Germany finds itself under the control of Adolf Hitler, this very fact demonstrates that his government is 'of God.'"[47] This abhorrent conclusion should be more than enough to dismiss such an approach. Nevertheless more subtle forms of positivistic logic in the guise of an historic appeal to particular patterns of governance (as self-evidently effective, and therefore preferable) still permeate the rhetoric of both conservative retrograde politics, and, conversely, of "revolutionary" utopianism.

The legitimistic reading of Romans 13 is perhaps more attractive for those seeking a theological basis for social criticism. Yoder locates the reading within a broadly Calvinistic tradition, flowing from Zwingli, through Cromwell, and on to Barth and Brunner. "What is ordained is not a particular government but the concept of proper government, the principle of government as such."[48] Thus each particular constellation of governmental power is subject to a critique on the basis of a prior standard or norm. Should one's state be found wanting in its performance of the essential tasks of maintaining peace and punishing evildoers, or if it aggregates the kind of all-encompassing role found in totalitarian regimes, then the duty of the Christian is to revolt against the unjust government. It is at this juncture that Yoder rejects "legitimacy" language as both monolithic and open to unbiblical justifications of revolutionary violence. Romans 13, he claims, cannot be used to justify revolt. It is clear that the duty of the Christian is to remain subordinate to the state, no matter how unjust that state may be. Thus,

> No state can be so low on the scale of relative justice that the duty of the Christian is no longer to be subject; no state can rise so high on that scale that Christians are not called to some sort of suffering because of their refusal to agree with its self-glorification and the resultant injustices.[49]

On the face of it, this is hardly the stuff of a theology capable of significant political critique. Indeed, here we encounter an ambiguity

---

47. Ibid., 199.
48. Ibid.
49. Yoder, *CWS*, 77.

particularly characteristic of Yoder's earlier writings. The ambiguity revolves around the verbs "to be subject," and "to revolt." Only when this earlier text is read in tandem with the important distinction, seen in the previous chapter, of subordination from subjection or submission (the phrasing of the text above would thereby replace "subject" with "subordinate") can any patrician or positivistic misconstruals be avoided.[50] To revolt then refers here specifically and exclusively to violent rebellion. Recall, by contrast, Yoder's claim that "'subordination' is itself the Christian form of rebellion. It is the way we share in God's patience with a system we basically reject."[51] Eschatology is the key to understanding how the Church is to respond to God's providential *ordering* of the powers—whether they are "legitimate" or not! As we have already heard him say:

> The willingness to suffer is then not merely a test of our patience or a dead space of waiting; it is itself a participation in the character of God's victorious patience with the rebellious powers of creation. We subject ourselves to government because it was in so doing that Jesus revealed and achieved God's victory.[52]

To name "revolution" as the hope of the world exhibits the fundamental limitation of all "carnal" or "worldly" power.[53] Yoder's disavowal of violent revolt is not, then, based in some concept of the duly established authority of a particular government. The regrettable ambiguity in Yoder is the result of an intermittent association of regime change with violent revolt. This fails to create the theological space necessary for his own defense of revolutionary subordination to flourish. When that association is broken, we can see more clearly how Yoder's theology of witness may allow for an ad hoc discernment of the alignment of the church with a particular political cause.

> The point is not that one can attain all of one's legitimate ends without using violent means. It is rather that our readiness to renounce our legitimate ends whenever they cannot be attained by legitimate means itself constitutes our participation in the triumphant suffering of the Lamb.[54]

50. Yoder, *PJ*, 172.
51. Ibid., 200 n. 10.
52. Ibid., 209.
53. Yoder, *OR*, 165–66.
54. Yoder, *PJ*, 237.

Despite his unease with the term, I suggest Yoder's cause would have been better served by a more explicit delineation of a "functional" from an "ontological" sense of a state's "legitimacy." He is persuasive in his critique of the monolithic sense of legitimacy. This continues the move we saw him make in relation to H. R. Niebuhr's construction of "culture." Yoder's theology of witness does not require one to reject *all* activities of a particular state, or accept them *all*.[55] He is also rightly cautious of the way language of legitimacy may base itself on an implied claim to attain an unrealistic level of clarity in judgment. There is no simple checklist, no unequivocal signal that allows us "to tell accurately the specific point at which a state would move from sobriety into idolatry."[56] For Yoder, the language of legitimacy runs the risk of imposing a simplistic polarity upon an infinitely complex setting. But need the language of legitimacy be entirely rejected?

The functional norms applying to the state are defined in relation to the eschatological and christological vision from which Yoder's theology of witness stems.

> The reign of Christ means for the state the obligation to serve God by encouraging good and restraining evil, i.e., to serve peace, to preserve the social cohesion in which the leaven of the gospel can build the church, and also render the old aeon more tolerable.[57]

That basic description allows for enormous diversity and room for debate. The option is not between the legitimate government of Romans 13, which Christians are to bless, or the idolatrous government of Revelation 13, which should be overturned.

For most biblical translations, the functional nature of this norm is compromised by reading Rom 13:6 along rather static ontological lines—"the authorities are God's servants, busy with this very thing." By contrast, for Yoder the state has no ontology in and of itself; the exercise of authority is only in the service of God *to the extent that* it fulfils these minimal functions.[58] We can therefore see something of this "functional" legitimacy in Yoder's personal decision to withhold a proportion of his income tax used in respect of those purposes "contrary to that which

---

55. Yoder, "Church and State," 282.
56. Yoder, *CWS*, 80.
57. Yoder, *OR*, 76.
58. Yoder, *PJ*, 205.

government is supposed to be serving," e.g., the development of weapons of mass destruction.[59] But what does it mean to say that the state has no ontology? It means that, for Yoder, there is no such thing as the state *as such*. The state exists only as a permissive ordinance of God. The state has no metaphysical existence above or beyond the particular constellation of governmental activities exercised in its name. This is why both Yoder and Barth can say that the New Testament contains no doctrine of the just state.[60]

It is on this basis that Yoder distinguishes his view from those concerned primarily with legitimacy.

> The logical implication of any concept of legitimacy—its *raison d'etre*, in fact—is the point where a given state may be declared not to be legitimate and its removal by war or revolution thereby justified.[61]

Yoder's eschatology is clear that our subordination to a government is not conditional upon its putative legitimacy. But Yoder equally affirms that the same cannot be said of our obedience to that ruler! We can, and indeed sometimes must, express our subordination through disobedience. Yoder's disavowal of the abstract or ontological functioning of the term "legitimate" allows him to maintain that the illegitimate state, no less than the legitimate one, exists solely by divine permission. Any totalitarian state continues to exist only because of divine patience and an overriding eschatological tension. We should not deny that God's sovereign purposes may be served even through a morally abhorrent regime. YHWH's use of the idolatrous Assyria or Rome is not a ratification of their legitimacy.[62] Those nations may serve the purposes of God, but in no way does this exonerate them from his judgment. But even if the notion of divine permission is adequately distanced from connotations of moral ratification, surely there is still room for a denunciation of a regime as, in a functional sense, illegitimate? It does not seem to follow that it is necessary to deny the functional illegitimacy of a totalitarian state

---

59. In order not to profit personally from withholding these funds Yoder made an equivalent contribution to the Mennonite Central Committee for use in overseas war sufferers" relief. See Yoder, "Why I Don't Pay."

60. Barth, "Christian Community and Civil Community."

61. Yoder, *CWS*, 43.

62. Yoder, *PJ*, 198.

Eschatology, Exile, and Election

in order to preclude violent revolt. Violent revolt, after all, is precluded already on other ecclesiological and christological grounds.

Ontologically speaking, no state is entirely legitimate or illegitimate —for the state no longer has an existence outside of the order of grace, and no authority outside the lordship of Christ. The state belongs to the "order of providence," whilst the church belongs to the "order of redemption."[63] However it would be a mistake to assume that Yoder locates grace solely within the Church. Rather, as we began to see in our discussion of Gutiérrez, the lordship of Christ over the world and his headship of the church are both of the order of grace, although they remain distinct.[64] The violence of the state, as part of the principalities and powers, is turned against itself in the kingdom of Christ. Equally, as we shall see below, even in its most democratized form the state can never escape a moment of self-deification.[65] But there are better or worse state forms. We shall see in the final chapter that this is no blessing of democracy per se (of course, there is no such thing as "democracy per se"). So, Yoder's eschatology and exousiology show us that the concept of "legitimacy" must be shorn of all ontological, abstract forms; it must not be taken to circumscribe God's free permissive action and patience; it must be adequately distanced from connotations of moral ratification— only then is there some use for the term. Then, Yoder claims, the Church's witness may utilize the language of legitimacy in a way that better fits the complexities of citizenship. Too often political theology juxtaposes accounts of state authority as requiring either subjection or rebellion—as if "sovereign power" were held by a singular, discrete, and identifiable body. That is, and has always been, a myth—and often an idolatrous one at that. Yoder's eschatological vision undermines such bald polarities while still permitting a functional account of legitimacy that may allow

---

63. This is a moment of divergence from the Barthian elements of Yoder's understanding of the state. For Barth allows a more positive role to the civil community. The state then remains part of the order of *redemption*. See Hunsinger, *Disruptive Grace*, 114–28.

64. Yoder, *CWS*, 12.

65. Ibid., 38. See also "Democracies are as much in need of demythologizing as are all the other oligarchies. The consent of the governed, the built-in controls of constitutionality, checks and balances, and the bill of rights do not constitute the fact of government; they only mitigate it." Yoder, *PK*, 137 and "The fact that certain agents are chosen by relatively democratic procedures does not modify the fact that the state is still defined by its claim to the use of violence for the maintenance of order." Yoder, *KBPW*, 109.

the Church to witness effectively to Christ's own sovereign lordship.[66] Such a functional distinction moves the language of legitimacy beyond the black and white polarity that Yoder detects in its common use and affords a more nuanced account of state practices.[67] This, as we shall see shortly, is precisely the kind of discernment that is at the heart of Yoder's exilic ecclesiology.

Violence and the State: Tactical and Strategic Readings

The functional sense of legitimacy I detect in Yoder's writings on the state runs counter to the commonplace reading of his texts as characterized by an exclusively negative tenor. Despite the negativity regarding state forms embedded in his critique of Constantinianism, there are signs that Yoder was not as pessimistic as he is often taken to be.[68] Taking Yoder's corpus

66. Yoder notes, for example, that "Prince versus emperor, state or province versus federal government, bureaucracy versus constitution, executive versus judiciary, revolutionary underground versus colonial occupation; Katanga versus Congo—repeatedly the choice is not between subjection and rebellion as two possible attitudes toward the same government, but between two 'lords' competing for recognition and support. The subjects themselves, and sometimes other parties as well, may then have to make decisions on some ground other than the *de facto* exercise of sovereignty since this is divided. Here legitimacy may well be the key. . . . an application of one form or another of the concept of legitimacy . . . [may] thereby [provide] a witness to both governments." Yoder, *CWS*, 43–44. We may add larger-scale international bodies to this list; given recent conflicts over meeting the "legitimate [competent] authority" in the declaration of a just war, one may add "Nation-state versus European Union" or "Coalition/NATO versus UN."

67. In asserting this, I note that Yoder's use of "legitimism" as an ideal type represents a somewhat simplistic construction. The notion of legitimacy is not always used monolithically, even by the authors he names, to describe a particular state as legitimate or illegitimate *in toto*. The term "functional normativism" should also be distinguished from accounts of legitimacy in relation to the notion of popular sovereignty, whereby the epithet "legitimate" is applied differentially dependent upon the impact of governmental activity upon oneself, rather than upon society as a whole; e.g., a state is legitimate for the rich, who benefit from its claim to sovereignty, and illegitimate for the poor who bear the burden of that claim. For a good critique of such a position, see Hoffman, *Beyond the State*, 76–93. For this form of functional normativism, the state is legitimate and/or illegitimate in relation to a christological and eschatological norm.

68. The anecdotal evidence on Yoder's own understanding of the degree of negativity in his view of the state is inconclusive. Koontz points to a memorandum in which Yoder is clear that, if he is seen by others as imbalanced on the side of pessimism in relation to his expectations for constructive participation by Christians in politics, this is a corrective to the optimism that has been a persistent problem in Western Protestantism. Yoder also suggests that others think he is more pessimistic than he really is. Koontz, "Confessional Theology," 129 n. 100. By contrast, David Hughes cites a conversation in

as a whole, there is an ambiguity to be found that may be described as a tension between a more dominant Weberian voice and a minor Barthian voice in his understanding of the relation of violence to the nature of the state. The Weberian conception sees violence as the very essence of state activity. In Weber's famous definition, the state is "a human community that (successfully) claims the *monopoly of the legitimate use of physical force* within a given territory."[69] By constrast, Barth's analogical view holds open the possibility of a minimally violent exercise of state power. I suggest that the functional understanding of legitimacy shares a greater affinity with the minor Barthian voice, while also being able to accommodate the skepticism in regard to state violence found in the dominant voice.

This theoretical tension is one that Yoder never explicitly identified and never found it necessary to overcome.[70] Of course, the balance between these two elements is itself subject to changes of emphasis in response to various political situations. The corrective dominance of a negative tenor sits alongside the recognition that to identify the sword as the essence of the civil order is tantamount to denying in principle

> the possibility of a progressive minimizing of the violence of the sanctions of the state and a progressive dismantling of the lethal sanctions of the state through considerations of social contract and checks and balances. It denies the vision of peace as the *prima ratio* of government, as held to by Catholicism, by liberalism, or by Karl Barth.[71]

In refusing to let violence define the essence of the state's functions, Barth invokes a distinction between its *opus proprium* and its

---

which Yoder concedes his equation of the state with "the sword" is essentially Hobbesian. Hughes, "Ethical Use of Power," 135. I take Yoder's use of the epithet to be a reference to the notion that state force operates in order to constrain retributive violence, and not to imply any broader anthropological parallel with Hobbes's notions of individual rights or an originary state of nature.

69. This account of the Weberian definition of the state is ubiquitous in writings on modern political thought. It is most famously found in Weber's essay on "Politics as Vocation." I cite here from the version published as "Profession and Vocation," 310–11. Emphasis in original. The concept is well critiqued in Held, *Political Theory and the Modern State*, 39–51.

70. This connection between violence and the form of the nation-state is explored in a way largely consistent with Yoder's account in Giddens, *Nation-State and Violence*.

71. Yoder, "Reformed Versus Anabaptist," 5.

opus alienum.[72] The proper functioning of the state is the fashioning of a circumscribed peace (more of a *pax Romana* than a *pax Christi / shalom*) and the nurturing of human life. It is only when that peace is inadequate that war becomes inevitable.[73] In Barth, of course, the terms are employed in order to delineate conditions under which war may be undertaken for the protection of life. Nevertheless, Yoder does make use of a phrase occurring in Barth here, that violence is the "*ultima ratio*" of the state.[74] Violence is its outer edge, justifiable for the state (never for the Church) only in extreme circumstances, and then only to a minimal degree.[75] The church cannot demand that the state be non-resistant, but only that it be minimally violent.

A comparison with the way Oliver O'Donovan employs a somewhat different schema may underline how Yoder's ecclesiology of nonviolence allows him to maintain a strong vision of social change alongside a high degree of skepticism with regards to the likelihood of a truly Christian state. In *The Desire of the Nations*, Oliver O'Donovan aims to recover the lost roots of a political theology and thus furnish a truer basis for political authority.[76] The *bene esse* of political authority is found in the exercise of judgment, the *esse* of the state, in ways faithful to its provisional (properly secular) eschatological status.[77] Just as in Yoder, then, eschatology circumscribes the claimed legitimacy of the state. The analogical principle

---

72. Barth, *CD* III/4, 456f. The terms are also used by Eberhard Jüngel in *Christ, Justice, and Peace*.

73. Ibid. See also Williams, "Barth, War and the State." Williams points to the outworking of this in Barth's response to contemporary events. For Barth, says Williams, "The church, in committing itself to support for the Riechstaat, commits itself to supporting political *potestas*, not *potentia*, power defined in terms of the purposive capacity to serve and effect law so as to realize harmony, as opposed to pure might, defining its own ends" (183).

74. It is debatable whether Yoder is correct in reading Barth's use of the terms *opus proprium* and *opus alienum* in *CD* III/4 as a divergent emphasis, rather than a substantial variance, with his more negative construal of the state in the earlier *Church and State*. See Biggar, *Hastening that Waits*, 178–79. For our purposes it is only necessary to note that, in many places, the more Calvinist Barth offered an account of the state with a more positive redemptive element to it.

75. Yoder, *CAW*, 294–95.

76. O'Donovan, *DN*. The critical response to this work has been extensive—among the best commentaries are the essays from the symposium on the text found in *Studies in Christian Ethics*; Wolterstorff, "A Discussion," with a critical response from O'Donovan, "Deliberation, History and Reading," and Bartholomew, et al., *A Royal Priesthood?*

77. O'Donovan, *DN*, 233.

appears here too.[78] For O'Donovan Church and society are in dialectical relation. Society represents the *penumbra* of the Church—that is, it is the "radiation" of the Church rather than a participation in it.[79] Importantly, O'Donovan's use of the schema of *esse* and *bene esse* differs from the Barthian division of the *opus proprium* and the *opus alienum* precisely in its relation to violence. The theological notion of the *bene esse* of state activity is conceived to provide "normal" state functions, including the "generally beneficent institution [of] the professional army," with "a sufficient confidence to exercise judgment with the redemptive decisiveness that the use of force implies."[80]

For both Yoder and O'Donovan the involvement and enculturation attendant upon successful mission does not lead to social conformity. An important point of divergence emerges in relation to the phenomenon of civil religion. O'Donovan defines the elements of civil religion simply as "serving the interests of the state at large, bolstering its legitimacy, supporting its political philosophy, inculcating virtues, both passive and active, which are useful to the political constitution of society."[81] For O'Donovan not everything the Church does along the lines of "serving the political constitution of society" is to be rejected. The problem occurs when such activities are seen as autonomous, set free from the authority of Christ that is the only true foundation of the exercise of political power. By contrast, for Yoder the activities associated with civil religion are fundamentally flawed—they impute a Constantinian notion of historical agency and render the faith community involuntary.[82] Whereas for O'Donovan the issues of religious coercion and civil religion are distinct, Yoder can admit no such division.

Both O'Donovan and Yoder pursue a typological investigation of the political theology of the Old Testament. It is here that different readings of power, authority, and witness emerge. The complexity of O'Donovan's

78. Ibid., 119.

79. Ibid., 251.

80. O'Donovan, *BI*, 263, 260. O'Donovan's use of the distinction between *esse* and *bene esse* owes a great deal to Paul Ramsey. See especially his "Karl Barth and Paul Ramsey's 'Uses of Power,'" in *BI*, 246–75. The equation of "power" with "force" (and the conflation of "force" with "violence") is not given explicit examination. Thus, "[f]or Ramsey power is *always* suspect and *always* necessary, while Barth considers it *usually* suspect and *occasionally* necessary" (270).

81. O'Donovan, *DN*, 224–26.

82. Yoder, *PK*, 187.

exegesis defies easy summary. For present purposes it is sufficient to consider some problems arising from his construction of the notion of "dual authority." In recovering the theological basis of "authority," O'Donovan argues that "Yhwh's authority as king is established by the accomplishment of victorious deliverance, by the presence of judicial discrimination and by the continuity of a community-possession."[83] In the monarchic period these three attributes of YHWH's rule over Israel—as judge, lawgiver, and king (Isa 33:22) were mediated through the critical interaction of kings and prophets.[84] Later exilic experience shows YHWH as setting aside the kingly role, as the prophet becomes the sole mediator of God's rule of his chosen people (Jer 22:24).[85] In exile Israel experiences a reality shaped by living under a "dual authority," a life simultaneously under the authority of YHWH and subject to the rule of empire.

For O'Donovan, the climax of Israel's history (which marks a transition in the locus of power) is enacted in Christ's refusal to afford loyalty to the rule of empire. The politics of empire is marked for disposal as the spatial division of the two rules gives way to the temporal division of two eras.[86] In inaugurating the Kingdom, Christ unites all authority in himself. The persistence of the institutions of rule is a providential act of divine permission for the sake of the outworking of God's purposes of reconciliation. Much of this is resonant with Yoder's account, for both take their cues from eschatological claims. However, O'Donovan's understanding of the continuing role for governmental power displays a tendency, against its own intention, to collapse the eschatological basis for political witness.

O'Donovan pictures the kingly rule of Christ as "reauthorizing" the political in the light of the eschatological horizon. Instead of permitting all three of the functions of YHWH's kingship to be mediated through the state, the function of judgment provides the only continuing rationale for governmental power.[87] In a pattern similar to that we have identified in Niebuhr, in *The Desire of the Nations* the common grace in which judgment is exercised is formally distinct from the forgiving grace of God's mercy. Herein lies the problem—behind O'Donovan's modal distinction

83. O'Donovan, *DN*, 36.
84. Ibid., 61–66.
85. Ibid., 77.
86. Ibid., 82–119.
87. Ibid., 146–57.

of justice and mercy lies an attenuated theology of witness.[88] His individualized reading of Matthew 18 precludes the exercise of penultimate judgment for any member of the Christian community.[89] In doing so, we can see that O'Donovan's eschatology is far too realized. Dangerously, this realized eschatology concedes the legitimacy of violent forms of penultimate judgment in state operations and thereby introduces a notion of sub-Christian justice as normative for the state.[90] There is some apparent moderation of the view in the subsequent work *The Ways of Judgment*—where the sphere of public judgment may be chastened by mercy. The division between judgment and grace may itself be broached by the work of the Spirit.[91] That true grace and forgiveness are radically excessive of mere clemency or amnesty is not in doubt. Nonetheless, to continue our visual metaphor, O'Donovan's approach places the separation of streams (mercy and judgment) so much in the foreground that the basis and extent of any capillary connections or tributaries between the two are lost in an unfocused region beyond depth of field. This stands in contrast to the picture given by Yoder's theological realism, with its affirmation of a single normative standard, from which we have seen him affirm the practice of fraternal admonition as the Church's practice of a reconciliatory form of *penultimate* and merciful judgment.

It is this same fault that compromises O'Donovan's reading of the Christendom model of mission. He bases his critical but largely positive account of Christendom on "the doctrine of the two," which is said to suppose "the vis-à-vis of church and secular government, as distinct structures belonging to distinct societies and, indeed, distinct eras of salvation-history."[92] However, with a rigid functional distinction prohibiting witness towards nonviolent practices of government one has to question whether underneath the vocabulary of "mutual service" and "exploratory partnership," the tension of already/not yet has ebbed away.

To draw on the understanding of social change outlined in the previous chapter, we can perhaps see the difference between O'Donovan and Yoder's readings of the way eschatology impinges on governmental

---

88. Ibid., 150, 233–34.

89. Ibid., 150–51.

90. O'Donovan's eschatology has been the subject of varied criticisms from Richard Neuhaus, "Commentary," and Hauerwas and Fodor, "Remaining in Babylon."

91. O'Donovan, *WJ*, 100.

92. O'Donovan, *DN*, 196.

power as a division of strategic from tactical approaches.[93] O'Donovan's strategic approach is found, for example, in his overriding concern for "authority" as the basic category of political theology, and his focus on issues of the self-conception of political *structures*. Yoder's more tactical vision of eschatological tension, as we have seen, revolves around the category of witness and a focus on the ad hoc world of *practices*—including, of course, practices of government. The point is not that practices and structures should be conceived as distinct, but that structures are to be addressed and critiqued through the practices in which they subsist.

Yoder provides examples of such practices. In examining the colonial government established by William Penn in 1681, he notes a substantial commitment to nonviolence, which, while it didn't extend to questioning the morality of colonial activities as such, engendered a number of nonviolent practices including open courts, religious liberty, peaceful relations with Native Americans, early forms of modern democratic governance, etc.[94] For Craig Carter, this provides a refutation of an exclusively negative construal of the nature of the state in Yoder.[95] I suspect that may be going too far. The bulk of Yoder's thought always displays an overriding skepticism in relation to the extent to which historic or present state forms may claim to operate within their eschatological mandate. It is unlikely, then, that an account of functional legitimacy would depart from a primarily skeptical tenor in its reading of the claims of states to embody the pursuit of some common good.[96] Yoder's exposition of the Penn experiment is best seen as a refutation not of negativity per se but of two related phenomena. Yoder's negativity is neither exclusive nor paralyzing. It does not yield any paralysis or stultification of action, indeed it impels a discernment of degrees of better or worse government. Equally, against an exclusive negativity construed as a persistent naysaying, a construc-

---

93. Subsequent to writing this section it has come to my attention that Scott Bader-Saye also invokes these Certeauean categories in his comparison of Yoder and O'Donovan. Bader-Saye, "Aristotle or Abraham?" 312. While the comparison was arrived at independently, Bader-Saye's work provides an excellent analysis of the central issues in relation to the danger of supersessionism, which will concern us below. However, Bader-Saye's passing comment does not relate the categories of strategy and tactic to the eschatological understandings that, I suggest, undergird the division.

94. Yoder, *CHRN*, chapter 7; *FTN*, 20–21.

95. Carter, *Politics of the Cross*, 22.

96. See also Cavanaugh, "Killing for the Telephone Company."

tive and critical moment is always present.[97] Likewise, Michel Foucault was often accused of a paralyzing negativity in his various accounts of the operations of power. I suggest that Yoder's exilic ecclesiology provides grounds for a form of Christian witness not only to "the state," but also to the wider functionings of power that Foucault diagnosed and named "governmentality." Furthermore, both Yoder and Foucault provide accounts of social critique and resistance that are particularly apposite to the current state of Western political regimes.

Exile

The second and third panels of our triptych then frame this demythologizing functional critique of state operations by relating it to the ongoing mission of the Church. We already noted in passing the way in which Yoder uses the motif of Jer 29:7—"seek the peace (salvation) of the city (or culture) where I have sent you into exile, and pray to the Lord on its behalf, for in its welfare you will find your welfare." The currency of exilic language for Christian ethics has increased substantially through the hyperbolic motifs—such as "resident aliens"—employed by Stanley Hauerwas.[98] Yet even here, and certainly in Yoder, the term goes much deeper than providing a convenient idiom in which to express Christian distinctiveness.

Certainly the lack of place (in the Certeauean sense) has a great deal of importance in conceiving of the relation of the Church to the operations of governmental power. Yet it is not rootlessness per se, but the normativity of the Jewish diaspora model in particular, that Yoder points to in a series of investigations into the Jewish-Christian schism. There are three elements of importance for our argument within Yoder's reading of diaspora citizenship (galuth in Hebrew) as a condition of Jewish, and consequently also Christian, identity. First, diaspora citizenship is *normative*, second the exile has *continued* since Babylon, and third, it is to be seen as an occasion of *blessing*.

---

97. Nicholas Wolterstorff fails to see how the exemplary nature of the Church in Yoder's ecclesiology counters any claim to a solely "naysaying" mode. Wolterstorff, "Review of *The Royal Priesthood*."

98. Hauerwas, *RA*.

Exile as Normative

Yoder, implicitly at least, is able to unite the demythologizing impact of Pauline cosmology with the political life of the exilic community—as exemplified in the model of prophetic figures like Joseph, Daniel, and Jeremiah. The Jeremianic model is possible only through a prior confession that it is God who is sovereign over history and over the powers.[99] The sense of dependence on YHWH that marks the identity of Israel is fundamental to their ability to live in exile. To draw a parallel once again with the language of Michel de Certeau, this dependence is, in part, a refusal of strategic space. The Mosaic tradition always insisted upon the mobility of the tabernacle as the representation of divine presence. This refusal of space is intended, we might suggest, to militate against the reification of divine presence. In Yoder's words,

> The transcendence of the Most High is acted out in the fact that the place of his manifestation is not our own turf.
>
> God's choosing to pitch his tent in our midst is his mercy, not our merit or our property. That God chooses neutral ground (or foreign ground) as the way to be graciously in our midst points to a truth which all three Abrahamic faiths have retained, though in different ways. God is never our God in the sense of our possessing him. . . . They all relativize the empirical, manipulable "reality." They relativize the given in favor of the gift.[100]

Indeed, the transcendence of the Most High God is seen in his choice of Jerusalem as his seat—a city belonging to none of the tribes of Judah. Yet, of course, Jerusalem becomes the site of the kingship experiment; for Yoder, the ill-fated slide into the proto-Constantinian "Solomonic temptation." Here, as in our earlier discussions of the War of YHWH, we encounter the selectivity (in a non-pejorative sense) of Yoder's exegesis. For here he elevates the Mosaic pattern as it is continued in the exilic writers, above the Davidic pattern of kingship that names a strand of Jewish identity continued in the Maccabees, the Bar Kochba revolt, and contemporary Zionism.[101] Indeed, for Yoder, the latter strand

---

99. Yoder, "See How they God with their Face to the Sun," in *FTN*, 51–78, also reproduced in *JCSR*, 183–202.

100. Yoder, "Earthly Jerusalem," in *JCSR*, 161–66.

101. From the perspective of exilic normativity, Zionism is not the rejection of Jewish assimilation in favour of independent identity, but, rather, is the assimilation of Israel to the modern vision of nationhood as nation-state. See Yoder, "Jesus the Jewish Pacifist," in

is inappropriate precisely because it undercuts the notion of Israel's dependence on the transcendent God, and thereby destabilizes the community's ability to affirm the prevenient sovereignty of God over the principalities and powers.

By noting the "selective" nature of this reading we must be cautious to avoid two undeserved implications. First, this selectivity is not in tension with the basic tenets of christocentric "biblical realism" explored in our third chapter.[102] Second, and more importantly for our present purpose, selectivity does not imply an arbitrary or anachronistic reading. There is, we could suggest, a strong parallel between Yoder's "hermeneutics of peoplehood" and the Talmudic practices of Jewish textual reasoning. Equally, Yoder prefigures what has recently been described as the "New Perspective" school of New Testament scholars, in conceiving of Pauline discussion of "the law" in Romans as an intra-Judaic debate.[103] On this reading Yoder may, as we shall see in our discussion of "election," begin to avoid the danger of supersessionism by insisting that the Jewish-Christian schism "did not have to be."[104] As Yoder puts it, "What goes on here is *not* that I am 'co-opting' Jews to enlist them in my cause. It is that I am finding a story, which is really there, coming all the way down from Abraham, that has the grace to adopt me."[105]

Yoder notes a number of central facets of diaspora Jewish identity mirrored in the free-church vision. Both are local, non-sacerdotal communities grouped around a shared text.[106] Neither "Judaism" nor "Christianity" name discrete, identifiable, and stable identities, for both Judaism and what we have earlier called the "becoming church" are

---

JCSR 69–89, at 85; "It Did Not Have to Be," ibid., 43–66; or, more generally, "Exodus and Exile: The Two Faces of Liberation." For an excellent discussion of these issues, see A. E. Weaver, "On Exile." See also A. E. Weaver, "Constantinianism, Zionism, Diaspora."

102. That is to say, selectivity is both inevitable and proper to the process of discernment. It is not convincing when particular political readings of scripture are accused of being "selective" or "culturally determined"—as if the mere assertion of these conditions is sufficient to refute the logic of the argument.

103. See Yoder, "Paul the Judaizer," in *JCSR*, 93–101.

104. Yoder, "It Did Not Have to Be," in *JCSR*, 43–66. For a comparison of Yoder to the New Perspective, as represented by N. T. Wright, see Harink, *Paul among the Postliberals*. Although Harink is largely fair to Yoder, his reading of Wright is occasionally somewhat over-egged and ungenerous.

105. Yoder, "Jewishness of the Free Church," in *JCSR*, 105–19, 115.

106. Yoder, *JCSR*, 187. Yoder also locates the free-church's restitutionism within the *halakahik* practices of Judaism. "Restitution of the Church," in *JCSR*, 133–43.

constantly negotiated through textual reasoning.[107] These commonalities grow out of a shared concern to maintain the "otherness" of the community (conceived not as interior purity, but as witnessing forms of holiness), or, as the Psalmist puts it, to sing the Lord's song in a foreign land (Psalm 137).

To frame the issue in this way may be seen to provide an important constructive counterbalance to the critical stance of anti-Constantinianism. Gerald Schlabach attempts to open a more explicit constructive element to Yoder's thought by positing Constantinianism as a particular form of a more basic issue—named as the "Deuteronomic problem." He defines this simply as

> . . . the problem of how to receive and celebrate the blessing, the *shalom*, the good, of "the land" that God desires to give, yet to do so without defensively and violently hoarding God's blessing.[108]

I suggest that, without abandoning the important and more directly political language of Constantinianism, Yoder's increasing interest in the politics of exile represents a parallel move to Schlabach's suggestion.[109] Indeed, it is precisely the exilic mode, with its continuation of the Mosaic refusal to reify God's blessing, that safeguard's against the dangers Schlabach appropriately identifies.

For Schlabach, the challenge of the Deuteronomists requires greater attention to the institutional existence of the community within "the land." If all the critics of Constantinianism can offer is a persistent suspicion of all institutions as coercive, coupled with a romanticized notion of the restoration of face-to-face communities, then "they are admitting that they really have no idea how to live long in the land that God would give them."[110] We have seen in previous chapters how Yoder's vision of social change refuses to be content with this stereotypical communitarian rhetoric. The motif of exile denotes a creatively engaged mode of life. It is emphatically not a mere subsistence within the world that eschews transformative engagement with existing institutions.

The life of diaspora citizenship, says Yoder, is one of "cosmopolitan homelessness." In many ways this correlates with the arguments for the

---

107. Yoder, "Judaism as a Non-non-Christian Religion" in ibid., 147–58, 150.

108. Schlabach, "Deutoronomic or Constantinian," 451.

109. Yoder appears to conceive of the Jeremianic turn as an equally basic moment to the Constantinian, see *FTN*, 8–9.

110. Schlabach, "Deuteronomic or Constantinian," 464–65.

prophetic nature of immanent criticism we encountered at the outset of our discussion. Yet the "cosmopolitan" focus of Yoder's view, I suggest, highlights a level of constructive involvement and diverse levels of engagement that is missing from philosophical invocations of the exilic nature of criticism, which often correlate "exile" solely with detachment or postmodern flux.[111] The recounting of missionary encounters, with which this book began, can now be placed within this wider context of continuing exilic presence. The missionary challenge to sing the song of the Lord in a foreign land led the Jews to become polyglots—to maintain loyalty to their own culture while learning the languages of Babylon and participating creatively within the city of exile.[112]

Exile as Continuous

The motif of exile is not denotative of a singular stance or rigid prescription of roles, but of the variety of ad hoc forms of response to various settings and power structures. The image of exile is fruitful for our reflections not simply because it places a welcome emphasis on adaptability and creative engagement with the state, but because the Jewish pattern of that adaptability allows greater critical reference to the fissiparous practices of governmental power *beyond* the state.

We turn next to Yoder's understanding of the contemporary situation as a *continuation* of exilic life and will note how it displays many important parallels with contemporary philosophical notions of "transversal" dissent and the wider exercise of governmental power. I shall then show how the connotations of blessing within Yoder's theology of exile both counter the failures within Michel Foucault's understanding of "governmentality" and lead on to the requirement for a more substantial theology of election than Yoder provided.

The normativity of the exilic pattern leads Yoder to affirm a singularly important occurrence of the way those outside of the Church may call it back to faithfulness. In so doing he also provides a dramatically non-supersessionist reading of Judaism. He argues that, through the development of rabbinic Judaism, the Jews

---

111. I am thinking here of slogans like Georg Lukacs's "transcendental homelessness" and even Adorno's discussion of the impossibility of "dwelling." For Adorno "dwelling" is no longer possible—"it is part of morality not to be at home in one's home." Adorno, *Minima Moralia: Reflections from Damaged Life*, 38–39. Both Lukacs and Adorno are cited in A. E. Weaver, "On Exile," 169–71.

112. Yoder, *JCSR*, 193.

were able to maintain identity without turf or sword, community without sovereignty. They thereby demonstrated pragmatically the viability of the ethic of Jeremiah and Jesus.

In sum, the Jews of the Diaspora were for over a millennium the closest thing to the ethic of Jesus existing on any significant scale anywhere in Christendom.[113]

In addition to his characteristic stress on the contingent and regrettable nature of the Jewish-Christian schism, this passage, like many others, demonstrates the important claim that the exilic condition has continued unabated since the time of the Jeremiah. Christ's own mission was undertaken within the setting of life within an occupied territory. Indeed the hope of return to the land (reflected, only in part, in messianic expectation)[114] is not fulfilled in the incarnation, but remains subject to eschatological tension.[115]

It is also possible to subject the continuing nature of exile to premature (Constantinian) foreclosure. Yoder's normative reading therefore runs contrary to the claims of contemporary Zionism, and indeed, to some readings of the "post-exilic" writings of Ezra and Nehemiah. For Yoder, the false return represented by these prophets is read as an inappropriate deviation from the Jeremianic line, for they "reconstituted a cult and a polity as a branch of the pagan imperial government."[116] The post-exilic writers are therefore taken as a return to that proto-Constantinian line that later continued into the Sadducean attempts at restoration. In denying the pacifism of "not being in charge," such approaches run counter to YHWH's will for his elect people, and therefore, claims Yoder, such attempts are not prospered by God.[117] Yoder combines normative and descriptive implications when he insists,

> To "seek the peace of the city where JHWH has sent you" meant for Jewry all the way from Jeremiah to Rosenzweig and Bucer the acceptance of a non-sovereign, non-territorial self-definition.[118]

113. Yoder, "Jesus," in *JCSR*, 69–89, 81–82. For further discussion of the claim, see *CAW*, 123–30.

114. Wright, *New Testament and the People of God*, 299–301.

115. We could speculate that the reading of the restoration of Davidic kingship and the reconstitution of Israel around Christ as a completed end of exile is the root of O'Donovan's eschatological foreclosure.

116. Yoder, *JCSR*, 194.

117. Yoder, "On Not Being In Charge," in *JCSR*, 168–79, 170.

118. Yoder, "To Serve God and to Rule the World," in *RP*, 133.

Eschatology, Exile, and Election

However, contrary to Yoder's own exegesis, a more sympathetic reading of some supposedly post-exilic writers may also allow us to gain valuable insights into how the life of galuth citizenship adapts in a variety of ways to the constellation of power in which it finds itself. The supposed return to the land under Persian rule was not an end to exile per se, but represented a structure of power that required a radically different response and mode of action from the exilic community. Admittedly, in the face of this new structure of power, a proto-Constantinian drift toward a more patrician politics may easily be detected. But even here the shift is not total. There remain anti-Constantinian moments. The continuing galuth status of the Jews is never far from view. Thus Neh 9:36 reads "Here we are, slaves to this day—slaves in the land that you gave to our ancestors to enjoy its fruit and its gifts."

Daniel Smith-Christopher provides a fascinating rereading of these "post-exilic" prophets, which understands their stance as, to use James Scott's term, a "hidden transcript" within the Persian court.[119] Undoubtedly some texts here, as in second and third Isaiah, present a positive picture of life under the Persian empire. Indeed, one could suggest that the accretion of messianic titles to Cyrus in Isaiah 45 provides something of a prototype for Eusebius of Caesarea's panegyric descriptions of Constantine.[120] Nevertheless, Ezra and Nehemiah also display parallels with the other occurrences of the motif of "standing before the king" in the account of figures like Joseph and Daniel, with which Yoder expresses greater affinity. In this motif the apparent power imbalance of ruler over prophet is reversed through the perception and faithfulness of the prophet. In the post-exilic writers the authority of the ruler is secondary to that of the prophets (Zechariah and Haggai) (Ezra 5:1–2, 6:14). Smith-Christopher allusively compares the context of restrictive requirements for permission from the King to the practices of domination seen in the "ever-present requirement to carry "papers" in authoritarian regimes."[121] The relationship of prophet to king is not one of easy

---

119. Smith-Christopher, *A Biblical Theology of Exile*, 35–45.

120. Of course, Eusebius's *Vita Constantini* 1.7, elevates Constantine well above the transitory and limited achievements of Cyrus. See Eusebius, "Life of Constantine," 483.

121. Smith-Christopher, *Biblical Theology of Exile*, 38. This is obviously a theme pregnant with potential. It is beyond the limits of this current discussion to elaborate on it. Suffice it to say for now that Georgio Agamben's biopolitical analysis of sovereignty and "bare life," extending Foucauldian concerns, may well be appropriately tempered by a reading of such themes. I offer here a theological IOU for a future exploration of

co-operation (note the fear Nehemiah experiences before his address to Artaxerxes, Neh 2:3). We could also suggest that the formal honorific mode of address to the King is subverted through a prior confession that YHWH is working his restorative purposes, in part, through "stirring the hearts" of rulers (Ezra 1:1).

Indeed, despite his equation of Ezra and Nehemiah with the proto-Constantinian nationalist line, Yoder notes that even here

> all that happens stays well within the constraints of submission to the Gentile empire. . . . Thus the reorientation of identity by the Jeremianic shift even comes back to give a new quality to the part of the story which returns to *Eretz* Israel.[122]

Two points arise from this brief consideration of post-exilic writings. First, that the practices of exilic politics are not to be exclusively associated with the anti-monarchist Mosaic strand with which Yoder aligns his thought. This is only to say, however, that the ecclesiological parallels to the free-church vision that Yoder draws bear a contingent, and not a necessary, relationship to the normativity of exilic politics. Even if we agree that the free-church vision most fully expresses central aspects of the Jeremianic mandate, we can also say that hierachical, established, and sacerdotal forms of ecclesiology may also exhibit important characteristics of exilic politics. Second, our discussion of exilic politics within more putatively co-operative modes of Church-state relations highlights the complex dynamics of governmental control that a politics of exile must attend to. I suggest a brief consideration of these wider operations of governmental power in contemporary society will allow us to see the importance of Yoder's insistence that the exile continues into the present.

Excursus on Foucault's Notion of "Governmentality"

In stressing the discernment required of the exilic community in relation to the operations of governmental power, I suggest that a fruitful comparison can be drawn with the political writings of the French postmodern philosopher and social critic Michel Foucault. Foucault's characteristic focus on the way all discourses exercise forms of power that constrain and discipline their subjects was frequently misconstrued

---

this. Agamben's account is found in English in an array of works, especially *Homo Sacer*; *Remnants of Auschwitz*; and *State of Exception*.

122. Yoder, *JCSR*, 188.

Eschatology, Exile, and Election

as providing a bleak picture of inescapably oppressive rationalities. Yet, Foucault responded

> My point is not that everything is bad, but that everything is dangerous, which is not exactly the same as bad. If everything is dangerous, then we always have something to do. So my position leads not to apathy but to hyper- and pessimistic activism.[123]

There are significant parallels between Jacques Ellul's notion of "active pessimism" in the face of the technocratic dominance of the powers and Foucault's language here.[124] Activism, for Foucault, is fostered in the discernment of the dangers inherent in all "technologies of the self."[125] These technologies take on multifarious forms, each exerting disciplinary power. For Foucault, the state exists solely as a constellation of these technologies. In his terms it is a "composite reality" and a "mythicized abstraction."[126] This fluctuating nature of state existence fits well with our previous insistence that the state has no ontology in and of itself. Foucault continues to argue that the state, as a discrete entity, has been afforded far too much attention. His famous aphorism that "in political theory we are yet to cut off the King's head" should be taken as an endeavor to broaden the examination of the operation of power and domination beyond concerns for sovereignty and obedience.[127] This, perhaps, is why a Foucaultian understanding of social criticism has been defended as so fruitful for our increasingly globalized and "post-statist" situation.[128]

In this aspect at least, Foucault provides scope for us to expand on Yoder's understanding of the nature and role of the state. I suggest that Foucault's notions of "governmentality" and what he calls "bio-power" can be held to be largely (though not entirely) consonant with Yoder's own concerns for the political nature of the life of the Church. Foucault's yearning for this proverbial decapitation of the monarch is born out of a

---

123. Foucault, *Ethics, Subjectivity and Truth*, 256.

124. Ellul, *Meaning of the City*, 181. However, one should not read Ellul's "active pesimism" and Foucault's "hyper- and pessimistic activism" too univocally. Foucault also names the modern nation-state "demonic." See Dean, *Governmentality*, 96.

125. Foucault, "Technologies of the Self," 223–51. See also Foucault, *Care of the Self*.

126. Foucault, "Governmentality," 87–104.

127 Dean, *Governmentality*, 24–25, quoting Foucault, *Power/Knowledge*, 121.

128. See for example, Bleiker, *Popular Dissent*. John Hoffman provides a clear and sober examination of the notion of post-statist politics, the problems of Weberian definitions of the state, and an exposition of the anti-statist nature of democratic ideals. Hoffman, *Beyond the State*. See also McGrew, Lewis, et al., *Global Politics*.

realization that government "is not just a power needing to be tamed or an authority needing to be legitimized. It is an activity and an art which concerns all and which touches each."[129] Through his genealogy of the subject he explains how, in modern Western civilization, techniques of domination interact with techniques of the self. External dominating practices are combined with an increasing level of self-government.[130]

The notion of "governmentality" springs from Foucault's response to critics for whom his writings, in their focus on specific events and genealogies, failed to account for the important role played by larger political systems like the state. Foucault's reply took the characteristic form of the exposure and denial of the supposedly self-evident importance of the state-form.[131] However, his premature death has prevented much of the embryonic writings on governmentality from receiving widespread attention. Even so, the concept has inspired a series of diverse studies of modern liberal society. Foucault defined government simply and profoundly as "the conduct of conduct." If the nature of the state institution is moulded by the sort of governmental practices it undertakes, rather than the reverse, then it is this governmental rationality, and not the structure of the state itself, which should assume primacy in a critical agenda. In this sense Foucault's approach is similar to the tactical approach to governmental practices we noted in the earlier contrast with O'Donovan.[132] Practices of government shape the field of action. Social critique therefore needs to be aware of the ubiquity of the disciplinary power through which persons and communities are placed in this field of action. That, of course, is the crux of Foucault's project—to enable dissent, to resist "what is," to encourage a "political spirituality."[133]

The genealogy of modern state power is traced to the "demonic" confluence of the Hebraic form of pastoral power (the shepherd-flock game) with the Greek civic model (the city-citizen game).[134] The specifics of these "games" need not concern us here; the point is to note

---

129. Burchell et al., *Foucault Effect*, x.

130. Lemke, "Birth of bio-politics."

131. Gordon, "Governmental rationality," 4.

132. Of course, it is clear that Certeau's language of tactics and strategies itself owes a great deal to Foucault's seminal writings.

133. "... the will to discover a different way of governing oneself through a different way of dividing up true and false—this is what I would call 'political *spiritualité*.'" Foucault, "Questions of Method," 82.

134. For a clear account of this, see Dean, *Governmentality*, 74–82, 96.

that in the combination of these two characters the state aggregates both an individualizing and a totalizing role.[135] That is to say, without conscious recognition of any inherent tensions, modern governmental rationality frames both the formation of the self and the nation. It is the understanding of the art of governing persons and populations.[136] Put simply, "government" comes to name the process by which the social is created as secure *and* the individual is created as free. The exercise of state power, from the eighteenth century on, has expanded well beyond the maintenance of peace and justice to "the disposition of society as a milieu of physical well-being, health, and optimum longevity." This in turn required the functioning of power beyond military and judicial apparatus, by "an ensemble of multiple regulations and institutions which in the eighteenth century takes the generic name of 'police.'"[137] Today this "science of police" is perhaps more clearly labeled as the exercise of technologies of policy.

Bio-politics, Foucault's phrase for that enormous terrain on which governance is exercised upon bodies (both individual and corporate, somatic and social) emerges in line with the problematization of "populations."[138] When "the population" comes to be seen as the context of the art of government, the state is no longer conceived as conforming to the model of the family. It is not, at least not any more, the practices of household management, the running of the *oikos*, writ large. "The family becomes an instrument rather than a model: the privileged instrument for the government of the population and not the chimerical model of good government."[139] It is population, and not geographical territory, which is the prime object of governmental activity. We might say that,

135. Bell provides a clear account of these two games in relation to the politics of forgiveness. See *Liberation Theology*. In particular, see Foucault, *Security, Territory, and Population*.

136. For the tracing of the governmental elements of these individualizing and totalizing moments in the formation of the modern welfare state, see Donzelot, "Mobilization of Society"; and Ashenden, "Questions of Criticism: Habermas and Foucault on Civil Society and Resistance." The connection between notions of governmentality and the (often enthusiastic) invocation of civil society in modern political ethics will concern us in the next chapter.

137. Foucault, "Politics of Health in the Eighteenth Century," 170.

138. Foucault, *Security, Territory, Population*; and *The Birth of Biopolitics*. Summary forms of these lectures are given in *Ethics: Subjectivity and Truth*, 67–71 and 72–79 respectively.

139. Foucault, *Governmentality*, 100.

though pastoral power is itself transformed in the process, sovereignty is now exercised over the flock, not (primarily) the field.[140] For Foucault, this marks a sea change. The bio-political domain emerges at the threshold of modernity, and there it establishes an "era of governmentality."

Both Foucault and Yoder, in slightly different ways, bring into question any assumption that the supposedly co-operative basis of modern political society is free from moments of oligarchic rule. Neither Yoder nor Foucault should be read through libertarian lenses—i.e., advocating a minimalist non-interventionist state *à la* Robert Nozick. Yoder is quite clear that it has always been the case that "government" is more than just "the sword"—and that "when modern social orders assign to 'government' the administration of many other kinds of services, it is by no means necessary to apply to them all the same church/world dualism which the New Testament applied to servanthood and the sword."[141] Indeed, it is not often appreciated by Yoder's critics that active participation in wider functionings of government, including wider exercises of "power" are not (necessarily and absolutely) antithetical to the non-Constantinian witness of the diaspora community. Thus, Yoder argues,

> The assumption that commitment to a minority ethic, derived from a minority faith, must issue logically in withdrawal from significant involvement in the social process, including the refusal of office holders or adversary roles, is itself an outworking of the establishment axioms which I am challenging. It assumes ... that the relevance of an ethical stance depends on the readiness of its constituency to fill *all* the posts in society. It assumes ... that the paradigm of the exercise of social responsibility is not the civil servant or the opposition legislator, the minority agitator or the political prisoner, but the sovereign.[142]

To affirm this is not a concession, but a challenge. With the "governmentalization of the state" the problem of sovereignty does not fade away, but becomes all the more acute. For Foucault,

> [d]iscipline was never more important or more valorised than at the moment when it became important to manage a population; the managing of a population not only concerns the collective

---

140. Foucault, *Security, Territory and Population*, esp. 87–114.
141. Yoder, *PK*, 165.
142. Ibid. Emphasis mine.

mass of phenomena, the level of its aggregate effects, it also implies the management of population in its depths and its details.[143]

In order to further explore the comparative account of Foucault's notion of governmentality on the one hand, and Yoder's motifs of eschatology and exile on the other, let us consider the way in which recent understandings of active citizenship have lead to a strongly disciplinary revision of social welfare policy. The dominance of a broadly neo-liberal agenda in both Britain and America means that the role of governing both individual and population through the series of discrete bio-political apparatus has been covertly transferred to the power of the market. The earlier model of the welfare state gives way, through persistent reform, to the neo-liberal construction of society along consumerist lines. As Thomas Lemke argues,

> [u]nlike the state in the classical liberal notion of rationality, for the neo-liberals the state does not define and monitor market freedom, for the market is itself the organizing and regulative principle underlying the state. . . . [*homo oeconomicus*] becomes a behaviouristically manipulable being and the correlative of a governmentality which systematically changes the variables of the "environment" and can count on the "rational choice" of individuals.[144]

Recent reform in the welfare state focuses on the rhetoric of a "stakeholder" society.[145] The consumer-self-with-a-social-conscience can find in this idiom an acceptable recasting of the welfare provision of the state. An element of compulsion attached to welfare initiatives is claimed to encourage an active and "self-responsible" form of citizenship. It is said that the paternalistic optimism of the earlier age of welfare traded on a deficient moral anthropology. Frank Field, one of the architects of stakeholder policy in the UK, asserts that "[s]elf-interest, not altruism,

---

143. Foucault, *Governmentality*, 102.

144. Lemke, "The birth of Bio-politics," 200.

145. There is an extraordinary utopianism surrounding the notion of stakeholder society. Witness the salvation from social division predicted in Ackerman and Alstott, *Stakeholder Society*. The rhetoric of stakeholding shows a strange conglomeration of Anglo-American free market capitalism with the language of Continental European social democracy. Patrick Minford is characteristic of the flip-side of this stakeholder optimism in sounding a vitriolic restatement of the triumph of capitalism, *a la* Fukuyama. Minford, *Markets not Stakes*.

is mankind's main driving force."[146] In compelling this "active" form of citizenship, government ensures that each citizen "owns" his or her share of the welfare capital that is generated.[147] It is a model of the production of an inclusive and just society that is fundamentally pessimistic about the capacity for individual altruism, and conversely optimistic regarding the sort of "collective responsibility" placed on those individuals when construed primarily as consumers. This consumerist version of collective responsibility trades the notion of mutual interdependence for a vision of self-interest vitiated through the benevolent administration of various "autonomous corporations." It does not appear to be the recovery of Christian Socialism that Field claims, but a grand and somewhat crude reversal of Reinhold Niebuhr's *Moral Man and Immoral Society*.

The increasingly overt disciplinary structures of this new politics of welfare do little to address the needs of those upon whom the role of "active citizen" places the highest burden. To be an active citizen, after all, means to participate in the formal economy. As the rhetoric of the moment has it, the "enabling state" at the heart of these programs must move beyond the monolithic provision of the paternalistic public sector to a series of consumer options.[148] In proselytizing mode, Tony Blair claims it is only by giving people the chance to save capital that social mobility will be driven up. This "social mobility" is, he claims, "the great force for equality in market economies."[149] Under the guise of enforced "participation," governmental process comes to be used to place the population within the frame of a consumerist construction of the social market.[150] Poorer communities are "freed" to become both producers and consumers of a never-satiated desire for the fruits of capital. The egalitarianism that underwrote the link between welfare and character made by Beveridge,

---

146. Field, *Stakeholder Welfare*, 19.

147. Ironically the "take-up" of stakeholder pensions in Britain, one of the mainstays of long-term welfare reform, has occurred predominantly within middle-class income groups. It remains uncertain that the intention to include those on the lowest incomes in such schemes, in order to combat social exclusion and facilitate reform of welfare provision, will be met through the combination of market forces and administrative compulsion.

148. The phrase comes from Tony Blair's 2002 Labor Party Conference address, cited in White, "Blair Message," 1.

149. Blair, "Speech on Welfare Reform."

150. Jordan, *New Politics of Welfare*, 222.

Tawney, and Temple withers in favor of an ever-more technical (in Ellul's sense) and governmental conception of economic justice.[151]

Foucault argues that in the eighteenth century "sovereignty" is a problem because it must now answer another set of questions than those addressed by Machiavelli. It is, he says,

> no longer a question of . . . How to deduce an art of government from theories of sovereignty, but rather, given the existence and deployment of an art of government, what juridical form, what institutional form, and what legal basis could be given to the sovereignty typical of a state.[152]

Nonetheless, Foucault is clear that the notion of sovereignty coming from Hobbes is no longer to be the focus of critique.[153] Foucault's language of governmentality can bring into sharp relief the disciplinary constraints operative behind the rhetoric of empowerment and freedom that dominate Western political discourse. Yoder's insistence that the exile continues to be normative in Christian social thought may safeguard against the more wholesale acceptance of any particular policy or extension of governmentality beyond the state—e.g., the defense of the social market found in some theological responses to recent social policy.[154] But the motif of exile does more than just maintain an appropriate level

---

151. The verdict of George and Wilding is damning, "stakeholder welfare will probably be no more effective in abolishing poverty than are today's schemes; it will be less redistributive, it is likely to be more supportive of work incentives, it will be just as complex administratively, it will have neutral effects on social cohesion, and it will be less costly to the state, although not to many individuals. . . . Playing on people's self-interest first and then appealing to their altruism may not prove convincing enough to win continued political support for subsidizing the weak in society." George, and Wilding, *British Society and Social Welfare*, 158–59.

152. Foucault, *Security, Territory and Population*, 106.

153. "We have to study power outside the model of Leviathan, outside the field delineated by juridical sovereignty and the institution of the State. . . . Truth to tell, if we are to struggle against disciplines, or rather against disciplinary power, in our search for a nondisciplinary power, we should not be turning to the old right of sovereignty; we should be looking for a new right that is both antidisciplinary and emancipated from the principle of sovereignty." Foucault, *Society Must be Defended*, 34, 39–40.

154. Theological responses to social policy often correspond to the prevailing construal of social benevolence. Thus theological justification has moved from the paternalism of F. D. Maurice, through the optimistic benevolence of William Temple's welfare state, and on to a sometimes insufficiently theological endorsement of a "social market economy." See, for example, Atherton, *Public Theology*. The correspondence between views of God and of the state is clearly shown in Nicholls, *Deity and Domination*.

of critical distance. We saw above how the Jeremianic mandate to "seek the peace of the city" is predicated upon a notion of peoplehood as utterly dependent on God. Indeed, the theological vision of true freedom is based precisely on this true dependence. As we saw in relation to the post-exilic prophets, the "prior loyalty of the people of God", as Yoder puts it, requires the exilic community to maintain a healthy skepticism in relation to even the most apparently benevolent of governments.[155] That is not to say that a Machiavellian account of political motivation takes precedence—the exilic mind is one of skepticism, not cynicism. Rather, it is to insist that the critical role of the galuth community has an integrity of its own, regardless of the more constructive elements sometimes present in the stance of cosmopolitan homelessness.

It is in the relation of critical to constructive elements that Yoder and Foucault diverge in a way most significant to our present concerns. Yet in their appreciation for local practices of resistance, both argue for the independence of critical from constructive imperatives. Foucault's displacing of the sovereign as the subject of discourse on power strongly corresponds to Yoder's anti-Constantinian denial of Caesar as "the only mover of history."[156] For Foucault and Yoder, this analysis does not lead to apathy and an acceptance of futility. Foucault's "cratology" (theory of power) of "carcereal society" is often taken to reveal a reformist, as opposed to revolutionary, practice of resistance.[157] He is even read as a neoconservative by Habermas.[158] But need the local practices of resistance that follow from Foucault's work necessarily lead to a hopelessness that in turn may yield a paralysis of action? We saw in the previous chapter that David Toole finds in Foucault a tendency towards a tragic politics, which, ultimately, cannot ground human meaning and hope. Certainly the lack of an overarching hope can stultify a long-term constructive vision; but those finding in Foucault the resources for reflecting on and empowering their own practices of dissent would dispute any connotation of futility. Even if Toole is right, the "lyricism of protest" discerned in Foucault should be given its due. Foucault denies the charges of paralysis and anaesthesia, again turning the tables—"[t]he necessity of reform mustn't be

---

155. Yoder, "Religious Liberty."

156. Yoder, AE, 56.

157. For a construal of Foucault as reformist, see Michael, "Politics of Michel Foucault," 51–68.

158. Habermas, *Philosophical Discourses*, 238–93.

allowed to become a form of blackmail serving to limit, reduce or halt the exercise of criticism."[159]

Foucault's thoroughgoing historicism contrasts here with Yoder's important christological circumscription of historical relativity. By contrast with Foucault's history of power, with its motifs of chance and arbitrary succession, we find in both Yoder's theology of the cross (with its revolutionary vision of powerlessness and patience in the face of contingency) and his exilic vision (with its emphasis on meaning in apparently powerless settings) a form of politics that refuses the absolute juxtaposition between revolution and reform. Yoder is certainly clearer than Foucault that critique and dissent are not just negative, but are oriented by the "pro" in protest—for Christian protest, the normative vision comes from the eschatological revelation of Christ as Lord.[160] It is in light of this confession that

> a minority group with no immediate chance of contributing to the ways things go may still by its dissent maintain the wider community's awareness of some issues in such a way that ideas which are unrealistic for the present come to be credible later.[161]

In emphasizing the gradual nature of radical social transformation, Yoder's understanding of dissent also fits well with the contemporary theories of anti-hegemonic politics as a politics of truth. It also fits well enough with the notion of "transversal" dissent—that is, those actions of protest which cut across normal boundaries such as nation or ethnicity, that are becoming increasingly influential as the diverse phenomena of globalization continue apace. So, for example, Roland Bleiker's important account of transversal dissent narrates the ways in which gradual cultural shifts contributed to the fall of the Berlin wall. The exilic motif may sit well with an account of the potency of the quiet transformations of perception provided, for example, by the East German Protestant churches' dissemination of music, novels, and poetry.[162] Such transformed perceptions may provide some grounds for hope even as the diverse phenomena of globalization continue apace. Nonetheless, one must be cautious in appropriating such parallels too quickly. Both the

---

159. Foucault, "Questions of Method."
160. Yoder, "Christianity and Protest."
161. Yoder, *PJ*, 96.
162. Blieker, *Popular Dissent, Human Agency and Global Politics*.

operations of governmentality, and resistance to it, emerge in local, particular and ad hoc ways; but just as Yoder would not have endorsed all forms of nonviolent resistance, so too, not all local practices would be acceptable—to be a critic of sovereignty is not necessarily to escape the danger of Constantinianism.

The ethos of critique found in Foucault's understanding of governmentality is not primarily a patrician one, by which I mean, as Foucault has it, "[c]ritique doesn't have to be the premise of a deduction which concludes: this then is what needs to be done. It should be an instrument for those who fight, for those who resist and refuse what is."[163] The parallel with Yoder's vision of ecclesial critique in relation to "transformation" is noteworthy. Yoder consistently rebuffs those who, through an imperative to the "responsible" presentation of constructive options, would confine pacifist witnesses to the margin of idealist conscience-pricking.[164] Indeed, Foucault's account of the local character of critique is expressed in an idiom that evokes strong associations with Yoder's normative vision of exilic citizenship.

> I think that the essentially local character of critique in fact indicates something resembling a sort of autonomous and noncentralized theoretical production, or in other words a theoretical production that does not need a visa from some common regime to establish its validity.[165]

Contrary to some readings, Yoder does not eschew all transformative agendas or purposive reasoning. Chris Huebner's otherwise impressive reading of Yoder's epistemology of nonviolence seems to me to compromise the constructive element in the exposition of exilic cosmopolitanism. Huebner asserts that Yoder rejected any instrumentalist thinking, and "did not seek a nonviolent way of transforming society or securing the future, but claimed that the peace of Christ involves a rejection of the possessive logic of security and social transformation."[166] Huebner's

---

163. Foucault, "Questions of Method," 84. On Foucault's notion of governmentality establishing a particular *ethos*, as opposed to a *method* or a *theory* of critique, see Barry, Osborne, and Rose, "Liberalism, Neo-liberalism and Governmentality: Introduction."

164. E.g., Yoder, *PK*, 178–79.

165. Foucault, *Society Must Be Defended*, 6.

166. Huebner, "Yoder and Virilio," 58. For a fuller account of Huebner's reading of Yoder's epistemological pacifism, with which I would be in broad agreement, see Huebner, "Unhandling History."

point seems to me to conflate Yoder's cautionary skepticism in regard to the Constantinian danger of "putting handles on history," as he put it, with a total rejection of transformative agendas. That may even be to imbibe precisely the sort of (Reinhold) Niebuhrian dichotomy between effectiveness and fidelity that Yoder deconstructs.

I suggest that, through attentiveness to what I have discerned as the "doxological" understanding of social change in Yoder's thought, critical and constructive modes can both be found in Yoder's exposition of exilic life. It is within this framework of galuth citizenship that the imperative for transformation may escape the imprecision Yoder criticizes in H. Richard Niebuhr. The exilic community's dependence on God for its own mission militates against the twin dangers of Niebuhr's implied account of moral agency—which was constrained by a monolithic understanding of culture and restricted to a singular (coercive) model of action. To talk of transformation in such limited terms is, says Yoder, "not so much wrong as empty."[167] Yoder does not deny the imperative to constructive social engagement. What he does deny are two misplaced understandings of transformation: first, that the meaning of the term is immediately discernible through reference to some ideal order—as opposed to focusing on specific situations or issues;[168] and second, that the constructive imperative can be said to constrain the critical obligation. Behind such a constriction of critique can lurk a covert liberal optimism in the beneficence of the state institution.

Exile as Blessing

Yoder's normative reading of the exile as a continuous condition of God's people refuses to see the Babylonian captivity as a temporary punitive hiatus from which a swift return would mark the continuation of the monarchic project. To take the idiom of the previous section, we should distinguish between the critical and constructive elements of the Jeremian reading of the exilic condition. The critical moment is seen in the way both the prophets and the Deuteronomists relate the exile to the failure of Israel's kingship experiment. Of course, exile entails suffering and loss. Yet in no way does this diminish the constructive rhetoric of Jeremiah's prophecy—the exile is an occasion for the continued mission of the chosen

---

167. Yoder, *AT*, 68.
168. Yoder, *CWS*, 38–39; *OR*, 79.

people of God.[169] It is the continuation of the promise made to Abraham in Gen 12:3—"in you all the families of the earth shall be blessed." Again the non-possessive logic of a peoplehood guaranteed only through dependence upon YHWH comes into view. Indeed, we might say, Israel is a peoplehood constituted not by the centripetal force of shared ethnicity, location, or political sovereignty, but by the centrifugal operation of divine blessing. As Yoder puts it, "Israel's very existence as a nation is not a self-guaranteeing institution but a recurrent gift of grace."[170]

The connotations of calling and blessing within exile are also found in Yoder's reflections on the gracious nature of the dispersal spoken of in the legend of the Tower of Babel. He finds the motif of exile preferable to Jeffrey Stout's advocacy of *bricolage* as a response to the fragmentation of moral language in modernity.[171] The *bricoleur* adapts to fragmentation only through a tentative approach that never risks costly involvement. The exile, by contrast, not only maintains their subculture through a greater degree of commitment to "the city," but thereby contributes to making the wider world viable.[172] Yet the diaspora people of God make their contribution, for Yoder, without engaging in the machinations of power politics.

> Not being in charge of the civil order is sometimes a more strategic way to be important for its survival or its flourishing than to fight over the throne. In dramatic and traumatic cases the Jews were murdered or banished; in more, quieter cases they were needed and appreciated despite (or thanks to) their nonconformity.[173]

That said, as we shall see in the next chapter, the exilic community's impact upon wider society should not lead us to read Yoder as providing support for the tendency of some theorists to limit the social impact of religious groups to civil society (as differentiated from the state itself).

---

169. Thus Yoder claims, "The general understanding, held by scholars today, of the editorial slant of the 'deuteronomic historian(s),' is that those narrator's reason for retelling the whole history of royal Israel was to show who was to blame for the exile. But the fact that there was unfaithfulness along the way does not make the mission to Babylon any less of a mission. It merely intensifies what we have already seen about the moral ambivalence of kingship." *JCSR*, 199 n. 30.

170. Yoder, *RP*, 133.

171. Stout, *Ethics After Babel*.

172. Yoder, *JCSR*, 194–95.

173. Ibid., 172.

Eschatology, Exile, and Election 251

The view of galuth Israel as a blessing to the nations is based in Yoder's reading of historical revelation. Thus Jesus's restructuring of Israelite peoplehood follows in continuity with the providential occurrence of exile. The normativity of nonviolent communal life is founded not upon some Marcionite narration of a capricious shift in divine will, but on the historical realization of the Abrahamic covenant.[174] It is worth quoting Yoder at length:

> From the ancient Hebrews through the later prophets up to Jesus there was real historical movement, real "progress"; but the focus of this progress was not a changing of ethical codes but rather in an increasingly precise definition of the nature of peoplehood. The identification of the people of Israel with the state of Israel was progressively loosened by all of the events and prophecies of the Old Testament. It was loosened in a positive way by the development of an increasing vision for the concern of Yahweh for *all* peoples and by the promise of a time when all peoples would come to Jerusalem to learn the law; it was loosened as well in a negative direction by the development of a concept of the faithful remnant, no longer assuming that Israel as a geographical and ethnic body would be usable for Jahweh's purposes. These two changes in turn altered the relevance of the prohibition on killing. Once all men are seen as potential partakers of the covenant, then the outsider can no longer be perceived as less than human or as an object for sacrificing. Once one's own national existence is no longer seen as a guarantee of Jahweh's favor, then to save this national existence by a holy war is no longer a purpose for which miracles would be expected. Thus the dismantling of the applicability of the concept of the holy war takes place not by promulgation of a new ethical demand but by a restructuring of the Israelite perception of community under God.[175]

Yet any endorsement of the exilic motif as useful for social ethics requires attentiveness to the tension between metaphorical and actual senses of the term. Yoder is sensitive to the tension here. Indeed, as we have seen before, the relevance of such models to contemporary situations operates analogously. Nonetheless Yoder stops short of describing any specific way in which the exilic model may "give hope to other refugees"

---

174. Thus John Miller's accusation of Marcionitism in Yoder's christocentric theology is entirely inappropriate. Miller "In the Footseps of Marcion."

175. Yoder, *OR*, 107–8.

or victims of imperial displacement.[176] Alain Epp Weaver has provided a suggestive account of the nonviolent strategies found in Yoder's theology of exile in relation to the present situation of Palestinian refugees.[177] In the final chapter I shall also suggest that the exilic model of citizenship provides Yoder with a suitable vocabulary for describing the mission of the Church in relation to the exclusionary aspects of modernity. Zygmunt Bauman provides a reading of global "modernization" as a process that, in striving for economic "progress," creates ever increasing numbers of migrants, refugees, and a variety of "human waste."[178] Yoder's reading of the Abrahamic promise continuing through the condition of diaspora may provide grounds for affirming the value of these "redundant populations" within the economy of God's blessing. It is to that promise itself that we now turn.

Election

The third panel in the triptych of a theology of governmental power will allow further clarification of the relation of metaphorical to actual exilic conditions. Perhaps the greatest discrepancy between the metaphorical and the actual is found in the largely voluntary nature of the former. Actual exilic existence, almost without exception, remains a condition imposed upon a populace by circumstance, or as a consequence of complex historical and political processes. I suggest that attention to the doctrine of election will deepen the understanding of exile as a condition of the continuation of the identity of Israel, and hence, the Church, as a blessing "for the nations."

While some readers detect in Yoder a deliberate aversion to the doctrine of election, I suggest that, while somewhat underdeveloped, there is a tacit understanding of election in relation to mission that may, with some critical revision, compliment the eschatological and exilic motifs of his theology of governmental power.[179] We shall pay attention to two elements of Yoder's thought in order to demonstrate the presence of a tacit understanding of election: these are Yoder's understanding of the

---

176. Yoder, *JCSR*, 195–96.
177. A. E. Weaver, "Constantinianism, Zionism, Diaspora."
178. Bauman, *Wasted Lives*.
179. See Harink, *Paul Among the Postliberals*, 195–98.

voluntariety of the exilic community, and his attempt to avoid supersessionistic readings of Judaism.

Voluntariety and a Tacit Doctrine of Election

Both Foucault and Yoder have, in rather different ways, been accused of utilizing accounts of human freedom and possessive individualism that owe too much to the liberal modernist vision they eschew. Foucault, the arch-critic of all humanisms still managed to write in favor of aspects of the Kantian vision.[180] Certainly there is a tension, which we cannot explore here, between the concern for (covertly liberal) defense of "freedom" in Foucault, and his Nietzschean disdain for metaphysics. Oliver O'Donovan argues that the critical potential of Yoder's thought is undermined by his detecting a single fault behind everything from "infant baptism, [to] the control of the church by civil authority, and the approbation of the violence of civil government within the doctrine of the just war."[181] O'Donovan claims that by centering such diverse issues on the maintenance of uncoerced voluntariety, Yoder conforms the Church to the model of a club or political party. In doing so, asks O'Donovan, "[i]s Yoder, in the name of non-conformity, not championing a great conformism, . . . just to prove that the church offers [the] late-modern order no serious threat?" For O'Donovan, Yoder maintains "voluntariety" at the expense of "belief." After all, a voluntary society is one that I could leave "without incurring grave or irremediable loss, which might seem a strange thing for a Christian to think about the church." Indeed, it would be strange. But Yoder would affirm neither the tendentious distinction between voluntariety and belief, nor the notion of an absence of grave loss at leaving the believing community.

Nevertheless, behind this atypically crass caricature lies a serious ecclesiological issue—O'Donovan's own *bête noir* of voluntarism. But why identify Yoder with it? By "voluntarism" O'Donovan means that tendency of modern (Western) moral thought to associate morality with the prior activity of man's will.[182] Its modern Christian variant is seen, he claims, in the rendering of Christian moral obligations as esoteric and a "function

---

180. Foucault, "What is Enlightenment?"; *Politics of Truth*.
181. O'Donovan, *DN*, 223–24.
182. O'Donovan, *RMO*, 116–19, 131–37.

of the believer's decision."[183] Yoder is not advocating the sort of moral relativism that renders "thou shalt not kill," and "thou shalt not commit adultery" as intra-ecclesial house rules that cannot be applied outside the Church. Quite the opposite! The problem is that, in seeking to protect political theology from this pernicious modern (and post-modern) myth, O'Donovan does not see in Yoder a sufficient differentiation between a thoroughgoing moral relativism (belief as commodity) and the affirmation of a moment of agapeic freedom in the gracious inclusion of believer into church.

In using the term "voluntary society" Yoder has invited misunderstanding in not distinguishing his account clearly from a "rationalist" understanding of faith.[184] However, I suggest that a rather tacit and underdeveloped theology of election could be elaborated to help, and, in turn, may also place in question the modern political myth of voluntariety. I agree that Yoder's language of voluntariety is problematic. A modernist understanding of the abstract "will" does not undergird it, but that is a misunderstanding his work does little to avoid. His intention in arguing for the voluntary nature of the Christian community is not the preservation of individual rational freedom, but the construction of a community of authentic nonviolent witness.[185] Nor then does Yoder line up with the modernist understanding that "social doctrine of whatever kind is coercive; [where] those who claim a social identity in terms of unnecessary belief do violence to those who do not share it."[186] To affirm the Church as a *voluntary* community is to say that the grace present in coming to belief, mediated as it is by formational traditions, entails an aspect (not necessarily a discernible punctiliar moment) of conscious and deliberate submission to communal life. This decision is then enacted in the rite of baptism. For Yoder, that there be a committed community is an essential precondition for authentic protest.[187] The freedom of Christ is not the fabricated liberty of the consumer, but the gracious embrace of the nonviolent life of the church.

Yoder's language of "coercing assent to the Gospel" is not some Pickwickian extension of "coercion" to all forms of rhetorical persuasion

---

183. Ibid., 16.
184. See Hauerwas and Fodor, "Remaining in Babylon."
185. Yoder, *PK*, 105–13. See also Biesecker-Mast, "Radical Christological Rhetoric."
186. O'Donovan, *DN*, 223.
187. Yoder, "Christianity and Protest."

(unlike Habermas's appeal to some chimerical pure, non-strategic communication). Yoder talks in these terms primarily in the exposition of what we have called his nonfoundationalist epistemology and the imperative to a stance of vulnerability in the face of the other. Here one cannot evade an obvious empirical discrepancy. Surely, it may be asked, in a modern, secularized situation, where any compulsory membership of the Church is but a dim memory, people aren't coerced into belief? Indeed the derision that religious belief can suffer at the hands of a "secularized" sacralizing of "autonomy" and "choice" would seem to point in the opposite direction. There is perhaps some divergence between the context of O'Donovan and Yoder. The U. S. certainly displays a more overt form of civil religion. Does this mean we should concede O'Donovan's critique? Not in its entirety. I have already suggested that Yoder's insistence upon voluntariety could have been articulated in ways that better guard against the miscontrual found in O'Donovan. Yoder can seem to speak of the voluntariety of both believer and unbeliever as a self-evident and irreducible good.[188] It is understandable that, without a fulsome engagement with the wider claims of Yoder's theology, this may well sound very much like the fetishization of "freedom" in modern liberal culture. This latter account is sustained in part by an abstract notion of arbitrary human will in which the capacity for choice is anthropologically basic, inviolable, and prior to social instantiation.

However, I suggest that the tacit account of election in Yoder's work, when suitably elaborated and expanded, may provide the beginnings (only) of a challenge to the political edifice now erected on this modern sovereign will. Indeed, I concur with Scott Bader-Saye's claim that the modern notion of political *voluntas* can emerge only with the "national supersessionism" found in Hobbes and Spinoza. In different ways these accounts combine a rejection of eschatology and the displacement (truly an inversion) of the doctrine of election from Israel and the Church and to the operation of the sovereign in the nation-state.[189] Thus for Spinoza the election of Israel ends not with the coming of Christ, but far earlier, with the loss of virtue presaging the exile. Without election Jewish attempts to maintain identity in exile are retrograde, stubborn, and seditious. They fail to recognize the divine elective blessing when

---

188. Yoder, "Burden and Discipline," 22–29.
189. Bader-Saye, *Church and Israel After Christendom*, 59–65.

transferred to the sovereign nation.[190] The same fault occurs in a politicized Christology, for the universal moral precepts taught by Christ, for Spinoza, promise only a spiritual reward of no temporal impact and thus do not in any way threaten or circumscribe the claims of the sovereign. Here covenant is reconfigured as contract. Divine initiative and the universal concern of YHWH's elective economy are replaced by the fearful social contracting of a newly-liberated people who through Moses divest their natural right to God at Sinai.[191] Whether this transferral to the sovereign is total, as in Hobbes, or partial, as in Spinoza, need not concern us here. The differences are significant, but in both cases the originary decision belongs to the sovereign but fearful will.

So how might a more robust theology of election lead in a different direction? In order to see the proper functioning of "election" underlying Yoder's thought we must first make an important distinction. For our purposes the doctrine of election is not to be taken as a soteriological category—i.e., that which was subjected to intense wranglings in Calvinist and Arminian thought.[192] Rather, it relates more directly to the narrative outlined above in relation to the ecclesiological and missiological aspects of the Abrahamic covenant. As mentioned previously, election here is a missiological and ecclesiological notion—because, as Barth rightly insisted in his creative reworking of the Calvinist approach, it is Christ who is the elect—and we who are incorporated into that election.[193] The election of Abraham, Isaac, and Jacob continues through the reconstitution of Israel around the person of Jesus, and, in and through him, is seen in the Church.[194]

The doctrine of election allows us to see YHWH's choice of Israel, Jesus and the Church as the means by which the reconciliation of the

---

190. See especially chapter 3, "On the Vocation of the Hebrews," in Spinoza, *Theological-political Treatise*, 43–56.

191. See especially chapter 17 of the *Theological-political Treatise*, which bears the somewhat cumbersome title "Where it is shown that no one can transfer all things to the sovereign power, and that it is not necessary to do so; on the character of the Hebrew state in the time of Moses, and in the period after his death before the appointment of the kings; on its excellence, and on the reasons why this divine state could perish, and why it could scarcely exist without sedition."

192. Although, it should not go unnoticed that the concepts of human freedom operative within those debates certainly has bearing on modern understandings of liberal freedom of choice.

193. Barth, *CD* II/2, 94–127.

194. Wright, *Jesus and the Victory of God*.

world with God is wrought.[195] As Colin Gunton puts it, "God elects the particular in order to achieve his universal purposes."[196] In this reconciliatory movement the Church is unashamedly partisan in its option for the poor; for, as is consonant with Yoder's assertion of the poor and oppressed as the bearers of the meaning of history, this partisanship is universal, i.e., catholic, in its scope.[197] Somewhat confusingly, O'Donovan notes the element of voluntariety inherent in the doctrine of election as it follows the Jeremianic pattern. Ever since Jeremiah taught a new covenant reaching into the hidden depths of the believer's heart (Jer 31:33ff) "an element of confessional voluntarism enters into Israel's sense of itself. . . . What Israel affords is a strong concept of the individual on a quite different basis from the individualism of the West."[198] It is precisely this sort of "voluntariety" that I contend best fits Yoder's description of the church. Furthermore, it is this different basis for individual and communal human freedom that empowers the resistance to the consumerist understanding we have detected in "stakeholder" governmentality.

What is missing in Yoder is an account of precisely how an understanding of voluntary decision is to escape an almost Pelagian denial of the prevenience of grace. Part of the problem lies in O'Donovan's mistaken reading of free-church ecclesiology as necessarily voluntarist in its view of the gathered community. To affirm the aspect of voluntariety in ecclesial election does not negate the divine work of constituting of the Church. It is not the individual's or the community's act of gathering that, in and of itself, *constitutes* the Church. Rather "the Spirit of God, acting through the word of God and the sacraments, is the real subject of the genesis of the church."[199] The act of constitution is not based in an ecclesiological form of the social contractarian theory. Likewise ecclesial voluntariety is not to be juxtaposed with a deterministic view of the effect of the formative community upon the will. The voluntariety of the

---

195. On the diaconal aspect of election see Lindbeck, "Gospel's Uniqueness," 223–52. Wright, *New Testament and the People of God*, 259–68.

196. Gunton, "Election and Ecclesiology." Gunton links this claim with "The dissenting stream of the Reformed tradition [which] offers models of a stronger distinction-in-relatedness between the Church and its social context than did Constantinianism, without falling into the voluntarist theologies of baptism and church membership which mark both Barth and modern Anabaptism alike." 213.

197. Moltmann, *Church in the Power of the Spirit*, 352.

198. O'Donovan, *DN*, 79–81. See also the discussion of this in Kroeker, "O'Donovan's Christendom."

199. Volf, *After Our Likeness*, 176ff.

associative element of the process of ecclesial constitution is to be combined with the "organic" nature of the formative community in a cyclical process through which a person is reborn into (rather than simply "joining") the Church.[200] In this way the modernist form of voluntarism is avoided, while Yoder's concern for the otherness of nonviolent Christian witness is maintained.

This missiological understanding of ecclesial election is consistent with how the voluntary nonviolent community envisaged by Yoder provides a construction of "the social" that is able to ground a significant theological critique, indeed we can properly call it a "demythologization," of the modern state. The exilic community (Israel and the Church) is the subject of God's elective blessing, and thus the conduit of his reconciling purposes. It is not the individual believer who is elect, but the community into which that believer is inducted in baptism. Election therefore differs from individual vocation in its ontological understanding of participation in Christ and incorporation into his body, the Church. The motif of the elect community marks a contrast with the voluntarist and consumerist reading of popular sovereignty. Just as Jesus cannot be easily reduced to "the ideal human being," the uniqueness of the chosen people cannot be emptied out into an ideal community of mankind; the kind of thing that Franz Rosenzweig detects in German Idealism that reinterprets the Jewish people as "the contingent bearer of a thought not bound up with its existence."[201]

Yet because in Yoder this is combined with the tactical reading of social change and the normativity of exilic forms of political engagement it also disallows any hint of theocratic politics. The emergence of modern political voluntarism, as we have it, is bound up with the transfer of sovereignty from God to self—most particularly flowing from nominalist assertions of divine potential power as absolute and unbound.[202] The monist deity whose latent power includes the ability to alter and undo any prior revelation of character has little to do with the Jesulogical norms defended here. Indeed it is only when the Father is viewed as possessing absolute sovereign power in excess of either Son or Spirit that the seeds

---

200. Ibid., 180ff.

201. Rosenzweig, "Atheistic Theology," in *Philosophical and Theological Writings*, 10–24, 16; as quoted in Hollander's excellent *Exemplarity and Chosenness*, 30.

202. Elshtain, *Sovereignty*, 50.

are sewn for modern views of human *voluntas*.[203] O'Donovan makes a similar point when he describes Christendom as having a sense that all political authority was the authority of the law of the ascended Christ. "Those theologians who insisted, against Abrosiaster, that the source of political authority was Christ, not the Father alone, understood something important: however much political authority survives from the old aeon, it does so upon terms set by the new."[204] I contend that a common fault appears in both the Barthian *grenzfall* and the Schmittian account of sovereignty that is proving so enticing for contemporary political theology. For both posit an excess or reserve of pure power, whether beyond the revelation in Christ (and thus in direct tension with Barth's own avowed actualism) or outside the claim of law. Either way the tyrannous underbelly of popular sovereignty is concealed from view. Here only a form of Jesulogical realism and a robust and fulsome doctrine of election can together turn politics from the mire of an anthropology spun from the excessive nature of sovereignty and the exceptionality of the capricious command.

Supersessionism and Political Critique

Through this incorporation into the body of Christ, believers (Gentiles) are, in the language of Romans 11, "engrafted" into the Jewish promise. But the interpretation of these central passages of Scripture has proved a minefield of potential miscontruals. Theological responses to the *Shoah* have heightened sensitivities to any hint of supersessionism in discussions of election.[205] We have already seen that Yoder's insistence on the Jewishness of his normative pacifism, and his exilic ecclesiology, largely avoid any explicit supersessionist move. Further, we can add that, for Yoder, the very possibility of exilic politics remaining realist (in the sense outlined previously as operating "with the grain of the universe"), is dependent on its remaining "Jewish." Without this element it seems unlikely that the confluence of the critical and constructive modes would survive. Yoder is emphatic that apologetic attempts to render the Christian message credible in ways that sloth off the Jewishness of the promise in which the Church's mission finds its guarantee, or

203. Ibid., 267 n. 35.

204. O'Donovan, *DN*, 233.

205. A strongly polemical account of the dangers of supersessionism is found in Soulen, *God of Israel*.

detached the message of Jesus from its Jewish matrix . . . thereby transposed it into an ahistorical moral monotheism with no particular peoplehood and no defenses against acculturation.[206]

Yet precisely because Yoder links emergent supersessionism with the loss of critical ability, some critics have argued that he reifies Jewishness and reduces it to a singular moral stance.[207] The combination of Yoder's typological form of analysis and his reliance on strongly normative language do indeed lead in this direction. Douglas Harink points to a residual supersessionism in Yoder's normative reading of Israel's history:

> Paul does not in Romans or his other letters engage in a moral history of Judaism. . . . Yoder [does], and a great deal of [his] judgments about the irrelevance or continuing relevance of Judaism for Christian theology [are] based on that moral history. . . . the biblical and Pauline doctrine of God's election of a specific, nonsubstitutable, fleshly historical people tends to disappear behind a set of "Jewish" ideas or practices.[208]

Harink's division between a "moral history" and a fuller (in some undisclosed way) Pauline view of election is somewhat arbitrary. It is unclear in what the marks of Israel's constantly negotiated identity would consist if we were to eliminate "ideas" and "practices" from the equation. That said, there is something of an idealism in the way Yoder invokes Jewish identity. By which, of course, I refer not to any sense of ivory-tower naïveté, but to an underlying historiographical method that assumes that it is within the detection of occurrences of the "idea"—or to use our earlier distinction, the metaphor—of exile within ecclesial practices that Christian communities demonstrate their continuity with normative Jewish identity. Daniel Boyarin has quite rightly objected to the dangers of Yoder's enterprise to locate an essence to Judaism *tout court*.[209]

As much as supersessionistic conclusions may be drawn from this, it should also be emphasized, contra Harink's tone, that this "moral history" is not a method alien to Jewish understandings of their identity, but, for Yoder, is implied within the Diaspora model itself. Dangers of supersessionism of a different kind would also lurk within the other strand

---

206. Yoder, *JCSR*, 152.

207. E.g., many of Peter Ochs's comments in Yoder, *JCSR*; see also Michael Cartwright's essay in the same volume, "Afterword," 211.

208. Harink, *Paul Among the Postliberals*, 201–3.

209. Boyarin, "Judaism as a Free Church."

of Yoder's typology of Jewish identity. For example, those emphasizing ethnic or liturgical continuity might also reify Judaism as a discrete group in possession of an identity and a blessing, and would be less able to clearly exposit how God's election of Israel is *both* for Israel themselves *and*, without any hint of paradox, through Israel to the world. We might say then that Yoder's language does not entirely escape supersessionistic implications, but it may point in the direction of a more appropriate understanding of the relationship of Christians to Jews. The further development of that direction would be a worthy, if complex, task. It is sufficient for our present purposes to note that a fuller understanding of election provides a reading of human freedom and political agency that is in marked contrast to the voluntarist rhetoric of choice that permeates contemporary Western society—both in terms of its consumerist understanding of the individual, and, consequently, its agenda for social change. When Yoder says that the Church is more truly political than the state, that is a politics not defined by concerns for legitimacy, sovereignty, and government—but is instantiated in ways closer to Foucault's vision of politics as "no more or less than that which is born with resistance to governmentality...."[210]

We turn in our final chapter to an exploration of contemporary theories of civil society in order to examine how a political theology marked by the three interrelated moments of eschatology, exile, and election may embody, within Western democratic settings, something of the understanding of social change and critique described so far in this book.

---

210. Foucault, *Security, Territory, Population*, 390.

CHAPTER 7

Towards a Peaceable Civility

"The problem with the tradition of civic virtue can be stated succinctly: that virtue is armed."[1]

—Jean Bethke Elshtain

"In the first instance, civil society replaced the Church in the role of defining tasks and positions, leaving the Church with only a marginal possibility of correcting or going beyond the delimitation of domains."[2]

—Michel de Certeau

MISSION AND EXEMPLARY POLITICS IN DEMOCRATIC CIVIL SOCIETY

Recall the stories of mission with which this book began. The challenge those accounts set before us was to provide a description of the public truth of the gospel that can adequately convey the theological basis for political critique and engagement in efforts for social change. I have suggested that John Howard Yoder's theological realism provides an attractive depiction of the way in which the peculiar contours of gospel truth, especially patience and nonviolence, impinge on our understanding of

1. Elshtain, "Citizenship and Armed Civic Virtue," 50.
2. Certeau, "Weakness of Believing," 226.

the political nature and mission of the Church. Furthermore, in contrast to those who would paint engagement in social change and the stance of witness as largely juxtaposed options, I have provided an account of the forms of social transformation that flow from Yoder's understanding of exemplary politics. I then began to develop and augment Yoder's analysis by expounding three moments of a theology of governmental power. Finally, I consider the way that the public truth of the gospel, as it is understood to flow from a christological and eschatological basis through the life and mission of the Church, may impact contemporary democratic society.

The near ubiquity of the construct of "civil society" in contemporary political theory often leads political theologians to treat it as a natural or essential constituent of social structure. While the existence of civil society is taken to be a given, its essence is assumed to be that of a benign amorphous and non-governmentalized space. It is the fertile social seedbed from which will emerge the sapling of true democracy. The role of the institutions and groups that form civil society is to nurture and protect this fragile growth. Such accounts often proceed by constructing a highly questionable form of public religious presence guided by the attenuated normative religious subjectivity of modernity—the apparently beneficent form of Milbank's policing of the sublime. That such accounts of civil society are highly governmentalized and far from benign should not lead us to easy dismissal. Such is the city into which the Church in the modern West has been sent. A brief investigation of "civil society" in contemporary political theory will enable us to explore the way that the exilic community may "seek the peace of the city," when that city, or "receptor culture," conceives of itself as democratic.[3] After a brief account of the historical development of the idea of civil society I shall explore the ways in which two contemporary strands of thinking on civil society, the neo-Marxist and the neo-republican, may relate to the understandings of mission, critique, and social change outlined previously. After summarizing each strand I shall briefly engage with theological works that cover the central concerns raised. I will then conclude with a few suggestions of how the theology of governmental power outlined in the previous

3. Of course, this is not to deny Yoder's concerns with the use of "theory." Rather, it is to suggest both that some aspects of contemporary understandings of civil society are liable to a strong critique from a Yoderian perspective, and that other aspects of such theorizations may be suggestive of some specific ways in which the vision of social change and the theology of governmental power outlined in previous chapters may apply to contemporary democratic polities.

chapter may contribute to the critique of three pathological tendencies of contemporary democratic society. I shall name these tendencies "colonization" (e.g., of civil society by the forces of global capitalism), "control" (a contrast of democratic "freedom" with the level of bureaucratic social control), and "confinement" (of the critical power of citizens through diverse phenomena of social exclusion).

A Brief History of Civil Society

In both communitarian and contemporary liberal circles the call for a revivified civil society has issued in a search for an institutional locus from which to exert a countervailing pressure against the encroaching domination by state and market. It is these civil institutions, variously (and contestably) listed as families, communities, voluntary associations, affinity groups, trade unions, friendship networks, and religious organizations, that provide the "social cement" necessary to sure up the foundations for any substantive agreement on the good.

A variety of religious voices have joined the call. Jonathan Sacks's *The Politics of Hope* appeals for a restoration of a politics of civil institutions in order to combat the variety of social ills and fragmentation symptomatic of libertarian politics. This vision of social change is focused upon "character and on the institutions that promote a strong sense of independent personhood and social concern."[4] Such emphases cannot be enforced by the power of the state, but only by the enlivening of institutional embodiments of spontaneous association. This is not a rallying cry for a retreat into small-scale communities, but for

> a restoration of valance in the body politic. Without a state there is anarchy. Without a respect for individuals as individuals there is tyranny. But without morality and the civil institutions within which it lives, breathes and has its being, there is too little to prevent the pendulum swinging between tyranny and anarchy.[5]

---

4. Sacks, *Politics of Hope*, 259–60. For Sacks, this is akin to the Victorian emphasis on character and independence. Sacks offers a surprisingly one-sided account of Victorian society (ibid., 254–56). He dismisses the stereotyped criticisms of the inequalities of Victorian society, noting the respect such society afforded, for the first time, to Jews. But surely its economic inequality, racism, sexism, and rampant cultural imperialism are not to be ignored because, as Sacks rightly notes, it was an era that afforded (some) Jews more respect and freedom than previous eras!

5. Ibid., 230.

The hope that Sacks aims to restore differs from mere optimism in so far as it leads not to a fragile utopianism but to a realistic and empowering moral courage. Sacks acknowledges the debt his account of moral agency owes to liberal conceptions of autonomy, which locate social change in the acts and relationships of individuals. The institutions of civil society are seen here primarily as mediating structures between the individual and the state. Sacks's contemporary religiously founded rhetoric displays notable parallels with the way that civil society was conceived in the early liberal tradition of the seventeenth and eighteenth centuries.[6]

The idea of civil society combines, from the first, issues of social structure, moral anthropology, the discernment and pursuit of public goods, and the basis for political solidarities. Etymologically, the term "civil society" is traced to the Latin *societas civilis* that functioned as a translation of Aristotle's *politike koinonia*.[7] The Aristotelian notion of the political man (*zôon politkon*), with all the exclusions that implied, participates in the public community of free and equal citizens, the polis. The telos of this political man is a form of "living well" that culminates in an ethic of friendship. Importantly, all particular friendships, be they friendships of utility or of virtue, are "subordinate to the association of the state, which aims not at a temporary advantage but at one covering the whole of life."[8] Thus in such roots the notion of civil society lacks the basic forms of differentiation between society and state or between economy and society, which are pivotal for many modern accounts of sociality. There is nothing in this early vision of the social, to move from Greek to German, of Tönnies's famous distinction of Gesellschaft (community) and Gemeinschaft (society).

A duality of state and non-political society arose as a result of the increasing differentiation that occurred through the depoliticization of the estates of classical feudalism, the simplification of political space, and consequently, the emergence of a form of sovereignty located in the modern state.[9] John Locke's *Two Treatises on Government*, written in justification of the Whig rebellion and revolution of 1688, marks the transition from an ancient to a modern view of civil society. For Locke, political and civil society remain identical, but are to be distinguished from the

6. Ibid., 266–68.
7. Cohen and Arato, *Civil Society*, 84–86.
8. Aristotle *Nicomachean Ethics* VIII: 9 1160a19f.
9. Cohen and Arato, *Civil Society*, 86–87.

original state of nature. This natural state of liberty therefore requires a rationalist contractarian account of the role of government. Thus "the social" and "government" are to be held, in some way, distinct—the former being the source of the latter. Such a contract aims to create a form of governmental authority capable of safeguarding the natural rights of its citizens. For Locke, these natural rights are particularly related to the possession of property.[10] He therefore speaks of slaves thus:

> These men, having, as I say, forfeited their lives and with it their liberties, and lost their estates, and being in a state of slavery not capable of any property, cannot in that state be considered as any part of civil society, the chief end whereof is the preservation of property.[11]

Though here, the bald claim of political "freedom," enabled by holding property, is loosed from the proper end in the common good and becomes more clearly an assertion of the power of the sovereign will.[12] In order to provide a theological basis to the exercise of government in the contract of formally equal citizens, Locke's view built upon a Calvinistic form of natural theology that identified God's will with the exercise of right reason.[13]

By the mid-eighteenth century this foundation for the social order was largely eroding. With the coming dominance of capitalist market relations a series of oppositions arose between public and private, the individual and the social, to which an account of the social order had to address itself. In the quest to hold these oppositions together, the moral vision of a civil society provided the conceptual space for a synthesis. The synthetic intent of the thinkers of the Scottish Enlightenment required an account of civil society largely freed of the theological basis of Locke's moral anthropology. The developing notion of the person as an autonomous self-interested social actor provided a radically new texture to the understanding of social relations. The confluence of divine will and human reason cedes dominance to the ideas of moral affection and

---

10. As MacIntyre shows, this construction of government around concerns for the natural rights to property trades on Locke's doctrine of tacit consent; whereby the majority of the population are presumed, with little coherence, to favour an oligarchy of property owners! MacIntyre, *Short History of Ethics*, 157–61.

11. Locke, *Two Treatises of Government*, Second Treatise, Chapter VII, para. 85, 162.

12. See by contrast St. Thomas Aquinas, *Summa Theologiae*, II.II. 66 1 and 2.

13. Seligman, *Idea of Civil Society*, 21–25.

natural sympathy as the basis for civil society. The heart of the moral vision of civil society expounded in the Scottish Enlightenment was a proposed union of a natural human benevolence and the exercise of reason. Civil society is thus seen as a "realm of solidarity" predicated on the benevolent character of moral sentiments and natural affections. For Adam Smith and, in different ways, Adam Fergusson, innate human mutuality leads to a basic need for what might, in today's "therapeutic" idiom, be termed "validation" ("sympathy" and "appreciation" for Smith, "vanity" for Fergusson). This need constitutes civil society as an ethical arena, which, through a complex mechanism of exchange, forms the individual as person.

Subsequently, with the thought of Hume any confluence of moral sympathy and the exercise of reason is shattered, and the project of the Scottish Enlightenment subverted from within.[14] The rift between moral affection and reason in ethics (with Hume on one side and Kant on the other) splits asunder the anthropological and moral basis of Fergusson's civil society. For Hume, reason may ascertain a great deal in the process of moral deliberation (primarily in terms of a cost-benefit calculus) but it can never account for "the ultimate ends of human reason." Motives can only be understood in terms of affection and sentiment—the passions. Indeed, for Hume, because reason can only bring us to a universal truth beyond morality itself, there can be no specific social good discerned by reason. Public good is merely the concatenation of private interests. Hume thereby foreshadows later themes of liberal politics (as MacIntyre notes in contrasting him to Aristotle) in presuming a society "structured in terms of modes of satisfaction of desire."[15]

For Hume, reasoned self-interest operates within a realm of social conventions—which are to be distinguished from the natural or transcendental order in which previous accounts of civil society were based. Norms of justice and public good are seen as artifices of only instrumental value in so far as, in following them, within the confines of law, one's own interests are served. Thus, in Hume, as Adam Seligman describes him,

---

14. Hume's account of moral affection and its problematic relation to reason, combined with his famous critique of the logical relationship between "is" and "ought" is said by MacIntyre to be a "subversion from within" of the Scottish Enlightenment. See Macintyre, *Whose Justice?* 281–325; also Seligman, *Idea of Civil Society*, 36–41.

15. MacIntyre, *Whose Justice?* 298.

> the distinction between justice and virtue, between a public sphere based on the workings of self-interest . . . and a strictly private sphere of moral action . . . is presented in its starkest form. . . . The ensuing dilemma, of how to posit a prescriptive and not just descriptive model of the social order . . . has defined the modern period from Hume onward.[16]

The division between justice and virtue is further absolutized in Kant. In providing his account of universal reason, Kant outlines the link between the individual and the social through the vision of the "kingdom of ends." His insistence that no person should ever "be used as a means except when it is at the same time an end" is realized in his account of a juridical community of citizens. It is this exclusively juridical vision of the "public" in which were synthesized his concerns for reason, equality, and freedom.[17] This division of the right from the good, the juridical from the ethical, as we have seen at the outset of this work, is key to the liberal understanding of the public sphere. It is here that Kant places the foundations for the realization of the kingdom of ends. Here we find, in the strongest terms yet, the division of the social from the state. It is in the civil structures of society that man's autonomy and reason are guaranteed. It is civil society, freed from the activities of political society, that can harbor the critical citizenry that alone can defend against the absolutist state.

But the separation of the ethical and the juridical has never been stable. Such boundaries are regularly and unavoidably traversed. The analytical division between society and state can never be so neatly discerned in practice. Who is to decide when an issue is of private ethical concern rather than a public issue of justice? How, for example, is one to decide that abortion or pornography are issues of private interest, or that the provision of medical care and the prosecution of war are fields where the language of justice must exclude the language of "right"? As writers from MacIntyre to William Galston have noted, the claim to neutrality of liberal politics in policing such distinctions itself conceals a vital tradition of liberal virtues based on its own conception of the good.[18] In criticizing the impermeability of Kant's division, subsequent

---

16. Seligman, *Idea of Civil Society*, 41.

17. Ibid., 41–44.

18. Galston, *Liberal Purposes*. Similar concerns drive the collection of essays published as Boxx and Quinlivan, *Public Morality*.

theorizations have begun to reinscribe normative visions of historical purposiveness into these juridical structures. It is with Hegel that the concept of civil society moves beyond Kant's separation of the juridical and the ethical (although, of course, the division is widely restored in liberal theory from Rawls to Habermas).[19]

In attempting to reintegrate the legal and the moral, Hegel and Marx mark the next stage in the development of the concept of civil society. The complexity and polyvalence of Hegel's thought cannot be engaged here. It is sufficient for our purposes to note that the general move he makes is to distinguish civil society from the state, only to offer an account of ethical community that subsumes the former into the latter. Hegel's attempt to outline a notion of ethical solidarity based on the unity of public right with private ethics is characterized by the participation of the particular and individual within the universal and social "idea of freedom." Civil society is seen as the sphere of social interaction and trade, which encompass the conflicts of interest seen in the administration of justice and the "system of needs." Thus, in his *Philosophy of Right*, Hegel outlines a threefold distinction of family, civil society, and state. The state, for Hegel, is not simply the institutional framework within which civil society exists. Rather civil society is located in those institutions and associations where the bourgeois schism of universal and particular is again united in a renewed model of participatory citizenship.

For Hegel such institutions are characterized by his idea of "corporations." These are primarily seen as professional or business associations, with some role accorded to churches and charitable bodies.[20] Nevertheless, it is only within the state that the "idea of freedom" is fully actualized, and where particular and universal are finally united. In overcoming the Kantian dichotomy via such a fundamentally statist trend, the autonomy of civil society is compromised. Civil society is, in that sense, merely a staging post in the historical unfolding of the "idea of freedom" to its fulfillment in the state.[21] Of course, insofar as the state is conceived

---

19. Of course this restoration must come to terms with Hegel's important critique of Kant, and his famous distinction of *moralität* from *sittlichkeit*. See, for example, Habermas, "Morality and Ethical Life," in *Moral Consciousness*, 195–216; and Rawls, *Political Liberalism*, 285–88.

20. Shanks, *Hegel's Political Theology*, 160–64.

21. Seligman, *Idea of Civil Society*, 50–51. Nevertheless it is important to note that, as is typical of the polyvalence of Hegel's thought, the strongly statist implication here is, to some extent (though perhaps not entirely happily) mitigated by the foundation

as either the source or the consummation of the operation of civil society it remains conceptually incompatible with the non-statist politics of exile outlined in previous chapters. In none of these classic theorizations do we find a vision of civil society with which an exilic form of political engagement may share much kinship. The Aristotelian sense lacks the important differentiations that would allow it to address modern society. The Lockean view remains theologically problematic and would be insufficient for the critique of capitalist systems. The Kantian view inscribes into social reality the kind of division of the juridical from the ethical that undermines enterprises for public theology, and the Hegelian account leads to a statist eschatology.

Nevertheless, I suggest there are two strands of contemporary usage of the notion of civil society that may point to a more ambivalent and, at times, constructive relation between these political theories and the Jeremianic model of political life. I shall briefly outline these two strands: first dealing with the model of hegemonic change and the threefold differentiation of state, economy, and civil society, which stem from neo-Marxist thought into critical theory; and second, the neo-republican or Tocquevillian argument that seeks a broadly communitarian agenda for "making democracy work." What unites both, at least in their contemporary manifestations, is an underlying commitment to the importance of civil society for the flourishing of a truly democratic polity.

The Neo-Marxist Strand: Hegemony and Anti-politics

In a highly plural and differentiated society a twofold distinction of state from civil society is far too generalized and vague to be of great use in ascertaining the locus of critical action. Civil society is not merely the sum total of all those aspects of collective existence that fall outside the explicit designation of state power. The emergence of a threefold schema of state, economy, and civil society provides more focus for the discernment of civic sites of resistance against what, with Walter Wink,

---

for possible critique of existing states in his normative accounts. Thus Cohen and Arato state "For Hegel, undoubtedly the highest purpose of public life is to generate a rational universal identity that he equates with the patriotic ethos of the state.... But Hegel also registers serious doubts about whether the modern state as such can be the locus of public freedom, doubts that run completely contrary to the statist strain of his thought." Cohen and Arato, *Civil Society and Political Theory*, 113.

we have previously called the "domination system."[22] Civil society is distinguished from "political society"—parties, quangos (though not more autonomous forms of non-governmental organization) and the like, and from "economic society," with its corporate institutions, unions, etc.[23] The roots of the distinction coincide with an increasingly critical mood in the notion of civil society. In Marx, Hegel's abstract and idealist tendencies are turned on their head. For Marx the realm of civil society is fundamentally a place of conflict between the (primarily economic) interests of private individuals (Hegel's "system of needs"). The state does not, indeed cannot, resolve these conflicts, for civil society is emphatically distinguished from the political public realm. It is only in the future (post-revolutionary) reunification of civil and political society that such conflicts will be resolved.[24] Yet here the earlier sense of civil society as the institutional locus for the flourishing of innate mutuality is subjected to Marxist "economic reductionism."

A significantly more fruitful account of civil society can be found in the work of the Italian neo-Marxist Antonio Gramsci. In seeking an explanation for the failure of the proletariat to revolt, Gramsci outlines why the Bolshevik strategy of violent attack on state apparatus was inevitably unsuccessful. For Gramsci, the stability of the systems of domination resides not merely in their techniques of violent discipline and corruption, but in the role of civil society in manufacturing consent. It is "hegemony" rather than force that Gramsci names as the cultural and political mechanism through which the dominant class remains in perpetuity.

Gramsci advocated a protracted "war of position" whereby the bourgeois hegemony in civil society is gradually replaced with a proletarian counter-hegemony.[25] In advocating the creation of alternative forms of association whose values engender this counter-hegemony, Gramsci distinguishes civil society not only from the state but also, in response to Marx's economic reductionism, from the economy. Certainly Gramsci's notion of hegemony opens the understanding of state operations to

22. It should be noted that the place of the family within or outside of civil society does not enjoy any significant consensus. Equally it would be foolish to attribute to civil society an innocuous or purified character *vis-à-vis* the domination system.

23. A clear account of such differentiations is found in Cohen, "Interpreting the Notion of Civil Society."

24. Seligman, *Idea of Civil Society*, 51–58.

25. Keane, *Civil Society*, 15–16; Cohen and Arato, *Civil Society and Political Theory*, 142–59; and Chambers, "Critical Theory of Civil Society."

the more subtle forms of disciplinary power that Foucault and, in different ways, Yoder so acutely analyzed. But it is necessary to note that, for Foucault, the notion of civil society arises as a technology of power peculiarly suited to the liberal vision of government. That is to say, it constructs a governmental domain wider than either a solely economic or exclusively juridical subjectivity could achieve.[26] Gramsci's notion of hegemony allows us some scope for the discernment of governmental functions within bourgeois society, while also permitting a politics of critique less pessimistic about the ubiquity of disciplinary power. Indeed, this flexibility is seen in Gramsci's use of the threefold division. For Gramsci, any division of civil society from state and economy is rightly seen as a purely analytic distinction that, in practice, is substantially blurred.[27] The point is to discern, in the maelstrom of ethical and political contestation that makes up civil society, those practices and organizations that can begin to alter the structures of domination.

By identifying civil society as both the ground of the status quo and the realm in which a new social order may be fostered, Gramsci is able to offer an account of social change that combines a sense of the responsive and ad hoc nature of the transformative enterprise with a realistic estimation of the complexity of the ways in which an ideological superstructure becomes embedded within a cultural setting. To this extent his analysis resembles the subversive practices and eschatological patience found in Yoder's vision of social change. Equally, even with the lack of a singular identifiable proletariat, the notion of counter-hegemonic politics may prove fruitful in resisting the hegemony of global capitalism.[28] Nonetheless, there are two elements of Gramsci's account, which, for our purposes, require more critical attention. First, it is questionable whether the Gramscian abolition of bourgeois civil society is the best way in which to reconstruct a viable civic sphere. Gramsci's understanding of civil society is characterized by an excessively functional motive. He argues that, subsequent to the triumph of the proletarian counter-hegemony, civil society loses the dynamism of its social movements (whose raison d'etre is, of course, the subversion of bourgeois hegemony). Critics therefore identify an antinomy in Gramsci between an account of civil society as a pluralistic, democratic, and free society and a single

26. Burchell and Miller, *Foucault Effect*, 22ff.
27. Neilsen, "Reconceptualizing Civil Society for Now."
28. Cox, "Civil Society at the Turn of the Millennium," 25.

unified state-society.[29] The new proletarian hegemony is more unified, but, in an inversion of Hegel's pattern, this form of civil society becomes the "normal continuation" and "organic compliment" of political society.[30] Thus political society—the realm of state power—is absorbed into a unified civil society, conceived as akin to the Marxist utopia of a society without institutions.

Second, and more important for the thrust of our argument, the temporary and functional value accorded to civil society does not provide sufficiently variegated and robust grounding for the diverse social practices of resistance that a revivified civil society is said to provide. Gramsci's account of the proletarian conquest of civil society privileges a monolithic rendering of the false consciousness found in hegemonic civic culture. This sits ill with both the apparent plurality of contemporary Western societies, and with the account of the potential for everyday resistance seen in Yoder's understanding of revolutionary subordination (see chapter 5). The threefold distinction of civil society from both state and economy provides a valuable though imperfect analytic structure for the continued resistance against the principalities and powers, as they manifest themselves in state power and capitalist domination.

The temporariness and functionalism that undermine something of the normative impact of Gramsci's schema are in marked contrast with the more permanent democratizing construal of civil society found in Jürgen Habermas. Habermas moves toward a model of criticism oriented to the reconstruction of the communicative rationality of the lifeworld. A division of economy and civil society has become an essential element of his critical analysis. Both state power and economic systems are characterized by instrumental or "functional" rationalities. By contrast, the "lifeworld" is seen as the locus of civil society, the latter being the institutional expression of the former.[31] It is the lifeworld that is the privileged locus of critical activity, by virtue of its (ideal-typical) operation according to the communicative rationality that alone may achieve a truly undistorted intersubjectivity.

We have already seen in previous chapters that there is less need than Habermas presumes to posit this universalistic counter-factual in order to provide for authentic forms of critique and emancipation. However,

29. Cohen and Arato, *Civil Society and Political Theory*, 142–74; Bobbio, "Gramsci."
30. Ibid., 156.
31. Chambers, "Critical Theory of Civil Society," 93.

the vision of a realm, or more properly, a fluctuating series of institutional loci, in which people can orient themselves toward resistance against the encroaching "colonization of the lifeworld" by logics of power, technique, or money is an important contribution to the description of those practices necessary for the sustenance of a vital public moral discourse. Habermas's own defense of a model of deliberative democracy highlights how the division of civil society from state and economy has shifted from Gramsci's revolutionary framework to Habermas's own reformist intention. Nevertheless, Habermas's liberal-Kantian intent may itself limit the usefulness of the idea of civil society in settings (the former Yugoslavia, Afghanistan, Iraq, Zimbabwe to mention only those that have grabbed headlines) whose religious and cultural complexion differs from that presumed in his account. Central elements of Habermas's view of civil society are unlikely to find acceptance in contexts where a different substantive view of the good predominates, or where the historical developments upon which his account of the "linguistification of the sacred"[32] is based, are either not present or, at least, hotly contested. Habermas is right to say that for his theory "a robust civil society can develop only in the context of a liberal political culture and the corresponding patterns of socialization, and on the basis of an integral private sphere; it can blossom only in an already rationalized lifeworld."[33] This, of course, is to beg the question regarding the governmentality enacted in the modern liberal construction of religious subjectivities. Here again we find the problematic eschatology, for which hope is grounded in the guiding notion of autonomy. This hope remains problematic for religious participation within civil society, for it perpetuates the division between public and private and locates the capacity of social action solely within "autonomy," liberally understood.[34]

32. This is the name given to the process whereby the sacred vision of the lifeworld gives way to the modern lifeworld via a process if differentiation and secularization. The means of "cultural reproduction, social integration, and socialization" are transferred from sacred foundations to communicative action. See Habermas, *Theory of Communicative Action*, 2:77–112.

33. Habermas, *Between Facts and Norms*, 371.

34. Kymlicka, *Multicultural Citizenship*, 161–62. Kymlicka here reflects on the exclusion from a liberal politics of those who, like the Hutterites and Amish, would reject the notion of "autonomy" as basic for human sociality. Yoder, of course, was often critical of the quietistic and sectarian tendencies of some such groups. Equally, my point is not that Yoder rejected outright the liberal notion of "autonomy." He did not. Rather, it is the placing of social hope on such a basis that should be approached with a certain amount of skepticism.

While "civil society" in its current usage is largely dependent on its liberal lineage, there are strong reasons to suppose a broader base of support within diverse normative traditions.[35]

The robust sense of long-term gradual social change through the cultivation of a counter-hegemonic civil society fits well with the experiences of resistance to totalitarian regimes found in the recent history of central and Eastern Europe. The distinction of civil society from state became fundamental for the self-understanding of the Polish opposition from 1976, and to the political movement (officially a trade union) Solidarity. The resurgence of civic actions, first promoted by Polish intellectuals, was supported and facilitated in its development by the Catholic Church. The relative independence of the Catholic Church from the socialist state, a democratizing turn subsequent to the Second Vatican council, and the presence of a primarily Catholic form of popular religiosity combined to encourage the Church and the intellectual left to forge an important alliance. The construction of this common purpose was essential to the character of the Workers Defence Committee (KOR), out of which Solidarity was to emerge.[36] The conception of civil society driving this movement was largely Gramscian. That said, Solidarity was primarily oriented to a more evolutionary or gradualist form of social change than Gramsci had envisaged.[37]

The Velvet Revolution in Czechoslovakia in 1989 was the culmination of the development of a popular momentum for change given voice through the "civic forum"—a body born out of a series of strikes, mass demonstrations, and public discussions (largely held in theaters). The driving force behind the "civic forum" was the philosopher and playwright Václav Havel. While Havel was later to become a somewhat troubled President of Czechoslovakia, his involvement within the mobilization of civil society stems from his role in the production of the landmark Charter 77.[38] The charter was a demand, signed by numerous

---

35. See Chambers and Kymlicka, *Alternative Conceptions*. Herbert, *Religion and Civil Society*.

36. Casanova, *Public Religions in the Modern World*, 92–133.

37. Pelczynski, "Solidarity." See also Luxmoore and Babiuch, "In Search of Faith."

38. Of course the momentum for change can be traced back further, to the liberalizing reforms proposed by Alexander Dubček, and their violent suppression by Soviet invasion in the "Prague Spring" of 1968. Havel's involvement in Charter 77 also earned him a conviction on charges of "subversion" and a sentence of four years hard labor. His tireless work in bolstering the resistance of civil society against the state coincided with the

Czech intellectuals, for the state to afford its citizens those basic human rights outlined in the Helsinki agreements.[39] In his reflections on the politics of civil society Havel offered a strongly philosophical account of a dissident politics as "the experience of life at the very ramparts of dehumanized power."[40] In contrast to the patrician techniques of statist politics, this civil mode is designated an "anti-political politics."

The defining characteristic of Havel's anti-politics is not given in a calculus of demonstrable effects, but in the very practice of "living in truth."[41] Indeed, as Havel expresses it with typically affective prose,

> That effect, to be sure, is of a wholly different nature from what the West considers political success. It is hidden, indirect, long term and hard to measure; often it exists only in the invisible realm of social consciousness, conscience and subconsciousness and it can be almost impossible to determine what value it assumed therein and to what extent, if any, it contributes to shaping social development. It is, however, becoming evident—and I think that is an experience of an essential and universal importance—that a single, seemingly powerless person who dares to cry out the word of truth and to stand behind it with all his person and all his life, ready to pay a high price, has, surprisingly, greater power, though formally disfranchised, than do thousands of anonymous voters.[42]

For Havel, modern forms of anonymous depersonalized power have replaced the human being, characterized by faculties of personal conscience and personal responsibility, with an impersonal object of

---

liberalizing shift in Soviet politics under Gorbacev's banner of Perestroika. The support for mass demonstrations culminated in nearly 750,000 people converging at Prague's Letna Park on the twenty-fifth and twenty-sixth of November in 1989, which, when combined with a general strike on the twenty-seventh, had a devastating effect on the communist regime. The "Velvet revolution" culminated, only days later, with the election of Dubček as "speaker of the federal assembly," imminently followed by the election of Havel as President of Czechoslovakia.

39. In 1975, representatives from 35 countries had attended a "Conference on Security and Cooperation in Europe." Its final document, the "Helsinki Agreement," set forth basic rights of equality; freedom of thought, conscience, and religion; and sought to "promote and encourage the effective exercise of civil, political, economic, social, cultural, and other rights and freedoms all of which derive from the inherent dignity of the human person and are essential for his free and full development" (453).

40. Havel, "Politics and Conscience," 155.

41. Havel, *Living in Truth*; the parallel with Yoder is striking, see *PJ*, 232.

42. Havel, *Living in Truth*, 156.

technologically achievable "universal welfare."[43] There is, for Havel, an inhuman, or what we might call a totalitarian, moment in every project of "general well-being." This is revealed "the moment it demands a single involuntary death—that is one which is not a conscious sacrifice of a life to its meaning." The task of dissident anti-politics is one of resisting "the irrational momentum of anonymous, impersonal and inhuman power." Furthermore the basis of the possibility of this anti-politics does not spring from its appeal as an intellectual thesis. Rather it grows from the "humdrum 'everydayness'" in which the massive civil mobilization of the Velvet Revolution had its roots. Havel wrote in 1984,

> I favour "anti-political politics": that is, politics not as the technology of power and manipulation, of cybernetic rule over humans or as the art of the useful, but politics as one of the ways of seeking and achieving meaningful lives, of protecting them and serving them. I favour politics as practical morality, as service to the truth . . .[44]

This strand of thought about civil society, as it has developed in Havel's work, is important for our conceptualization of the social significance of a theology of witness. It has been central to the claims of this book that the notions of truth and realism I have discerned in Yoder's thought lead us to reconceive social change in ways that directly affect how we can understand the relation of the Church to governmental power. I suggest the "anti-political" practices of "living in truth" inaugurate the kind of "counter-hegemonic" politics that Yoder describes in his account of the witnessing community. I further suggest that the nonviolence of both the Velvet Revolution and the concommitant Polish experience in Solidarity bear witness to a deeper confluence with the political model we have found so powerfully expressed in Yoder's theology.[45] In accordance with

---

43. Havel, "Politics and Conscience," 141–43.

44. Ibid., 155–57. See also Havel's famous essay "Power of the Powerless." Havel here claims the form of solidarity inherent in "living within the truth" is a sign of a "rudimentary moral reconstitution" A prefiguration of the political structures that might become the foundation for a better society.

45. The nonviolence of Solidarity is largely attributable to the monumental influence of Cardinal Wyszyński. However, after Wyszyński's death the relation of the Catholic Church to the Polish state has been significantly more ambiguous. Divisions between the privatizing aspects of a liberal program on the one hand, and attempts to instigate a more strongly Catholic hegemony in political society, on the other, bring into question the possibility of the long-term activity of such a highly mobilized form of civil society.

the typological method that so often characterized Yoder's social analysis, he suggestively remarks that Havel's practice of nonviolent resistance marks him out as the successor of the distinctively pacifistic strand of the Czech Reformation seen in Peter Chelčický (1390?–1460?).[46]

Nevertheless, there are elements of the metaphysics that underlie Havel's thought that would be entirely inimical to an adequately theological account of civil society. The basis of Havel's anti-politics is a rather romanticized personalism that places civil dissent in a restitutionary idiom. The dignity of those engaged in "anti-political" action is derived, for Havel, from the avoidance of the sort of instrumentalism and "lust for certainty" that erodes a pre-social "natural" wholeness. Havel draws heavily on the philosophy of a fellow chartist, Jan Patočka. Patočka articulates a notion of the "solidarity of the shaken" viewed as a level of collaboration that transcends all metaphysical differences through the identification of a prior (i.e., putatively pre-metaphysical) unity of all those victimized by dehumanizing political practices. Andrew Shanks attempts to construct a form of "civil religion" upon the civic solidarity understood in these terms.[47] But through his endorsement of a supposedly demythologized post-metaphysical basis for this civil religion, Shanks makes a problematic division of civil and confessional forms of theology. Confessional forms are said to be restricted by their theological loyalties—they can only ever yield a "solidarity of shaken Christians," never a full "solidarity of the shaken."[48]

Shanks conceives of true civility as emerging in what we can identify as a largely Hegelian pattern, albeit shorn of its statist bent, where metaphysical forms of religion are subjected to a universalizing historical movement that alone can free citizens from the constraints of a (Nietzschean) consolatory God.[49] He persists in this problematic dichotomy by characterizing all those who would stress the ecclesial resources for solidarity as "recoil theologians." The pejorative notion of a defensive retreat from the liberating processes of modernity conceals a tacit, and entirely metaphysical, notion of common grace that Shanks fails to defend. The confessional understanding of social change this book has

---

46. Yoder, "On Not Being in Charge," in *JCSR*, 169–70, 176 n. 8. For an account of the life and thought of Chelčický, see Durnbaugh, *Believers' Church*, 39–63, especially 53–57.

47. Shanks outlines his distinctive take on civil solidarity in a number of works, most notably in *Civil Society, God and Modernity*, and *"What Is Truth?"*

48. Shanks, *God and Modernity*, 42–64.

49. Shanks, *Civil Society*, 135.

discerned in Yoder's thought simply undermines the assumption on which Shanks trades—that commitment to a particular community necessarily requires exclusivity and the circumscription of solidaristic intent. Yoder's vision of the church as a community of vulnerable dialogue, as Romand Coles puts it, "allows the truth to manifest itself ever anew in the specificities of historical encounter and discernment."[50] This patience and vulnerability is essential to the way in which confessional theology may understand its capacity to aid the Church in its counter-hegemonic mission in democratic civil societies.

The Neo-republican Strand: Making Democracy Work

Current calls for a reviving of the body politic through the structures of civil society rightly point to the way these institutions provide the social cohesion and formation required for the legitimation of democratic states. Such a view has been central to democratic self-understanding for well over a century and a half. It was with the prescient comments of Alexis de Tocqueville, in the middle of the nineteenth century, that the practices for the sustenance of a democratic polity were associated with the idea of civil society. Tocqueville, in his classic *Democracy in America*, argues that the statist implications of the (Hegelian) elevation of the state to a role governing civil society may lead to a form of "elected state despotism."[51] The "great democratic revolution" sweeping modern life fosters an egalitarian passion that can, when combined with a dangerous "individualism" (a term coined by Tocqueville), all too easily degenerate into a tyranny of the majority. In order to prevent the build-up of undemocratic monopolies of power, Tocqueville argues that the forms of voluntary association that together comprise civil society provide the crucial bulwark against these novel forms of pseudo-democratic despotism.

Civil society may depend on the state for its own survival, in the negative sense that without the basic functioning of the state, the conditions required for free association would flounder. Importantly, for Tocqueville, the reverse is equally true. It is only in a vital civil society that true democracy can be nurtured.[52] The central facets of this

---

50. Coles, "Wild Patience," 311.

51. Tocqueville, *Democracy in America*; Keane, "Despotism and Democracy," 55.

52. Tocqueville's moral anthropology therefore affirms the innate sociality of human beings—a sociality, moreover, which is undermined by individualism and the natural vices

argument echo through to recent sociological studies such as Robert Putnam's *Making Democracy Work*.[53] Through a substantial study of Italian regional government, Putnam discovered that the "social capital" derived from a vibrant civic culture correlates strongly with the democratic success of a government.

A range of contemporary initiatives aim at harnessing the ability of religious communities to perform this function of the *eirenikon* or social glue.[54] Not only will a revived civil society bolster the legitimation of democratic governments, but the standing of religious groups within a local community is coming to be viewed as a resource to be exploited as an alternative to interventionist state provision. Yet the exclusively functional language in which such a role is expressed may give us pause. One case in point is recent attempts in the U.S., and to a lesser degree, in the U.K., to render "faith-based organizations" as alternative social-service providers, who may compete for a share of central government funds and yet maintain their religious identity. In this way religious communities are encouraged to trade on their role in civil society and their ability to repair "the ties that bind," in order to efficiently deliver welfare services. However, critics rightly express concerns over the possibility, when provision is regulated and overseen by the state, of these same bodies maintaining prophetic criticism of the systems of domination and exclusion that make such welfare provision necessary in the first place.[55] That is not, in itself, to disallow such collaborative efforts. Rather, as with the eschatological principles outlined in the previous chapter, here too the Church's political life takes its cues from the lordship of Christ. Not only does the eschatological framework of Christian politics relativize the standing of all secular institutions, it also, therefore, places a note

---

of excessive material desire. See Mahoney, "Moral Foundations of Liberal Democracy." For brief summaries of Tocqueville's account of religion, see Elshtain, "Religion and American Democracy"; and Sloat, "Subtle Significance."

53. Putnam, *Making Democracy Work*.

54. Most recently in the U.K. the report produced by the Home Office Communities Unit in February of 2004 *Working Together*; in the U.S. see Wuthnow, *Saving America?*

55. Other critics highlight the potential reduction of philanthropic spirit and private giving if state funding dominates provision; concerns over the constitutional basis of the move, problems of perception, in the sense that recipients may object to explicitly religious provision, and thereby reject the only services open to them, etc. See Glennon, "Blessed Be the Ties That Bind?"; Davis, "President Bush's Office."

of caution on the spaces those institutions "create" for the functions of religious communities.[56]

Similar concerns may be expressed regarding the requirements for legal recognition placed on churches in, for example, Chile. Previously, legal recognition had been reserved for the Roman Catholic church, but since March 2000 provisions in the "law on religion" (*ley de culto*) require all religious bodies to submit their statement of faith and constitution for government approval.[57] The benefits of such approval, from tax status through to new opportunities for chaplaincy, are conferred on all bodies who meet the criteria set by the state. Such measures are justified as a move to restrict the dangerous influence of cults and some new religious movements. Both the benefits and costs of recognition, and the nature of criteria, should be assessed on their specific merits. Similar requirements for registration are made throughout the globe (Armenia, Bulgaria, China, and Russia, amongst others). Naturally in some settings these measures have dramatically more detrimental impact than in others. It is common, given the commercial idioms of social policy (e.g., the provision of a "choice" of "services" to "clients"), to construct the allocation of funds and contracts to "faith-based groups" through practices of competitive tender. Such agonistic mechanisms encourage a divisive focus on confessional distinctiveness construed as a measure of competitive advantage—precisely the opposite of the non-possessive identity given in Christian "distinctiveness." In such ways bureaucratic procedures may militate against the formation of convivial ad hoc relations oriented to the common good. Such moves serve to illustrate the impact on religious witness of the substantial and inevitable blurring, in practice, of the division between state and civil society. It creates a field of action in which such groups must confirm the liberal account of religion as essentially exclusive and divisive in order to participate in the state's own schemes of inclusion.

---

56. An excellent example of this is seen in Sam Wells's reflections on the churches role in the British government's "New Deal for Communities" (which is largely underpinned by humanistic values). Wells, "No Abiding Inner City."

57. I am grateful to Paul Avis for highlighting this practice with regard to Chile. For a broad, though both relatively superficial and value-laden, account of such requirements, see the U. S. State Department's *Annual Report on International Religious Freedom*. The most recent report (2008) is currently available at the online archive of the Department of State: http://2001–2009.state.gov/g/drl/rls/irf/2008/index.htm.

Any generation of a particularly critical form of social capital is an effect of the Church's faithfulness to its mission, not, in the first instance, a sign of its conformity to a particular model of civil society. To place the everyday witness of the Church solely within the notion of civil society allocates to the Church a functional value dependent on the sort of social capital it is able to generate. But, of course, the value and role of the Church are ascertained only in relation to their mission in the divine economy. From the Yoderian perspective advocated here, the way in which the Church can help make democracy work is through the witness to an "alternative construction of society and history."[58]

The neo-Tocquevillean thrust of this strand of thinking about civil society yields partial but profound insights, and yet houses equally precarious dangers for our account of the social-critical witness of the Church. Churches, in so far as they are to be located within civil society, contribute in both direct and indirect ways to the development of social capital through which the despotic and oligarchic tendencies of democratic polities are critiqued and countered. In terms of direct impact this may be taken as a partial de facto refutation of some of the concerns of isolationism noted in connection with Yoder's ecclesiology. The very nature of being the Church can indeed help make democracy work.[59] Indirectly, of course, there is significant evidence that religious belief motivates participation in a wide range of voluntary and charitable activities.[60] I suggest that in order to escape the limitations of a purely functional view of the place of religion within democratic societies it is necessary to adopt the sort of stance in respect of the normative social practices of democratic citizenship that Yoder expresses in the motif of exilic life. Given the constraints of space, a brief survey of some of the most important trends in theological reflection on civil society and democratic participation will have to suffice to conclude this section, after which we shall engage in more detail with an assessment of the way the approach developed in this book may contribute to the critique of the condition of contemporary democratic societies.

---

58. Yoder, *PK*, 43.

59. Hollenbach, *Common Good*, 107; Rasmusson, *Church as Polis*, 369; Harris, "Civil Society," 48.

60. Gill, *Churchgoing and Christian Ethics*.

Religion and Democratic Citizenship

The danger of reducing the civil role of the Church to a largely instrumental and functional good can be seen, for example, in Richard John Neuhaus's *The Naked Public Square*. There is, says Neuhaus, a moral vacuum created by the exclusion of religion from public life. This in turn has led to "a rupture between public policy and moral sentiment" that all too readily invites totalitarianism. It can only be healed by the restoration of those elements in which reside the moral heart of American culture.[61] What is required is a recovery of, in Peter Berger's famous phrase, "the sacred canopy."[62]

Neuhaus advocates a recovery of the "culture-forming" potential of religion, for, contra the liberalism of Rawls or Rorty, only religious mediating structures are capable of legitimating the law on which a just society rests.

> There is in store a continuing and deepening crisis of legitimation unless a transcendent moral purpose is democratically asserted by which the state can be brought under critical judgment, unless it is made clear once again that the state is not the source but the servant of the law.[63]

A passing comparison with other theological ethicists is sufficient to highlight the main bone of contention in Neuhaus's appeal. There is a certain parallel with the move made, in very different ways, by both Yoder and O'Donovan. Both of whom, as we saw in the previous chapter, place the state in a framework of circumscribed authority and providential order. Problematically, Neuhaus's appeal lacks the substantial theological framework with which to avoid the dangers of civil religion. The faith required for Neuhaus's goal is, ironically for a Roman Catholic, the chastened reinvigoration of the earlier liberal Protestant vision of the Christianizing of America (and the concomitant Americanizing of Christianity).[64]

The problem with the appeal to republican virtue in Neuhaus can also be seen in the groundbreaking sociological studies of Robert Bellah.

---

61. Neuhaus, *Naked Public Square*.

62. Berger, *Sacred Canopy*. For useful discussions of Berger, see Woodhead, Heelas, and Martin, *Peter Berger and the Study of Religion*.

63. Neuhaus, *Naked Public Square*, 248–64.

64. To be strictly accurate, Neuhaus did not convert from Lutheranism to Catholicism until 1990.

Bellah and the co-authors of both *Habits of the Heart* and *The Good Society* outline the diversity of civic traditions operating in American society. In so doing they note three trends: the (Lockean) "individualist," which is eroding social commitment to a common good, and the (Rousseauean) "civic republican" and the "biblical" traditions, in which may be found a renewal of the common concern for society. These are the traditions that, it is claimed, may open up "spaces for reflection, participation, and the transformation of our institutions."[65]

Jean Bethke Elshtain notes an important caveat to the predominantly positive bias in the Tocquevillian atmosphere of Bellah's work. For Elshtain, as the epigram to this chapter shows, "the problem with the tradition of civic virtue can be stated succinctly: that virtue is armed."[66] For the Ancient Greeks, as later for Machiavelli and Rousseau (the progenitors of the republican tradition that Bellah et al. appeal to) the nature of citizenship is derived from the model of the soldier-citizen. Elshtain stresses that the Rousseauean citizen and the Christian are, from the outset, conceived as exclusive options. The writers of *Habits of the Heart* were, it seems, too sanguine in their conception of the compatibility of the biblical and republican traditions of civic virtue. It is with Christ, she claims, that the "pacific ontology" leads, for the first time, to a "principled resistance to public power," found in both Christian pacifism and Augustinian just-war thought.[67]

It should hardly need pointing out that even the (putatively) most highly democratized states still operate oligarchically, wage unjust wars, and engage in a wide variety of pathological global economic and political activities. It is far from clear that Bellah's account is sufficiently attentive to the different ways republican and biblical civic traditions, with all the diversity they contain, may either critique or indeed contribute to these harmful tendencies. Therefore, in place of any strong notion of civic virtue and a single common good, Elshtain defends a more circumscribed form of civic formation. She bases this not on a shared

---

65. Bellah et al., *Habits of the Heart*; and Bellah et al., *Good Society*.

66. Elshtain, "Citizenship and Armed Civic Virtue," 50.

67. Elshtain, *Women and War*, 45–159. Despite divergent readings of Augustine, there is a strong parallel between Elshtain and Yoder. Elshtain critiques contemporary forms of just-war thought that display a propensity for a "crusading impulse" utterly absent from its earliest intentions. Yoder, for his part, frequently reproached the tendency for a rationalist politics with an ultimately utilitarian ethic to masquerade as a utilization of just-war criteria. See especially *WWU*.

conception of the common good, but on "a shared sense of pathos and tragedy." For Elshtain, it is the evocation of the negative episodes of the communal memory that may safeguard fledgling practices of civic virtue. In this way the complex interrelation of Bellah's three civic traditions is not constrained by the normative synthetic and restorative impetus that Bellah himself desires. The diversity of civic traditions may not yield a singular vision of the common good, but it may still pursue a number of goods in common.

Jeffrey Stout has recently developed an account of the virtues and norms found in contemporary American democracy.[68] For Stout, the ethical norms of democratic citizenship are creatures of the social practices by which the goods we seek in common are subjected to discursive justification. Stout explores the democratic pragmatism of Emerson, Whitman, and Dewey as a third way between the liberalism of Rawls and Rorty and the "traditionalism" of MacIntyre and Hauerwas. In a move that draws heavily on Hegel's criticism of Kantian *moralität*, Stout criticizes Rawls and Rorty for their refusal to admit religious reasons into the processes of public justification. In place of the abstractive enterprise of these theorists, Stout offers a passionate defense of the democratic (Emersonian) virtue of "piety"—a self-reliance born of a grateful yet critical stance in relation to one's tradition.[69]

For Stout, it is the combination of MacIntyre's anti-modern account of tradition with Yoder's pacifism and conception of the division of church from world that undermines any constructive possibility in Hauerwas's relation to democracy.[70] Stout traces the development of Hauerwas's thought and laments the development of this confluence of Yoder and

68. Stout, *Democracy and Tradition*. The notion of civil society is notable by its absence from Stout's book. This may, in part, be attributable to the fact that Stout's primary concern is to provide an account of how religious *individuals* can participate, in good conscience, within democratic discursive exchanges. Nonetheless, the lack of reflection on the institutional locus of the virtues he seeks to defend may compromise the persuasiveness of his account.

69. Ibid., 19–41, and 63–91.

70. Ibid., 148. It is somewhat ironic that, in a book dedicated to the virtuous practice of reason giving in justificatory arguments, Stout fails to move beyond mere assertion of the "unconvincing" nature of Yoder's exegesis on the central matter of nonviolence; see 323 n. 26. Equally, it seems odd that, despite admitting Yoder had "a more subtle position on justice than Hauerwas thought he did," at least in 1974, Stout then continues to read Yoder "as understood by Hauerwas," rather than on his own terms. Indeed, it is only Yoder as *mis*understood by Hauerwas in 1974! See 321 n. 7. Hauerwas has, of course, subsequently corrected this reading.

MacIntyre. In particular he argues that Hauerwas has fallen foul of the very danger he identified in Yoder's work in an essay dating back to 1974—that the "rigid dualism" of Church and world precludes "some forms of justice based on the possibilities open to unbelief."[71] Of course, Hauerwas has made clear in subsequent writings that the permeability of the division between Church and world is central to Yoder's distinction between the aeons, properly understood as a duality of agents.[72] The language of agency in this division allows Yoder to affirm the duality present in eschatological tension without descending into the kind of unhelpful dualism Stout seeks to avoid.[73] Indeed, as we saw earlier, it is precisely this "duality without dualism" that undergirds the analogical nature of ecclesial politics by which some forms of "justice" may be affirmed.

Stout may be correct that Hauerwas's idiom has depended so heavily on MacIntyre's anti-liberalism that what I have identified as the analogical basis of critique is compromised in such a way as to ossify the division of Church and world. Nonetheless, the critique is overplayed; even in his strongest rhetorical flourishes, Hauerwas's intent is not to dismiss all efforts for justice and democracy. Rather, his concern is that, in what he names "liberalism," what is valued as "freedom" is not really free, and what is designated "justice" remains unjust.[74] Thus, he says,

> If "democracy" names those forms of social and political life committed to the ongoing testing of the stories that legitimate or at least make intelligible the cooperation necessary to discover the goods in common, then I certainly think Christians have a stake in sustaining forms of life so constituted. Yet I continue to share John Howard Yoder's concern that governments that claim to rule in the name of "the people" are adept at hiding not only from "the people" but themselves the violence inherent in the order they have learned to call "peace."[75]

The theology of governmental power outlined in the previous chapter differs from the neo-republican strand of thought about civil society

---

71. Hauerwas, *VV*, 217.

72. The claim is made repeatedly in Hauerwas's reading of Yoder; see, for example, *State of the University*, 157; *PF*, 229–30.

73. Yoder, *CWS*, 28–32.

74. In particular, see *AC* and *BH*. For Hauerwas's response to Stout, see "Postscript" in *PF*, 215–41.

75. Hauerwas, *PF*, 19.

in its caution over the purely functional language in which religion is there described. An instrumental conception of ecclesial presence within civil society compromises the ability of the exilic community to critique the pseudo-peace (*pax romana*) of contemporary society in the light of the true peace (*shalom*) promised in God's election of Israel. The exilic model of citizenship, both in its resemblance of, and its distinction from, the two strands of thought on civil society just examined, can subject the claimed peace of a democratic order to an immanent critique. Yoder's highly cautious account of the preferability of a democratic polity emphasizes the way democracies make greater use of the vocabulary of accountability and public justification.[76] His point is not that modern democratic regimes represent a real though imperfect form of the self-government of the people, for the people, and by the people; but that to conduct government on such terms is to open oneself up to a greater degree of counter-hegemonic subversion of the oligarchic structures through the Christian's use of this "pagan" terminology. I suggest, then, that Yoder's approach to democracy can combine elements of both neo-Marxist and neo-republican readings of civil society in such a way as to begin to flesh out the exilic motif he expounded in the later years of his career.

Witness and the Pathologies of Democracy

The exilic metaphor finds some support from the historical stake the Christian church has in the development of democratic mechanisms. To affirm the Church's historical stake in democratization is to argue that, contrary to Habermas's analysis of a deliberative and participatory democracy, the modern idea of public space is derived first from the doctrine of the communion of saints and the free and open meeting (Yoder's "rule of Paul" as a public sign), and only secondarily (and with an ambiguous degree of independence) from settings like London's coffee houses in the eighteenth century.[77] Of course, tracing the complex genealogy of the concept of modern democracy, with Greek, ecclesial, and early modern antecedents, is insufficient, in and of itself, to provide a basis for the Christian presence within a democratic polity. Any such presence

---

76. Yoder, *PK*, 158–59.

77. Mayhew, *New Public*, 161. See also chapters 3 and 6 above, and Lindsay, *Churches and Democracy*; De Gruchy, *Christianity and Democracy*, 57–94; and Maddox, *Religion and the Rise of Democracy*.

requires precisely the sort of combination of critical and constructive elements we have detected in the motifs of eschatology, exile, and election that together make up our theology of governmental power. It is not only inappropriate, but in fact impossible, to provide a theological endorsement of democracy per se. For just as the state, in and of itself, does not exist, neither is there a singular distinct entity named "democracy" that is to become the object of ecclesial approval or censure. Yoder expresses this well when he argues

> [I]f we claim for democracy the status of a social institution *sui generis*, we shall inflate ourselves and destroy our neighbors through the demonic demands of the claims we make for our system and we shall pollute our Christian faith by making of it a civil religion. If on the other hand we protect ourselves from the Constantinianism of that view of democracy, we may find the realistic liberty to foster and celebrate relative democratization as one of the prophetic ministries of a servant people in a world we do not control.[78]

To foster relative democratization is, however, a function of the prophetic ministry of the church, which immediately brings it into critical encounter with the pathological tendencies of a number of contemporary social trends. Nonetheless, Oliver O'Donovan is wide of the mark when he identifies Yoder's emphasis on evangelical freedom with the theological consecration of a narrative of "irreversible ideological progress" of democracy found, for example, in Jacques Maritain.[79] I contend that the understanding of social change we have been at pains to outline in previous chapters is peculiarly well suited to provide an adequate theological means for the identification and critique of a consumerist trend in modern Western democracies. Given the constraints of space, it will be necessary to eschew in-depth empirical analysis, without wishing to deny its importance in actual ecclesial engagement with the issues. Instead, it is sufficient for now to demonstrate how the themes central to our theology of social change and the critique of governmental power bring three elements of consumerism into critical relief.

---

78. Yoder, *PK*, 165–66.
79. O'Donovan, *Ways of Judgment*, 171.

Colonization

I borrow the language of colonization from Habermas's conceptualization of the way the "instrumental logics" of power and money encroach on the functioning of the lifeworld, although a similar sense may be found in Jacques Ellul's exposition of the principalities and powers in the modern phenomena of "technique." I suggest that the eschatological perspective we have outlined allows us to conceive of "colonization" as something more pernicious than Habermas's sense of the incursive maneuvers and transgression of proper boundaries that characterize the spread of economic rationality. Habermas hardens the threefold division of civil society from state and economy through the use of systems theory. What, for Gramsci, was an analytic device, becomes, in Habermas, a set of descriptive and normative divisions. Both economic and state apparatus have become "systemically integrated action fields which can no longer be transformed democratically from within."[80]

In order to provide a fuller account of the mediation between lifeworld and colonizing systems, Habermas turns, in *Between Facts and Norms*, to the interstices of civil society. It is in the political public sphere that those institutions of civil society act as a "sluice" for moral insight and thus enact democratic processes of will formation. Civil society, in the mechanistic idiom of systems theory, represents the "input" side of the process of the democratic legitimation of law. It is not possible, under Habermas's construction, to critique the damaging logic of capitalist market economics; rather, through the moral discourses of civil society one can "erect a democratic dam against the colonizing encroachment of system imperatives on areas of the lifeworld."[81]

Here we must object to the circumscription of critical bite that springs from Habermas's overly schematized structures. Habermas's division of systems from lifeworld means that the democratizing activities found in civil society themselves only impact civil society itself. That is to say, civil society is both the terrain and the sole target of democratizing practices.

---

80. Habermas, "Further Reflections," 444.

81. Ibid. Habermas distances his reading of the systems of economics and power from that of systems theorist Niklas Luhmann. The "autopoietic turn" renders systems as entirely self-contained (both linguistically and, hence, normatively) and thus cuts them off entirely from deliberative legitimation. Systems theory cannot, therefore, offer its own theory of democracy as the basis of an ethically responsive society. Habermas, *Between Facts and Norms*, 330–42.

> Civil society can directly transform only itself, and it can have at most an indirect effect on the self-transformation of the political system; generally, it has an influence only on the personnel and programming of this system.[82]

Habermas frequently stresses the importance of excluding meddlesome incursions from the lifeworld into the self-steering mechanism of the systems.[83] This seems to be a privileging of efficacy over accountability, the balance of which cuts to the heart of modern systems of representative democracy.[84] As William Forbath notes, it also fails to take account of the basic status of all market orders as political artifacts "based on and constituted by highly plastic cultural norms and legal rules."[85]

It seems that, in the wake of the failure of state socialism, the market economy is deemed, almost by default, the proper, efficacious, and legitimate economic system. The exclusion of incursions from the lifeworld provides no basis for the development of the new and more participatory forms of redistributive welfare that Habermas wishes to defend. More critically, pace his defenders, Habermas therefore fails to accommodate the negative side of existing forms of civil society accentuated by Foucault.[86] The counter-hegemonic witness that we have identified as springing from the eschatological constraint of the powers both diagnoses a deeper level of colonization and suggests a stronger sense of the ability to resist it. Habermas's account can do little to counter what we might call the "colonization" that occurs within the notion of moral and political agency when the economic system is insulated from internal critique. This is the structural basis upon which, in Stanley Hauerwas's words, "we have let capitalism privatize our economic lives in a way that's detrimental to the public character of the church."[87]

Here the freedom gained by "living in truth" is traded for the capitalist freedom to make money. Yet as we saw in our discussion of Václav

---

82. Ibid., 372.

83. Ibid., 150.

84. For example, debates surrounding the preferability of various forms of proportional representation versus the regnant "first-past-the-post" system of British electoral procedure, operate on an equation whereby the degree of representational accuracy is inversely proportionate to the political efficacy of the system.

85. Forbath, "Short-Circuit," 280.

86. Cohen and Arato, *Civil Society*, 442–51.

87. Hauerwas, "Christianity." Hauerwas also notes the deleterious effects of the liberal division of economic from political and cultural systems in "In Praise of *Centessimus Annus*."

Havel, it is truthful living that represents "the chief breeding ground for independent, alternative political [and, we might add, economic] ideas."[88] The anti-political model of civil society acknowledges life's "humdrum everydayness" as a site of significant dissent in its own right, rather than merely a seedbed for sporadic mobilization of protest. Living in truth is as much an imperative in democratic societies as in totalitarian regimes. Havel claims that the personal freedoms and securities enjoyed in a democratic society do not escape "the automatism of technological civilization and the industrial-consumer society."[89]

How then are we to conceive of a Christian resistance to consumerist colonization found in civil society? Both new social movements and so-called new "spiritual" movements occupy a concern with what Anthony Giddens has called "life-politics."[90] The increasingly widespread concern of such groups with the deleterious effects of global capitalism highlights a more critical orientation to the economic and state systems than Habermas's theorizations would allow. Nevertheless, one could suggest that such new "spiritual" movements, in so far as they represent a readily privatized and consumerized "religious" product, lack the critical rigour and coherence that is required to bring the present structure of the domination system, as a whole, under scrutiny. The trend of colonization is best resisted by a more basic refusal of the consumerist logic of choice. Here the theological realism we have identified in Yoder's thought can bolster our understanding of the resistance to economic colonization. Not only can we affirm that, as the utopian language of the World Social Forum has it, "another world is possible,"[91] but furthermore, the eschatological element of our theology of the Church's relation to governmental power grounds such resistance in the knowledge that another, more true and more real, social order is there made present.

Control

The logic of consumer choice, which affects both capitalist colonization and, ironically, some of the rhetoric with which movements *opt* for a

---

88. Havel, "Power of the Powerless," 62.
89. Ibid., 115–16.
90. Heelas and Woodhead, "Homeless minds today?"
91. See for example the report of The International Forum on Globalisation, *Alternatives to Economic Globalization*; Fisher and Ponniah, *Another World is Possible*.

resistant *style* of life, may reflect an almost Pelagian understanding of political agency. That is not to say that these phenomena are equally suspect—for there is, as Yoder rightly insists, an important element of voluntariety in the stance of resistance to the principalities and powers. I suggest that the model of the exilic citizenship of the elect, with its non-Constantinian vision of a life lived "out of control," may counter the dangers inherent in the rationalist core of much understanding of civil society. Just as, as seen in chapter 5, René Girard's rationalist (as opposed to ontological) understanding of Christ's work is insufficient to ground the tactical transformations required in the field of a theological response to practices of punishment, so in order to critique the pathologies of democratic civil society something more than a sheer act of will is necessary.

The structures of social control are increasingly affected by an economic rationality—with its managerialism, actuarial calculation, and notions of efficiency. In relation to crime the notion of control is especially seen in crime prevention initiatives, but also appears in the loss of rehabilitative models of punishment in favor of motifs of control and risk management.[92] This logic of control coincides with the prominence of a model of criminality that downplays factors of social condition in favor of a model of opportunism and rational choice. Indeed that freedom to choose, and the notions of autonomy and control on which it trades, have become basic to the language of political reform from education through to health care. As with our earlier discussion of social change, the point is not that recognizing the dubious character of this myth of "control" leads us to reject all purposive reasoning. It does not.[93] Rather, the longer and broader understanding of efficacy that springs from Yoder's doxological account of social change might provide a corrective to the rhetoric of choice that is overdetermined by a consumerist understanding of freedom.

Ironically, existing somewhat unhappily alongside the consumerist logic of choice is an increasingly complex practice of governmentality that

---

92. Garland, *Culture of Control*.

93. In addition to the discussion on the redefinition of efficacy in chapter 5, see, for example, Hauerwas, *TPK*, 105, where he states—"To live out of control, however, does not mean that we do not plan and/or seek to find the means to promote justice in the world, but that such planning is not done under the illusion of omnipotence. We can take the risk of planning that does not make effectiveness our primary goal, but faithfulness to God's kingdom. To plan in such a manner involves breaking the self-deception that justice can only be achieved through a power and violence that seeks to assure its efficacy."

escapes the processes of democratic legitimation.[94] What governmentalization and consumerism share is a complex attenuation of the meaning of "freedom." A significant level of critique may spring from the counterposing of what we might call a Yoderian "politics of grace" with the consumerist "politics of will." The former is tactical, patient, responsive, and gracious in the face of contingency; the latter is strategic, governmental, managerial, and supposedly autonomous. Scott Bader-Saye's argument for the "freedom of election" strikes the appropriate note here.

> Election relieves one of the need to determine one's own destiny, and thus it frees one from the peculiarly modern anxiety that arises from having to be a self-creator. . . . The grace of divine election sets one free for the service of God and others. It sets one free to be out of control of one's destiny, and thus opens space for risky engagements, for throwing in our lot with the poor and the outcast, for befriending the sinner. It frees us to risk lifelong commitments such as marriage and holy orders, since such commitments can only be sustained if they are viewed within a larger story that relieves them of their arbitrariness. In short, election sets one free for covenant life.[95]

The contrast with consumerist "freedom of choice" is obvious. With Milbank we can assert that modern capitalism is heretical because it denies the ontological primacy of gift, and replaces it with what we might call the lust for control. "[T]he politics of endless acquisition and of deferred enjoyment in expectation of an absolute future rest upon an illusory ontology which seeks to erect a secure spatial edifice in defiance of death."[96] Despite the strong sense of human dependence on prevenient grace in such comments, the exilic model of citizenship has been seen to require substantially more than a simple rhetorical opposition. The doxological character of Yoder's vision of social change allows a suitable degree of skepticism in regard to the level of control that is simultaneously

---

94. See, for example, the diffuse power now afforded to the voluntary sector. Morison "Government-Voluntary Sector."

95. Bader-Saye, "Aristotle or Abraham," 352–55.

96. Milbank, *BR*, 177. Just as this ontology of gift surpasses the politics of consumption, for Milbank it also moves beyond neo-liberal conception of the common good as a set of legally guaranteed freedoms. "Today then, we need to surpass liberal democracy and search again for the common good in ceaseless circulation and creative development, a search that may involve laws, but more fundamentally involves charity beyond the law." Milbank, "Gift of Ruling." For a fuller Radical Orthodox reading of economics characterized by the strategy of rhetorical and ontological opposition, see Long, *Divine Economy*.

presumed and striven for in the economic idiom of social policy. It is equally cautious in regard to the exclusionary and possibly violent methods with which such control may be asserted.

Confinement

I have demonstrated that the analogical element of eschatological witness leads Yoder to emphasize the importance of ecclesial practices for social change. In relation to our example of consumerism within civil society, I suggest that if we combine that emphasis on practices with a caution over notions of control we can see how the three motifs of eschatology, exile, and election can inform a restatement of the ecclesial hospitality. We have already seen how procedural models of the social contract operate, in part, as an attempt to control public discourse through the confinement of religious language to a private arena of motivation.[97] However, within consumerism there is an even more ferocious form of confinement and exclusion—one dramatically at odds with the eucharistic logic of economic solidarity.[98]

Critics of modern consumerism point to the vapid excesses of consumption that thrive on the transience (shelf-life) of the product consumed. Whether it happens to be sushi or spouses, fruit or friendship, cars or careers, cravings are fabricated and manipulated in such a way as to leave only one constant—desire itself. The ecological concerns arising from this unsustainable cultural practice are well known. Yet, of course, the cost is borne not only by the environment, but also by the workers in sweat-shops, the refugees and "economic migrants"—many of whom either become, through a Girardian process, the demonic "other," or simply disappear from view altogether. The presumed "right" to satiate one's hunger for "products" itself produces a culture of disposal—including ever-growing detritus of "wasted lives."[99]

This is highly impassioned language, but behind the zeal lie a diverse range of phenomena, from insecure employment to mounting issues of consumer credit. The confinement and exclusion at the heart of the critics' objections is not so much an unforeseen side-effect of consumer culture

---

97. Stout reaches a similar verdict in his defense of the pragmatist tradition of reason-giving. Stout, *Democracy and Tradition*, 81.

98. In addition to Yoder, *BP*, see Cavanaugh, *Theopolitical Imagination*, "World in a Wafer," and *Being Consumed*.

99. Bauman, *Wasted Lives*.

as it is an innate part of the production process. Most of the excluded are not confined a priori, nor do they opt out through an act of will; they are produced through the fabrication of desire. Let us, once again, take the example of crime. Jock Young evokes the image of a bulimic culture—a seemingly uncontrollable and continuous hunger is compensated for by a forced emetic expulsion. In the social order of late modern capitalism, Young claims, "[c]rime occurs where there is cultural inclusion and structural exclusion."[100] There is a remarkable assimilative power to the culture of desire. The American, or, with some differences, the European, "dream" performs the function of cultural inclusion. Yet crime's relation to structural exclusion is not only found in the isolation arising from the inability of the poor to attain the goals and aspirations set for them by this vision. As the supposedly meritocratic society remains blind to the dynamics of class and racial inequality, so crime appears in the creation of subcultures that invert, yet remain steadfastly guided by, the values of competition and self-reliance. The final moment of the bulimic process, when the offending "others" are more fully expunged, occurs through the likes of "zero-tolerance" initiatives and ever-increasing levels of imprisonment—both of which disproportionately affect those on the wrong side of racial, educational, and class divisions.

None of this is to deny the appropriate level of individual culpability, but it does point to the way the logic of consumption contributes to a variety of pathological trends in modern British and American society. To a large degree the fabrication of desire is maintained through the complex mechanisms of the production of "brand identity."[101] We noted above the contrast of consumerism with the identity established in the eucharistic logic of solidarity. To use Certeau's distinction once more, through a variety of direct intitiatives (projects for children, shelter and acceptance for the homeless, prison visiting; as well as alternative economic practices from fair trade and "buying local" to credit unions, etc.) and a more nebulous, though no less important, strengthening of communal life, the Church may begin to open up hospitable spaces within this unwelcoming place. The *ethically* realist (that is to say efficacious and practicable) character of such ecclesial practices, as we saw in chapter 3,

---

100. Young, *Exclusive Society*, 81.

101. See most famously Klein, *No Logo*. For a fascinating attempt to outline the theological critique of the aesthetics of branding, see Maeseneer, "Saint Francis Versus McDonald's".

is based in a prior *theological* realism with its analogical and participatory motifs. I suggest, therefore, that the hospitality engendered in the mission and witness of the exilic community participates within the achievement of the incarnation. To echo the words of Rowan Williams, the point of the incarnation is

> above all the establishing of human communion by showing what the ultimate foundation of common life is, and actively drawing us—with all the forms of common life we are already involved in and which define our existence—into the common life of God.[102]

None of this fits with the now common assertion of ecclesial ethics as mere gesture politics, removed from the hard choices and institutional complexities of political rule. To "seek the peace of the city" places a burden of responsibility upon the exilic community that only faithfulness to its dependence on YHWH's prevenient grace can sustain. Theological calls for a recovery of hospitality and asylum within the Church point to an important counter-hegemonic gesture in a civil society deeply riven with exclusionary pathologies.[103] In the forgoing discussion we have begun to trace a theology of social change and governmental power from their origins in the theological realism of Christology and eschatology. We have seen in the reconciling purposes of a nonviolent God the promise of a Christian politics that is public, realist, and transformative. In such a horizon the theological response to civil society does not deny the importance or complexity of "normal" politics but affirms the theological norms under which political rule must conduct itself. There is nothing *mere* about such gestures—or more properly, such a witness.

---

102. Williams, "Incarnation," 226.

103. In addition to Milbank's call for such a recovery at the end of *TST*, see also Pohl, *Making Room*.

Bibliography

Ackerman, Bruce, and Anne Alstott. *The Stakeholder Society*. New Haven: Yale University Press, 1999.
Adams, Nicholas. *Habermas and Theology*. Cambridge: Cambridge University Press, 2006.
Adorno, Theodor W. *Minima Moralia: Reflections from Damaged Life*. London: New Left, 1951.
Adorno, Theodor W., and Max Horkheimer. *The Dialectic of Enlightenment*. London: Verso, 1997.
Agamben, Giorgio. *Homo Sacer: Sovereign Power and Bare Life*. Translated by Daniel Heller-Roazen. Meridien. Stanford: Stanford University Press, 1998.
———. *Remnants of Auschwitz: The Witness and the Archive*. Translated by Daniel Hller-Roazen. New York: Zone, 1999.
———. *State of Exception*. Translated by Kevin Attel. Chicago: University of Chicago Press, 2005.
———. *The Time that Remains: A Commentary on the Letter to the Romans*. Meridien, Crossing Aesthetics. Translated by Patricia Dailey. Stanford: Stanford University Press, 2005.
Allen, Jonathan. "The Situated Critic or the Loyal Critic? Rorty and Walzer on Social Criticism." *Philosophy and Social Criticism* 24 (1998) 25–46.
Anderson, Benedict. *Imagined Communities: Reflections on the Origin and Spread of Nationalism*. Rev. ed. London: Verso, 1991.
Anglican Roman Catholic International Commission (ARCIC) II. *Life in Christ: Morals, Communion and the Church*. London: CTS and CHP, 1994.
Aquinas, Thomas. *Summa Theologiae*. Edited by T. Gilby. London: Eyre & Spottiswoode, 1963–1975.
Arendt, Hannah. *The Human Condition*. 2nd ed. Introduction by Margaret Canovan. Chicago: University of Chicago Press, 1999.
———. *On Revolution*. London: Faber & Faber, 1963.
Aristotle. *The Nicomachean Ethics*. Translated by Harris Rackman. Wordsworth Classics of World Literature. Ware, UK: Wordsworth, 1996.
Asad, Talal. *Formations of the Secular: Christianity, Islam, Modernity*. Cultural Memory in the Present. Stanford: Stanford University Press, 2003.

Ashenden, Samantha. "Questions of Criticism: Habermas and Foucault on Civil Society and Resistance." In *Foucault Contra Habermas: Recasting the Dialogue Between Genealogy and Critical Theory*, edited by Samantha Ashenden and David Owen, 143–65. London: Sage, 1999.

Ashenden, Samantha, and David Owen, editors. *Foucault Contra Habermas: Recasting the Dialogue between Genealogy and Critical Theory*. London: Sage, 1999.

Atherton, John. *Public Theology for Changing Times*. London: SPCK, 2000.

Avis, Paul. *Church, State and Establishment*. London: SPCK, 2001.

———. *God and the Creative Imagination: Metaphor, Symbol and Myth in Religion and Theology*. London: Routledge, 1999.

Bader-Saye, Scott. "Aristotle or Abraham? Church, Israel, and the Politics of Election." PhD diss., Duke University, 1997.

———. *Church and Israel after Christendom: The Politics of Election*. 1999. Reprint, Eugene, OR: Wipf & Stock, 2005.

Badiou, Alain. *Being and Event*. Translated by Oliver Feltham. London: Continuum, 2007.

———. *Saint Paul: The Foundation of Universalism*. Translated by Ray Brassier. Cultural Memory in the Present. Stanford: Stanford University Press, 2003.

Balthasar, Hans Urs von. *The Glory of the Lord: A Theological Aesthetics*. Vol. 5, *The Realm of Metaphysics in the Modern Age*. Edited by Brian McNeil and John Riches. Translated by Oliver Davies et al. Edinburgh: T. & T. Clark, 1991.

Banner, Michael. *Christian Ethics and Contemporary Moral Problems*. Cambridge: Cambridge University Press, 1999.

———. "Christianity and Civil Society." In *Alternative Conceptions of Civil Society*, edited by Simone Chambers and Will Kymlicka, 113–30. Princeton: Princeton University Press, 2002.

Barber, Daniel. "The Particularity of Jesus and the Time of the Kingdom: Philosophy and Theology in Yoder." *Modern Theology* 23 (2007) 63–89.

Barry, Andrew, Thomas Osborne, and Nikolas Rose. "Liberalism, Neo-liberalism and Governmentality: Introduction." *Economy and Society* 22 (1993) 265–66.

Barth, Karl. *Against the Stream: Shorter Post-war Writings, 1946–1952*. London: SCM, 1954.

———. "The Christian Community and the Civil Community." In *Against the Stream: Shorter Post-war Writings, 1946–1952*, 15–50. London: SCM, 1954.

———. *Church Dogmatics, Volumes I-IV*. Translated by G. W. Bromiley and T. F. Torrance. Edinburgh: T. & T. Clark, 1956–1975.

———. *Dogmatics in Outline*. London: SCM, 1968.

———. *The Epistle to the Romans*. Oxford: Oxford University Press, 1968.

Bartholomew, Craig, Jonathan Chaplin, Robert Song, and Al Wolters. *A Royal Priesthood? The Use of the Bible Ethically and Politically—A Dialogue with Oliver O'Donovan*. Grand Rapids: Zondervan, 2002.

Bauckham, Richard. *Bible and Mission: Christian Witness in a Postmodern World*. Milton Keynes, UK: Paternoster, 2003.

———, editor. *God Will Be All In All: The Eschatology of Jürgen Moltmann*. Edinburgh: T. & T. Clark, 1999.

———. "Time and Eternity." In *God Will Be All In All: The Eschatology of Jürgen Moltmann*, edited by Richard Bauckham, 155–226. Edinburgh: T. & T. Clark, 1999.

Bauckham, Richard, and Trevor Hart. "The Shape of Time." In *The Future as God's Gift: Explorations in Christian Eschatology*, edited by David Fergusson and Marcel Sarot, 41–72. Edinburgh, T. & T. Clark, 2000.

Bauerschmidt, Frederick Christian. "The Abrahamic Voyage: Michel de Certeau and Theology." *Modern Theology* 12 (1996) 1–26.

———. "The Word Made Speculative? John Milbank's Christological Poetics." *Modern Theology* 15 (1999) 417–31.

Bauman, Zygmunt. *Intimations of Postmodernity*. London: Routledge, 1992.

———. *Wasted Lives: Modernity and Its Outcasts*. Cambridge: Polity, 2004.

Beckford, James. *Religion and Advanced Industrial Society*. Controversies in Sociology 23. London: Unwin, 1989.

Bell, Jr., Daniel. "Badiou's Faith and Paul's Gospel." *Angelaki* 12 (2007) 97–111.

———. *Liberation Theology after the End of History: The Refusal to Cease Suffering*. London: Routledge, 2001.

Bellah, Robert, Richard Madsen, William M. Sullivan, Ann Swidler, and Steven M. Tipton, editors. *The Good Society*. New York: Knopf, 1991.

———. *Habits of the Heart: Individualism and Commitment in American Life*. Berkeley: University of California Press, 1985.

Bender, Harold S. *The Anabaptist Vision*. Scottdale, PA: Herald, 1944.

Benhabib, Seyla. *Situating the Self: Gender, Community and Postmodernism in Contemporary Ethics*. New York: Routledge, 1992.

Benjamin, Walter. "Theological-Political Fragment." In *Selected Writings: Volume 3 1935–1938*, 305–6. Cambridge: Harvard University Press, 2002.

———. "Theses on the Philosophy of History." In *Illuminations*, 245–55. London: Pimlico, 1999.

Berger, Peter, L. *The Sacred Canopy: Elements of a Sociological Theory of Religion*. New York: Doubleday, 1967.

Berkhof, Hendrik. *Christ and the Powers*. Translated by John H. Yoder. 2nd ed. Scottdale, PA: Herald, 1977.

Berns, Walter. "The Morality of Anger." In *Capital Punishment: A Reader*, edited by Glen Stassen, 14–22. Cleveland: Pilgrim, 1998.

Berry, Philippa, and Andrew Wernick, editors. *Shadow of Spirit: Postmodernism and Religion*. London: Routledge, 1992.

Best, T. F., and G. Gassmann, editors. *On the Way to Fuller Koinonia: The Official Report of the Fifth World Conference on Faith and Order*. Geneva: WCC, 1994.

Best, T. F., and M. Robra, editors. *Ecclesiology and Ethics: Ecumenical Ethical Engagement, Moral Formation and the Nature of the Church*. Geneva: WCC, 1997.

Biesecker-Mast, Gerald. "The Radical Christological Rhetoric of John Howard Yoder." In *A Mind Patient and Untamed: Assessing John Howard Yoder's Contributions to Theology, Ethics and Peacemaking*, edited by Ben C. Ollenburger and Gayle Gerber Koontz, 39–55. Telford, PA: Cascadia, 2004.

Biggar, Nigel. *Burying the Past: Making Peace and Doing Justice after Civil Conflict*, Washington, DC: Georgetown University Press, 2003.

———. *The Hastening that Waits: Karl Barth's Ethics*. Oxford: Clarendon, 1993.

———, editor. *Reckoning with Barth: Essays in Commemoration of the Centenary of Karl Barth's Birth*. Oxford: Mowbray, 1988.

Black, Rufus. *Christian Moral Realism: Natural Law, Narrative, Virtue and the Gospel*. Oxford: Clarendon, 2000.

Blair, Tony. "Speech on Welfare Reform–June 10th 2002." No Pages. Online: http://www.number10.gov.uk/Page1716.

Bleiker, Roland. *Popular Dissent, Human Agency and Global Politics*. Cambridge: Cambridge University Press, 2000.

Blum, Peter C. "Foucault, Genealogy, Anabaptism: Confessions of An Errant Postmodernist." In *Anabaptists and Postmodernity*, edited by Susan Biesecker-Mast and Gerald Biesecker-Mast, 60–74. Telford, PA: Pandora, 2000.

Bobbio, Norberto, "Gramsci and the Concept of Civil Society." In *Civil Society and the State: New European Perspectives*, edited by John Keane, 73–100. London: Verso, 1988

Bodin, Jean. *Six Books of the Commonwealth*. Translated by M. J. Tooley. Oxford: Blackwell, 1955.

Boersma, Hans. "Being Reconciled: Atonement as the Ecclesio-Christological Practice of Forgiveness in John Milbank." In *Radical Orthodoxy and the Reformed Tradition: Creation, Covenant, and Participation*, edited by James K. A. Smith and James H. Olthius, 183–202. Grand Rapids: Baker, 2005.

———. *Violence, Hospitality and the Cross: Reappropriating the Atonement Tradition*. Grand Rapids: Baker, 2004.

Boff, Leonardo. *Ecclesiogenesis: The Base Communities Reinvent the Church*. Maryknoll, NY: Orbis, 1986.

———. *Trinity and Society*. Tunbridge Wells, UK: Burns & Oats, 1988.

Bonhoeffer, Dietrich. *Act and Being: Transcendental Philosophy and Ontology in Systematic Theology*. Translated by H. Martin Rumscheidt. Minneapolis: Fortress, 1996.

———. *Christology*. London: Collins, 1966.

———. *Creation and Fall: A Theological Exposition of Genesis 1–3*. Translated by Douglas Stephen Bax. Minneapolis: Fortress, 1997.

———. *Ethics*. New York: Touchstone, 1995.

———. *Letters and Papers from Prison*. Enlarged edition. New York: Simon & Schuster, 1997.

Boxx, T. William, and Gary M. Quinlivan, editors. *Public Morality, Civic Virtue, and the Problem of Modern Liberalism*. Grand Rapids: Eerdmans, 2000.

Boyarin, Daniel. "Judaism as a Free Church: Footnotes to John Howard Yoder's *The Jewish-Christian Schism Revisited*." *Cross Currents* 56 (2007) 6–21.

Braithwaite, John. *Crime, Shame, and Reintegration*. Cambridge: Cambridge University Press, 1989.

Brink, David O. *Moral Realism and the Foundations of Ethics*. Cambridge Studies in Philosophy. Cambridge: Cambridge University Press, 1989.

Brown, Callum, G. *The Death of Christian Britain: Understanding Secularisation 1800–2000*. Christianity and Society in the Modern World. London: Routledge, 2001.

Browning, D., and Francis Schüssler Fiorenza, editors. *Habermas, Modernity, and Public Theology*. New York: Crossroads, 1992.

Brubacher, Gordon. "Just War and the New Community: The Witness of the Old Testament for Christians Today." *Princeton Theological Review* 35 (2006) no pages. Online: http://www.princetontheologicalreview.org/issues_web/35_text.html#article3.

Bruce, Steve. *God is Dead: Secularisation in the West*. Oxford: Blackwell, 2002.

Brueggemann, Walter, *Old Testament Theology: Essays on Structure, Theme and Text*. Minneapolis: Fortress, 1992.

———. *Theology of the Old Testament: Testimony, Dispute, Advocacy*. Minneapolis: Fortress, 1997.

Burchell, Graham, Colin Gordon, and Peter Miller, editors. *The Foucault Effect: Studies in Governmentality*. Chicago: University of Chicago, 1991.

Calhoun, Craig, editor. *Habermas and the Public Sphere*. Studies in Contemporary German Social Thought. Cambridge: MIT Press, 1992.

Carrette, Jeremy, and Richard King. *Selling Spirituality: The Silent Takeover of Religion*. London: Routledge, 2004.

Carroll, M. Daniel, David J. A. Clines, and Philip R. Davies, editors. *The Bible in Human Society: Essays in Honour of John Rogerson*. JSOT Supplements 200. Sheffield: Sheffield Academic, 1995.

Carter, Craig. *The Politics of the Cross: The Theology and Social Ethics of John Howard Yoder*. Grand Rapids: Brazos, 2001.

Cartwright, Michael G. "Afterword: Stanley Hauerwas' Essays in Theological Ethics: A Reader's Guide." In *The Hauerwas Reader*, edited by Michael Cartwright and John Berkman, 623–72. Durham: Duke University Press, 2001.

———. "Afterword: 'If Abraham is Our Father . . .': The Problem of Christian Supersessionism *After* Yoder." In John Howard Yoder, *The Jewish-Christian Schism Revisited*, edited by Michael G. Cartwright and Peter Ochs, 204–40. London: SCM, 2003.

———. "Radical Reform, Radical Catholicity." In John Howard Yoder, *The Royal Priesthood: Essays Ecclesiological and Ecumenical*, 1–49. Grand Rapids: Eerdmans, 1994.

———. "Sharing the House of God: Learning to Read Scripture with Anabaptists." *Mennonite Quarterly Review* 74 (2000) 593–621.

Cartwright, Michael G., and John Berkman, editors. *The Hauerwas Reader*. Durham: Duke University Press, 2001.

Casanova, José. *Public Religions in the Modern World*. Chicago: University of Chicago, 1994.

Cavanaugh, William, T. "'A Fire Strong Enough to Consume the House': The Wars of Religion and the Rise of the State." *Modern Theology* 11 (1995) 397–420.

———. *Being Consumed: Economics and Christian Desire*. Grand Rapids: Eerdmans, 2008.

———. "Killing for the Telephone Company: Why the Nation-State Is Not the Keeper of the Common Good." *Modern Theology* 20 (2004) 243–74.

———. *Theopolitical Imagination: Discovering the Liturgy as a Political Act in an Age of Global Consumerism*. Edinburgh: T. & T. Clark, 2002.

———. *Torture and Eucharist: Theology, Politics, and the Body of Christ*. Oxford: Blackwell, 1998.

———. "The World in a Wafer: A Geography of the Eucharist as Resistance to Globalization." *Modern Theology* 15 (1999) 181–96.

Certeau, Michel de. "History: Science and Fiction." In *The Certeau Reader*, edited by Graham Ward, 37–52. Oxford: Blackwell, 2000.

———. *The Practice of Everyday Life*. California: University of California Press, 1984.

———. "The Weakness of Believing: From the Body to Writing, A Christian Transit." In *The Certeau Reader*, edited by Graham Ward, 214–43. Oxford: Blackwell, 2000.

Chambers, Simone, and Will Kymlicka, editors. *Alternative Conceptions of Civil Society*. Princeton: Princeton University Press, 2002.

Chambers, Simone. "A Critical Theory of Civil Society." In *Alternative Conceptions of Civil Society*, edited by Simone Chambers and Will Kymlicka, 90–110. Princeton: Princeton University Press, 2002.

Cohen, Jean L. "Interpreting the Notion of Civil Society." In *Towards a Global Civil Society*, edited by Michael Walzer, 35–40. Oxford: Berghahn, 1995.

Cohen, Jean. L., and Andrew Arato. *Civil Society and Political Theory*. Cambridge, MA: MIT Press, 1992.

Cohen, Mitchell. "An Empire of Cant: Hardt, Negri and Postmodern Political Theory." *Dissent* 493 (2002) 17–28.

Coleridge, Samuel Taylor. *Aids to Reflection: Moral and Religious Aphorisms*. London: George Bell and Sons, 1904.

Coles, Romand. "Communicative Action and Dialogical Ethics: Habermas and Foucault." *Polity* 25 (1992) 71–94.

———. "Identity and Difference in the Ethical Positions of Adorno and Habermas." In *The Cambridge Companion to Habermas*, edited by Stephen K. White, 19–45. Cambridge: Cambridge University Press, 1995.

———. "'The Wild Patience of John Howard Yoder: 'Outsiders' and the 'Otherness of the Church.'" *Modern Theology* 18 (2002) 305–31.

Collins, Adela Yarbro. "The Function of 'Excommunication' in Paul." *Harvard Theological Review* 73 (1980) 251–63.

Connolly, William. *Why I am Not a Secularist*. Minneapolis: University of Minnesota Press, 1999.

Cooke, Maeve. "Salvaging and Secularising the Semantic Contents of Religion: The Limitations of Habermas' Postmetaphysical Proposal." *International Journal of the Philosophy of Religion* 60 (2006) 187–207.

———. "A Secular State for a Postsecular Society? Postmetaphysical Theory and the Place of Religion." *Constellations* 14:2 (2007) 224–38.

Couzens Hoy, David, editor. *Foucault: A Critical Reader*. Oxford: Blackwell, 1986.

Cox, Robert, W. "Civil Society at the Turn of the Millennium: Prospects for an Alternative World Order." *Review of International Studies* 25 (1999) 3–28.

Crowder, Colin, editor. *God and Reality: Essays on Christian Non-Realism*. London: Mowbray, 1997.

Cullmann, Oscar. *Christ and Time: The Primitive Christian Conception of Time and History*. London: SCM, 1962.

Cunningham, David, S. *Faithful Persuasion: In Aid of a Rhetoric of Christian Theology*. Notre Dame: University of Notre Dame Press, 1990.

———. *These Three Are One: The Practice of Trinitarian Theology*. Challenges in Contemporary Theology. Oxford: Blackwell, 1997.

Dalferth, Ingolf U. "Karl Barth's Eschatological Realism." In *Karl Barth: Centenary Essays*, edited by S. W. Sykes, 14–45. Cambridge: Cambridge University Press, 1989.

Davie, Grace. *Religion in Britain Since 1945: Believing without Belonging*. Oxford: Blackwell, 1994.

Davies, Oliver. *The Creativity of God: World, Eucharist, Reason*. Cambridge Studies in Christian Doctrine 12. Cambridge: Cambridge University Press, 2004.

———. *A Theology of Compassion*. London: SCM, 2001

Davis, Creston, John Milbank, and Slavoj Žižek, editors. *Theology and the Political: The New Debate*. Durham: Duke University Press, 2005.

Davis, Derek H. "President Bush's Office of Faith-Based and Community Initiatives: Boon or Boondoggle?" *Journal of Church and State* 43 (2001) 411–22.

Dawn, Marva Jenine Sandberg. "The Concept of 'The Principalities and Powers' in the Works of Jacques Ellul." PhD diss., University of Notre Dame, 1994.

D'Costa, Gavin, editor. *Christian Uniqueness Reconsidered: The Myth of a Pluralistic Theology of Religions*. Faith Meets Faith Series. Maryknoll, NY: Orbis, 1990.
De Gruchy, John W. *Christianity and Democracy: A Theology for a Just World Order*. Cambridge Studies in Ideology and Religion. Cambridge: Cambridge University Press, 1995.
———. *Reconciliation: Restoring Justice*. London: SCM, 2002.
Dean, Mitchell. *Governmentality: Power and Rule in Modern Society*. London: Sage, 1999.
Dillon, Michelle. "The Authority of the Holy Revisited: Habermas, Religion and Emancipatory Possibilities." *Sociological Theory* 17 (1999) 290–306.
Dodaro, Robert. *Christ and the Just Society in the Thought of Augustine*. Cambridge: Cambridge University Press, 2004.
Donzelot, Jacques. "The Mobilization of Society." In *The Foucault Effect: Studies in Governmentality*, edited by Graham Burchell, Colin Gordon, and Peter Miller, 169–79. Chicago: University of Chicago, 1991.
Dostert, Troy Lewis. "Beyond Rawlsian Politics: Towards A Post-Secular Ethics of Public Life." PhD diss., Duke University, 2001.
Drake, H. A. *Constantine and the Bishops: The Politics of Intolerance*. Baltimore: John Hopkins University Press, 2000.
Duff, Paul Brooks. "René Girard in Corinth: An Early Christian Social Crisis and a Biblical Text of Persecution." *Helios* 22 (1995) 79–99.
Duquoc, Christian. "The Forgiveness of God." In *Forgiveness*, edited by C. Floristan and C. Duquoc, 35–44. Edinburgh: T. & T. Clark, 1986.
Durnbaugh, Donald F. *The Believers' Church: The History and Character of Radical Protestantism*. Scottdale, PA: Herald, 1985.
Durnbaugh, Donald F., editor. *On Earth Peace*. Elgin, IL: Brethren, 1978.
Eagleton, Terry. *The Illusions of Postmodernism*. Oxford: Blackwell, 1996.
Eberle, Christopher J. *Religious Conviction in Liberal Politics*. Cambridge: Cambridge University Press, 2002.
Elliott, Neil. *Liberating Paul: The Justice of God and the Politics of the Apostle*. Maryknoll, NY: Orbis, 1994.
Ellul, Jacques, *Autopsy of Revolution*. New York: Knopf, 1971.
———. *The Ethics of Freedom*. Grand Rapids: Eerdmans, 1976.
———. *False Presence of the Kingdom*. New York: Seabury, 1963.
———. *The Meaning of the City*. Grand Rapids: Eerdmans, 1970.
———. *The New Demons*. New York: Seabury, 1975.
———. *The Technological Society*. London: Cape, 1965
———. *Violence: Reflections from a Christian Perspective*. New York: Seabury, 1969.
Elshtain, Jean Bethke. "Citizenship and Armed Civic Virtue: Some Questions on the Commitment to Public Life." In *Community in America: The Challenge of Habits of the Heart*, edited by Charles H. Reynolds and Ralph Norman, 47–55. Berkeley: University of California Press, 1988.
———. "Religion and American Democracy." In *Public Morality, Civic Virtue, and the Problem of Modern Liberalism*, edited by William T. Boxx and Gary M. Quinlivan, 14–23. Grand Rapids: Eerdmans, 2000.
———. *Sovereignty: God, State, and Self*. New York: Basic, 2008.
———. *Women and War*. Brighton: Harvester, 1987.
Eusebius of Caesarea. "The Life of Constantine." In *A Select Library of Nicene and Post-Nicene Fathers of the Christian Church*, edited by Philip Schaff and Henry Wace, 1:481–560. New York: Christian Literature, 1890.

Bibliography

Farrow, Douglas. *Ascension and Ecclesia: On the Significance of the Doctrine of the Ascension for Ecclesiology and Christian Cosmology*. Edinburgh: T. & T. Clark, 1999.
Fergusson, David. *Community, Liberalism and Christian Ethics*. Cambridge: Cambridge University Press, 1998.
Field, Frank. *Stakeholder Welfare*. Philadelphia: Coronet, 1996.
Finger, Thomas, N. *Christian Theology: An Eschatological Approach*. 2 vols. Scottdale, PA: Herald, 1983-89.
Fiorenza, Francis Schüssler. "The Church as a Community of Interpretation: Political Theology Between Discourse Ethics and Hermeneutical Reconstruction." In *Habermas, Modernity and Public Theology*, edited by Don Browning and Francis Schüssler Fiorenza, 66-91. New York: Crossroad, 1992.
———. *Foundational Theology: Jesus and the Church*. New York: Crossroad, 1985.
Fisher, William F., and Thomas Ponniah, editors. *Another World is Possible: Popular Alternatives to Globalization at the World Social Forum*. London: Zed, 2003.
Fitz-Gibbon, Andrew L. *In the World, But Not of the World: Christian Social Thinking at the End of the Twentieth Century*. Oxford: Lexington, 2000.
Floristan, C., and C. Duquoc, editors. *Forgiveness*. Edinburgh: T. & T. Clark, 1986.
Forbath, William E. "Short-Circuit: A Critique of Habermas's Understanding of Law, Politics, and Economic Life." In *Habermas on Law and Democracy: Critical Exchanges*, edited by Michel Rosenfeld and Andrew Arato, 272-86. Berkeley: University of California Press, 1998.
Forrester, Duncan, B. *Christian Justice and Public Policy*. Cambridge Studies in Ideology and Religion 10. Cambridge, Cambridge University Press, 1997.
Foster, Hal, editor. *Postmodern Culture*. London: Pluto, 1985.
Foucault, Michel. *The Birth of Biopolitics: Lectures at the Collège de France*. Translated by Graham Burchell. Basingstoke: Palgrave MacMillan, 2008.
———. *Dits et Ecrits t.II*. Paris: Gallimard, 1994.
———. *The Essential Works, 1954-84*. Vol. 1, *Ethics, Subjectivity and Truth*. Translated by Robert Hurley et al. Edited by Paul Rainbow. New York: New York Press, 1997.
———. "Governmentality." In *The Foucault Effect: Studies in Governmentality*, edited by Graham Burchell, Colin Gordon, and Peter Miller, 87-104. Chicago: University of Chicago, 1991.
———. *The History of Sexuality*. Vol. 3, *The Care of the Self*. Translated by Robert Hurley. New York: Vintage, 1988.
———. "Politics and the Study of Discourse." In *The Foucault Effect: Studies in Governmentality*, edited by Graham Burchell, Colin Gordon, and Peter Miller, 53-72. Chicago: University of Chicago, 1991.
———. "The Politics of Health in the Eighteenth Century." In *Power/Knowledge: Selected Interviews and Other Writings 1972-1977*, 164-82. Brighton: Harvester, 1980.
———. *The Politics of Truth*. Translated by Lysa Hochroth and Catherine Porter. New York: Semeiotexte, 1997.
———. *Power/Knowledge: Selected Interviews and Other Writings, 1972–1977*. Translated by Colin Gordon et al. Brighton: Harvester, 1980.
———. "Questions of Method." In *The Foucault Effect: Studies in Governmentality*, edited by Graham Burchell, Colin Gordon, and Peter Miller, 73-86. Chicago: University of Chicago, 1991.
———. *Security, Territory, and Population: Lectures at the Collège de France*. Translated by Graham Burchell. Basingstoke: Palgrave MacMillan, 2007.

———. "Society Must be Defended": Lectures at the College de France, 1975–1976. Translated by David Macey. London: Penguin, 2003.

———. "What is Enlightenment?." In *The Foucault Reader: An Introduction to Foucault's Thought*, edited by Paul Rabinow, 32–50. London: Penguin, 1986.

Galston, William, A. *Liberal Purposes: Goods, Virtues, and Diversity in the Liberal State*. Cambridge: Cambridge University Press, 1991.

Garland, David. *The Culture of Control: Crime and the Social Order in Contemporary Society*. Oxford: Oxford University Press, 2001.

———. *Punishment and Modern Society: A Study in Social Theory*. Oxford: Clarendon, 1990.

Garrett, J. L., editor. *The Concept of the Believers' Church*. Scottdale, PA: Herald, 1969.

Gascoigne, Robert. *The Public Forum and Christian Ethics*. New Studies in Christian Ethics 19. Cambridge: Cambridge University Press, 2001.

Geffré, Claude, and Jean-Pierre Jossua, editors. *The Debate on Modernity*. London: SCM, 1992.

George, Vic, and Paul Wilding. *British Society and Social Welfare: Towards a Sustainable Society*. London: MacMillan, 1999.

Giddens, Anthony. *The Nation-State and Violence*. Vol. 2 of *A Contemporary Critique of Historical Materialism*. Berkeley: University of California Press, 1987.

Gilkey, Langdon. *On Niebuhr: A Theological Study*. Chicago: University of Chicago Press, 2001.

Gill, David, W. *The Word of God in the Ethics of Jacques Ellul*. Metuchen, NJ: Scarecrow, 1984.

Gill, Robin. *Churchgoing and Christian Ethics*. Cambridge: New Studies in Christian Ethics 15. Cambridge University Press, 1999.

Gingerich, Ray C. "Theological Foundations for an Ethic of Nonviolence: Was Yoder's God a Warrior?" *Mennonite Quarterly Review* 77 (2003) 417–35.

Girard, René. *Things Hidden Since the Foundation of the World*. Translated by Stephen Bann and Michael Metleer. London: Athlone, 1987.

———. *Violence and the Sacred*. Translated by Patrick Gregory. Baltimore: John Hopkins University Press, 1978.

Glennon, Fred. "Blessed Be the Ties That Bind? The Challenge of Charitable Choice to Moral Obligation." *Journal of Church and State* 42 (2000) 825–43.

Gordon, Colin. "Governmental rationality: an introduction." In *The Foucault Effect: Studies in Governmentality*, edited by Graham Burchell, Colin Gordon, and Peter Miller, 1–51. Chicago: University of Chicago Press, 1991.

Gormally, Luke, editor. *Moral Truth and Moral Tradition: Essays in Honour of Peter Geach and Elisabeth Anscombe*. Dublin: Four Courts, 1994.

Gorringe, Timothy. "Eschatology and Political Radicalism." In *God Will Be All In All*, edited by Richard Bauckham, 87–114. Edinburgh: T. & T. Clark, 1999.

———. *God's Just Vengeance: Crime, Violence and the Rhetoric of Salvation*. Cambridge Studies in Ideology and Religion 9. Cambridge: Cambridge University Press, 1996.

———. *Karl Barth: Against Hegemony*. Oxford: Oxford University Press, 1999.

Green, Clifford. *Bonhoeffer: A Theology of Sociality*. Revised edition, Grand Rapids: Eerdmans, 1999.

Gunton, Colin, "Election and Ecclesiology in the Post-Constantinian Church." *Scottish Journal of Theology* 53 (2000) 212–27.

———. "Reinhold Niebuhr: A treatise of Human Nature." *Modern Theology* 4 (1987) 71–81.

Gutiérrez, Gustavo. *The Power of the Poor in History*. Translated by Robert R. Barr. Maryknoll, NY: Orbis, 1983.

———. *A Theology of Liberation*. Revised edition. Translated and edited by Sister Caridad Inda and John Eagleson. Maryknoll, NY: Orbis, 1988.

Gwyn, Douglas, George Hunsinger, Eugene F. Roop, and John Howard Yoder. *A Declaration of Peace: In God's People the World's Renewal Has Begun*. Scottdale, PA: Herald, 1991.

Habermas, Jürgen. *Between Facts and Norms: Contributions to a Discourse Theory of Law and Democracy*. Cambridge: Polity, 1996.

———. *Between Naturalism and Religion*. Oxford: Polity, 2008.

———. "Further Reflections on the Public Sphere." In *Habermas and the Public Sphere*, edited by C. Calhoun, 421–61. Cambridge: MIT, 1992.

———. *The Future of Human Nature*. Oxford: Blackwell, 2003.

———. *Justification and Application: Remarks on Discourse Ethics*. Cambridge: Polity, 1993.

———. *Legitimation Crisis*. Oxford: Polity, 1988.

———. *The Liberating Power of Symbols*. Cambridge: MIT, 2001.

———. "Modernity: An Incomplete Project." In *Postmodern Culture*, edited by Hal Foster, 3–15. London: Pluto, 1985.

———. *Moral Consciousness and Communicative Action*. Cambridge: Polity, 1989.

———. *The Philosophical Discourse of Modernity: Twelve Lectures*. Cambridge: MIT, 1987.

———. *The Postnational Constellation: Political Essays*. Translated, edited and with an introduction by Max Pensky. Cambridge: Polity 2001.

———. *Religion and Rationality: Essays on Reason, God, and Modernity*. Oxford: Polity, 2002.

———. *The Structural Transformation of the Public Sphere*. Cambridge: Polity, 1989.

———. *The Theory of Communicative Action*. Vol. 1, *Reason and the Rationalization of Society*. Cambridge: Polity, 1984.

———. *The Theory of Communicative Action*. Vol. 2, *Lifeworld and System: A Critique of Functionalist Reason*. Cambridge: Polity, 1987.

Haddorff, David. "The Postmodern Realism of Barth's Ethics." *Scottish Journal of Theology* 57 (2004) 269–86.

Hardin, Michael. "Sacrificial Language in Hebrews: Reappraising René Girard." In *Violence Renounced: René Girard, Biblical Studies and Peacemaking*, edited by Willard Swartley, 103–19. Telford, PA: Cascadia, 2000.

Hardt, Michael, and Antonio Negri. *Empire*. Cambridge: Harvard University Press, 2000.

———. *Multitude: War and Democracy in the Age of Empire*. London: Penguin, 2005.

Hardy, Daniel W., and David F. Ford. *Jubilate: Theology in Praise*. London: Darton Longman & Todd, 1984.

Harink, Douglas. *Paul Among the Postliberals: Pauline Theology beyond Christendom and Modernity*. Grand Rapids: Brazos, 2003.

Harrington, Austin. "Habermas' Theological Turn." *Journal for the Theory of Social Behaviour* 37 (2007) 45–61.

Harris, Harriet. A. "Should We Say That Personhood is Relational?" *Scottish Journal of Theology* 51 (1998) 214–34.

Harris, Margaret. "Civil Society and the Role of the UK Churches: An Exploration." *Studies in Christian Ethics*, 15 (2002) 45–59.

Harvey, Barry A. "Insanity, Theocracy, and the Public Realm: Public Theology, The Church, and the Politics of Liberal Democracy." *Modern Theology* 10 (January 1994) 27–57.
Harvey, David. *The Condition of Postmodernity: An Enquiry into the Origins of Cultural Change*. Oxford: Blackwell, 1990.
Hauerwas, Stanley. *After Christendom: Why Freedom, Justice, and a Christian Nation Are Bad Ideas*. Nashville: Abingdon, 1991.
———. *Against the Nations: War and Survival in a Liberal Society*. Minneapolis: Winston, 1985.
———. *A Better Hope: Resources for a Church Confronting Capitalism, Democracy, and Postmodernity*. Grand Rapids: Brazos, 2000.
———. *Christian Existence Today: Essays on Church, World and Living in Between*. Durham: Labyrinth, 1988.
———. "Christianity: It's Not a Religion: It's an Adventure." Interview appearing in *US Catholic* 56 (1991) 6–13.
———. *Dispatches from the Front: Theological Engagements with the Secular*. Durham: Duke University Press, 1994.
———. "In Praise of *Centessimus Annus*." *Theology* 95 (1992) 416–32.
———. "On Being 'Placed' by John Milbank: A Response." In *Christ, Ethics and Tragedy: Essays in Honour of Donald MacKinnon*, edited by Kenneth Surin, 197–201. Cambridge: Cambridge University Press, 1989.
———. *The Peaceable Kingdom: A Primer in Christian Ethics*. Notre Dame: University of Notre Dame Press, 1983.
———. *Performing the Faith: Bonhoeffer and the Practice of Nonviolence*. Grand Rapids: Brazos, 2004.
———. *Sanctify Them in Truth: Holiness Exemplified*. Edinburgh: T. & T. Clark, 1998.
———. *The State of the University: Academic Knowledges and the Knowledge of God*. Oxford: Blackwell, 2007.
———. *Unleashing the Scriptures: Freeing the Bible from Captivity to America*. Nashville: Abingdon, 1993.
———. *Vision and Virtue: Essays in Christian Ethical Reflection*. Notre Dame: University of Notre Dame Press, 1981.
———. *Wilderness Wanderings: Probing Twentieth-Century Theology and Philosophy*. Boulder, CO: Westview, 1997.
———. *With the Grain of the Universe: The Church's Witness and Natural Theology—Being the Gifford Lectures Delivered at the University of St. Andrews in 2001*. London: SCM, 2002.
Hauerwas, Stanley, and Romand Coles. *Christianity, Democracy, and the Radical Ordinary*. Theopolitical Visions. Eugene, OR: Cascade, 2008.
Hauerwas, Stanley, and James Fodor. "Remaining in Babylon: Oliver O'Donovan's Defence of Christendom." *Studies in Christian Ethics* 11 (1998) 30–55.
Hauerwas, Stanley, Chris K. Huebner, Harry J. Huebner, and Mark Theissen Nation, editors. *The Wisdom of the Cross: Essays in Honour of John Howard Yoder*. Grand Rapids: Eerdmans, 1999.
Hauerwas, Stanley, and William, H. Willimon. *Resident Aliens: Life in the Christian Colony*. Nashville: Abingdon, 1989.
Hauerwas, Stanley, and Alasdair MacIntyre, editors. *Revisions: Changing Perspectives in Moral Philosophy*. Notre Dame: University of Notre Dame, 1983.

Hauerwas, Stanley, Nancey Murphy, and Mark Theissen Nation, editors. *Theology Without Foundations: Religious Practice and the Future of Theological Truth.* Nashville: Abingdon, 1994.

Havel, Václav. *Living in Truth: Twenty-two Essays Published on the Occasion of the Award of the Erasmus Prize to Václav Havel.* Edited by Jan Vladislaw. London: Faber, 1987.

———. "Politics and Conscience." In *Living in Truth: Twenty-two Essays Published on the Occasion of the Award of the Erasmus Prize to Václav Havel*, edited by Jan Vladislaw, 136–57. London: Faber, 1987.

———. "The Power of the Powerless." In *Living in Truth: Twenty-two Essays Published on the Occasion of the Award of the Erasmus Prize to Václav Havel*, edited by Jan Vladislaw, 36–122. London: Faber, 1987.

Hays, Richard, B. *The Moral Vision of the New Testament: Community, Cross, New Creation: A Contemporary Introduction to New Testament Ethics.* San Francisco: Harper Collins, 1998.

———. "'Why Do You Stand Looking Up Toward Heaven?' New Testament Eschatology at the Turn of the Millennium." *Modern Theology* 16 (2000) 115–35.

Heelas, Paul, and Linda Woodhead. "Homeless minds today?." In *Peter Berger and the Study of Religion*, edited by Linda Woodhead, Paul Heelas, and David Martin, 43–72. London: Routledge, 2001.

Heelas, Paul. "Introduction: On Differentiation and Dedifferentiation." In *Religion, Modernity and Postmodernity*, edited by Paul Heelas, David Martin, and Paul Morris, 1–18. Oxford: Blackwell, 1998

Heelas, Paul, David Martin, and Paul Morris, editors. *Religion, Modernity and Postmodernity.* Religion and Modernity. Oxford: Blackwell, 1998.

Heilke, Thomas. "Yoder's Idea of Constantinianism: An Analytical Framework Toward Conversation." In *A Mind Patient and Untamed: Assessing John Howard Yoder's Contributions to Theology, Ethics, and Peacemaking*, edited by Ben C. Ollenburger and Gayle Gerber Koontz, 89–125. Telford, PA: Cascadia, 2004.

Heim, S. Mark. *Saved From Sacrifice: A Theology of the Cross.* Grand Rapids: Eerdmans, 2006.

Held, David. *Political Theory and the Modern State: Essays on State, Power and Democracy.* Cambridge: Polity, 1989.

"The Helsinki Agreement." In *The Human Rights Reader: Major Political Essays, Speeches and Documents from Ancient Times to the Present*, edited by Micheline Ishay, 452–61. London: Routledge, 1997.

Herbert, David. "Getting By in Babylon: MacIntyre, Milbank and a Christian Response to Religious Diversity in the Public Arena." *Studies in Christian Ethics* 10 (1997) 61–81.

———. *Religion and Civil Society: Rethinking Public Religion in the Contemporary World.* Aldershot, UK: Ashgate, 2003.

Higton, Mike, A. "Hans Frei and David Tracy on the Ordinary and the Extraordinary in Christianity." *The Journal of Religion* 79 (1999) 566–91.

Hill, David. *New Testament Prophecy.* London: Marshall, Morgan and Scott, 1979.

Hobbes, Thomas. *Leviathan.* Edited by Richard Tuck. Cambridge: Cambridge University Press, 1996.

Hoffman, John. *Beyond the State: An Introductory Critique.* Cambridge: Polity, 1995.

Hollander, Dana. *Exemplarity and Chosenness: Rosenzweig and Derrida on the Nation of Philosophy.* Stanford: Stanford University Press, 2008.

Hollenbach, David. *The Common Good and Christian Ethics.* New Studies in Christian Ethics 22. Cambridge: Cambridge University Press, 2002.

Home Office Communities Unit. *Working Together: Cooperation Between Government and Faith Communities.* London: Home Office Communities Unit, 2004.

Hooker, Morna. *The Signs of a Prophet: The Prophetic Actions of Jesus.* London: SCM, 1997.

Horsley, Richard A. *Jesus and Empire: The Kingdom of God and the New World Disorder.* Minneapolis: Fortress, 2003.

———, editor. *Paul and Empire: Religion and Power in Roman Imperial Society.* Harrisburg: Trinity , 1997.

———, editor. *Paul and the Roman Imperial Order.* London: Continuum, 2004.

Horsley, Richard A., and Neil Asher Silberman, *The Message and the Kingdom: How Jesus and Paul Ignited a Revolution and Transformed the Ancient World.* New York: Grosset/Putnam, 1997.

Horton, John, and Susan Mendus, editors. *After MacIntyre.* Oxford: Polity, 1994.

Hovey, Craig. "Free Christian Speech: Plundering Foucault." *Political Theology* 8 (2007) 63–81.

Howard-Brook, Wes, and Anthony Gwyther. *Unveiling Empire: Reading Revelation Then and Now.* Bible & Liberation Series. Maryknoll, NY: Orbis, 1999.

Huebner, Chris, K. "Can a Gift be Commanded? Theological Ethics Without Theory by Way of Barth, Milbank and Yoder." *Scottish Journal of Theology* 53 (2000) 472–89.

———. "Knowledge, Politics, and Speed: Yoder and Virilio on the Reconfigurations of Peace." *A Mind Patient and Untamed: Assessing John Howard Yoder's Contributions to Theology, Ethics and Peacemaking,* edited by Ben C. Ollenburger and Gayle Gerber Koontz, 56–74. Telford, PA: Cascadia, 2004.

———. *A Precarious Peace: Yoderian Explorations on Theology, Knowledge, and Identity.* Polyglossia. Scottdale: Herald, 2006.

———. "Unhandling History: Anti-Theory, Ethics, and the Practice of Witness." PhD diss., Duke University, 2002.

Hughes, David Michael. "The Ethical Use of Power: A Discussion with the Christian Perspectives of Reinhold Niebuhr, John Howard Yoder, and Richard J Barnet." PhD diss., The Southern Baptist Theological Seminary, 1984.

Hunsinger, George. *Disruptive Grace: Studies in the Theology of Karl Barth.* Grand Rapids: Eerdmans, 2000.

Hütter, Reinhard. *Suffering Divine Things: Theology as Church Practice.* Grand Rapids: Eerdmans, 2000.

Hyman, Gavin. *The Predicament of Postmodern Theology: Radical Orthodoxy or Nihilist Textualism.* Louisville: Wesminster John Knox, 2001.

The International Forum on Globalisation. *Alternatives to Economic Globalization: A Better World is Possible.* San Francisco: Berrett-Koehler, 2002.

Jameson, Frederic. *Postmodernism, or, the Cultural Logic of Late Capitalism.* London: Verso, 1991.

Jeanrod, Werner G., and Jennifer L. Rike, editors. *Radical Pluralism and Truth: David Tracy and the Hermeneutics of Religion.* New York: Crossroad, 1991.

John Paul II. *Redemptoris Missio.* 1990. No pages. Online: http://www.vatican.va/holy_father/john_paul_ii/encyclicals/documents/hf_jp-ii_enc_07121990_redemptoris-missio_en.html

Johns, Loren. "'A Better Sacrifice' or 'Better than Sacrifice'? Response to Michael Hardin's 'Sacrificial Language in Hebrews.'" In *Violence Renounced: Rene Girard, Biblical Studies and Peacemaking*, edited by Willard Swartley, 120–31. Telford, PA: Cascadia, 2000.

Jones, Christopher, and Peter Sedgwick, editors. *The Future of Criminal Justice: Resettlement, Chaplaincy and Community*. London: SPCK, 2002.

Jones, L. Gregory. *Embodying Forgiveness: A Theological Analysis*. Grand Rapids: Eerdmans, 1995.

Jordan, Bill. *The New Politics of Welfare: Social Justice in a Global Context*. London: Sage, 1998.

Jüngel, Eberhard. *Christ, Justice and Peace: Toward a Theology of the State*. Edinburgh: T. & T. Clark, 1992.

Kallenberg, Brad. "The Gospel Truth of Relativism." *Scottish Journal of Theology* 53 (2000) 177–211.

Keane, John, editor. *Civil Society and the State: New European Perspectives*. London: Verso, 1988.

———. *Civil Society: Old Images, New Visions*. Cambridge: Polity, 1998.

———. "Despotism and Democracy." In *Civil Society and the State: New European Perspectives*, edited by John Keane, 35–71. London: Verso, 1988.

Kee, Alastair. *Constantine Versus Christ: The Triumph of Ideology*. London: SCM, 1982.

Kelly, Michael, editor. *Critique and Power: Recasting the Foucault/Habermas Debate*. Cambridge: MIT Press, 1994.

———. "Foucault, Habermas, and the Self-Referentiality of Critique." In *Critique and Power Recasting the Foucault/Habermas Debate*, edited by Michael Kelly, 365–400. Cambridge: MIT Press, 1994.

Kettle, David. "Lesslie Newbigin, Christendom and the Public Truth of the Gospel." *Anvil* 18 (2001) 107–15.

Klassen, A. J. *Consultation on Anabaptist-Mennonite Theology: Papers Read at the 1969 Aspen Conference*. Fresno, CA: Council of Mennonite Seminaries, 1970.

Klassen, William. "Jesus and the Zealot Option." In *The Wisdom of the Cross: Essays in Honour of John Howard Yoder*, edited by Stanley Hauerwas et al., 131–49. Grand Rapids: Eerdmans, 1999.

Klein, Naomi. *No Logo*. London: HarperCollins. 2000.

Koontz, Gayle Gerber. "Confessional Theology in a Pluralistic Context: A Study of the Theological Ethics of H. Richard Niebuhr and John H. Yoder." PhD diss., Boston University, 1985.

Kovacs, Judith, and Christopher Rowland. *Revelation Through the Centuries: The Apocalypse to Jesus Christ*. Oxford: Blackwell, 2003.

Krasner, Stephen D. "Globalization and Sovereignty." In *States and Sovereignty in the Global Economy*, edited by David A. Smith, Dorothy J. Solinger, and Steven C. Topik, 34–52. London: Routledge, 1999.

Kroeker, P. Travis. "Why O'Donovan's Christendom is not Constantinian and Yoder's Voluntariety is not Hobbesian: A Debate in Theological Politics Re-defined." *Annual of the Society of Christian Ethics* 20 (2000) 41–64.

Kymlicka, Will. *Multicultural Citizenship*. Oxford: Oxford University Press, 1995.

Lactantius. *Divine Institutes*. In *The Ante-Nicene Fathers: The Writings of the Fathers Down to A.D. 325*. Vol. 7, *Fathers of the Third and Fourth Centuries*, edited by Alexander Roberts, 9–223. New York: Cosimo, 2007.

Lalonde, Marc, P. *Critical Theology and the Challenge of Jürgen Habermas: Toward a Critical Theory of Religious Insight*. Studies in Religion, Politics, and Public Life 1. New York: Lang, 1999.
Lash, Nicholas. "Conversation in Gethsemane." In *Radical Pluralism and Truth: David Tracy and the Hermeneutics of Religion*, edited by G. Jeanrod Werner and Jennifer, L. Rike, 51–61. New York: Crossroads, 1991.
Le Masters, Philip. "The Import of Eschatology in John Howard Yoder's Critique of Constantinianism." PhD diss., Duke University, 1990.
Lehmann, Paul. *The Transfiguration of Politics: Jesus Christ and the Question of Revolution*. London: SCM, 1975.
Lemke, Thomas, "'The Birth of Bio-politics': Michel Foucault's Lecture at the Collège de France on Neo-liberal Governmentality." *Economy and Society* 30 (2001) 190–207.
Levenson, Jon D. *The Death and Resurrection of the Beloved Son: The Transformation of Child Sacrifice in Judaism and Christianity*. New Haven: Yale University Press, 1993.
Levinas, Emmanuel. *Difficult Freedom: Essays on Judaism*. Baltimore: John Hopkins University Press, 1990.
Lieu, Samuel N. C., and Dominic Montserrat, editors. *Constantine: History, Historiography and Legend*. London: Routledge, 1998.
Lilla, Mark. *The Stillborn God: Religion, Politics and the Modern West*. New York: Knopf, 2007.
Lincoln, Andrew. "Liberation from the Powers: Supernatural Spirits or Societal Structures." In *The Bible in Human Society: Essays in Honour of John Rogerson*, edited by R. M. Daniel Carroll, David J. A. Clines, and Philip R. Davies, 335–54. JSOT Supplements 200. Sheffield: Sheffield Academic, 1995.
Lind, Millard. *Yahweh is a Warrior: The Theology of Warfare in Ancient Israel*. Scottdale, PA: Herald, 1980.
Lindbeck, George, A. *The Church in a Postliberal Age*. London: SCM, 2002.
———. *The Nature of Doctrine: Religion and Theology in a Postliberal Age*. Philadelphia: Westminster, 1994.
Lindsay, A. D. *The Churches and Democracy*. London: Epworth, 1934.
Locke, John. *Two Treatises of Government*. New York: Hafner, 1947.
Long, D. Stephen. *Divine Economy: Theology and the Market*. London: Routledge, 2000.
———. *The Goodness of God: Theology, the Church and the Social Order*. Grand Rapids: Brazos, 2001.
Looney, Thomas, P. "*Koinonia* Ecclesiology: How Solid a Foundation?" *One in Christ* 36 (2000) 145–66.
Lossky, N. *Dictionary of the Ecumenical Movement*. Geneva: WCC, 1991.
Loughlin, Gerard. "Christianity at the End of the Story or the Return of the Master Narrative." *Modern Theology* 8 (1992) 365–84.
Lovin, Robin. *Christian Faith and Public Choices: The Social Ethics of Barth, Brunner, and Bonhoeffer*. Minneapolis: Fortress, 1984.
———. *Christian Realism and the New Realities*. Oxford: Oxford University Press, 2008.
———. *Reinhold Niebuhr and Christian Realism*. Cambridge: Cambridge University Press, 1995.
Lubac, Henri de. *The Drama of Atheist Humanism*. San Francisco: Ignatius, 1995.
———. *The Mystery of the Supernatural*. New York: Crossroad, 1998.
Luxmoore, Jonathan, and Jolanta Babiuch. "In Search of Faith: The Metaphysical Dialogue Between Poland's Opposition Intellectuals in the 1970s." *Religion, State and Society* 23 (1995) 75–95.

Lyotard, Jean-François. *The Postmodern Condition: A Report on Knowledge*. Manchester: Manchester University Press, 1984.

MacIntrye, Alasdair. *After Virtue: A Study in Moral Theory*. 2nd ed. London: Duckworth, 1985.

———. "Moral Relativism, Truth and Justification." In *Moral Truth and Moral Tradition: Essays in Honour of Peter Geach and Elizabeth Anscombe*, edited by Luke Gormally, 6–24. Dublin: Four Courts, 1994.

———. "A Partial Response to My Critics." In *After MacIntyre*, edited by John Horton and Susan Mendus, 283–304. Oxford: Polity, 1994.

———. *A Short History of Ethics: A History of Moral Philosophy from the Homeric Age to the Twentieth Century*. London: Routledge, 1967.

———. *Three Rival Versions of Moral Enquiry: Encyclopaedia, Genealogy and Tradition*. Notre Dame: University of Notre Dame, 1990.

———. *Whose Justice? Which Rationality?* Notre Dame: University of Notre Dame, 1988.

Maddox, Graham. *Religion and the Rise of Democracy*. London: Routledge, 1996.

Maeseneer, Yves de. "Saint Francis Versus McDonald's: Contemporary Globalization Critique and Hans Urs Von Balthasar's Theological Aesthetics." *Heythrop Journal* 44 (2003) 1–14.

Mahmood, Saba. "Secularism, Hermeneutics and Empire: The Politics of Islamic Reformation." *Public Culture* 18 (2006) 323–47.

Mahoney, Daniel J. "The Moral Foundations of Liberal Democracy." In *Public Morality, Civic Virtue, and the Problem of Modern Liberalism*, edited by William T. Boxx and Gary M. Quinlivan, 24–39. Grand Rapids: Eerdmans, 2000.

Maritain, Jacques. *Integral Humanism*. New York: Scribner, 1968.

———. *The Things That Are Not Caesar's*. London: Sheed & Ward, 1932.

Markham, Ian. *Plurality and Christian Ethics*. New Studies in Christian Ethics. Cambridge: Cambridge University Press, 1994.

Markus, R. A. *Christianity and the Secular*. Notre Dame: University of Notre Dame, 2006.

———. *Saeculum: History and Society in the Theology of St Augustine*. Cambridge: Cambridge University Press, 1970.

Marshall, Bruce D. *Trinity and Truth*. Cambridge: Cambridge University Press, 2000.

Marshall, Christopher. *Beyond Retribution: A New Testament Vision for Justice, Crime and Punishment*. Grand Rapids: Eerdmans, 2001.

Martin, David. "The Secularisation Issue: Prospect and Retrospect." *British Journal of Sociology* 42 (1991) 465–74.

Martinez, Gaspar. *Confronting the Mystery of God: Political, Liberation, and Public Theologies*. New York: Continuum, 2001.

Marx, Anthony W. *Faith in Nation: Exclusionary Origins of Nationalism*. Oxford: Oxford University Press, 2003.

Mathewes, Charles. *A Theology of Public Life*. Cambridge: Cambridge University Press, 2008.

Mayhew, Leon. *The New Public: Professional Communication and the Means of Social Influence*. Cambridge: Cambridge University Press, 1997.

McClendon, James Wm. Jr. *Systematic Theology: Ethics—Volume 1*. Nashville: Abingdon, 1986.

———. *Systematic Theology: Doctrine—Volume 2*. Nashville: Abingdon, 1994.

———. *Systematic Theology: Witness—Volume 3*. Nashville: Abingdon, 2000.

McDowell, John C. *Hope in Barth's Eschatology: Interrogations and Transformations Beyond Tragedy*. Aldershot, UK: Ashgate, 2000.

McFadyen, Alistair. *The Call to Personhood: A Christian Theory of the Individual in Social Relationship*. Cambridge: Cambridge University Press, 1990.

McGrath, Alister E. *A Scientific Theology*. Vol. 3, *Theory*. Edinburgh: T. & T. Clark, 2003.

McGrew, Anthony G., and Paul G. Lewis. *Global Politics: Globalization and the Nation State*. Cambridge: Polity, 1992.

Meilander, Gilbert. "Against Consensus: Christians and Public Bioethics." *Studies in Christian Ethics* 18 (2005) 75–88.

Mendieta, Eduardo. "Introduction." In *Religion and Rationality: Essays on Reason, God, and Modernity*, by Jürgen Habermas, 1–36. Oxford: Polity, 2002.

Milbank, John. *Being Reconciled: Ontology and Pardon*. London: Routledge, 2003.

———. "Between Purgation and Illumination: A Critique of the Theology of Right." In *Christ, Ethics, and Tragedy: Essays in Honour of Donald MacKinnon*, edited by Kenneth Surin, 161–96. Cambridge: Cambridge University Press, 1989.

———. "Can a Gift Be Given? Prolegomena to a Future Trinitarian Metaphysic." *Modern Theology* 11 (1995) 119–61.

———. "Christian Peace: A Conversation between Stanley Hauerwas and John Milbank." In *Must Christianity Be Violent? Reflections on History, Practice, and Theology*, edited by Kenneth R. Chase and Alan Jacobs, 207–23. Grand Rapids: Brazos, 2003.

———. "Enclaves, or Where Is the Church?" *New Blackfriars* 73 (1992) 341–52.

———. "The End of Dialogue." In *Christian Uniqueness Reconsidered: The Myth of a Pluralistic Theology of Religions*, edited by Gavin D'Costa, 174–91. Faith Meets Faith Series. Maryknoll, NY: Orbis, 1990.

———. "The End of Enlightenment: Post-Modern or Post-Secular?" In *The Debate on Modernity*, by Claude Geffré and Jean-Pierre Jossua, 39–48. London: SCM, 1992.

———. "The Gift of Ruling: Secularization and Political Authority." *New Blackfriars* 85 (1996) 212–38.

———. "Intensities." *Modern Theology* 15 (1999) 445–97.

———. "Materialism and Transcendence." In *Theology and the Political: The New Debate*, edited by Creston Davis, John Milbank, and Slavoj Žižek, 393–426. Durham: Duke University Press, 2005.

———. "The Midwinter Sacrifice: A Sequel to 'Can Morality be Christian?'" *Studies in Christian Ethics* 10 (1997) 13–38.

———. "The Name of Jesus: Incarnation, Atonement and Ecclesiology." *Modern Theology* 7 (1991) 311–33.

———. "Postmodern Critical Augustinianism: A Short *Summa* in Forty-Two Responses to Unasked Questions." *Modern Theology* 7 (1991) 225–37.

———. "Problematizing the Secular: The Post-modern Agenda." In *Shadow of Spirit: Postmodernism and Religion*, edited by Philippa Berry and Andrew Wernick, 30–44. London: Routledge, 1992.

———. "Radical Orthodoxy and the Radical Reformation: What is Radical about Radical Orthodoxy: A Forum with John Milbank." *Conrad Grebel Review* 23 (2005) 41–54.

———. "The Return of Mediation, or the Ambivalence of Alain Badiou." *Angelaki* 12 (2007) 127–43.

———. "Socialism of the Gift, Socialism by Grace." *New Blackfriars* 77 (1996) 532–48.

———. "Stories of Sacrifice: From Wellhausen to Girard." *Theology, Culture and Society* 12 (1995) 15–46.

———. "The Soul of Reciprocity Part One: Reciprocity Refused." *Modern Theology* 17 (2001) 335–91.

———. "The Soul of Reciprocity Part Two: Reciprocity Granted." *Modern Theology* 17 (2001) 485–507.

———. *The Suspended Middle: Henri de Lubac and the Debate concerning the Supernatural*. Grand Rapids: Eerdmans, 2005.

———. "Testing Pacifism: Questions for John Milbank." In *Must Christianity Be Violent? Reflections on History, Practice, and Theology*, edited by Kenneth R. Chase and Alan Jacobs, 201–6. Grand Rapids: Brazos, 2003.

———. *Theology and Social Theory: Beyond Secular Reason*. Oxford: Blackwell, 1990.

———. *The Word Made Strange: Theology, Language, and Culture*. Oxford: Blackwell, 1997.

Miller, Adam S. "Universal Truths and the Question of Religion: An Interview with Alain Badiou." *Journal of Philosophy and Scripture* 3 (2005) 38–42.

Miller, John W. "In the Footseps of Marcion: Notes Toward an Understanding of John Yoder's Theology." *Conrad Grebel Review* 16 (1998) 82–92.

Minford, Patrick. *Markets Not Stakes: The Triumph of Capitalism and the Stakeholder Fallacy*. London: Orion Business, 1998.

Moltmann, Jürgen. *The Church in the Power of the Spirit: A Contribution to Messianic Ecclesiology*. London: SCM, 1981.

———. *The Coming of God: Christian Eschatology*. London: SCM, 1996.

———. "The Liberation of the Future and Its Anticipations in History." In *God Will Be All In All: The Eschatology of Jürgen Moltmann*, edited by Richard Bauckham, 265–89. Edinburgh: T. & T. Clark, 1999.

———. *Theology of Hope: On the Ground and the Implications of a Christian Eschatology*. London: SCM, 1967.

Morison, John. "The Government-Voluntary Sector Compacts: Governance, Governmentality, and Civil Society." *Journal of Law and Society* 27 (2000) 98–132.

Moss, Jeremy. "Foucault, Rawls and Public Reason." In *The Later Foucault*, 149–63. London: Sage, 1998.

———. *The Later Foucault*. London: Sage, 1998.

Myers, Ched. *Binding the Strong Man: A Political Reading of Mark's Story of Jesus*. Maryknoll, NY: Orbis, 1988.

Nagel, Thomas. *The View from Nowhere*. Oxford: Oxford University Press, 1986.

Nation, Mark Thiessen. "The Ecumenical Patience and Vocation of John Howard Yoder: A Study in Theological Ethics." PhD diss., Fuller Theological Seminary, 2000.

———. "John H Yoder, Ecumenical Neo-Anabaptist: A Biographical Sketch." In *The Wisdom of the Cross: Essays in Honour of John Howard Yoder*, edited by Stanley Hauerwas et al., 1–23. Grand Rapids: Eerdmans, 1999.

———. "John Howard Yoder: Mennonite, Evangelical, Catholic." *Mennonite Quarterly Review* 77 (2003) 357–70.

———. *John Howard Yoder: Mennonite Patience, Evangelical Witness, Catholic Convictions* Grand Rapids, Eerdmans, 2006.

Nation, Mark Thiessen, and Samuel Wells, editors. *Faithfulness and Fortitude: In Conversation with the Theological Ethics of Stanley Hauerwas*. Edinburgh: T. & T. Clark, 2000.

Negri, Antonio. *The Politics of Subversion: A Manifesto for the Twenty-First Century*. New York: Polity, 2005.

Neilsen, Kai. "Reconceptualizing Civil Society for Now: Some Somewhat Gramscian Turnings." In *Towards a Global Civil Society*, edited by Michael Walzer, 41-67. Oxford: Berghahn, 1995.

Neuhaus, Richard John. "Commentary on *The Desire of the Nations*." In *Studies in Christian Ethics* 11 (1998) 56-61.

———. *The Naked Public Square: Religion and Democracy in America*. Grand Rapids: Eerdmans, 1984.

Newbigin, Lesslie. *The Gospel in a Pluralist Society*. London: SPCK, 1989.

———. *Truth to Tell: The Gospel as Public Truth*. London: SPCK, 1991.

———. *Unfinished Agenda*. London: SPCK, 1985.

Nicholls, David. *Deity and Domination: Images of God and the State in the Nineteenth and Twentieth Centuries*. London: Routledge, 1989.

Niebuhr, Reinhold. *An Interpretation of Christian Ethics*. London: SCM, 1936.

———. *Moral Man and Immoral Society: A Study in Ethics and Politics*. New York: Scribners, 1932.

———. *The Nature and Destiny of Man*. 2 vols. London: Nisbet, 1941.

———. "Why the Christian Church Is Not Pacifist." In *Christianity and Power Politics*. New York: Scribners, 1940.

Nisbet, Robert A. *The Quest for Community*. Oxford: Oxford University Press, 1969.

O'Donovan, Joan Lockwood. "Nation, State and Civil Society in the Western Biblical Tradition" in *Bonds of Imperfection: Christian Politics, Past and Present*, by Oliver O'Donovan and Joan Lockwood O'Donovan, 276-95. Grand Rapids: Eerdmans, 2004.

O'Donovan, Oliver. "Deliberation, History and Reading: A Response to Schweiker and Wolterstorff." *Scottish Journal of Theology* 54 (2001) 127-44.

———. *The Desire of the Nations: Rediscovering the Roots of Political Theology*. Cambridge: Cambridge University Press, 1996.

———. "The Political Thought of the Book of Revelation." *Tyndale Bulletin* 37 (1986) 61-94.

———. *Resurrection and Moral Order: An Outline for Evangelical Ethics*. Leicester: InterVarsity, 1986.

———. *The Ways of Judgment*. Grand Rapids: Eerdmans, 2005.

O'Donovan, Oliver, and Joan Lockwood O'Donovan. *Bonds of Imperfection: Christian Politics, Past and Present*. Grand Rapids: Eerdmans, 2004.

Ollenburger, Ben C., and Gayle Gerber Koontz, editors. *A Mind Patient and Untamed: Assessing John Howard Yoder's Contribution to Theology, Ethics and Peacemaking*. Telford, PA: Cascadia, 2004.

Outhwaite, William, editor. *The Habermas Reader*. Cambridge: Polity, 1996.

Owen, David. *Maturity and Modernity: Nietzsche, Weber, Foucault, and the Ambivalence of Reason*. London: Routledge, 1997.

Panagopoulos, J., editor. *Prophetic Vocation in the New Testament and Today*. Leiden: Brill, 1977.

Patterson, Sue. *Realist Christian Theology in a Postmodern Age*. Cambridge: Cambridge University Press, 1999.

Pelczynski, Z. A. "Solidarity and 'The Rebirth of Civil Society' in Poland, 1976-81." In *Civil Society and the State: New European Perspectives*, edited by John Keane, 361-80. London: Verso, 1988.

Peukert, Helmut. *Science, Action and Fundamental Theology: Toward a Theology of Communicative Action*. Massachusetts: MIT Press, 1984.

Pfeil, Margaret R. "John Howard Yoder's Pedagogical Approach: A Just War Tradition with Teeth and a Hermeneutic of Peace." *Mennonite Quarterly Review* 76 (2002) 181–88.

Pickstock, Catherine. *After Writing: On the Liturgical Consummation of Philosophy*. Oxford: Blackwell, 1998.

Pinches, Charles. "Christian Pacifism and Theodicy: The Free Will Defence in the Thought of John H. Yoder." *Modern Theology* 5 (1989) 239–55.

Placher, William, C. "Revisionist and Postliberal Theologies and the Public Character of Theology." *Thomist* 49 (1985) 392–416.

———. *Unapologetic Theology: A Christian Voice in a Pluralistic Conversation*. Louisville: Westminster John Knox, 1989.

Plant, Raymond. *Politics, Theology, and History*. Cambridge: Cambridge University Press, 2001.

Pohl, Christine D. *Making Room: Recovering Hospitality as a Christian Tradition*. Grand Rapids: Eerdmans, 1999.

Porter, Jean. *Natural and Divine Law: Reclaiming the Tradition for Christian Ethics*. Grand Rapids: Eerdmans, 1999.

Preston, Ronald Haydn. *Church and Society in the Late Twentieth Society*. London: SCM, 1983.

———. *Religion and the Persistence of Capitalism*. London: SCM, 1977.

Putnam, Robert D. *Making Democracy Work: Civic Traditions in Modern Italy*. Princeton: Princeton University Press, 1993.

Rabinow, Paul, editor. *The Foucault Reader: An Introduction to Foucault's Thought*. London: Penguin, 1986.

Ramsey, Paul. *Basic Christian Ethics*. London: SCM, 1950.

Ramseyer, Robert L., editor. *Mission and the Peace Witness*. Scottdale, PA: Herald, 1979.

Rasmusson, Arne. *The Church as Polis: From Political Theology to Theological Politics as Exemplified by Jürgen Moltmann and Stanley Hauerwas*. Notre Dame: University of Notre Dame Press, 1995.

Rawls, John. "The Idea of Public Reason Revisited." In *The Law of Peoples*, 129–80. Cambridge: Harvard University Press, 1999.

———. *The Law of Peoples*. Cambridge: Harvard University Press, 1999.

———. *Political Liberalism*. New York: Columbia University Press, 1993

———. *A Theory of Justice*. Oxford: Oxford University Press, 1971.

Reader, John. *Local Theology: Church and Community in Dialogue*. London: SPCK, 1994.

Reimer, A. James. "Mennonites, Christ, and Culture: The Yoder Legacy." *Conrad Grebel Review* 16 (1998) 5–14.

———. *Mennonites and Classical Theology: Dogmatic Foundations for Christian Ethics*. Ontario: Pandora, 2001.

———. "Theological Orthodoxy and Jewish Christianity: A Personal Tribute to John Howard Yoder." In *The Wisdom of the Cross: Essays in Honour of John Howard Yoder*, edited by Stanley Hauerwas et al., 430–48. Grand Rapids: Eerdmans, 1999.

Reynolds, Charles H. and Ralph Norman, editors. *Community in America: The Challenge of Habits of the Heart*. Berkeley: University of California Press, 1988.

Rieger, Jeorg. *Christ and Empire: From Paul to Postcolonial Times*. Minneapolis: Fortress, 2007.

Rogers, Eugene F. Jr. *After the Spirit: A Constructive Pneumatology from Resources Outside the Modern West.* Grand Rapids, Eerdmans, 2005.

———. *Sexuality and the Christian Body: Their Way into the Triune God.* Oxford: Blackwell, 1999.

Rogerson, John, Margaret Davies, and M. Daniel Carroll Rodas, editors. *The Bible in Ethics: The Second Sheffield Colloquium.* JSOT Supplements 207. Sheffield: Sheffield Academic, 1995.

Rorty, Richard. *Philosophy and Social Hope.* London: Penguin, 1999.

———. "Religion in the Public Square: A Reconsideration." *Journal of Religious Ethics* 31 (2003) 141–49.

Rowland, Christopher. *The Open Heaven: A Study of Apocalyptic in Judaism and Early Christianity.* London: SPCK, 1982.

Sacks, Jonathan. *The Politics of Hope.* London: Jonathan Cape, 1997.

Sagovsky, Nicholas. *Ecumenism, Christian Origins and the Practice of Communion.* Cambridge: Cambridge University Press, 2000.

Schindler, David L. *Heart of the World, Center of the Church: Communio Ecclesiology, Liberalism and Liberation.* Edinburgh: T. & T. Clark, 1996.

Schipani, Daniel S., editor. *Freedom and Discipleship: Liberation Theology in Anabaptist Perspective.* Maryknoll: Orbis, 1989.

Schlabach, Gerald W. "The Christian Witness in the Earthly City: John H. Yoder as Augustinian Interlocutor." In *A Mind Patient and Untamed: Assessing John Howard Yoder's Contributions to Theology, Ethics and Peacemaking,* edited by Ben C. Ollenburger and Gayle Gerber Koontz, 221–44. Telford, PA: Cascadia, 2004.

———. "Deuteronomic or Constantinian: What is the Most Basic Problem for Christian Social Ethics?" In *The Wisdom of the Cross: Essays in Honour of John Howard Yoder,* edited by Stanley Hauerwas et al., 449–71. Grand Rapids: Eerdmans, 1999.

The Schleitheim Confession. Translated by John Howard Yoder. Scottdale, PA: Herald, 1977.

Schüssler Fiorenza, Elizabeth. *In Memory of Her: A Feminist Theological Reconstruction of Christian Origins.* New York: Crossroad, 1983.

Schwager, Raymund. *Jesus in the Drama of Salvation: Toward a Biblical Doctrine of Redemption.* New York: Crossroads, 1999.

Schweitzer, Albert. *The Quest of the Historical Jesus: A Critical Study of its Progress from Reimarus to Wrede.* Translated by W. Montgomery. London: A. & C. Black, 1954.

Scott, James C. *Domination and the Arts of Resistance: Hidden Transcripts.* New Haven: Yale University Press, 1990.

———. *Weapons of the Weak: Everyday forms of Peasant Resistance.* New Haven: Yale University Press, 1985.

Seligman, Adam. *The Idea of Civil Society.* Princeton: Princeton University Press, 1992.

Shaffer, Thomas L., editor. *Moral Memoranda From John Howard Yoder: Conversations on Law, Ethics, and the Church between a Mennonite Theologian and a Hoosier Lawyer.* Eugene, OR: Wipf & Stock, 2002.

Shanks, Andrew. *Civil Society, Civil Religion.* Oxford: Blackwell, 1995.

———. *God and Modernity: A New and Better Way To Do Theology.* London: Routledge, 2000.

———. *Hegel's Political Theology.* Cambridge: Cambridge University Press, 1991.

———. *'What Is Truth?': Towards a Theological Poetics.* London: Routledge, 2001.

Sigmund, Paul E. *Liberation Theology at the Crossroads: Democracy or Revolution?* Oxford: Oxford University Press, 1990.

Simpson, Gary M. *Critical Social Theory: Prophetic Reason, Civil Society, and Christian Imagination*. Minneapolis: Fortress, 2002.

Sloat, James M. "The Subtle Significance of Sincere Belief: Tocqueville's Account of Religious Belief and Democratic Stability." *Journal of Church and State* 42 (2000) 759–79.

Smith, David A., Dorothy J. Solinger, and Steven C. Topik, editors. *States and Sovereignty in the Global Economy*. London: Routledge, 1999.

Smith, James K. A. "Will the Real Plato Please Stand Up? Participation versus Incarnation." In *Radical Orthodoxy and the Reformed Tradition: Creation, Covenant, and Participation*, edited by James K. A. Smith and James H. Olthius, 61–72. Grand Rapids: Baker Academic, 2005.

Smith, James K. A., and James H. Olthius, editors. *Radical Orthodoxy and the Reformed Tradition: Creation, Covenant, and Participation*. Grand Rapids: Baker Academic, 2005.

Smith-Christopher, Daniel L. *A Biblical Theology of Exile*. Overtures to Biblical Theology. Minneapolis: Fortress, 2002.

Sobrino, Jon. *The True Church and the Poor*. London: SCM, 1985.

Soulen, R. Kendall. *The God of Israel and Christian Theology*. Minneapolis: Fortress, 1996.

Spinoza, Baruch. *Theological-political Treatise*. Edited by Jonathan Israel. Cambridge, Cambridge University Press, 2007.

Spjuth, Roland. "Redemption Without Actuality: A Critical Interrelation Between Eberhard Jüngel's and John Milbank's Ontological Endevours." *Modern Theology* 14 (1998) 505–22.

Stassen, Glen. "Biblical Teaching on Capital Punishment." In *Capital Punishment: A Reader*, 119–30. Ohio: Pilgrim, 1998.

———, editor. *Capital Punishment: A Reader*. Cleveland: Pilgrim, 1998.

Stassen, Glen. H, Dianne M. Yeager, and John Howard Yoder. *Authentic Transformation: A New Vision of Christ and Culture*. Nashville: Abingdon, 1996.

Stewart, Robert B., editor. *The Resurrection of Jesus: The Crossan-Wright Dialogue*. London: SPCK, 2006.

Stout, Jeffrey. *Democracy and Tradition*. Princeton: Princeton University Press, 2004.

———. *Ethics after Babel: The Languages of Morals and Their Discontents*. Princeton: Princeton University Press, 1990.

———. *Flight From Authority: Religion, Morality, and the Quest for Autonomy*. Notre Dame: University of Notre Dame, 1981.

———. "The Spirit of Democracy and the Rhetoric of Excess." *Journal of Religious Ethics* 35 (2007) 3–21.

———. "Survivors of the Nations: A Response to Fergusson and Pecknold." *Scottish Journal of Theology* 59 (2006) 210–34.

Swartley, Willard M. *Covenant of Peace: The Missing Peace in New Testament Theology and Ethics*. Grand Rapids: Eerdmans, 2006.

———, editor. *The Love of Enemy and Nonretaliation in the New Testament*. Louisville: Westminster John Knox, 1992.

Swartley, Willard, M. editor. *Violence Renounced: Rene Girard, Biblical Studies and Peacemaking*. Telford, PA: Cascadia, 2000.

Sykes, Stephen. *The Identity of Christianity: Theologians and the Essence of Christianity from Schleiermacher to Barth*. London: SPCK, 1984.

———, editor. *Karl Barth: Centenary Essays.* Cambridge: Cambridge University Press, 1989.

Taubes, Jacob. *The Political Theology of Paul.* Stanford: Stanford University Press, 2004.

Taylor, Charles. *Modern Social Imaginaries.* Durham: Duke University Press, 2004.

———. "Modes of Secularisation." In *Secularism and Its Critics*, edited by Rajeev Bhargava, 31–53. Delhi: Oxford University Press, 1998.

———. *A Secular Age* Cambridge: Harvard University Press, 2007.

Thiemann, Ronald. F. *Constructing a Public Theology: The Church in a Pluralistic Culture.* Louisville: Westminster John Knox, 1991.

Thompson, J. B. and D. Held, editors. *Habermas: Critical Debates.* Cambridge: MIT Press, 1982.

Thompson, J. B. "Universal Pragmatics." In *Habermas: Critical Debates*, edited by J. B . Thompson and D. Held, 116–33. Cambridge: MIT Press, 1982.

Tillard, J-M, R. *Church of Churches: The Ecclesiology of Communion.* Collegeville, MN: Liturgical, 1987.

Tilley, Terrence, W. "Incommensurability, Intratextuality, and Fideism." *Modern Theology* 5:2 (1989) 87–111.

Tillich, Paul. *Systematic Theology Volume III.* London: SCM, 1963.

Tocqueville, Alexis de. *Democracy in America.* London: Campbell, 1994.

Toews, Paul. "The Concern Movement: Its Origins and Early History." *Conrad Grebel Review* 8 (1990) 102–26.

Toole, David. *Waiting For Godot In Sarajevo: Theological Reflections on Nihilism, Tragedy, and Apocalypse.* Bolder, CO: Westview, 1998.

Tombs, David, and Joseph Liechty, editors. *Explorations in Reconciliation: New Directions in Theology.* Aldershot, UK: Ashgate, 2006.

Toulmin, Stephen. *Cosmopolis: The Hidden Agenda of Modernity.* Chicago: University of Chicago, 1990.

Tracy, David. *The Analogical Imagination: Christian Theology and the Culture of Pluralism.* London: SCM, 1981.

———. *Blessed Rage for Order: The New Pluralism in Theology.* New York: Seabury, 1975.

———. *Plurality and Ambiguity: Hermeneutics, Religion, Hope.* London: SCM, 1987.

———. "Theology, Critical Social Theory and the Public Realm." In *Habermas, Modernity and Public Theology*, edited by Don Browning and Francis Schüssler Fiorenza, 19–42. New York: Crossroad, 1992.

Trappenburg, Margo. "In Defence of Pure Pluralism: Two Readings of Walzer's *Spheres of Justice*." *Journal of Political Philosophy* 8 (2000) 343–62.

Troeltsch, Ernst. *The Social Teaching of the Christian Churches.* 2 vols. London: George Allen and Unwin, 1931.

United States State Department. *2008 Report on International Religious Freedom.* No pages. Online at http://2001–2009.state.gov/g/drl/rls/irf/2008/index.htm.

Visser't Hooft, W. A., and J. H. Oldham. *The Church and Its Function in Society.* London: Allen and Unwin, 1937.

Vodola, Elizabeth. *Excommunication in the Middle Ages.* Berkeley: University of California Press, 1986.

Volf, Miroslav. *After Our Likeness: The Church as the Image of the Trinity.* Grand Rapids: Eerdmans, 1998.

———. *Exclusion and Embrace: A Theological Exploration of Identity, Otherness, and Reconciliation.* Nashville: Abingdon, 1996.

———. "'The Trinity is our Social Program': The Doctrine of the Trinity and the Shape of Social Engagement." *Modern Theology* 14 (1998) 403-23.
Volf, Miroslav, Carmen Krieg, and Thomas Kucharz, editors. *The Future of Theology: Essays in Honour of Jürgen Moltmann*. Grand Rapids: Eerdmans, 1996.
Walzer, Michael. *The Company of Critics: Social Criticism and Political Commitment in the Twentieth Century*. New York: Basic, 1988.
———. *Exodus and Revolution*. New York: Basic, 1986.
———. *Interpretation and Social Criticism*. Cambridge: Harvard University Press, 1987.
———. *On Toleration*. New Haven: Yale University Press, 1997.
———. "The Politics of Michel Foucault." In *Foucault: A Critical Reader*, edited by David Couzens Hoy, 51-68. Oxford: Blackwell, 1986.
———. *Spheres of Justice: A Defence of Pluralism and Equality*. Oxford: Blackwell, 1983.
———. *Thick and Thin: Moral Argument at Home and Abroad*. Notre Dame: University of Notre Dame, 1994.
———, editor. *Towards a Global Civil Society*. Oxford: Berghahn, 1995.
Wannenwetsch, Bernd. *Political Worship: Ethics for Christian Citizens*. Oxford: Oxford University Press, 2004.
Ward, Graham. *The Certeau Reader*. Oxford: Blackwell, 2000.
———. *Cities of God*. London: Routledge, 2000.
———. "Michel de Certeau's 'Spiritual Spaces.'" *New Blackfriars* 79 (1998) 428-42.
Weaver, Alain Epp. "After Politics: John Howard Yoder, Body Politics, and the Witnessing Church." *Review of Politics* 61 (1999) 637-73.
———. "Constantinianism, Zionism, Diaspora: Toward a Political Theology of Exile and Return." Philadelphia: Mennonite Central Committee Occasional Paper 28, 2002.
———. "Missionary Christology: John Howard Yoder and the Creeds." *Mennonite Quarterly Review* 74 (2000) 423-39.
———. "On Exile: Yoder, Said, and a Theology of land and Return." In *A Mind Patient and Untamed: Assessing John Howard Yoder's Contribution to Theology, Ethics, and Peacemaking*, edited by Ben C. Ollenburger and Gayle Gerber Koontz, 161-86. Telford, PA: Cascadia, 2004.
———. "Unjust Lies and Just Wars: A Christian Pacifist Conversation with Augustine." *Journal of Religious Ethics* 29 (2001) 51-78.
Weaver, J. Denny. "The John Howard Yoder Legacy: Whither the Second Generation?" *Mennonite Quarterly Review* 77 (2003) 451-71.
———. *The Nonviolent Atonement*. Grand Rapids: Eerdmans, 2001.
Weber, Max. "The Profession and Vocation of Politics." In *Political Writings*, 309-69. Cambridge: Cambridge University Press, 1994.
Wells, Samuel. "No Abiding Inner City: A New Deal for the Church." In *Faithfulness and Fortitude: In Conversation with the Theological Ethics of Stanley Hauerwas*, edited by Mark Theissen Nation and Samuel Wells, 117-37. Edinburgh: T. & T. Clark, 2000.
———. *Transforming Fate into Destiny: The Theological Ethics of Stanley Hauerwas*. Carlisle: Paternoster, 1998.
Werpehowski, William. "Ad Hoc Apologetics." *Journal of Religion* 66 (1986) 282-301.
White, Michael. "The Blair Message: Be Bold." *The Guardian* (2002) 1.
White, Stephen K., editor. *The Cambridge Companion to Habermas*. Cambridge: Cambridge University Press, 1995.
Williams, Bernard. *Truth and Truthfulness: An Essay in Genealogy*. Princeton: Princeton University Press, 2002.

Williams, Rowan. "Barth, War and the State." In *Reckoning with Barth: Essays in Commemoration of the Centenary of Karl Barth's Birth*, edited by Nigel Biggar, 170–90. Oxford: Mowbray, 1988.
———. "Incarnation and the Renewal of Community." In *On Christian Theology*, 225–38. Oxford: Blackwell, 1999.
———. "Politics and the Soul: A Reading of the City of God." *Milltown Studies* 19 (1987) 55–72.
Wilson, Bryan. *Religion in Sociological Perspective*. Oxford: Oxford University Press, 1982.
Wink, Walter. *Engaging the Powers: Discernment and Resistance in a World of Domination*. Vol. 1 of *The Powers*. Minneapolis: Fortress, 1992.
———. "Neither Passivity Nor Violence: Jesus' Third Way Matt 5:38–42." In *The Love of Enemy and Nonretaliation in the New Testament*, edited by Willard M. Swartley, 102–25. Louisville: Wesminster John Knox, 1992.
———. *Naming the Powers: The Language of Power in the New Testament*. Vol. 3 of *The Powers*. Philadelphia: Fortress, 1984.
———. *Unmasking the Powers: The Invisible Forces that Determine Human Existence*. Vol. 2 of *The Powers*. Minneapolis: Fortress, 1986.
Witherington, Ben III. *Conflict and Community in Corinth: A Socio-Rhetorical Commentary on 1 and 2 Corinthians*. Grand Rapids: Eerdmans, 1995.
Wolterstorff, Nicholas. "A Discussion of Oliver O'Donovan's *The Desire of the Nations*." *Scottish Journal of Theology* 54 (2001) 87–109.
———. "An Engagement With Rorty." *Journal of Religious Ethics* 31 (2003) 129–39.
———. "Review of *The Royal Priesthood*." *Studies in Christian Ethics* 10 (1997) 142–45.
Wood, Chris. *The End of Punishment: Christian Perspectives on the Crisis in Criminal Justice*. Edinburgh: St Andrew's, 1991.
Woodhead, Linda, Paul Heelas, and David Martin, editors. *Peter Berger and the Study of Religion*. London: Routledge, 2001.
Wright, N. T. *Jesus and the Victory of God*. London: SPCK, 1996.
———. *The New Testament and the People of God*. London: SPCK, 1992.
———. *The Resurrection of the Son of God*. London: SPCK, 2003.
Wright, Nigel Goring. *Disavowing Constantine: Mission, Church and the Social Order in the Theologies of John Howard Yoder and Jürgen Moltmann*. Carlisle, UK: Paternoster, 2000.
Wuthnow, Robert. *Saving America? Faith-based Services and the Future of Civil Society*. Princeton: Princeton University Press, 2004.
Yoder, John Howard. "Absolute Philosophical Relativism is an Oxymoron." Unpublished paper, June 1993.
———. "Against the Death Penalty." In *The Death Penalty Debate: Two Opposing Views on Capital Punishment*, by H. Wayne House and John Howard Yoder. Dallas: Word, 1991.
———. "The Anabaptist Dissent: The Logic of the Place of the Disciple in Society." *Concern* 1 (1954) 45–68.
———. "Anabaptist Vision and Mennonite Reality." In *Consultation on Anabaptist-Mennonite Theology: Papers Read at the 1969 Aspen Conference*, edited by A. J. Klassen, 1–46. Fresno: Council of Mennonite Seminaries, 1970.
———. *Anabaptism and Reformation in Switzerland: An Historical and Theological Analysis of the Dialogues Between Anabaptists and Reformers*. Ontario: Pandora, 2004.

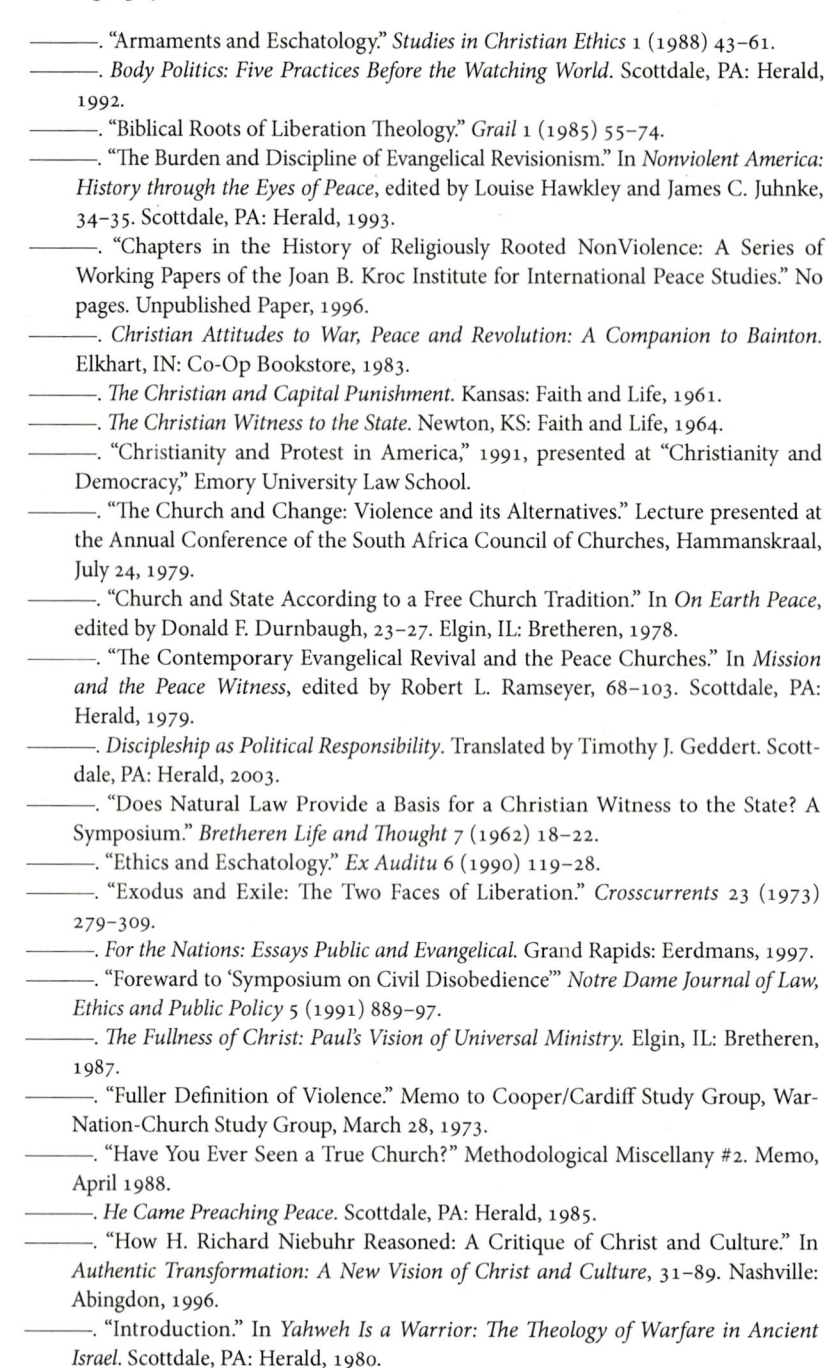

———. "Armaments and Eschatology." *Studies in Christian Ethics* 1 (1988) 43–61.
———. *Body Politics: Five Practices Before the Watching World*. Scottdale, PA: Herald, 1992.
———. "Biblical Roots of Liberation Theology." *Grail* 1 (1985) 55–74.
———. "The Burden and Discipline of Evangelical Revisionism." In *Nonviolent America: History through the Eyes of Peace*, edited by Louise Hawkley and James C. Juhnke, 34–35. Scottdale, PA: Herald, 1993.
———. "Chapters in the History of Religiously Rooted NonViolence: A Series of Working Papers of the Joan B. Kroc Institute for International Peace Studies." No pages. Unpublished Paper, 1996.
———. *Christian Attitudes to War, Peace and Revolution: A Companion to Bainton*. Elkhart, IN: Co-Op Bookstore, 1983.
———. *The Christian and Capital Punishment*. Kansas: Faith and Life, 1961.
———. *The Christian Witness to the State*. Newton, KS: Faith and Life, 1964.
———. "Christianity and Protest in America," 1991, presented at "Christianity and Democracy," Emory University Law School.
———. "The Church and Change: Violence and its Alternatives." Lecture presented at the Annual Conference of the South Africa Council of Churches, Hammanskraal, July 24, 1979.
———. "Church and State According to a Free Church Tradition." In *On Earth Peace*, edited by Donald F. Durnbaugh, 23–27. Elgin, IL: Bretheren, 1978.
———. "The Contemporary Evangelical Revival and the Peace Churches." In *Mission and the Peace Witness*, edited by Robert L. Ramseyer, 68–103. Scottdale, PA: Herald, 1979.
———. *Discipleship as Political Responsibility*. Translated by Timothy J. Geddert. Scottdale, PA: Herald, 2003.
———. "Does Natural Law Provide a Basis for a Christian Witness to the State? A Symposium." *Bretheren Life and Thought* 7 (1962) 18–22.
———. "Ethics and Eschatology." *Ex Auditu* 6 (1990) 119–28.
———. "Exodus and Exile: The Two Faces of Liberation." *Crosscurrents* 23 (1973) 279–309.
———. *For the Nations: Essays Public and Evangelical*. Grand Rapids: Eerdmans, 1997.
———. "Foreward to 'Symposium on Civil Disobedience'" *Notre Dame Journal of Law, Ethics and Public Policy* 5 (1991) 889–97.
———. *The Fullness of Christ: Paul's Vision of Universal Ministry*. Elgin, IL: Bretheren, 1987.
———. "Fuller Definition of Violence." Memo to Cooper/Cardiff Study Group, War-Nation-Church Study Group, March 28, 1973.
———. "Have You Ever Seen a True Church?" Methodological Miscellany #2. Memo, April 1988.
———. *He Came Preaching Peace*. Scottdale, PA: Herald, 1985.
———. "How H. Richard Niebuhr Reasoned: A Critique of Christ and Culture." In *Authentic Transformation: A New Vision of Christ and Culture*, 31–89. Nashville: Abingdon, 1996.
———. "Introduction." In *Yahweh Is a Warrior: The Theology of Warfare in Ancient Israel*. Scottdale, PA: Herald, 1980.
———. "Is there Such a Thing as Being Ready for Another Millennium?" In *The Future of Theology: Essays in Honour of Jürgen Moltmann*, edited by Miroslav Volf, Carmen Krieg, and Thomas Kucharz, 63–69. Grand Rapids: Eerdmans, 1996.

———. *The Jewish-Christian Schism Revisited*. Edited by Michael G. Cartwright and Peter Ochs. London: SCM, 2003.

———. *Karl Barth and the Problem of War*. Nashville: Abingdon, 1970.

———. "Karl Barth, Post-Christendom Theologian." Unpublished paper presented to the Karl Barth Society. Elmhurst, IL, June 8, 1995.

———. *The Legacy of Michael Sattler*. Scottdale, PA: Herald, 1973.

———. "Meaning after Babble: With Jeffrey Stout Beyond Relativism." *Journal of Religious Ethics* 24 (1996) 125–38.

———. *Nevertheless: Varieties of Religious Pacifism*. Revised Edition. Scottdale, PA: Herald, 1992.

———. "Noah's Covenant, the New Testament, and Christian Social Order." In *The Death Penalty in America: Current Controversies*, edited by Hugo Adam Bedau, 429–44. Oxford: Oxford University Press, 1997.

———. "On Not Being Ashamed of the Gospel: Particularity, Pluralism, and Validation." *Faith and Philosophy* 9 (1992) 285–300.

———. *One Flesh Until Death: Conversations on the Meaning and Permanence of Marriage*. Elkhart, IN: Shalom Desktop Publications, 1996.

———. "Orientation in Midstream: A Response to the Responses." In *Freedom and Discipleship: Liberation Theology in Anabaptist Perspective*, edited by Daniel S. Schipani, 159–68. Maryknoll, NY: Orbis, 1989.

———. *The Original Revolution: Essays on Christian Pacifism*. Scottdale, PA: Herald, 1998.

———. "'Patience' as Method in Moral Reasoning: Is an Ethic of Discipleship 'Absolute'?" *The Wisdom of the Cross: Essays in Honour of John Howard Yoder*, edited by Stanley Hauerwas et al., 24–42. Grand Rapids: Eerdmans, 1999.

———. "Peace." In *Dictionary of the Ecumenical Movement*, edited by N. Lossky, 786–89. Geneva: WCC, 1991.

———. *The Politics of Jesus: Vicit Agnus Noster*. 2nd ed. Grand Rapids: Eerdmans, 1994.

———. "The Politics of Jesus Revisited." Unpublished paper, 1997. An assigned lecture at Toronto Mennonite Studies Center. March 1997.

———. *Preface to Theology: Christology and Theological Method*. Grand Rapids: Brazos, 2002.

———. *The Priestly Kingdom: Social Ethics as Gospel*. Notre Dame: University of Notre Dame, 1984.

———. "Primitivism in the Radical Reformation: Strengths and Weaknesses." In *The Primitive Church in the Modern World*, edited by Richard T. Hughes, 74–97. Urbana: University of Illinois Press, 1995.

———. "Reinhold Niebuhr and Christian Pacifism." *Mennonite Quarterly Review* 29 (1955) 101–17.

———. "Religious Liberty and the Prior Loyalty of the People of God." Unpublished paper presented at the Fifth Annual Institute on Law and Pastoral Ministry, Valparaiso University School of Law, January 16, 1990.

———. *The Royal Priesthood: Essays Ecclesiological and Ecumenical*. Grand Rapids: Eerdmans, 1994.

———. "That Household We Are." Unpublished paper presented at the conference "Is There a Believers' Church Christology?" Bluffton College, Bluffton, OH, October 1980.

———. "A Theological Critique of Violence." *New Conversations* 16 (1994) 2–5.

———. "A Theological Point of Reference for an Approach to Conflict, Intervention, and Conciliation." Unpublished Paper. November 1996 revision of presentation given at the Mennonite Central Committee Peace Theology Colloquium, Kansas City, KS, April 6–8, 1978.

———. *To Hear the Word*. Eugene, OR: Wipf & Stock, 2001.

———. "'To Your Tents, Oh Israel': The Legacy of Israel's Experience with Holy War." *Studies in Religion* 18 (1989) 345–62.

———. "Walk and Word: The Alternatives to Methodologism." In *Theology Without Foundations: Religious Practice and the Future of Theological Truth*, edited by Stanley Hauerwas et al., 77–90. Nashville: Abingdon, 1994.

———. "What Are Our Concerns?" *Concern* 4 (1957), 20–32.

———. *What Would You Do? A Serious Answer to a Standard Question*. Expanded edition. Scottdale, PA: Herald, 1992.

———. *When War Is Unjust: Being Honest in Just-War Thinking*. Rev. ed. Maryknoll, NY: Orbis, 1996.

———. "The Wider Setting of 'Liberation Theology.'" *Review of Politics* 52 (1990) 285–96.

———. "The Wrath of God and the Love of God." Unpublished paper presented to Historic Peace Churches and IFOR Conference, England, September 11–14, 1956.

———. "Why I Don't Pay All My Income Tax." *Gospel Herald*, January 22, 1963, 81–92.

———. "Withdrawal and Diaspora: The Two Faces of Liberation." In *Freedom and Discipleship: Liberation Theology in Anabaptist Perspective*, edited by D. S. Schipani, 76–84. Maryknoll, NY: Orbis, 1989.

———. "You Have It Coming: The Legitimate Social Function of Punitive Behaviour." No pages. Elkhart, IN: Shalom Desktop Publications, 1995.

Yoder, John Howard, and James Wm. McClendon Jr. "Christian Identity in Ecumenical Perspective." *Journal of Ecumenical Studies* 27 (1995) 561–80.

Yoder, John Howard, and H. Wayne Pipkin. *Balthasar Hubmaier: Theologian of Anabaptism*. Scottdale, PA: Herald, 1989.

Yoder Neufeld, Tom R. *"Put on the Armour of God": The Divine Warrior from Isaiah to Ephesians*. Sheffield: Sheffield Academic, 1997.

Young, Jock. *The Exclusive Society: Social Exclusion, Crime and Difference in Late Modernity*. London: Sage, 1999.

Zehr, Howard. *Changing Lenses: A New Focus for Crime and Justice*. Scottdale, PA: Herald, 1990.

Ziegler, Philip. "Dietrich Bonhoeffer: An Ethics of God's Apocalypse?" *Modern Theology* 23 (2007) 579–94.

Zimbleman, Joel. "The Contribution of John Howard Yoder to Recent Discussions in Christian Social Ethics." *Scottish Journal of Theology* 45 (1992) 367–99.

———. "Theological Ethics and Politics in the Thought of Juan Luis Segundo and John Howard Yoder." PhD diss., University of Virginia, 1986.

Žižek, Slavoj. "Class Struggle or Postmodernism? Yes Please!" In *Contingency, Hegemony, Universality: Contemporary Dialogues on the Left*, by Judith Butler, Ernesto Laclau, and Slavoj Žižek, 90–135. London: Verso, 2000.

Index of Names and Subjects

Aristotle, 31, 265, 267
Adorno, Theodor, 47, 49, 60, 235n111
Agamben, Giorgio, 27n89, 237n121,
analogy, 28, 42, 82–83, 122–24, 127,
   130, 132, 136, 137, 139–41, 142–46,
   148, 154, 155, 158, 160, 164, 175,
   179, 194, 195, 207, 211, 225–27,
   251, 286, 294, 296
apocalyptic, 57, 102, 103n91, 107–9,
   112–17, 177–79, 208n3,
Aquinas, Thomas, 123, 266n12
Arendt, Hannah, 112, 155, 215n29,
Asad, Talal, 9, 156n145,
Augustine, 118n153, 155–56, 162,
   190n113, 196, 284n67

Bader-Saye, Scott, 230n93, 255, 293
Badiou, Alain, 87–93, 150
Balthasar, Hans Urs von, 28, 123n2,
   147n95, 159
Banner, Michael, 30–33
baptism, 124, 134, 160–61, 253–54,
   257n196, 258
Barber, Daniel, 54n41, 109n112,
Barth, Karl, 33, 37, 38, 58, 63, 71,
   81, 84–87, 92–93, 96, 97, 98n70,
   106n100, 107–8, 110, 112–14, 123,
   124, 141n69, 172n47, 219, 222,
   223n63, 226–27, 256, 257n196, 259
Bauckham, Richard, 60n67, 88
Bauerschmidt, Frederick Christian,
   148n101, 181, 182n87, 183,
Bell, Daniel, Jr., 92n51, 186n93,
   199n147, 202, 241n135
Bellah, Robert, 283–85
Bender, Harold, 125–26

Benhabib, Seyla, 19, 50–51,
Benjamin, Walter, 26, 59,
Berkhof, Hendrikus, 157, 211
Biggar, Nigel, 93n55, 170n41, 226n74,
Bodin, Jean, 215, 218n44,
Boersma, Hans, 154
Boff, Leonardo, 140, 198n141,
Bonhoeffer, Dietrich, 91–93, 98n70,
   106n100, 109, 116n145, 194,
   202n157, 216n35,
Boyarin, Daniel, 260
Braithwaite, John, 164–65
Brown, Callum, 8

Carter, Craig, 15, 85n12, 93n55, 95,
   104n94, 125n7, 126n9, 141, 187n98,
   188n99, 230,
Cartwright, Michael G., 60n69, 94n59,
   129n23, 133n43, 137–38, 260n207,
Casanova, José, 6–7, 275n36,
catholicity, 121, 129, 138n57, 143–44
Certeau, Michel de, 158, 179–83,
   184, 193n126, 230n93, 231, 232,
   240n132, 262, 295
change, social, *See* transformation,
   social
Christ, and nonviolence, 53, 85, 93,
   105–6, 108, 113, 115, 128, 131, 132,
   139n62, 142, 158, 187n98
Christ, lordship of, 32–34, 38, 39,
   55n48, 61, 73–75, 111, 115–16,
   117, 118, 119, 123, 130, 134, 143,
   145, 151, 154, 161, 162, 186, 191,
   194, 196, 197, 201, 206, 207, 213,
   223–24, 280

Index of Names and Subjects

Christ, normativity of, 92–5, 100–105, 113, 115, 158
Christocentrism, 43n8, 53–54, 67, 68, 70, 85–95, 97, 105, 107, 113, 116, 120, 166, 215n28, 233, 251n174,
Church and world, 24, 31, 33–34, 38, 39, 60, 63, 69, 78–80, 99n75, 106, 108, 112, 115n144, 116, 119–20, 122–56, 157, 164, 175, 196, 199, 202–5, 242, 250, 285–86, 288
civil disobedience, 177n65, 203–5, 222,
civil religion, 227, 255, 278, 283, 288
civil society, ix, 55n48, 64, 156, 181, 241n136, 250, 261, 262–96
Coles, Romand, 51n33, 60n67, 79n121, 152, 279,
Constantinianism, 34, 35, 37, 55, 104, 113, 116–21, 125, 127,128, 129, 133, 135–36, 156n143, 161, 163–64, 179, 182, 186–90, 200, 208–9, 218n44, 224, 227, 232, 234, 236, 237, 238, 246, 248–49, 257n196, 288, 292,
consumerism, 11, 243, 244, 257, 258, 261, 287–96
Cooke, Maeve, 45n11, 65,
criticism, immanent, 13–38, 73, 234–35, 287
Cullmann, Oscar, 114

democracy, 2, 10, 20, 41, 44–46, 47n16, 63, 65, 67, 76–80, 155, 215n29, 216, 217, 218, 223, 230, 239n128, 243n145, 261, 262–64, 270, 272, 274, 275, 279–96
democracy, pathologies of, 287–96
Derrida, Jacques, 181
Descartes, René, 3, 28, 49, 147,
doxology, and politics, 157–206, 209, 249, 292, 293

ecumenism, 122, 124–25, 135, 136–39, 141, 143, 163
election, theology of, 24, 71, 86–87, 89, 124, 201, 208, 209, 233, 236, 252–61, 287, 288, 292, 293, 294
Ellul, Jacques, 117, 211–14, 239, 245, 289

Elshtain, Jean Bethke, 258n202, 262, 280n52, 284–85,
empire, 1, 108–9, 118, 121, 164n22, 189–90, 218, 228, 237, 238
eschatology, 4, 16, 24, 26–27, 32, 34, 42, 52, 57, 59–62, 66, 68, 70, 73, 75, 81–82, 84, 85, 88, 99, 103n91, 105, 106–21, 122, 123, 124, 127–28, 130, 132, 133, 135–36, 143–44, 148, 153, 155, 160, 165, 172–75, 176–79, 180, 183, 184, 188–89, 191, 195, 196–97, 203, 208, 209, 210–31, 236, 243, 247, 252, 255, 261, 263, 270, 272, 274, 280, 286, 288, 289, 290, 291, 294, 296
eschatology, and analogy, 82, 122, 148, 155, 160
eschatology, and realism, 106–21, 132, 136, 184, 188, 208, 209, 215,
Eusebius of Caesarea, 118n153, 218, 237
exile, 24, 135, 166, 184, 209, 228, 231–28, 243, 245, 249–52, 255, 260, 261, 270, 288, 294

Fergusson, Adam, 267
Fergusson, David, 20n57, 29n95, 31
Fiorenza, Francis Schüssler, 58n60, 67, 72–3,
Forgiveness, ix, 28, 80, 106, 107, 109, 143–46, 159–65, 173, 176–85, 186, 191–94, 202, 228–29, 241n135
Foucault, Michel, 10, 40, 43, 51–52, 79, 177, 207, 208–9, 231, 235, 238–49, 253, 261, 272, 290

Garland, David, 169n40, 171, 292n92
Girard, René, 158, 165, 167–72, 183, 214n24, 292, 294
Gorringe, Timothy, xi, 112, 164n23, 168n35,
governmentality, 209n3, 231, 235, 238–49, 257, 261, 274, 292
grace, 3, 85, 88, 89, 101, 109, 116, 130, 143, 148, 151, 152, 153, 161, 167, 185, 190–97, 200–203, 210, 223, 228–29, 233, 250, 254, 257, 278, 293, 296

Index of Names and Subjects

Gutiérrez, Gustavo, 111, 199n146, 200-202, 223

Hütter, Reinhard, 156,
Habermas, Jürgen, 20, 21-22, 43, 44, 46-77, 210n6, 216n34, 246, 255, 269, 273-74, 287, 290-91
Hardt, Michael, 189-90, 218
Harink, Douglas, 233n104, 252n179, 260-61
Harrington, Austin, 65, 66n87,
Harvey, David, 11-12
Hauerwas, Stanley, ix, xi, 13, 35, 60, 73n108, 76, 78-80, 90n36, 93n54, 97, 106, 115, 120n161, 132, 135, 136, 145, 152, 153-55, 157, 158n5, 161n14, 180-81, 186n93, 193n117, 202, 229n90, 231, 254n184, 285-86, 290, 292n95
Havel, Václav, 275-78, 291
Hegel, G. W. F., 14, 63, 66, 182, 188, 269-70, 271, 273, 278, 279, 285
Herschberger, Guy, 126
historicism, 13, 15-16, 26-27, 54, 72, 73, 121, 216, 247
historicism and historicity, 16, 26-27, 54
Hobbes, Thomas, 196, 215, 217, 225n68, 245, 255-56,
Huebner, Chris, 35n115, 36n117, 150n123, 208n3, 248-49
Hume, David, 267-68

Jameson, Frederic, 11-12
Jaspers, Karl, 58, 63

Kant, Immanuel, 5, 10, 18, 31, 47, 59, 60, 62, 63, 65-67, 72, 106n100, 253, 267, 268-70, 274, 285

Lactantius, 218
Levinas, Emmanuel, 161
liberalism, justificatory, 14, 18, 21, 44-46, 58,
liberation theology, 130, 157, 159, 186, 197-206
Lindbeck, George, 34, 43n8, 115, 257n195

Locke, John, 10, 217, 265-66, 270, 284,
Lovin, Robin, 106n100, 186n93
Lubac, Henri de, 28n90,
Lyotard, Jean-François, 10

MacIntyre, Alasdair, 14, 16-17, 19-20, 25, 27-32, 34, 35n115, 73, 78-79, 104, 165, 187, 266n10, 267, 268, 285-86
Maritain, Jacques, 198-201, 288
Marx, Karl, 87, 263, 269, 270-73
Mathewes, Charles, 10, 101n83
McClendon, James, 70n97, 84, 126-27, 140n65,
Milbank, John, 14, 27-35, 54-55, 59, 61, 65, 75, 76, 78, 89, 92n46, 120n163, 123, 141, 146-55, 156n145, 158, 162, 166n29, 177-79, 190, 195-97, 202, 215n31, 263, 293, 296n103,
mimesis, 165-70, 171,
Moltmann, Jürgen, 81, 84, 107, 111, 112, 113, 114, 117, 143n76, 257n197

Nagel, Thomas, 20, 44n9
Negri, Antonio, 189-90, 218
Neuhaus, Richard, 229n90, 283-84
Newbigin, Lesslie, 2-4,
Niebuhr, H. Richard, 70n95, 102, 103n92, 130n29, 131n33, 139n62, 150, 221, 249,
Niebuhr, Reinhold, 84, 113, 116, 135, 136, 179, 186, 190-97, 228, 244, 249,
Nietzsche, Friedrich, 11, 87, 89, 90, 117, 177, 253, 278
nonviolence, 4, 37-38, 54, 55, 75, 115, 116-18, 122-56, 158, 161, 162, 176, 179, 181, 191, 204-5, 226, 229, 230, 248, 251-52, 254, 258, 262, 277, 278, 285n70,
nonviolence, as character of God, ix, 16, 27, 37, 80, 81-82, 93, 95-100, 106, 140, 145, 156, 296
nonviolence, of Jesus, *See* Christ, and nonviolence

O'Donovan, Joan Lockwood, 215n29

Index of Names and Subjects

O'Donovan, Oliver, 24, 83, 107n102, 119, 120–21n64, 160, 163, 207, 215n29, 217, 218, 226–30, 236n115, 240, 253–59, 283, 288

participation, 16, 26, 61, 70, 94, 101, 115, 122–24, 132, 134, 136–37, 139–55, 167, 179, 182, 194–95, 203, 220, 258, 269, 296
particularity, 1, 6, 13–19, 20–21, 23, 25–27, 29, 32–39, 40–80, 85–93, 97, 101, 103, 120, 132, 134–35, 142, 148–51, 164, 177n65, 179, 189n107, 208n3, 248, 260, 269, 279,
Peukert, Helmut, 59–62
Plato, 28, 92n46, 123n2, 148, 149,
Preston, Ronald, 135–36
Principalities and Powers, 34, 99, 111–12, 130n30, 134, 138, 157, 172, 184, 189n106, 191, 197, 203n157, 205, 210–16, 220, 223, 232, 233, 239, 273, 289, 290, 292
public, Church as, 7–9, 81, 121, 131–36, 145, 150, 155–57, 176–79, 195, 208, 291, 296
public, definition and nature of, 25–26, 31–32, 41–43, 47, 54, 121, 155–57, 267, 268, 287–88
public, theology as, 1–39, 41–43, 45, 55–80, 121, 202, 207, 262, 270
punishment, capital, 158, 167–70,

Rawls, John, 17, 20n59, 44–46, 50, 51n31, 64, 72, 77, 78, 269, 283, 285
Reader, John, 67, 73–75,
realism, biblical, 82, 93–104, 233,
realism, moral, 13, 31–32, 60, 80, 83, 91, 106–21, 140
realism, political, 83, 113, 155,
realism, theological, 13, 65, 80, 82–95, 100–116, 122–23, 144, 148, 150, 158, 179–83, 229, 262, 291, 295–96
reconciliation, ix, 16, 39, 40, 75, 80, 85, 93–94, 100, 106, 124, 133, 134–46, 150, 158, 159–65, 170, 184, 192, 203, 228–29, 256–58, 296
Reimer, A. James, 85n11, 109n114, 133n42,
relativism, 14–15, 151, 254

restitutionism, 122, 125, 126–31, 138, 168, 209, 253n106, 278,
Rogers, Eugene, 110n129, 187n98
Rorty, Richard, 29, 41, 76, 283, 285
Rousseau, Jean-Jacques, 10, 284

Sacks, Jonathan, 264–65
sacrament, as social practice, 74, 101n83, 109–10, 133–36, 203, 205
Scott, James C., 21–22, 176–77, 179, 237,
secularization, 3, 5–12, 35, 52n35, 62, 77, 113n130, 137, 151, 200, 274n32
Shanks, Andrew, 269n20, 278–79
Smith, Adam, 135, 267
Smith-Christopher, Daniel, 237–38
Spinoza, Baruch, 255–56
state, and violence, 224–31
state, legitimacy of, 41, 62, 65, 156, 199–200n148, 209, 210–31, 261, 279, 280
Stout, Jeffrey, 14n38, 32, 46, 76–89, 82–83, 135n47, 155, 250, 285–87, 294n97
strategy and tactic, 180–82, 183–86, 224–31, 232, 240n132, 293
supersessionism, 52n35, 201, 230n93, 233, 235, 253, 255, 259–61

tactic, See strategy and tactic
Taylor, Charles, 8n16, 9, 156n145
Tocqueville, Alexis de, 279–82
Tracy, David, 56–58, 59, 61, 62, 123
transformation, social, 6, 7, 8, 16, 20, 32, 47, 61, 92, 102, 117, 122, 125, 128, 129, 130, 136, 140, 142, 145, 148, 155, 156, 157–206, 208, 209, 226, 229, 234, 247, 248–49, 258, 261, 262–65, 270, 272, 275–79, 288, 292, 293, 294, 296
trinity, 58, 70n95, 101, 103, 120, 123, 139–55, 163–64, 182, 187–88n98
Troeltsch, Ernst, 120, 185n92, 186, 193

universal, 3, 11, 13, 14, 15, 16, 18, 19, 21, 23, 24, 25, 26, 31, 34–6, 40–80, 85–95, 97n68, 121, 129, 143, 144, 146, 149, 150–51, 164n22, 189n107, 215, 217, 256–57, 267–70, 273, 278

Volf, Miroslav, 20–21, 123, 141, 142–46, 257n199

Walzer, Michael, 10n24, 14, 17–27,
Weaver, Alain Epp, 85n11, 96n65, 104n94, 156n143, 204n165, 233n101, 235n111, 252
Wells, Samuel, xi, 60n69, 281n56
Williams, Bernard, 2n2
Williams, Rowan, 155, 226n73, 296
Wink, Walter, 174, 211–14, 270–71
witness, xi, 3, 4, 41, 46, 59, 61, 68, 69, 78, 102, 106, 118, 119, 121, 122–56, 159, 160n8, 161, 163, 175, 183–90, 194, 195, 201, 203, 204, 209n3, 216–17, 220–4, 227–31, 234, 242, 248, 254, 258, 263, 277, 281, 282, 287–96

Wolin, Sheldon, 79, 155
Wolterstorff, Nicholas, 41n4, 45, 226n76, 231n97
Wright, N. T., 24n73, 100n77, 107n102, 108, 173n51, 233n104, 236n114, 256n194, 257n195
Wright, Nigel Goring, 71n99, 111n123, 139n62, 141n69, 145n83

Žižek, Slavoj, 16
Zehr, Howard, 164–65, 168n33
Zimbleman, Joel, 145n84, 199–200n148, 204